The Netherlands as an EU Member: Awkward or Loyal Partner?

The Netherlands as an EU Member: Awkward or Loyal Partner?

Adriaan Schout
Jan Rood
(eds.)

eleven
international publishing

Published, sold and distributed by Eleven International Publishing
P.O. Box 85576
2508 CG The Hague
The Netherlands
Tel.: +31 70 33 070 33
Fax: +31 70 33 070 30
e-mail: sales@budh.nl
www.elevenpub.com

Sold and distributed in USA and Canada
International Specialized Book Services
920 NE 58th Avenue, Suite 300
Portland, OR 97213-3786, USA
Tel: 1-800-944-6190 (toll-free)
Fax: +1-503-280-8832
orders@isbs.com
www.isbs.com

Eleven International Publishing is an imprint of Boom uitgevers Den Haag.

ISBN 978-94-9094-799-6
ISBN 978-94-6094-696-7 (E-book)

Printed in The Netherlands

Preface

Normally, a book will be interesting if it has something new to offer. However, this book may be of interest because it concludes exactly the opposite: not much has actually changed in the Dutch European Union (EU) debate. And this is precisely the big news. But it also says a lot about the superficiality of the Dutch debate on the EU in recent years.

This book started off in autumn 2010 to find an answer to the question whether the Netherlands had lost its way in 'Europe'. By the end of the first decade of the new century, we saw a country where disparaging the EU in politics had become common practice, also within traditionally pro-European political parties, and even involved a certain amount of populism. Aversion to the EU thus seemed considerable, both within politics and in society at large. In 2005, the Netherlands rejected the proposed European constitution in a referendum. Meanwhile, the anti-Europeanism propagated by Pim Fortuyn was taken over by the PVV and SP – and these parties did well in the polls over the past few years. Among the great majority of citizens, the introduction of the euro created the impression that prices had risen, and by 2006, only 40% believed the euro had brought benefits. However, criticism not only focused on the euro but also seemed levelled at the integration project as a whole, whether this involved the impending accession of Turkey, the European budget, European regulation or concerns over preserving our own identity. It seemed Europe was under heavy fire.

This was all the more remarkable because, to the outside, the Netherlands has always had the image of a country with an open economy, which is therefore tied hand and foot to trade with the rest of the EU and which, as a transit country for the EU, is at the forefront of trade contacts with the rest of the world. In addition, the Netherlands is regarded as a representative and defender of international law. Both in trade and international law and justice, our roots go back centuries. The combination of international economic relations and international law is fully in line with the traditional Dutch foreign policy orientation: that of a merchant who is doing well by legally guaranteed international relations, i.e., a strong international legal order.

So, what happened with this country that had always prided itself on such an exemplary international reputation? How could a country that has so much to gain by open and harmonized markets become so critical – on such a large scale – of the European integration project?

This paradoxical situation raised a number of questions. First, with this book project, we wanted to get behind the facade of the daily political tumult. How deep did and does the aversion to the EU go – would we encounter such aversion also at the level of individual policy areas? Was the aversion in the public field linked to developments that are problematic for the Netherlands within these sectors? The famous book by Surowiecki *Wisdom of the Crowds* suggests that there would be wisdom behind the public outcry.[1] If that were true, we should be able to see such wisdom also in the sectors where policy is really taking shape, as this is also the level where social problems are actually being dealt with. Therefore, this book takes stock of the current state of affairs in a number of areas, particularly focusing on the role the Netherlands plays and has played.

Our second aim was to compare the findings of this sectoral thermometer with longer-term perspectives on, first, the discussion about the Dutch position on European integration and, second, the Dutch support for the EU. Would we really find that the Netherlands has indeed changed from a Europhile to a Eurosceptic country? Did the Netherlands used to be so pro-EU and pro-supranational, and has it suddenly transformed into a supporter of more intergovernmental cooperation and less Europe?

Third, we were curious whether changes could be observed at the political level of political parties and of the organization of democratic scrutiny in the Dutch House of Representatives. Could these changes be linked to the growing irritation with the EU?

Despite the considerable political commotion about the EU at the time this book was written, such as the ongoing stalemates over the euro crisis and discussions on further European integration, the chosen approach led to a number of remarkably mild insights into the relationship between the Netherlands and the EU. If we look beyond the fierce – and often superficial – discussions in the media and statements by politicians about the EU, the chapters do not indicate that the Netherlands is turning its back on the EU. None of the chapters on the policy sectors cast any doubt on the importance of joint action at EU level. The chapters provide a cross section of policy areas, and these sectors are often regarded as 'Europe sensitive', such as asylum policy, police cooperation, EU budget or economic policy. Nevertheless, they show a high degree of continuity in policy development and in the perceived need to continue along these lines.

The chapters also demonstrate that the Netherlands has always taken a pragmatic approach to European integration and its finality. In the short-term perception of the media and politicians, the Netherlands may have switched direction from unconditional support for a supranational body like the European Commis-

1 Surowiecki, J. (2004). *The wisdom of crowds: Why the many are smarter than the few and how collective wisdom shapes business, economies, societies and nations*. Little: Brown.

sion to a form of intergovernmental cooperation with other countries that is more dictated by self-interest, and from support for further integration to keeping European policy at bay or even reversing it. The chapters underline, however, that the Netherlands was generally not dogmatic and made all its decisions mostly on pragmatic grounds in terms of usefulness and necessity. Sometimes this happened at intergovernmental level; other times, at supranational level. Sometimes the aim was regulation; other times, deregulation and coordination. Nor did the Netherlands suddenly change course in 2005 or become critical of the EU. The Dutch were already critical of the EU in its early years. The Netherlands is pragmatic, which is echoed in each chapter.

This book thus shows that there is a high degree of continuity in the Dutch pragmatism. The parliamentary elections of 2012 are also in line with this trend: the Netherlands and the Dutch are not ready for experiments with the EU, nor are they looking for break-ups in the EU. Apparently, their wish is for the EU to form the basis of a stable Europe where solutions are sought to cross-border problems – and this is precisely what is being done at the level of various policy sectors.

Thus, in many respects, the Netherlands has not been a fickle country but, quite the contrary, a rather predictable EU partner. Important lessons can be drawn from this. Perhaps politicians should try less hard to please the anti-European public, since that public may well be more pragmatic than they think, as Geert Wilders found out at the last elections. Political commentators should know the longer-term context of EU discussions: Dutch EU debates get quite heated sometimes, and of course, major fights take place in the EU and about the Dutch position. That is politics; that is how it should be. Such fights do not imply that the Netherlands is turning its back on the EU. It is just a fact that politics involves fighting over more or less European regulation, more or less intergovernmental cooperation or more or less money to the EU. But behind those disputes hides the simple fact that the Netherlands is closely intertwined with the EU, which is reflected in all kinds of interrelations and in the initiatives which the Netherlands takes in the EU. Headlines labelling the Netherlands as a 'pain in the neck' do not do justice to this fact.[2]

We do not claim to have written the definitive book on the relationship between the Netherlands and the EU, but we do hope to have exposed the underlying continuity in the relation between the Netherlands and the EU. While working on this book, many people advised and assisted us. First of all, we thank the authors for sharing their many years of practical experience and academic insights. Many thanks also to Ali Molenaar, who helped us a great deal by carefully reading the texts and putting them in the right format. Finally, we thank Joris Bekkers of Boom Lemma publishers for his assistance, his help in arranging for the English translation and his patience.

2 *See* the chapter by Schout & Rood.

Table of contents

1 Europe Beyond its Image

Adriaan Schout en Jan Rood

1.1 Introduction: the Netherlands in Search of a European Foothold

There never seems to be a good time for a book on the Netherlands and the European Union (EU). As a result of large-scale integration projects such as '1992', the EMU, enlargements and the constitutional treaty, or, currently, the euro crisis, the EU is in a constant state of flux. In these dynamic and hectic circumstances, there has not been one opportunity for the European dust to settle in the Netherlands. Consequently, it is difficult to assess where the Dutch population and politicians stand on Europe and where the inevitable rhetoric surrounding the elections of September 2012 indeed has substance to it. Moreover, in looking for conflict, debates in the press and the Dutch House of Representatives only seem to complicate and magnify the lack of clarity regarding the position of the Netherlands in the European integration debate. The Netherlands is portrayed as a divided and recalcitrant country that is sliding into Euroscepticism. The debates about Prime Minister Rutte's positions at the many European summits suggest that the Netherlands has completely lost its way in Europe. Prime Minister Rutte, as the mouthpiece of the Netherlands, is depicted as someone who does not want to transfer sovereignty, does not want to talk about European vistas and says no to everything.[1] But he is also the man who is in favour of Community cooperation because otherwise the Netherlands will be overshadowed by the big countries, and he supports far-reaching independent European surveillance of the economic policies of countries and their banks. The House of Representatives wants to maintain sovereignty, but the EU – particularly the eurozone – seems to have moved on to the next phase and is working hard on deepening integration, heading for discussions about an elected president of the European Commission or European Council, a European minister of Finance, a banking union and a transfer union.

In response to such contradictions, politicians are often accused of saying one thing at national level, for instance, that national sovereignty is being defended

1 European integration is unravelling. (2011, May 30). *Financial Times*; Mark Rutte zegt nee tegen alles [Mark Rutte says no to everything]. (2012, June 23). *NRC Handelsblad*.

tooth and nail, but doing something else at European level, like following the choices of 'Brussels'. This image of politicians agreeing to further European integration while, at the same time, the population seems to be turning its back on the EU suggests that the Netherlands is heading for a repeat of the veto of the constitution in 2005.[2] The progressing integration is also creating the image of a country that – in the words of former Minister of Finance De Jager – despite all Dutch objections, is being 'hustled' deeper into Europe.[3] This image of politicians lacking a foothold and not keeping their word and of the Netherlands being hustled into the EU is certainly not conducive to public and political support for the EU.

Prime Minister Rutte's approach seems to fit the existing impression about the Netherlands and the Dutch. The prevailing image is that of a country that rather keeps the EU at bay. This is perhaps best expressed in the wide-spread expectations in the media that the elections of 2012 would be about the EU. For instance, Wilders shifted his focus from Islam to European despotism, arguing that the Netherlands should leave the EU. The SP, too, has taken firm stances to save the Netherlands from the EU's neoliberal claws and from the power of big business. The PvdA also criticizes Europe's lack of a social face and the imposed cuts. The VVD has – with a few exceptions – long been critical of further (political) integration, as was apparent in the 1990s during the leadership of Bolkestein, who argued against Dutch payments to the EU budget and against deepened integration beyond the internal market.[4] Even the usually EU-biased CDA, in its election programme of 2010, switched from European integration to 'European cooperation' and called, through Member of the European Parliament Van der Camp, for a substantial reduction of the EU budget and for setting up an *'Oranjeberaad'* to thus watch over the Dutch interests also in the European Parliament (EP).

It is the appearance of Euroscepticism under which the Dutch 'no' to the European constitution in 2005 is often presented as a watershed in Dutch European policy. Since then, the Netherlands has had the image of a Eurosceptic country. What confuses this image is that Rutte has nevertheless committed himself to transferring "cartloads" of sovereignty to the EU[5] and that, in his first weeks as PvdA leader, Samsom argued that the Netherlands should have the courage to choose Europe.[6] Everyone is attacking one another over lack of support for the

2 Sommer, M. (2012, July 8). Waarom doe je in Brussel alleen maar mee als je ja en amen zeg? [Why do you only count in Brussels when you say amen to everything]. *Volkskrant*.

3 *Financieel Dagblad*, 2 July 2012.

4 Goslinga, H. (1996, October 22). Inspelen op anti-Europastemming gevaarlijk [Taking advantage of anti-Europe sentiments is dangerous]. *Trouw*.

5 Dutch House of Representatives. (2011, March 23). *Handelingen Tweede Kamer* 2010-2011, No. 64.

6 Dutch House of Representatives. (2012, June 27). *Handelingen Tweede Kamer* 2011-2012, No. 101.

EU, but in the meantime, even the SP has transformed into a self-proclaimed supporter of the EU, provided it is social.[7]

Another confusing element is the PVV's failed attempt to make the Dutch membership of the EU an issue in the last elections. In fact, the more Eurosceptic flanking parties were not rewarded for their position by the voters and, in the case of the PVV, suffered a major loss. At the same time, two traditional middle parties – VVD and PvdA – won these same elections. Both parties have, although not always enthusiastically and for different motives (the VVD as the governing party and the PvdA from the opposition), supported the European project and have backed measures considered necessary to save the euro. In short, 'pro-European' parties won the voters' favour, where, according to many observers, those same voters are consumed by suspicion and distrust of Europe.

So, on the face of it, confusion abounds, with a clear undertone: the Netherlands and the Dutch have become more Eurosceptic. The Netherlands is performing a balancing act: increasingly critical of Europe, it is reluctantly being sucked into a deepening EU. This image dominates the debate. To the extent that this is actually the case, pursuing an effective Europe policy that can be defended in both The Hague and Brussels thus becomes more difficult. An increasingly critical home front limits the government's room for manoeuvre in the European playing field and may irritate partners, which may ultimately result in loss of reputation and influence.

But the question is, of course, whether the picture painted above is correct. Has the Netherlands (the Dutch) exchanged its traditionally pragmatic position towards Europe for a much more reticent, possibly even hostile attitude? That is the key question here. This book aims to find out whether a coherent story can be told about the Netherlands and the EU without lapsing into paradoxes, balancing acts and contradictions. If a uniform picture can be presented, for instance, of a Netherlands that is, by and large, for or against the EU, the media, politicians and our European neighbours will have a better idea of the actual situation. Should a large majority in the Netherlands indeed be against the EU, parties will not have to pretend as if they are looking for a positive European story. But if the Netherlands is predominantly positive about European integration, politicians need not painstakingly voice anti-European sentiments simply to please the public.[8]

This book therefore analyses the Dutch position on the EU in everyday practice. Instead of examining nicely elaborated (party-political) views, we will consider developments in actual policy areas. According to Geert Mak, people do not

7 Schout, A. (2012, July 3). In de praktijk zijn politieke partijen vóór Europese integratie – ook de PVV [In practice, political parties are in favour of European integration – including the PVV]. *Volkskrant*.

8 Schout, A. (2011, July 14). Oh dat verongelijkte toontje in de EU [Oh that 'I've been wronged' tone in the EU]. *NRC Handelsblad*.

wish to be swamped with institutional stories; they want to know what the added value of the EU is,[9] and hence the chapter's attention to developments in policy practice. In this context, we look at what has been achieved in these fields and what is at stake for the Netherlands. The EU deals with many issues and affects our political structures in many ways. The trends at policy level help us see what lies behind the rhetoric for or against the EU. For this, a number of policy areas were selected: EU and foreign policy, EU and prosperity, and EU and legitimacy.

This introductory chapter distinguishes three images. Section 2 of this chapter deals with the (self-)image of the Netherlands as a Eurosceptic country. Section 3 paints the possibly reverse picture: the Netherlands as a pro-EU country. The fourth section focuses specifically on what research says about the population's aversion to the EU. The concluding section depicts the Netherlands as a country that knows full well that it is intricately intertwined with the EU. The people seem to support the EU as long as it is clear what practical added value it has to offer. At the time of writing, this chapter was based on reports about the Netherlands and the EU in the (international) media, on the subsequent chapters, and on interviews with officials and politicians who have been involved in European negotiations for many years.

1.2 The Anti-European (Self-)image of the Netherlands

For a moment, it seemed as if the Netherlands knew what it wanted with European integration. After the EU constitution fiasco in 2005, the political discourse changed its tune, calling for less EU, more attention for subsidiarity and a smaller EU budget.[10] Against this background, the Netherlands has had to put up with a lot over the past turbulent years of euro crisis and successive European summits. What is striking in this context, as stated earlier, is the combination of Eurosceptic language that could be heard and, at the same time, the support for deepened integration and the commitment of tens of billions of euros to European emergency funds, approved by Parliament. Dutch politicians find it hard to steer a clear course in this respect, which, again, became apparent in June 2012 when Germany put the inevitable political Union on the agenda[11] and Van Rompuy took a first step in that direction. Prime Minister Rutte replied that he would not be tempted into presenting institutional vistas, thus voicing the reticence also expressed by the House of Representatives whenever the subject of a more politically integrated Union comes up. The fact that in the run-up to an EU summit the

9 Mak, G. (2012). *Kom van die ijsschots af!* [Get off that ice floe!] [Essay]. <www.geertmak.nl>.

10 Coalition agreement. (2010, September 30). <www.rijksoverheid.nl/regering/het-kabinet/regeerakkoord>.

11 Halting Europe's downward spiral: a master plan to save the euro. (2012, June 26). *Der Spiegel*.

need to maintain sovereignty is repeatedly emphasized in plenary House debates is typical in this respect. In these same debates, the Prime Minister indicated that countries may judge, but not lay down the law to each other.[12] Focusing on the euro crisis, the government mainly indicated that the EU should not interfere in Dutch economic policy and that 'the South' should conform.

Still, leaving aside the vague concept of Political Union, the fact is that a sustainable EMU also demands the *E* of economic union, with emergency funds for governments, eurobonds, banking supervision and bank guarantees.[13] It is the logical implication of far-reaching monetary unification. But, here too, the Netherlands showed its current reluctance, arguing that these are the final steps of the EMU, which can only be taken once Member States have proved they are capable of managing their economies. The Netherlands, even more than Germany, has thus wanted to delay and fend off deeper European integration.

Meanwhile, the possibility of binding supervision has been reinforced – also at the insistence of the Netherlands – by, for instance, the independent European Commissioner for Economic Policy, the Six-Pack, the new Fiscal Compact and many other crisis measures,[14] no longer even guaranteeing national control over the use of the European emergency fund (ESM). As a result, over the coming years and despite all the rhetoric, European control of the symbol of national sovereignty (the national budget) is only likely to increase.

There are more fields where, within the EU, the Netherlands has presented itself as a conservative EU member. The Nederland is, in any case, one of the countries saying 'no' most often during European negotiations; this was the outcome of a study by Votewatch widely covered by foreign media.[15] In addition, the Netherlands has tried to again gain control over its borders (see the chapter by Groenendijk), to reduce the EU budget (see van Nispen and Blankenstein), is no longer at the forefront of further police cooperation (see den Boer) and has major reservations about further enlargement of the EU and the Schengen area (see Wiersma). To also keep the European Commission at bay, the Netherlands indicated that it especially did not want the emergency fund (EFSF) to be managed by the Commission and that the IMF should play an important role in monitoring Greece (see Verdun). All this fits the position which, amongst others, Prime Minister Rutte adopted when, fully in line with the VVD's views in recent years, emphasizing that European integration was a project that should, in particular,

12 Schout, A., Wiersma, J.M. & Ebben, I. (2012). De EU-paradox van kabinet-Rutte: zowel voor als tegen [The EU paradox of the Rutte cabinet: Both for and against]. *Internationale Spectator, 66*(9), 416-420.

13 De Grauwe, P. (2011). *Governance of a fragile eurozone* (CEPS Working Documents).

14 Borger, V. (2011). De eurocrisis als katalysator voor het Europese noodfonds en het toekomstig permanent stabilisatiemechanisme [The euro crisis as a catalyst for the European emergency fund and the future permanent stabilisation mechanism]. *Tijdschrift voor Europees en Economisch Recht, 59*(5), 207-216.

15 *See*, for instance, *De Stem*, 9 July 2012.

have economic added value.[16] These Dutch views may be understandable in the case of each separate issue, but together they create an image to the outside world of a country turning its back on European integration.

Moreover, the tone in the media and the House of Representatives hardened: the VVD now wants an opt-out from Schengen, like the United Kingdom, "garlic eaters" should leave the euro, and the Netherlands wants its money back. In the Volkskrant, a "well-mannered diplomat" said to have had it with "that stalling by those f*** Greeks".[17] The House of Representatives has repeatedly given the government restricting negotiation instructions. One day before a European Council, the Slob Motion[18] stated that no action shall be taken towards European political union and no sovereignty shall be transferred. The Plasterk/Voordewind Motion[19] limits budget negotiations to the effect that the EU budget is to be kept at the same level, without even inflation adjustment, and refers, as an aside, to cuts on "the travelling circus to Strasbourg". Former Minister De Jager was not afraid of becoming 'immensely unpopular' in the negotiations, all in "the Dutch interest".[20] Still, these firm statements have not been able to prevent him from having to bite the Brussels dust on several occasions, if only because Germany – in consultation with France – proved more flexible during the negotiations.[21]

Apart from taking this attitude in European negotiations, the Netherlands was firmly against accepting the mirror held up by the EU semester to Dutch policy-makers. Over recent years, Prime Minister Rutte has always repeated that economic supervision only applies to problem countries and that the Netherlands is not one of them. The VVD called the Commission recommendations in this field "inappropriate" and stated that the Commission should stay out of our economic policy.[22] The PVV and SP considered the EU semester a diktat from Brussels, and the PvdA backed the measures but wanted the Netherlands to define its own timetable. Thus, an important part of the discussion on the economic recommendations revolved around the question to what extent the Commission should have a say in Dutch policy choices and was characterized by resistance to EU interference.

16 Arts, G. & Bos, M. (2010). Het Europa-gehalte van de Nederlandse verkiezingsprogramma's [The Europe level of the Dutch election programmes]. *Internationale Spectator, 64*(6), 328-331.

17 Peeperkorn, M. (2011, September 14). Europa heeft het gehad met dat getalm van die kut-Grieken [Europe has had it with that stalling by those f*** Greeks]. *Volkskrant.*

18 Dutch House of Representatives. (2011, March 23). *Vergaderjaar* 2010-2011, *Kamerstuk* 21 501-20, No. 516.

19 Dutch House of Representatives. (2011, May 26). *Vergaderjaar* 2010-2011, *Kamerstuk* 32 502, No. 6.

20 De Jager wil best 'immense impopulair' zijn [De Jager does not mind being 'immensely unpopular']. (2011, July 10). *Trouw.*

21 Visser, M. (2012). *De eurocrisis: politieke strijd om de redding van de euro* [The euro crisis: Political struggle to save the euro]. Business Contact.

22 VVD vindt dat EU boekje te buiten gaat [VVD believes EU oversteps the mark]. (2012, May 31). <www.nu.nl/politiek/2823734/vvd-vindt-eu-boekje-buiten-gaat.html>.

Content and tone fed the anti-European image of the Netherlands at home and abroad. The Dutch NRC Handelsblad placed the Netherlands in the anti-European camp twice in one article,[23] and opinions are becoming more extreme. For instance, speculations are made about the following two extreme possibilities: the EU either becomes a Euro-federal state, in line with the ideas of former Belgian Prime Minister Verhofstadt, or will be no more than a form of cooperation between sovereign states; "everything else will merely be a stay of execution".[24] Putting it in such black and white terms, a pro-European choice can easily be presented as the wrong one: in case of European unity, we will have a "revolt" on our hands.[25] In addition, the media do not stop going on about the problems of Greece and the lazy Greeks and the fact that 7 out of 10 Dutch people would balk at paying for them.[26]

This EU-critical tone has also been noticed abroad. According to the *Financial Times*, the leading newspaper in the EU, the Netherlands is the most obstructionist country in the EU.[27] It was always considered a constructive country, allowing it to punch above its weight. Now, the FT is presenting politicians like Wilders and De Jager as prominent examples of the not very diplomatic Dutch behaviour in the euro crisis. In Brussels, the Netherlands is seen as a 'swing state' – not written off yet, but close – which may adversely affect the EU's internal cohesion and stability. An otherwise cautious politician like Polish Prime Minister Tusk, in his capacity as new President of the Council, referred to the Netherlands as a 'detracting' country, and reluctant countries are difficult to work with for an EU president. Commission President Barroso always has to navigate between leading the EU and avoiding statements about political developments in Member States. Nevertheless, on several occasions he indirectly referred to the Netherlands: leaders should not pander to populists, extremists or xenophobes.[28] In discussions on the EU's collapse, the Netherlands is often presented as one of those to be blamed[27] and, due to emerging extreme left and right wings, is an example of rising nationalism within the EU, together with Finland and Denmark.[29]

The general picture of the Dutch attitude also has consequences for the Dutch influence within the EU. Insiders in European negotiations from official and business circles are very concerned sometimes about the hardening political tone on Europe. Image matters and impacts not only on domestic political relations and choices but also on the relationship with Europe and the room for manoeuvre in Brussels. Abroad, close attention is paid to EU debates in the media

23 *NRC Handelsblad*, 7 September 2011.

24 Baudet, T. (2011, September 9). Minder EU of juist meer, iets anders is er niet [Less or more EU, there is nothing else]. *NRC Handelsblad*.

25 Heijne, B. (2011, September 3). Crisis. *NRC Handelsblad*.

26 *De Telegraaf*, 14 June 2011.

27 European integration is unravelling. (2011, May 30). *Financial Times*.

28 Speech by Barroso to the EP, 5 December 2011, *Financial Times* Blog, 6 January 2011.

29 Finland highlights unease about bail-outs. (2011, April 18). *Financial Times*.

and the House of Representatives. The domestic EU debate thus forms part of Dutch (economic) diplomacy, sending signals that affect the negotiating position. A Dutch top negotiator indicated that, in his field, the United Kingdom sometimes sidelines itself in Brussels negotiations because of its non-constructive and inflexible attitude; he feared the same fate awaits the Netherlands. Many Dutch commentators, too, have warned that the Netherlands might become a pariah.[30] Even ambassadors have publicly stated that the Netherlands should not hide behind its dykes and that it seems as if the Netherlands has become a confused and introvert country.[31]

The general opinion abroad is that the political attitude of the Netherlands lacks substantiation. As a result, Ministers Leers' and Kamp's wish to partly close the borders to workers from the East and to limit family reunification led to problems with the European Commission which were not just legal. For instance, in the Dutch press, European Commissioner Andor complained that there were no figures on the number of East Europeans abusing the social security system. It was not until nearly a year later (August 2011) that the Cabinet decided to investigate the alleged disturbance resulting from the free movement of persons. The image of a withdrawing Netherlands was completed by that of a country practising 'fact-free politics'.

The Dutch position not only concerns the 'Brussels' agenda. The EU also has (potential) consequences for national policy space. Sensitivities range from the fear that the mortgage interest tax relief will be abolished (see the chapter by van Witteloostuijn and Hendriks) to the concern that increased European budgetary surveillance will provoke criticism of the low level of participation of women in the labour market.[32]

Moreover, beyond the attention of the general public, a discussion has started about the extent to which the European Court of Justice should have a say in the Dutch justice system. Baudet believes Europe interferes too much.[33] The Court has played an important part in the creation and monitoring of the internal market, which also produces benefits for the Netherlands, but the limits of its undisputed legitimacy are beginning to show.

30 Sommer, M. (2011, December 24). Hadden ze dijken gehad, dan zou de rest van Europa erachter hebben gezeten [Had they had dykes, the rest of Europe would have been behind them]. *Volkskrant*.

31 Ambassadeurs vinden Nederland een verward en introvert land [Ambassadors find the Netherlands a confused and introvert country]. (2011, October29). *NRC Handelsblad*.

32 *Handelingen Tweede Kamer, Vergaderjaar* 2010-2011, No. 52, 15 February 2011.

33 Baudet, T.H.P. (2010, November 13). Het Europees Hof voor de Rechten van de Mens vormt een ernstige inbreuk op de democratie [The European Court of Human Rights forms a serious encroachment of democracy]. *NRC Handelsblad*.

1.3 The Image of the Netherlands as a Pro-European Country

In the light of the previous section, there is no denying the image of the Netherlands as a Euro-critical country, and it is not hard to add to the list of examples. But what is striking first and foremost is that over the past few years, despite all the criticism, the Netherlands has agreed to many European measures. So, besides this Euro-critical image, another image emerges. It may be stated that the anti-European attitude described above does not necessarily mean that the Netherlands is against the EU or further integration.

For instance, the Netherlands has become more assertive about further enlargement (see the chapter by Wiersma in this volume). Having learnt from the earlier experience of Greece, Bulgaria and Romania acceding to the EU too soon, the Netherlands has stipulated extra demands before countries can actually become members, for instance, about the existence of an independent justice system in the country concerned. The Netherlands is prepared, if need be alone, to stick to its guns on enlargement, for example, during the Serbian negotiations when it demanded that Mladic be extradited for trial to the Yugoslavia Tribunal. Earlier pressure on the Netherlands to water down its extradition demand and criticism in 2009 from, amongst others, Carl Bildt (Minister of Foreign Affairs and, at that time, Swedish President of the EU) about "moving the goalposts during the match" turned to international recognition for the Dutch position when, in 2011, Mladic was actually extradited[34] and, in addition, steps were finally taken in regard to Serbia's recognition of Kosovo. When Schengen was enlarged with Romania and Bulgaria, the Netherlands also fought hard for stricter application of the legal and administrative requirements.

This also applies when it comes to solving the euro crisis, where, in recent years, the Netherlands has focused all its efforts on stricter agreements about, e.g., budgetary discipline and tighter and more effective supervision of enforcement of the agreed rules. In a later chapter, Wiersma refers, in this context, to the Dutch pursuit of the 100% Union, a Union where countries have to stick to agreements reached. Eurobonds and a banking union, to name a few examples, may be possible, but the Netherlands believes that countries should first prove that they can fulfil their agreements. It is of the opinion that the EU has been too flexible and permissive. It is precisely because adequate supervision has been lacking that all kinds of necessary adaptations have not been made, which, according to the Netherlands, goes a long way in explaining the current crisis. Since so much store is set by enforcement and by strict application of the agreed *acquis*, it should come as no surprise that within the EU the Netherlands initiated the establish-

34 Schout, A. & Wiersma, J.M. (2012, August 8). *Reinventing Europe: The Dutch paradox*. European Council on Foreign Relations.

ment of a common rule of law monitor[35] to ensure uniform application of the law.

This focus on enforcement can also be seen in the institutional choices advocated by the Rutte Cabinet to strengthen independent supervision of Member States.[36] This initiative, supported by Germany, is fully in line with the traditional choice of working with the Commission and the Community method. A strong European Commission is to our advantage, which even Rutte's minority cabinet admitted at the time of alleged Euroscepticism. In this respect, it is striking that the Netherlands has called for independent supervision of (macro-)economic policy, budgetary policy and the total public debt as well as the banking sector.[37]

Calling the Netherlands anti-European in other EU matters where the Netherlands has been strongly criticized would be taking a limited view as well. Together with others, the Netherlands is campaigning against a higher European budget (see the chapter by van Nispen and Blankenstein), but considering all the criticism of money being pumped around via regional funds and the spending of European agricultural funds, the Dutch approach could also be regarded as constructive (see the chapter by Oskam), especially against the background of the 'modernization' of the European budgetary system advocated by the Netherlands.

In recent years, leaving aside the rhetoric, the government as well as substantial majorities in the House of Representatives have shown their pro-European colours at crucial moments, displaying a distinct preference for Community cooperation and particularly for strengthening independent supervision by the European Commission. The House has clearly endorsed the choice for a 100% Union. The Dutch political parties – except for the PVV – have committed themselves to saving the euro and supporting further integration.[38] Of course, these preferences are not to everyone's liking, but they do put the Dutch image as an anti-European country into perspective. In fact, the image created by the above examples taken together is that of a country in favour of an EU based on rules that are enforced, whether these concern Schengen, enlargement or the eurozone; the reasoning behind this is that, without rules and supervision, the European integration process will grind to a halt, with all the negative consequences. In short, an

35 Botero, J.C., Janse, R., Muller, S. & Pratt, C.S. (Eds.). (2012, June 26). *Innovations in rule of law*. The Hague: The Hague Institute for the Internationalisation of Law and the World Justice Project. <www.hiil.org/data/sitemanagement/media/WJP&HiiL%20UN%20Report-UNGA%20Event.pdf>.

36 Dutch House of Representatives. (2011, September 7). *Vergaderjaar* 2011-2012, *Handelingen Tweede Kamer* 21 501-07, No. 839, Kamerbrief over de Visie Toekomst Economische en Monetaire Unie [Letter from the House of Representatives on views on the future of Economic and Monetary Union].

37 Dutch House of Representatives. (2012, June 27). *Handelingen Tweede Kamer, Vergaderjaar* 2011-2012.

38 Schout (2012).

attitude inspired by a good understanding of the importance of an effective EU to the Netherlands.
Considered from this perspective, it is mainly the *tone* of the Dutch attitude that has fuelled the perception of the Netherlands as a Eurosceptic country. But the question is whether this tone, which mainly seems meant to please the public, has been used by politicians in response to the allegedly crumbling support for the EU among the population. Has this support really dwindled that much? This question is addressed below.

1.4 The Perception that Support among the Population Is Waning

Especially after the 'no' to the European constitution, it was widely believed that support for European integration among the population had dwindled and had turned into distrust. Somewhere along the way the political elite – or so the story went – had lost the citizen where Europe was concerned. The discussion then focused on the question how the population could be more involved in Europe again, how to bridge the gap between the citizen and the EU.[39] A popular approach in this context, especially in response to the euro crisis, is to tell that citizen what major economic advantages Europe has to offer.[40] However, the mantras of the Netherlands Bureau for Economic Policy Analysis (*Centraal Planbureau*, CPB) that the internal market accounts for one extra month's salary and the euro for one extra week's salary no longer seem to work and provoke daily and weekly newspapers into directing sneering remarks at Euro believers.[41] On further consideration, the CPB figures proved less clear anyway, which is why, when the benefits of trade liberalization within the EU were published, the CPB stated, "However, we cannot rule out that the effect of the internal market policy on trade between these countries [the six founding fathers] has been minor".[42] In

39 *See, e.g.*, Wetenschappelijke Raad voor het Regeringsbeleid (WRR) (Scientific Council for Government Policy). (2007). *Europa in Nederland* [Europe in the Netherlands]. Amsterdam: Amsterdam University Press.

40 Kroes, N. (2012, July 9). Kabinet moet stoppen met kritiek Europa [Cabinet should stop criticising Europe]. *Trouw*; Sommer (2012); Adviesraad Internationale Vraagstukken/Advisory Council on International Affairs. (2012, February). Towards enhanced and financial governance in the EU (Advisory Letter 19).

41 Wynia, S. (2011, September 5). Redders van Griekenland bezigen drogredeneringen [Saviours of Greece use fallacies]. *Elsevier*; Heck, W. (2012, June 15). Next.checkt: 'Europa' kost 230 euro per persoon per jaar, maar levert 1.500 tot 2.000 euro op' ['Europe' costs 230 euro per person per year, but brings in 1,500 to 2,000 euro']. D66 leader Alexander Pechtold in the television programme 'Buitenhof'.

42 SCP (*Sociaal-Cultureel Planbureau* – Netherlands Institute for Social Research), CPB. (2007). *Marktplaats Europa: vijftig jaar ongenoegen* [Marketplace Europe: fifty years of discontent]. Europese Verkenningen no. 5, The Hague, p. 100.

short, initially much was made of the advantages of integration, but the euro crisis has drawn our attention to the question what the costs and benefits of the EU really are.

But against this background, has Dutch support for the EU really dwindled that markedly? Have periods of waning support, followed by recovery, occurred more often? Insofar as the latter is true, the 'no' of 2005 was more of an incident than the turning point it is often said to be. An argument substantiating this interpretation is that, over the years, support for the EU has, by and large, been quite constant. In this volume, Paul Dekker demonstrates that even during the euro crisis the European attitude of the Dutch shows much more nuance. Despite differences between, e.g., levels of education, he concludes that support for EU membership has remained more or less the same over a longer period. For instance, in spite of everything, the euro can still count on the support of around 70% of the population.

On the basis of a further analysis of the figures (see the chapter by Dekker), we can also interpret this image of a country turning its back on the EU in the sense that the Netherlands has in fact always taken a *pragmatic* approach to European integration. Over the past 30 years, between 70% and 80% of the Dutch population have considered the EU a good thing (Eurobarometer). Around '1992', support for the EU was substantial. However, in 1993, surveys showed that still 45% would have voted against the Treaty of Maastricht. Like in France, all we, too, could have hoped for at the time would have been a 'petit oui' for the Maastricht Treaty. Rejecting a treaty has, in itself, not much to do with being for or against the EU. In 1993, the Netherlands was strongly in favour of the (at the time) highly visible '1992' project aimed at removing trade barriers between the Member States. However, even then, the advent of the euro and the corresponding federal vistas were less popular. After that, a clear dip can be seen in support for the EU, particularly around 2003, i.e., in the run-up to the 2004 enlargement (see Dekker). In spring 2005, however, support increased, even though in that period a large majority threw out the European constitution. Many explanations are circulating as to why the constitution was rejected, but the fact that the Dutch have little affinity with the symbolism of a European constitution, European flag and European president (quite apart even from the aversion to the Balkenende Cabinet at that time[43]) will certainly have something to do with it.

Moreover, in relative terms, the Netherlands can still be found in the top regions of European supporters. At the same time, it is not uncritical of the EU, or as Dekker puts it in a later chapter, "support for EU membership may continue to be considerable, but this should not be interpreted as enthusiasm for Europe". The picture that emerges from interviews is that the European 'narrative' of the Netherlands is less clear than in some other, surrounding countries. For decades, Germany has been quite cooperative, because Europe has been a means to escape

43 Survey by Maurice de Hond. (2005). <https://n9.noties.nl/peil.nl/>.

the shadow of the past. Luxembourg has always felt very European as it is small and surrounded by other countries and because it used to be a sort of monetary province of – of all countries! – monetarily weak Belgium.
The Dutch 'narrative' is characterized by economic pragmatism and has, since the 1950s, been linked to the removal of trade barriers,[44] quite understandable for a trade nation. SCP/CPB studies have also concluded that economic pragmatism rather than idealism has dominated the debate here.[45] This pragmatism goes together with differences in support for the various policy areas. The Eurobarometer (December 2011) shows that such support mainly concerns defence cooperation (62%), migration (58%), environmental policy (80%), combating terrorism (89%) and, quite remarkably, disadvantaged regions (72%), while we prefer dealing with other fields ourselves: social security (21%), employment policy (30%) and taxes (22%). This underlines that voters take a pragmatic view of the EU's added value, which holds particularly true of trade, security and transnational issues. Thomassen[46] takes a similar approach when pointing out that the internal market-oriented thinking of the Dutch is well in line with the wish to protect labour markets: we focus on the direct economic benefits of the EU. Perhaps our pragmatism also shows in the remarkably low scores on 'proud of our own nationality/proud to be European'.[47]
However, the crisis does lead – throughout the EU – to a declining trust in the European institutions.[48] This falling trust does not necessarily mean that the Netherlands is turning its back on the EU. In 2011, trust in the EU dropped by 11% to 51%.[49] These figures match the falling trust in the Dutch government, by 12% to 51%,[50] which might suggest that trust in the European institutions follows the fluctuations in trust in the national institutions. In any case, levels of trust in Dutch institutions and in those of the EU have been converging. Also in terms of trust and distrust, Europe seems quite normal in this light.

1.5 Conclusion: a Country Intertwined with the EU

The Netherlands seems to be struggling with the EU, and unfortunately, it is precisely now that it is beset by the wish and/or need to deepen integration. The euro crisis demands European controls and support funds, but it seems that support for this is diminishing. Voters see the House of Representatives' doubts

44 Griffiths, R.T. (Ed.). (1990). *The Netherlands and the integration of Europe, 1945-1957*. Amsterdam: NEHA.
45 SCP, CPB (2007), p. 70.
46 Thomassen, J. (2007). *Citizens and the legitimacy of the European Union*. The Hague: WRR.
47 SCP, CPB (2007), p. 44.
48 Eurobarometer December 2011.
49 Ibid., p. 46.
50 Ibid., p. 44.

about European measures, and motions have asked successive governments to develop convincing European perspectives. The Netherlands no longer seems to have a foothold in the EU debate. The story about the benefits of European integration is no longer automatically accepted. Citizens are distrustful. The government hesitates and is putting on the brakes. And abroad, the Netherlands is considered a penitent.

But next to this picture of a county turning its back on the Union, another picture emerges: Europe has become *normal*. The fact that there is more criticism and discussion is part of the EU maturing as a political and administrative layer in the edifice of Member States and European institutions. The question whether there is a 'permissive consensus' among the population is no longer relevant, since the EU has now become a broad part of all kinds of policy areas. This makes EU policy just as controversial as national policy issues concerning cuts, asylum, reforms of the welfare state and the future of defence – especially also because the national and European dimensions are strongly intertwined. Rather, it would have been odd had the EU remained unchallenged. Now that the EU is dealing with policy-sensitive issues, it has gained political relevance, and themes which used to be dealt with through a technocratic, Community approach, are inevitably politicizing. Those days are over. At the same time, surveys on policy preferences among the population can be interpreted as proof of a continuing pragmatic view on the EU's added value. In this context, the outcome of the recent parliamentary elections in 2012 is an indication of the ultimately pragmatic attitude of many voters. The electoral fight did not end in a choice for or against Europe, and parties that had been pro-European in the euro crisis were not punished for it.

Nor do the chapters in this book depict a country withdrawing from European integration. On the contrary, their discussions show that, in a range of policy areas, the Netherlands is strongly intertwined with the EU and closely involved in European developments. However, developments are different in each policy field. European agricultural policy is clearly an area that needs to be changed, and discussions to that effect are well under way, with active Dutch input. As Oskam argues, it would be good for the Netherlands were agricultural policy to shift from (income) support to innovation measures. Police cooperation is a policy field where fights over sovereignty are to be expected because national security is involved. But because this security strongly depends on cooperation with other Member States, it is precisely this policy field where a vibrant Europeanization process has taken place, with the Netherlands taking the initiative in certain phases (see the chapter by den Boer). The chapters on economic cooperation show the same trend of ongoing European integration, with further developments in the internal market, finding ways to make markets more competitive and attempts to monetarily discipline Member States. Moreover, the economic chapters by Pelkmans, van Witteloostuijn and Verdun show that further economic growth is hard to imagine without the EU and deepening economic integration.

Normalization can also be seen in foreign policy. Gerrits dispels the image of the EU only playing a marginal role in the relations with Russia because Member States mainly compete with each other for access to the Russian market. Quite the reverse, Gerrits broadly describes the logical division of roles that has developed between the EU and the Member States, whereby the EU determines the political context in which the Member States negotiate with Russia. Van Staden shows that the limits of a meaningful national foreign policy have been reached and that Dutch bilateral visits and contacts are better integrated into a European approach. Wolff, upon searching for workable support for the democratization challenges in North Africa, also concludes that joint European action adds value. The Netherlands wants to support democratization in our neighbouring countries, but will achieve nothing on its own. Meanwhile, there is more clarity as to cooperation with the United States. As described by van Eekelen, the old conflict between the Atlantic and European approach has been replaced by more pragmatic defence cooperation within NATO. In this context, the EU and forms of cooperation (bi-, tri- and multilateral) between European countries (will) increasingly claim, by trial and error, a place of their own.

This intertwining with the EU has also left its mark on the changes that Parliament has recently undergone to be able to act sooner and more effectively in matters of EU policy. Van Keulen describes the new procedures instituted to ensure that European policy processes are scrutinized at national level. However, these are by no means the only obstacles that political parties need to solve in integrating European reality into their debates and choices (see the chapter by Corbey). The fact that Europe is not finished yet thus also applies to the way political parties deal with the EU.

In short, the Netherlands is not performing a balancing act between deepened integration and crumbling European support. European policy issues have become part of 'national' choices and are discussed just as vehemently. The consequences of the picture of European normalization are considerable, if only because, as a result, politicians no longer have to bend over backwards pretending to be Euro-critical to please the public and commentators no longer need to interpret every remark of a politician in terms of for or against Europe.

So, is everything fine between the Netherlands and European integration? Certainly not. In 1988, Paul Scheffer described the Netherlands as a content nation, a country which, in its relations with the surrounding world, mainly focused on maintaining the status quo since this afforded stability, security and prosperity.[51] In the matter of Europe, this status quo was based on close ties with the United States as guardian of stability and security in Europe, and was reflected in NATO's doctrine as the cornerstone of Dutch security policy. In addition, and

51 Scheffer, P. (1988). *Een tevreden natie: Nederland en het wederkerend geloof in de Europese status quo* [A content nation: The Netherlands and the recurring belief in the European status quo]. Amsterdam: Bakker.

serving as a second anchor, there was European integration, which, however, was mainly meant to promote Dutch interests in free trade and – through Community cooperation – prevent dominance by the big Member States. The fact that the Netherlands has always been averse to political integration in the European context – this being a threat to its ties with the United States – was perfectly in line with this view. The Netherlands fully endorsed a EC/EU governed on a depoliticized and functional-technocratic basis. Both foundations of the Dutch status quo policy are under pressure. The ties with the United States are loosening, and Europe is becoming more political.

As a result, our anchors have broken loose, the new challenge being to prevent this 'content nation' from turning into a 'discontent nation', which carries the challenge of debating the Dutch position in Europe. These chapters demonstrate there is no mistaking that this future lies in Europe.

2 Public Opinion

Paul Dekker

2.1 Introduction

This chapter deals with public opinion as the sum of opinions of individual citizens. These opinions are far less public than the public opinion that emerges in the media via statements by politicians, representatives of civil society organizations, commentators and other opinion leaders. It rather involves opinions of the public, of the audience of opinion makers, and sometimes hardly even the latter. As we will see, until recently, Europe was barely a subject of discussion. However, this 'silent' public opinion is important, not only for citizens to find out what their own collective preferences are, but certainly also for representatives of their interests and for politicians to get a better idea of what the beliefs and feelings are of the population they wish to represent. Such information may be a reason to adjust one's own opinions as well as to be better prepared for resistance and to work harder to convince others, to 'gain support'. The latter is a dominant perspective in studies on public opinion about the European Union (EU). It generally involves 'support' (for membership, the euro, enlargement, etc.), which is practically taken for granted as normal or desirable, or both. Lack of support is a 'shortcoming', and explicitly labelling it as 'Euroscepticism' or 'Europhobia' does not help. For the sake of readability, all indicators in this chapter have been formulated pro-Europe: higher is more, but more need by no means be better. We will come back to this in Section 6. First, an overview in figures is provided of Dutch public opinion in a European comparative perspective (Section 2) and over time (Section 3), followed by analyses of differences between populations (Section 4) and ambivalences and developments in opinions of individuals (Section 5).

2.2 The Netherlands in Europe

I use population surveys from three international studies: various Eurobarometers (EB; population of 15+), the fourth wave of the European Values Study (EVS; 18+) and the fourth wave of the European Social Survey (ESS; 15+). The advantage of the EB surveys, often commissioned by the European Commission, is that current data are available for all EU Member States regarding a large number of subjects. A disadvantage is that sometimes the questions are rather biased towards a Brussels policy perspective and focus on the EU such that they probably put off many people who are not that interested in Europe, and the remaining respondents, giving the matter more thought, become more positive about Europe than before the surveys. In the EB, sentiments about Europe often seem somewhat more favourable or milder than in other studies. This does not mean that it is of no use. With a probably quite constant bias, it still lends itself to comparing countries and times. The advantage of the more academically inspired EVS and ESS is that they are more general. They offer little specifically about the EU, and the data are also slightly older (the surveys used here date from 2008-2009), and in the ESS many EU Member States have not been included.

2.2.1 *Europe between the Netherlands and the World*

Table 2.1 uses EVS data to situate attitudes towards Europeans and the EU between the national and the global level. This has been done for the 27 EU Member States, as well as for Iceland, Norway and Switzerland. The result is a voluminous table, but which has the advantage of also including the country codes, which are subsequently used in less-cluttered diagrams.

Table 2.1 Concern with Europeans and Other People and Trust in the EU and in Other Institutions in 30 Countries in 2008/9, Arranged According to Decreasing Concern with Europeans

Country	Code	Concern[a]			Trust[b]		
		Europeans	Deviation from fellow countrymen	Deviation from people worldwide	The EU	Deviation from national parliament	Deviation from United Nations
Switzerland	CH	**35**	+18	+19	**40**	+24	+17
Germany	DE	**29**	+17	+16	**37**	+ 0	+ 3
Portugal	PT	**27**	+18	+17	**69**	–28	+ 3
Romania	RO	**22**	+11	+ 0	**61**	–37	– 2
Denmark	DK	**22**	+18	+18	**44**	+26	+31
Malta	MT	**21**	+11	– 1	**67**	–13	– 2
Lithuania	LT	**18**	+11	+ 6	**71**	–57	– 2
Luxembourg	LU	**18**	+ 3	+ 8	**67**	+ 2	+ 2
France	FR	**16**	+10	+17	**53**	– 1	+11
Greece	GR	**16**	+21	+ 5	**49**	–18	–13
Sweden	SE	**15**	+12	+ 7	**41**	+19	+30
Italy	IT	**15**	+10	+15	**65**	–30	+ 0
Bulgaria	BG	**14**	+17	+ 1	**59**	–48	–13
Poland	PL	**14**	+12	+ 1	**55**	–36	+ 0
Iceland	IS	**14**	+18	+17	**33**	+ 6	+38

Country	Code	Concern[a]			Trust[b]		
		Europeans	Deviation from fellow countrymen	Deviation from people worldwide	The EU	Deviation from national parliament	Deviation from United Nations
Spain	ES	**13**	+14	+14	**55**	− 7	− 8
Ireland	IE	**13**	+11	+14	**58**	− 9	+ 3
Norway	NO	**13**	+14	+10	**43**	+21	+40
Cyprus	CY	**12**	+18	+ 3	**56**	+ 0	−21
Austria	AT	**12**	+ 5	+ 4	**30**	+ 0	+ 3
Belgium	BE	**12**	+ 9	+ 1	**60**	−18	+ 2
Finland	FI	**10**	+ 6	+33	**38**	+ 6	+20
Slovenia	SI	**10**	+19	+ 5	**71**	−25	− 7
United Kingdom	UK	**10**	+12	+21	**25**	− 2	+25
Slovakia	SK	**10**	+ 6	+ 3	**67**	−18	− 7
Czech Republic	CZ	**9**	+ 3	+ 9	**43**	−26	+ 3
Hungary	HU	**7**	+ 9	− 1	**51**	−30	+ 0
Estonia	EE	**7**	+11	+ 1	**55**	−27	− 2
Latvia	LV	**5**	+ 6	+ 1	**42**	−22	+ 9
Netherlands	NL	**5**	+ 6	+ 4	**45**	+ 4	+10
Averages of countries		**15**	+12	+ 9	**52**	−11	+ 6

[a]'To what extent do you feel concerned with the living conditions of [...] your fellow countrymen, Europeans, all people worldwide?' For Europeans, the % '(very) much' is given, and for fellow countrymen and all people, the deviation from this percentage is shown in % points.

[b]'Please indicate for each of the institutions on this card whether you trust it very much, quite a lot, not that much or not at all. [...] the parliament [...] the European Union [...] the United Nations.' For the EU, the % '(very/quite) much' is given, and for the parliament and the United Nations, the deviation from this percentage is shown in % points.

Source: EVS 4 (2008/9).

The Swiss say they are most concerned with Europeans; the Dutch and Latvians are least concerned. In nearly all countries, citizens are less concerned with Europeans than with their fellow countrymen and humankind as a whole. The question of concern probably appeals to feelings of both kinship and pity. For the former to apply, Europeans are too far away, and for the latter they are doing too well. To measure the 'European identity', the EB asks to what extent respondents feel European (or as inhabitants of their own neighbourhood or their own country or as world citizens). Regarding this question, in the EU the citizens of Luxembourg, Sweden, Estonia and Denmark feel most European and those of Cyprus, Italy, the United Kingdom and Greece least. The strongest rejection of the European identity – not feeling European 'at all' – can be seen in the United Kingdom.[1]

1 Creusen, H., Dekker, P., de Goede, I., Kox, H., Schyns, P. & Stolwijk, H. (2010). *Europa's Welvaart* [Europe's prosperity]. The Hague: Sociaal en Cultureel Planbureau/Centraal Planbureau [The Netherlands Institute for Social Research/Netherlands Bureau for Economic Policy Analysis], p. 15.

Trust in the EU ranges from 25% in the United Kingdom to 71% in Slovenia. It is compared with trust in the national parliament (somewhat less on average)[2] and trust in the United Nations (slightly more on average). The national level of trust in the EU is unrelated to the level of concern with Europeans (r = 0.08) and trust in the national parliament (0.01), but is positively linked to trust in the United Nations (0.28). In the Netherlands, trust in the EU is slightly below the average of countries, just as in other countries in north-western Europe.

2.2.2 *The EU: Concern and Knowledge*

Figure 2.1 compares two indications of concern with the EU: participation in discussions on European affairs and the claim to have knowledge of how the EU works. Relatively speaking, Europe very often is a topic of discussion in our country, and the level of knowledge is at the European average, at least in people's own perception.

Figure 2.1 Participation in Discussions on Europe[a] and Perceived Understanding of the EU, 2011

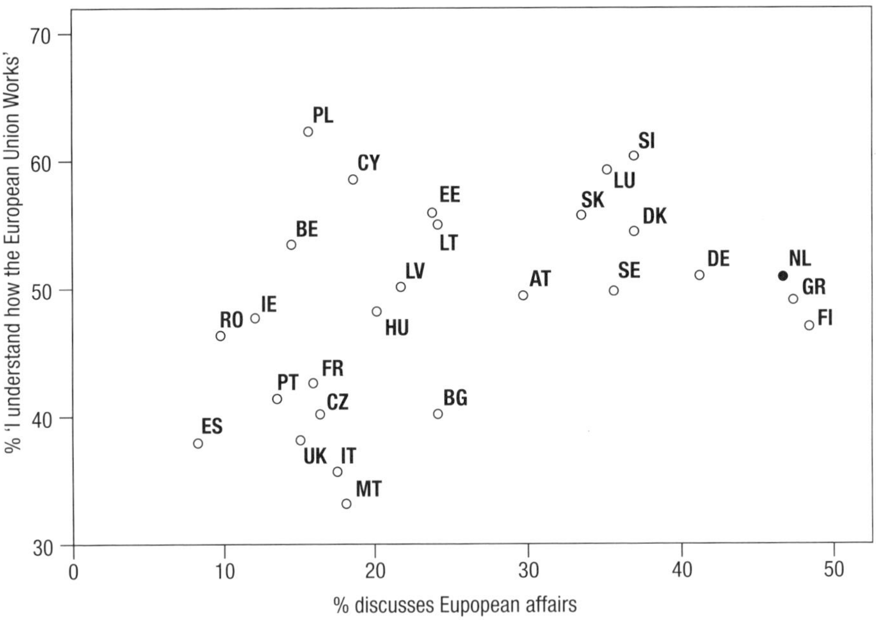

[a] Regularly or sometimes talks about European political affairs when among friends or family.

Source: EB 75.3 (May 2011).

2 'National government' would have been better as a comparative reference, but this term is not used everywhere. 'Parliament' has political connotations, which, in general, are not conducive to trust.

The question is, of course, what the level of actual knowledge is. This is regularly surveyed by the EB by means of a few simple factual questions. Most of the time, the Dutch score below average but do have an above-average impression that they are well-informed. The Dutch are unjustifiably optimistic about how well-informed they are.[3]

2.2.3 *The EU: Support for Membership and Policy Preferences*

Figure 2.2 shows the percentage of the population of the EU Member States who believe membership is a good thing and offers benefits. Both standard measurements of support for the EU are strongly correlated (r = 0.86 for percentages of the 27 Member States). Support is highly dispersed: in Latvia, not even a quarter of the population believe membership is a good thing, while in Luxembourg, the Netherlands and Ireland, almost three quarters believe membership is good. The percentages believing membership offers 'benefits' range from 37% in Latvia and the United Kingdom to 83% in Ireland.

Figure 2.2 Two Positive Assessments of EU Membership of One's Own Country, 2011

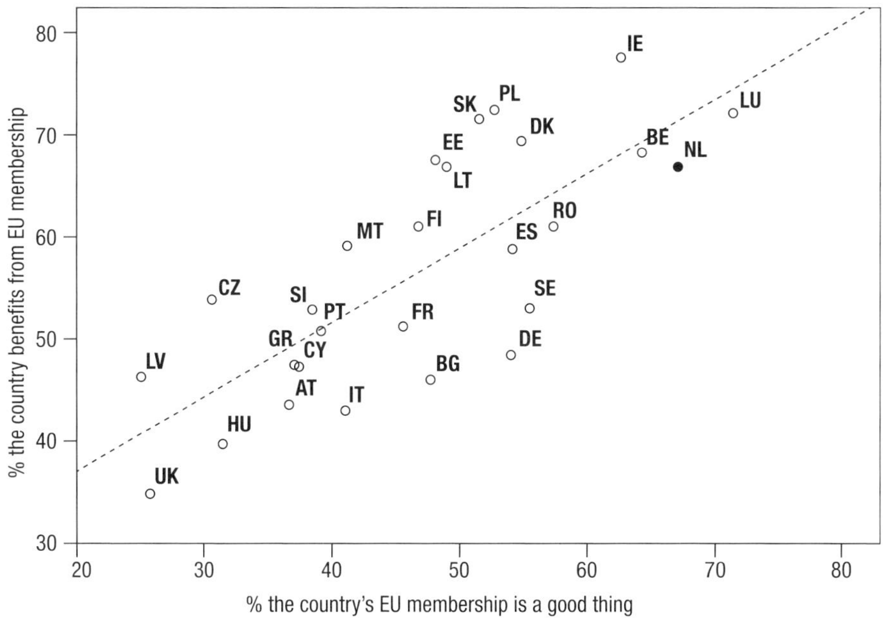

Source: EB 75.3 (May 2011).

3 *Cf.* Dekker, P., Horst, A. van der, Kok, S., Noije, L. van & Wennekers, C. (2008). *Europa's buren* [Europe's neighbours]. The Hague: Sociaal en Cultureel Planbureau/Centraal Planbureau, p. 15; Dekker, P., Horst, A. van der, Koutstaal, P., Kox, H., Meer, T. van der, Wennekers, C., Brosens, T. & Verschoor, B. (2009). *Strategisch Europa* [Strategic Europe]. The Hague: Sociaal en Cultureel Planbureau/Centraal Planbureau, p. 31; Creusen et al. (2010), p. 16.

As demonstrated by earlier measurements, the Netherlands is one of the countries where support for the EU is considerable, which has especially been measured as a 'good thing'. Developments in the Netherlands are discussed below. As stated above, the EB may paint a slightly too positive picture of support for the EU.[4] This need not be a problem in comparative analyses, but it does not hurt to look at another survey: Figure 2.3 contains data from the ESS of 2008-2009 regarding trust in the European Parliament and the desired level of European integration (the latter question is not included in the ESS of 2010/11). According to both criteria, the British are the least positive about Europe. This is well in line with the conclusions of the EB. Contrary to Figure 2.2, Figure 2.3 shows a lot of support for European integration in Romania and Bulgaria, while the Netherlands is found somewhere in the middle. Of course, asking about the desired level of unification of Europe is something else than asking about membership of one's own country. One may be satisfied with membership and still not want more Europe.

Figure 2.3 Support for European Unification and Trust in the European Parliament, 2008/9 (in Average Scores)[a]

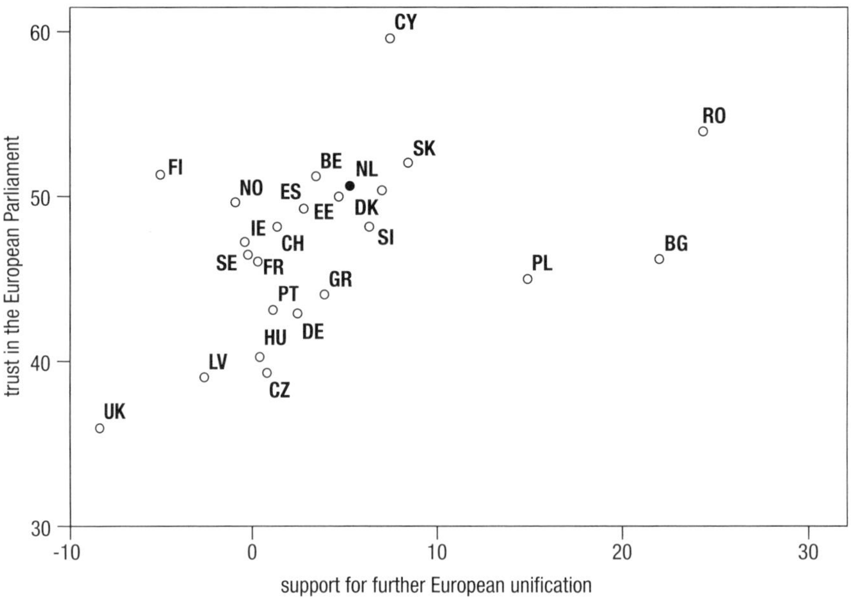

[a]Horizontally on a scale of –50 ('unification has already gone too far') to +50 ('unification should go further') ('Now thinking about the European Union, some say European unification should go further. Others say it has already gone too far. Using this card, what number on the scale best describes your position? Unification refers to further integration rather than further enlargement'); vertically on a scale of 0 ('no trust at all') to 100 ('complete trust').
Source: ESS 4 (2008/9).

4 *Cf.* Aldrin, P. (2011). The Eurobarometer and the making of European opinion. In D. Gaxie, N. Hubé & J. Rowell (Eds.), *Perceptions of Europe*. Colchester: ECPR, pp. 17-35.

To conclude this comparative section, Table 2.2 provides a further few elements of public opinion in the EU as a whole and in three northern and three southern countries of the eurozone. I show balances of percentages of the population with opposite views so as to take into account the sometimes strongly differing number of people who do not have a preference.[5]

Table 2.2 Democracy, Prospects and Various Policy Preferences End 2011 (and Early 2008): Net Majorities in Percentage Points[a]

	EU-27	NL	FI	DE	ES	IT	GR
Satisfaction (% satisfied – % dissatisfied) with the way national democracy works	+ 6	+51	+55	+37	– 8	–31	–66
Satisfaction (% satisfied – % dissatisfied) with the way democracy in the EU works	+ 2	+ 1	+ 1	+ 5	– 1	– 7	–37
Optimism (% optimists – % pessimists) about the future of the EU	+ 2	+ 9	+ 5	+ 6	+ 6	+13	–28
(Idem early 2008)	(+35)	(+55)	(+27)	(+28)	(+55)	(+31)	(+15)
Preference (% supporters – % opponents) for 'further enlargement of the EU to include other countries in future years'	–17	–33	–43	–59	+ 9	– 8	– 3
(Idem early 2008)	(+ 8)	(+ 4)	(– 4)	(+ 7)	(+46)	(+ 4)	(+24)
Preference (% supporters – % opponents) for 'a European monetary union with one single currency, the euro'	+13	+45	+45	+37	+33	+28	+55
(Idem early 2008)	(+27)	(+62)	(+61)	(+41)	(+41)	(+27)	(+ 2)
Preference (% supporters – % opponents) for the introduction of eurobonds (European bonds)	+20	+ 8	+ 9	–19	+37	+35	+42
Preference (% supporters – % opponents) for European decision-making on reducing public debt[b]	– 7	–23	–48	8	4	10	8
Preference (% supporters – % opponents) for European decision-making on pensions[b]	–49	–75	–89	–69	–34	–27	–48
Preference (% supporters – % opponents) for European decision-making on defence and foreign policy[b]	+34	+25	–53	+53	+51	+44	+12

[a]Positive – there are more satisfied people, optimists or supporters; negative – there are more dissatisfied people, pessimists or opponents.

[b]The choice is between decision-making by the national government or 'jointly within the EU'.

Source: EB 76.3 (November 2011) and EB 69.2 (April-May 2008).

5 This applies more to policy preferences than to the more general attitudes presented so far. For instance, when asked about eurobonds, 20% (Greeks) to 45% (Spanish) have no opinion.

First is satisfaction with the functioning of democracy in one's own country and in the EU. In the north, people are far more content with their own country than in the south. In southern countries, people even judge European democracy more kindly than they do democracy in their own country. The subsequent three opinions are about the future of the EU, enlargement and the euro. Between brackets, data are added from early 2008, i.e., before the banking crisis hit Europe. They show that, both in the EU as a whole and in the individual countries, people have become more negative about the EU's future and enlargement, but not about the euro. In Italy and Germany, opinions have not or hardly changed, and in Greece they have become more *positive*.

All six euro countries remain more positive than the EU as a whole. In countries outside the eurozone – with the United Kingdom again taking the lead (–65) – the population is, on average, less in favour of the single currency. It hardly comes as a surprise that eurobonds are more popular in the three southern euro countries than in the three northern ones. Finally, the level of support for more common policy in three areas is indicated. This varies between countries as far as public debt is concerned, but a common policy on pensions is rejected overall, while there is much support for an EU policy on defence and foreign policy. The latter is not the case in Finland.[6] The Dutch position is not exceptional, which is no different in more extensive comparisons. There is much support for a common policy on cross-border problems (such as the fight against terrorism and environmental protection), but little as far as social achievements and identity-sensitive matters are concerned.[7]

In terms of opinions on the EU and European affairs, comparisons often show the Netherlands to be a quite average country on many issues.[8] Support for EU membership may continue to be considerable, but this should not be interpreted as enthusiasm for Europe. Rather, it is evidence of mass acceptance of what is simply inevitable economically.

2.3 Developments

2.3.1 *The Long Term*

For the two positive assessments of EU membership in Figure 2.2, Figure 2.4 shows the developments in the Netherlands over the past decades. We see, with fluctuations, an increase in 'a good thing' until the early 1990s, a decrease until 2004 and then another upward trend until 2009. Then another downward trend

6 Traditionally: Dekker et al. (2008), p. 30.

7 Social security, education; *see also* Cerniglia, F. & Pagani, L. (2009). The European Union and the member states. *CESinfo Economic Studies, 55*(1), 197-232.

8 Dekker et al. (2008, 2009); Creusen et al. (2010).

seems to be setting in. The measurement of 'benefits' starts later, but follows the same pattern.

Figure 2.4 Support for Dutch EU Membership, 1973-2011

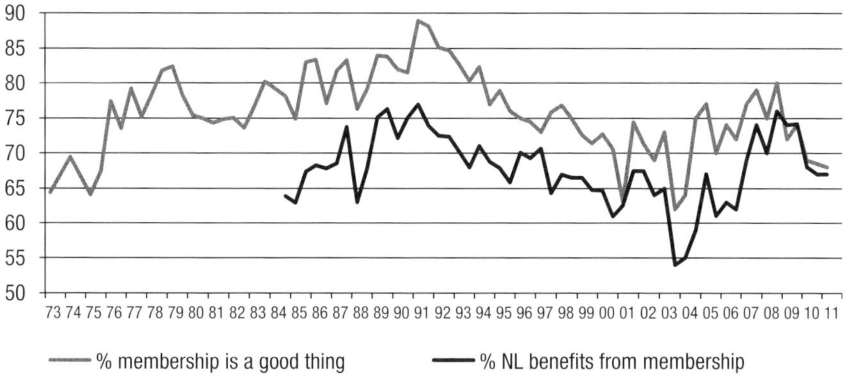

Source: EB 0 (1973)-EB 76.3 (November 2011).

There is no simple explanation for the changes. The downward trend that reached an all-time low in the 1990s and 2003/4 (after the introduction of the euro, during the enlargement by 10 new, mainly central and eastern European, countries) may be due to a growing (silent) unease about the 'runaway train' of European integration in those years.[9] Following the expression of dissatisfaction about this development before and at the referendum of 2005, it might perhaps have become easier again to acknowledge that, all in all, membership is the best option. However, that is not to say that the mood is turning more positive overall.

2.3.2 *The 2000s*

The latter is demonstrated by four other indicators, shown in Figure 2.5, for the years 2001-2012. Support for the euro increases again between 2004 and 2008, and then drops. Support for enlargement decreases quite significantly throughout the whole period and in recent years. This downward trend stops in the measurement of May 2012. The EU's image does not get worse either, but trust in the EU goes down further.

9 Cuperus, R. (2009). *De wereldburger bestaat niet* [The world citizen does not exist]. Amsterdam: Bert Bakker, p. 159 *et seq.*

Figure 2.5 Support for the EU, the Euro and Enlargement, 2001-2012

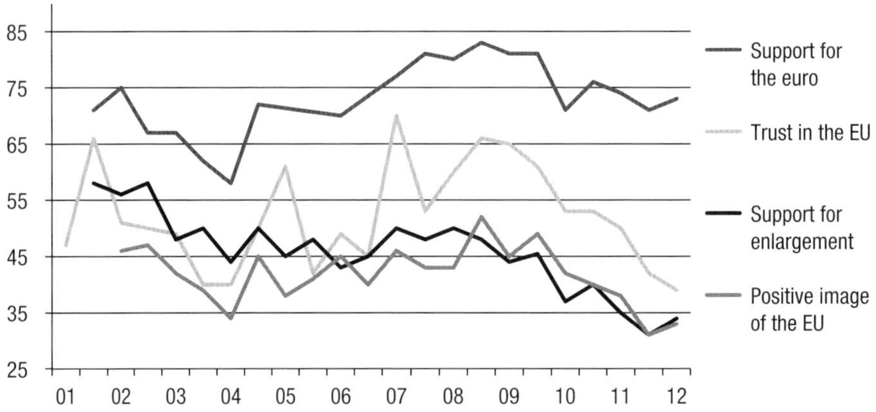

Source: EB 55.1 (April-May 2001)-77.3 (May 2012).

2.3.3 *From Banking Crisis to Euro Crisis*

Finally, Figure 2.6 shows the latest developments in the support for 'a good thing' according to the quarterly surveys of the *Continu Onderzoek Burgerperspectieven* (COB – Citizens' Outlook Barometer).[10] In anticipation of the next section, I also show, beside the curve for the entire population, the developments for three levels of education. The curves show fluctuations but not the downward trend in Figures 2.4 and 2.5 as of 2009. This difference cannot be simply explained by a difference in questions asked, and before we further interpret this, we should first wait and see how the curves will develop further. Apart from the trend, there is an ongoing substantial difference in appreciation of EU membership between levels of education. Throughout the entire period, 31% of the lower educated (up to and including *vmbo* = lower secondary professional education) and 66% of the higher educated (*hbo+* = higher vocational education and higher) agreed with the statement that membership is a good thing.

10 The question is different from that in the EB, where people are asked if membership is a good or bad thing. The question now is whether they agree with the statement that it is a good thing. Consequently, the response percentages cannot be compared with those in Figure 2.4.

Figure 2.6 EU Membership is a Good Thing: Agreement in %, 2008/1-2012/3

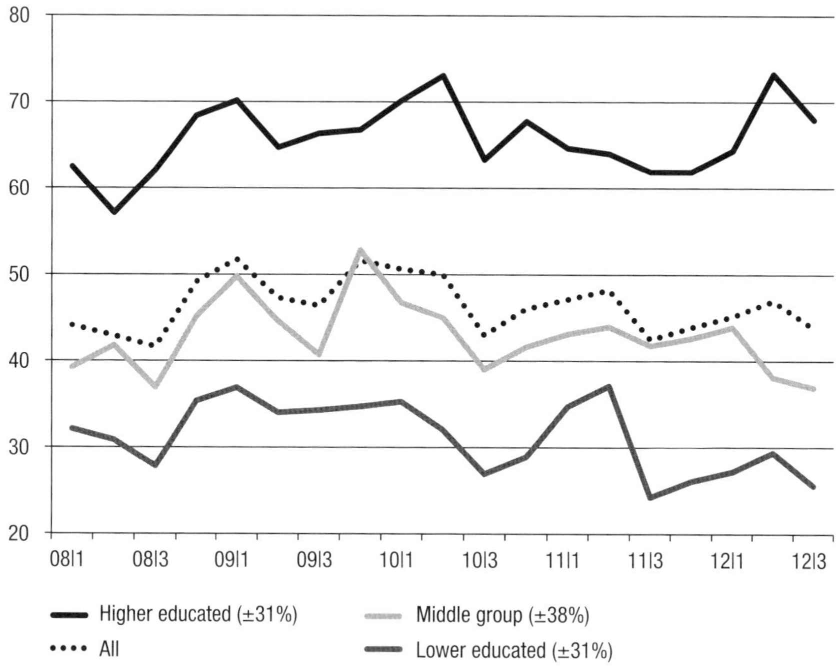

Source: COB 2008/1-2012/3.

The COB not only comprises surveys but also engages quarterly focus groups where 'Europe' has been raised several times. At first, this did not lead to much discussion, but the euro crisis certainly has increased interest in Europe. In the groups, the EU and European countries in financial difficulty are now spontaneously raised as an issue of concern.[11] During the discussions, lower-educated people are moreover markedly more negative about Europe than are higher-educated participants.[12]

2.4 Differences between Groups and Personal Backgrounds

In all EU Member States, higher-educated people are more positive about Europe than those with a lower education.[13] In addition, men are, across the board,

11 Dekker, P., den Ridder, J. & Schnabel, P. (2012). *Burgerperspectieven 2012/1* [Citizens' outlook 2012/1]. The Hague: Sociaal en Cultureel Planbureau, p. 29 *et seq.*; for earlier COB quarterly reports, *see* <www.scp.nl>.

12 Den Ridder, J. & Dekker, P. (2012). *Burgerperspectieven 2012/2* [Citizens' outlook 2012/1]. The Hague: Sociaal en Cultureel Planbureau, pp. 19-20.

13 Den Ridder & Dekker (2012), p. 22. This is not specific to Europe. Higher-educated people generally have more confidence in the national government as well.

somewhat more positive than women.[14] In this section, I discuss differences in attitudes towards the EU in more detail. A lot of research has been done on this subject, focusing on differences in (perceived) personal and national interests in Europe, as well as on differences in the extent to which people regard Europe as a threat to their own culture or national identity. So far, these studies have failed to arrive at any unambiguous conclusions. There are differences between countries and much depends on the operationalization of concepts.[15] For the Netherlands I have studied who to a lesser or greater extent is in favour of European integration on the basis of a combination of reactions to the four statements in Table 2.3. The figures relate to the first two quarters of 2012.

Table 2.3 Views on the EU and the Euro[a]

		Levels of education		
	All	**Low**	**Middle**	**High**
The Dutch membership of the EU is a good thing: 0 = strongly disagree → 100 = strongly agree	58	49	56	70
It is a bad thing that the guilder has been replaced by the euro: 0 = strongly agree → 100 = strongly disagree	49	36	45	65
In the current economic crisis, it is a good thing that the Netherlands has the euro: 0 = strongly disagree → 100 = strongly agree	52	47	49	60
Politicians in The Hague have transferred too much power to Europe: 0 = strongly agree → 100 = strongly disagree	41	33	38	51
Average score = support for European integration[a]	50	42	47	61

[a]The four measurements together form a reliable scale (Cronbach's alpha = 0.85).
Source: COB 2012/1+2.

Next to the population as a whole, the three levels of education are listed separately. Again, we keep seeing big differences there, especially as regards the replacement of the guilder by the euro.[16] This subject also keeps cropping up in the focus group discussions on Europe.

14 Nelsen, B.F. & Guth, J.L. (2000). Exploring the gender gap. *European Union Politics, 1*(3), 267-291.

15 *See, e.g.,* Scheuer, A. (2005). *How Europeans see Europe* [thesis]. Amsterdam: University of Amsterdam; Hooghe, L. & Marks, G. (Eds.). (2007). Understanding Euroscepticism: Special issue. *Acta Politica, 42*(2/3); Boomgaarden, H.G., et al. (2011). Mapping EU attitudes. *European Union Politics, 12*(2), 241-266.

16 With a view to further calculations, the table shows average support for this replacement. More appealing are the percentages of agreement with 'It is a bad thing that the guilder has been replaced by the euro': 52% of the lower educated and 17% of the higher educated agree. About 55% of the lower educated and 29% of the higher educated agree with the statement 'Politicians in The Hague have transferred too much power to Europe'. With the statement that was put to respondents only in the second quarter of 2012, 'It is good for our economy that Europe interferes more in the budgets of the Member States of the European Union', 34% of the lower educated and 67% of the higher educated agree (Den Ridder & Dekker (2012), p. 19).

2.4.1 Backgrounds

The average approval or rejection of the four statements in Table 2.3 can be considered to measure the support for European integration. Table 2.4 outlines the differences in that support, showing socio-demographic backgrounds, economic situations and views that say something about attitudes towards life and politics. The first column of figures shows the average support for European integration in the various categories mentioned. Support is lowest among those who believe the government is not doing enough for them (39) or who are unemployed or disabled for work (40), and highest among the higher educated (61) and those with an above-average income (61). Of course, these are not mutually exclusive categories, and the question is what remains of the differences if the overlap of characteristics is taken into account. This is shown in the columns with regression coefficients. If lower-educated and higher-educated people did not differ as regards the other characteristics, the difference in support would diminish from 19 (61 – 42 in the column with average scores) to 12 (–3 + 9 in the last column). This is certainly not negligible. Besides, through economic traits and prospects, (self-)confidence and attitudes towards politics, differences in education apparently also operate in other ways.[17] If we then look at the last column of Table 2.4, social distrust and the feeling of being ignored by politics appear to be relatively important negative factors. This has been established before by studies on attitudes towards Europe. Perhaps the fact that 'Europe' is so far removed from many people's lives is exactly the reason why their attitude towards Europe is firmly anchored in their outlook on life, with (self-)confidence and optimism stimulating a positive attitude.[18]

17 For example, different (work) experiences with 'Europe' and differences in how people follow European news (different intensity and different sources), but with the available data nothing can be said about this.

18 Dekker et al. (2009), pp. 53-64.

Table 2.4 Support for European Integration, Population of 18+, 2012 (in Averages and Regression Coefficients)

	Average (all = 50)	Unstandardized regression coefficients[a]		
		Demographic	+ Economic	+ Attitudes
Constant		46	45	57
Man (49%)	52	Ref.	Ref.	Ref.
Woman (51%)	48	– 3**	– 2*	– 2**
Aged 18-34 (27%)	53	+ 2*	+ 1	+ 1
Aged 35-54 (38%)	48	Ref.	Ref.	Ref.
Aged ≥55 (35%)	50	+ 5***	+ 5***	+ 5***
Lower education (31%)	42	– 6***	– 4***	– 3*
Middle group (36%)	47	Ref.	Ref.	Ref.
Higher education (32%)	61	+14***	+13***	+ 9***
Family income below average (23%)	47		– 4***	– 2
About average (34%)	48		Ref.	Ref.
Above average (40%)	61		+ 5***	+ 3**
Student (10%)	54		+ 4*	+ 4**
Employee, (semi-)government (10%)	57		+ 2	+ 3
Employee, private sector (41%)	50		Ref.	Ref.
Self-employed (5%)	52		– 1	– 0
Unemployed or disabled for work (6%)	40		– 5**	– 2
Housework (10%)	42		– 3	– 3
Retired (17%)	51		+ 2	+ 1
Expects to be worse off financially next year (26%)	44			– 4***
Feels that s/he has little control of his/her own future (28%)	45			+ 0
Believes one cannot be too careful when dealing with people (38%)	42			– 6***
Finds national politics often too complicated to understand (28%)	42			– 2**
Believes that 'people like me' have no influence on the government whatsoever (58%)	43			– 9***
Believes that the government is not doing enough for 'people like me' (34%)	39			– 7***
Explained variance		15%	18%	30%

[a]The constant is the estimated score of someone in the reference categories (Ref.), i.e., a man from the middle group in terms of age, education and income, employed in the private sector etc. Example: considering only the demographic factors, the estimated score of an older, higher-educated woman is 46 – 3 + 5 + 14 = 62. Small residual categories have been omitted from the presentation, but have been included in the analyses. Statistical significance: * <0.05, ** <0.01 and *** <0.001 (two-sided).

Source: COB 2012/1-2.

2.4.2 *Political Preferences*

Statistically, voting intentions may help explain differences in support – the 'explained variance' increases from 30% to 36% – but not when it comes to content, since for voters, party preferences and preferences for Europe probably interact in ways that are difficult to disentangle.
Figure 2.7 shows the differences in voting intentions. The group that plans to vote but does not know for which party yet (20% at the time of the survey) is not far off the average support, but those who are not planning on voting (6%) are far below that. They will more likely be seduced to vote by Eurosceptic parties than by pro-European parties.

Figure 2.7 Support for European Integration According to Voting Intentions, Population of 18+, 2012[a]

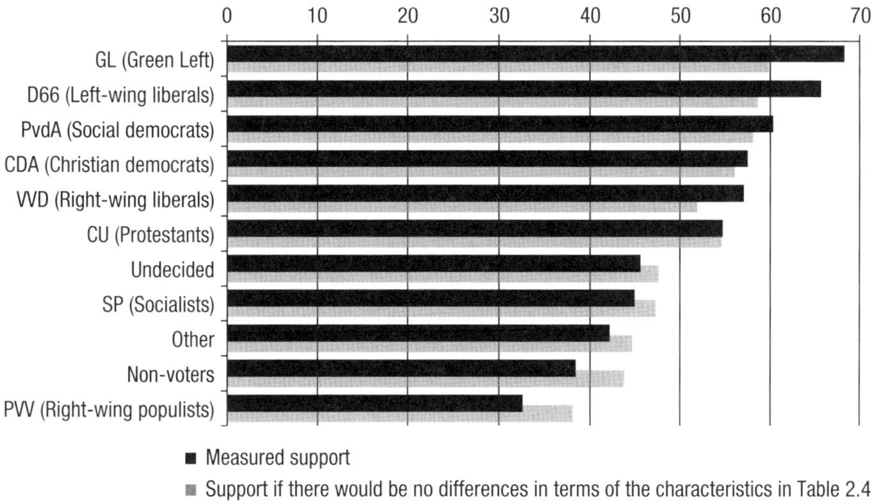

[a] Voting intentions are the choices made if at the time of the survey (January-May 2012) parliamentary elections were held. Example: of those who would be voting for D66, average support amounts to 66 points; of those who would not plan on voting, 38 points. When a statistical correction is made for the differences in terms of the characteristics listed in Table 2.4, those voting for D66 score 59 points and the non-voters 44.
Source: COB 2012/1-2.

Among people with a party preference, the biggest difference can be found between PVV voters (score of 33) and GL voters (score of 68). If they did not differ in all characteristics of Table 2.4, the differences would still be considerable (with scores of 38 and 60). This is the situation in the first months of 2012. Depending on the development of the euro crisis and on Europe's role in the campaigns and debates in the run-up to the parliamentary elections of September 2012, major changes may have taken place after that (as was the case prior to the referendum of 2005).

According to some political scientists, Europe as an issue of debate has, already for some time, been gaining in importance. Together with the multicultural society, it is a key point of conflict on a new, cultural divide in Dutch politics, next to the old socio-economic left-right divide.[19] According to Kriesi et al.,[20] winners and losers of globalization would be on opposite sides of the divide: cosmopolites who benefit from disappearing borders and feel comfortable in the multicultural context versus those who care about protecting the nation state and who see their culture threatened. Europe lends itself well as an issue to make this contradiction politically manifest, but this might change as a result of the euro crisis and disputes over crisis policies. If Europe becomes more real in terms of consequences for employment, taxes and cuts in government spending etc., it could become more controversial along the lines of the old left-right opposition.

2.5 Fleeting and Fickle

An argument sometimes raised against survey data is that they often say little, because people do not think their answers through, and when they actually have to make a serious choice in real life, they often do something completely different to what might have been expected on the basis of surveys. An example is the European referendum of 1 June 2005: a convincing majority voted against the European constitution, whereas shortly before that, in the EB, an even larger majority had stated they believed EU membership was a good thing. Although this 'say and do behaviour' was not necessarily contradictory (people might have all sorts of good reasons for being in favour of EU membership or against the constitution, or, if not that, against the politicians who were in favour), it undeniably and quickly changed public sentiments about Europe before the referendum. The unpredictability of public opinion is less a shortcoming of the survey method used than a consequence of a weak anchoring of support for Europe. Many Dutch people had – and still have – a quite superficial positive attitude: rationally, on balance, Europe is a good thing, but people are not really involved. Opinions are often ill thought through and not rooted in more general ideological preferences and political loyalties and emotions. This makes for fragile support.
Within the study on public opinion, this can be seen clearly in the focus groups, where random groups of citizens discuss all sorts of topics. In the *Europese Verkenningen,*[21] we often pointed out that there was little interest in the EU and

19 *E.g.,* Andeweg, R. & Thomassen, J. (2011). *Van afspiegelen naar afrekenen* [From reflection to settlement]. Leiden: Leiden University Press.

20 Kriesi, H., Grande, E., Lachat, R., Dolezal, M., Bornschier, S. & Frey, T. (2006). Globalization and the transformation of the national political space. *European Journal of Political Research, 45*(6), 921-956; *cf.* Cuperus (2009).

21 Most recently, Creusen et al. (2010); *see* further at <www.scp.nl>.

less-than-enthusiastic agreement, which became more negative as the issue was discussed. As a result, abstract support does not hold up to concrete and emotionally stronger objections (the expensive euro, examples of waste, interference and nonsense measures), uniting people in a common unease about Europe. We also observed such negative dynamics when we asked people to relate their individual stories on Europe and then talk about them in groups.[22] The stories were often quite neutral, but the common interpretation was still negative. In another approach, survey respondents indicated a preference and were then given extra information in order to see how firm they were in their opinions.[23] Apparently, under the influence of extra information or considerations, many people change their views on European issues. People with pro-European opinions are easier to turn into opponents on concrete issues than vice versa. People with a fundamentally negative attitude on Europe prove more steadfast in their views than those with a basically neutral or positive attitude.

Across the board, support for Europe often proves fleeting and fragile. Negative facts frequently prevail over vague advantages and ideals. In case of doubt, most people prefer being realistic or cynical instead of being naive.

2.6 Where Do we Go from Here?

To sum up, rationally, Dutch people are positive but anything but enthusiastic about European integration. Their opinions are ill thought through, stale and, for lack of involvement and knowledge, susceptible to counterarguments and negative emotions.

These summarizing sentences do, however, somewhat convey the dominant research perspective where support for European integration is taken for granted (and considered a good thing) and scepticism requires an explanation. As stated in the introduction, that was not the intention. Fortunately, the contradiction between overall support and scepticism is becoming less relevant. Due to the developments over the past decades and recently accelerated by the crisis, the question focuses increasingly on what we want and do not want for Europe and not on whether we want Europe and how much of it, just as for the Netherlands we ask ourselves and survey respondents what we want in our society and what policy should be pursued, rather than to what extent we are for or against the Netherlands.

As a result of the euro crisis, Dutch people's concern with Europe has increased and has become less a simplistic matter of being 'for or against' the EU. In addition, questions of what, at this point, is financially/economically wise and neces-

22 Dekker et al. (2009), p. 12 *et seq.*

23 Wennekers, C. (2008). *Veranderlijkheid van opvattingen over de EU* [Variability of opinions on the EU]. The Hague: Sociaal en Cultureel Planbureau.

sary have perhaps come to overly dominate the political debate and the media, and thus also public opinion. There is little attention for what we further believe is and is not desirable, and for how financial measures will affect democracy in Europe. Controversy over further integration as an 'irreversible' development is not conducive to democratic self-confidence and involvement in political debate. TINA (there is no alternative) is not a nice person, and the fact that the fate of more than 50% unemployed young people in Spain has become linked to her does not help make her any more likeable or interesting. Even though Dutch public opinion now revolves less around a clear 'for or against' Europe, the contradiction between rational agreement and instinctive aversion threatens to become sharper.

Avoiding this is a task for politicians as opinion leaders. The formation of public opinion on Europe would greatly benefit by politicians who refrain from double-speak, resort less to the old cliché that restrictions come from Brussels and successes from national politics, are more consistent in their statements about the European and national interests for different constituencies, and resist the temptation to act tough on the national stage while obeying Brussels. This would help reduce unease among the public about Europe and improve public debate on the future of the Netherlands and Europe.

I conclude this chapter mid-October 2012, following an electoral campaign in which Europe was not the big issue that some hoped and others feared it would be, and after an election result on 12 September which showed that the most Eurosceptic parties – PVV and SP – had not received as many votes as expected in the preceding months. Foreign media interpreted this result as something 'Europe' could be pleased with, and expectations are that soon a VVD-PvdA cabinet will take office that will be less obstructive in Europe, or at least will have to pretend less hard that it is with a view to party-political relations. Public opinion will initially give this cabinet the benefit of the doubt, but it would be unwise to regard the elections as an electoral acceptance of the European crisis policy. Rather, it is an acceptance of the inevitable. The combination of foreign (European) financial obligations and national cuts continues to be a source of dissatisfaction, even if it cannot be clearly expressed as public opinion.

3 The European Union: International Actor with Handicaps

Fred van Staden

3.1 Introduction

Can the European Union (EU) really be regarded as an independent participant in international relations, 'an actor in its own right'? After all, it lacks the features that characterize a state which – at least formally – can make its own decisions and generally has an army of its own. This question is usually answered in two ways.[1] Firstly, despite the strong autonomy of the Member States, the EU indeed tries to achieve common goals in its relations with third countries. These goals are laid down in the Treaties and in policy documents. The EU moreover has diplomatic and – though relatively modest – financial means allowing it to play a discernible role on the world stage. In many areas, the EU representatives may be bound by the collective mandate of the Member States, but the limits of this mandate do not entirely rule out individual interpretation and positioning. Secondly, present-day external relations comprise more than traditional foreign policy, which is governed by interactions between foreign ministries; they also involve trade relations, development cooperation, humanitarian assistance, combating terrorism and neighbourhood policy. In these fields, the Community method applies, which means that the European representatives (in particular the President and Members of the European Commission) have more room for manoeuvre than with foreign policy in the narrow sense, where intergovernmental cooperation predominates. However, the different allocation of responsibilities between Member States and European institutions among the various branches of external relations does make the EU a split personality.

The EU is often referred to as a 'soft power'. Such a power does not derive its influence from exercising force ('command power'), but from the ability to persuade and convince and from the appeal of its ideas and the positive example it sets ('leadership by example').[2] The EU, as a postmodern entity, would therefore aspire to be a world power which, as the *Wetenschappelijke Raad voor het Rege-*

1 *See, for instance,* Hill, C. & Smith, M. (Eds.). (2011). *International relations and the European Union* (2nd ed.). Oxford: Oxford University Press, Ch. 1.

2 *See* Nye, J.S. (2004). *Soft power: The means to success in world politics.* New York: Public Affairs, pp. 5-7.

ringsbeleid (WRR – Scientific Council for Government Policy) puts it, exercises influence based on values which Europe considers fundamental.[3] This statement may cause confusion though, because it intertwines instruments and objectives. Indeed, it can easily be claimed that the defence of democracy and human rights may require, by force of circumstances, the use of military force, i.e., 'hard power'. Göran Therborn even believes that

> without the backing of force and a willingness to use it, 'Europe' is unlikely to become a normative power, telling other parts of the world what political, economic and social institutions they should have.[4]

Conversely, one can also imagine that political entities try to protect material interests by using soft diplomatic instruments. Likewise, confusion may arise when the contrast between soft and hard power is put on exactly the same footing as that between civilian and military power. The EU is usually regarded as 'civilian', because it has no geopolitical ambitions. 'Civilian Europe' is thus set in opposition to *l'Europe-puissance*, Europe as a traditional power block. The EU's strategic culture may be characterized by a tendency to avoid confrontation and seek compromise, but it is a misunderstanding to think that civilian instruments are by definition 'soft' and military ones 'hard'. For instance, withdrawing economic aid and refusing access to the EU internal market are near-coercive measures. In addition, universal values may be propagated as a pretext for expanding influence or increasing national prestige. Furthermore, by setting strict requirements for accession, the Union is to a large extent capable of imposing its will on countries that want to accede. However, training military staff or reforming the security sector in a country can be classified as military assistance, but no one can claim that this involves coercion.

Thus, the distinctions made are less clear-cut than is often assumed. It is therefore easy to understand Karen Smith who writes that behind the broad category of 'civilian power' sometimes, in reality, lies hidden a hybrid figure of civilian power and a (traditional) power block.[5] This has certainly been the case since, at the end of the last century, European leaders had come to realize that the EU

3 Wetenschappelijke Raad voor het Regeringsbeleid. (2010). *Aan het buitenland gehecht. Over verankering en strategie van het Nederlands buitenlands beleid* [Attached to foreign countries. On the anchoring and strategy of the Dutch foreign policy]. Amsterdam: Amsterdam University Press, p. 79.

4 Therborn, G. (1997). Europe in the twenty-first century: The world's Scandinavia?. In P. Gowan & P. Anderson (Eds.), *The question of Europe*. London: Verso, p. 380.

5 Smith, K.E. (2008). *European Union foreign policy in a changing world* (2nd ed.). Cambridge: Polity Press, p. 23.

should have the military capabilities to carry out certain security tasks.[6] In short, there are reasons for putting into perspective the real meaning of the labels that are so easily stuck on the EU as an international player.

This chapter broadly evaluates the EU's progress in realizing a Common Foreign and Security Policy (CFSP), including the policy themes that are part of the Community institutional framework. The need for and desirability of a separate foreign policy for the Netherlands is strongly determined by how the current state of the CFSP is judged. What parts should the Netherlands preferably still handle itself and what elements are better off being propagated collectively through European channels? Before discussing these questions, the background of the EU policy will be outlined first, focusing, respectively, on objectives, instruments, decision-making and implementation.

3.2 Objectives and Instruments

Compared with most national constitutions, the EU has included in its basic Treaty an extensive catalogue of objectives that it wants to realize in the framework of its foreign policy.[7] Before listing these objectives, it is stated that the Union's action on the international scene shall seek to advance in the wider world the principles which have inspired its own creation, development and enlargement, namely democracy, the rule of law, the universality and indivisibility of human rights and fundamental freedoms, respect for human dignity, the principles of equality and solidarity. The emphasis on these principles, in connection with provisions on the Union's external action, makes clear that the EU wants to present itself to the outside world mainly as a normative power – a power which impresses its own basic principles and standards on third countries and, moreover, projects them on to a model of the ideal international order. It is also striking that of the eight objectives set out in the Treaty, only one (the first) falls in the category of what Arnold Wolfers once called 'possession goals', i.e., objectives that serve the specific interests or benefits of the state and are not

6 The most important milestone in this regard was the European summit in Berlin in June 1999, when the leaders committed themselves to developing "the capacity for autonomous action, backed up by credible military forces, the means to decide or use them, and a readiness to do so, in order to respond to international crises". France and the UK had already reached agreement on this goal at a bilateral meeting in St. Malo (December 1998). Earlier, the so-called Petersberg tasks had been laid down in the Treaty of Amsterdam (1997), which meant that the EU should be capable of carrying out "humanitarian and rescue tasks, peacekeeping tasks, and tasks of combat forces in crisis management, including peacemaking".

7 Treaty on European Union (TEU), as last amended in Lisbon, 2008, Title V, Art. 21.

shared with others.[8] This objective is: the Union shall "safeguard its values, fundamental interests, security, independence and integrity".

The other objectives lie more in the sphere of what Arnold Wolfers designated as 'milieu goals', objectives that involve influencing the environment in which the relations between states and other international players operate. These range from maintaining peace and preventing conflict to supporting economic development in poor countries and taking international measures to protect the natural environment. In addition, the "promotion of an international system based on stronger multilateral cooperation and good global governance" is explicitly mentioned as a separate objective.[9] Already earlier, in the European Security Strategy (2003), the establishment of an international order based on effective multilateralism (related to upholding international law and strengthening the United Nations) had been identified as one of the three 'strategic objectives' of the EU. The other two goals are to address security threats (terrorism, proliferation of weapons of mass destruction, regional conflicts, state failure and organized crime) and to increase the stability in the EU's neighbourhood.[10]

The EU's strong focus on the formulation of milieu goals provides a basis for the view that the EU's policy can serve as an example of a new type of foreign policy. In this context, Stephan Keukeleire and Jennifer MacNaughton make a distinction between – what they call – *conventional* foreign policy and *structural* foreign policy. The former type is aimed at states, military security, crises and conflicts. The latter refers to a foreign policy, characteristic of the EU, which, in the long run "seeks to influence or shape sustainable political, legal, socio-economic, security and mental structures".[11] These structures concern not only states and interstate relations, but also national societies, the position of individuals, relations between states and societies, and the international system as a whole. The so-called structural foreign policy is a typical product of the post-Westphalian order. In this order, national sovereignty has lost its absolute meaning, domestic and foreign policy are no longer strictly separate, supranational institutions can intervene in countries' internal affairs, state and non-state actors are interconnected in cross-border networks, and there is no fixed hierarchy of objectives. All these qualities strongly characterize the mutual relations between EU Member States, and, here too, the EU's view of the ideal international order is a reflection of its own internal structures.

A treaty-based catalogue of generally defined objectives is an indication of the level and nature of an actor's ambitions. However, it says nothing about the rela-

8 Wolfers, A. (1962). *Discord and collaboration. Essays on international politics*. Baltimore, MD: Johns Hopkins University Press, pp. 73-6.

9 TEU, Title V, Art. 21.

10 A secure Europe in a better world. (2003). Brussels, p. 12 *et seq*.

11 Keukeleire, S. & MacNaughton, J. (2008). *The foreign policy of the European Union*. London: Palgrave Macmillan, p. 25.

tive weight and the compatibility of these objectives, let alone about the actual commitment to realize them. A decisive factor in this context is, of course, the availability and choice of appropriate instruments, or, in other words, the means that are closely linked to the political resources an actor can deploy. What means can be employed if the EU wants to exert influence, i.e., tempt or stimulate other parties to act in a certain way? The above mentioned concept of Europe as a civilian power implies that the focus of the EU's range of policy instruments has been firmly on economic instruments and diplomacy. Of course, this need not come as a surprise seeing that the EU originated from the (European) Economic Community, which was primarily a trade power.[12] The economic instruments can be divided into agreements with third countries and regional groups (which, in turn, can be subdivided into regular trade agreements, cooperation agreements and association agreements) and the provision of technical assistance and financial aid to countries.[13] Economic sanctions, a pressure tactic par excellence, may take the form of both rewards (aid and other privileges, such as reducing import tariffs and providing loans on favourable terms) and penalties (ban on EU exports, boycott of products from countries that are penalized and suspension of aid). Sanctions are subject to the Community decision-making rules.
This is not the case with the second, most generally used policy instrument, diplomacy. Berridge has defined diplomacy as

> the conduct of international relations by negotiation, rather than by force, propaganda, or recourse to law, and by other peaceful means [...] which are either directly or indirectly designed to promote negotiation.[14]

Although negotiating is an essential part of diplomacy, the concept involves more than that. It includes all forms of communication, verbal and non-verbal, the most important influencing techniques being the ability to persuade and convince as well as the capacity to inspire emulation.[15] The specific instruments deployed in the framework of EU diplomacy are the same as those available to countries, the only exception being, of course, the offer of EU membership. In concrete terms, all this means that by or on behalf of the EU, *démarches* are made, statements are given, visits are paid, dialogues are entered into, countries are or are not recognized, peace proposals are made, special envoys are sent, conferences are organized or supported, etc. The EU, moreover, sends EU observers to certain countries or regions to monitor elections and ceasefires.

12 The European Political Cooperation launched after 1970 was given a treaty basis by the Single European Act.

13 Smith (2008), p. 55.

14 Berridge, G.R. (1995). *Diplomacy. Theory and practice*. London: Prentice-Hall/Harvester Wheatsheaf, p. 1.

15 'Coercive diplomacy', the special branch of diplomacy based on the threat to use (more) military force, is not considered here.

The limited scale of the use of military means has already been pointed out. The EU has no military capabilities of its own. This is not unusual in itself: NATO also relies on voluntary contributions from the individual Member States. But unlike the Atlantic Alliance, the EU lacks an extensive command structure and common logistics facilities. NATO could, moreover, heavily rely on US leadership. Initially, by adopting the so-called Headline Goal in Helsinki in December 1999, the EU had set the bar high for the Union's military capability: a rapid reaction force of 50,000 to 60,000 men and women should be deployable within 60 days to carry out the Petersberg Tasks[16] for the duration of at least one year.[17] This goal should have been reached by 2003. This proved impossible, since a year later, the EU countries were forced to considerably rein in their military ambitions. The new Headline Goal 2010 aimed to create relatively small 'battlegroups' (around 2500 troops per unit), which could be dispatched within 10 days of a decision to mount a mission. A number of battlegroups have been operational for some years now. For instance, the Netherlands formed a battlegroup together with the United Kingdom in 2010, and another one with Germany and Poland in 2011.

3.3 Capacity to Act

Foreign policy is not just about well thought-out objectives and choosing the right instruments, but also and mainly about the 'the capacity to act'. It has already been stated in the introduction that the EU can be typified as a split personality because foreign relations are governed by two different decision-making regimes. This is partly the reason why the organization of the decision-making is highly complex and diffuse. There is no discernible political body, a centre of power, which can provide strong leadership. Despite the fact that the Lisbon Treaty was created in order to, amongst other things, streamline the organization and enhance the effectiveness of external actions, the EU's capacity to act is still limited, particularly in vital matters of peace and security. As a result, the EU is falling behind other powers, especially when it comes to acting decisively and quickly in crisis situations.

Within the institutional structure, tension can be seen between the position of the Commission and that of the Council, particularly the Council for External Relations. As stated earlier, in matters of trade policy, development policy and enlargement the initiative lies with the Commission (although its proposals require the Council's ultimate approval). Where political and security issues are concerned, the institution in charge is undeniably the Council, being the representative of

16 *See* note 6.

17 *See also* van Eekelen, W. (2006). *From words to deeds. The continuing debate on European security.* Brussels/Geneva: CEPS/DCAF, pp. 47-48.

the Member States. In practice, however, it is by no means always clear where the line between both domains can be drawn. Only few economic subjects have no political dimension and, to a certain extent, the reverse is true as well. The uncertainty as to which institution was primarily or solely competent to define and conduct policy in concrete cases has led to "continuing turf wars between the Commission and the Council which are detrimental to the aim of a more coherent foreign policy and which are confusing to the outside world".[18] The promotion of cohesion in policy was an important reason for merging the post of High Representative of the CFSP with that of Commissioner for External Relations, as foreseen in the Treaty of Lisbon. With a view to increasing the clout of the policy, the same Treaty also provided for the creation of a European External Action Service (EEAS), which was officially launched on 1 December 2010.

Generally, the European Council of Heads of State and Government is only occasionally involved in matters of foreign policy. This is the case despite the fact that it is the highest decision-making body and, pursuant to the Treaty, determines the strategic interests of the Union as well as the principles and general guidelines of the CFSP, "including for matters with defence implications".[19] Statements that the European Council periodically issues about developments in the world are not seldom perfunctory and ritualistic. It is moreover telling that the European Council, apart from approving the Headline Goals, has so far never actually involved itself with defence issues. Apparently, the political leaders do not consider these as *Chefsache*. The appointment of a semi-permanent president of this body, as provided for by the Treaty of Lisbon, did however raise the expectation that this person, being the figurehead of the Union, would, also to the outside world, at his own level (i.e., government leaders of other countries), assert himself as interlocutor for important international topics.

Finally, the role of the European Parliament (EP) is quite limited, also in international matters that have to be dealt with in the Community framework. The EP's approval is required for the conclusion of international agreements that create a specific institutional framework for cooperation with third countries, as well as for agreements that have significant budgetary effects or contain amendments to agreements approved earlier by the EP. It is almost self-evident that accession treaties must also be reviewed by the EP. For the rest, the EP's involvement in the policy area discussed is mostly of a consultative nature. In this respect, one should bear in mind that legislation is of secondary importance in foreign policy, whilst in quite a few countries the position of national parliaments in foreign policymaking is also relatively weak.

The Treaty of Lisbon has not led to changes in the decision-making rules in the field of CFSP. This means that decisions on substantial issues require unanimity. Minor deviations from this strict rule are only possible by applying the procedure

18 Cameron, F. (2007). *An introduction to European foreign policy*. London: Routledge, pp. 40-41.

19 TEU, Art. 26.

of constructive abstention. Finding consensus among 27 Member States on often controversial issues is not an easy task. It takes a lot of time and often produces outcomes that comprise not much more than the greatest common denominator of different national positions. Given the fact that none of the Member States seems prepared to give up its veto (completely), creative solutions are necessary to still ensure that the EU can respond in time to international situations that require swift action. A solution could be to agree that a small group of countries should no longer be in a position to block decisions and actions that are supported by the vast majority of Member States. These countries would then no longer be obliged to participate in the implementation of such decisions and actions. Another, more far-reaching option is to use the possibility, offered by the Treaty, of enhanced cooperation.[20]

3.4 On Balance, What Has Been Achieved?

The above shows that the EU is an international actor with handicaps: its internal organization is weak and it has only limited military capabilities. In addition, the Member States do not agree on the scope of European ambitions. For instance, should the EU primarily focus on the 'near abroad' or does it also want to go further afield? Nor is there agreement over the right mix of military and civilian instruments. Below, an attempt is made to give a qualitative judgment of the progress which, despite everything, has been made nearly two decades after the Treaty of Maastricht entered into force, i.e., the formal starting point of the common policy. Two criteria are important in this respect: the level of coherence and of effectiveness. Policy coherence mainly concerns the extent to which actions are geared to one another. The latter is often regarded – and rightly so – as a condition for effectiveness, the capacity to realize set objectives. A few years ago, Fraser Cameron concluded that over the past years the EU had already achieved much:

> [...] the EU has developed steadily as an international actor during the past decade. More and more the EU operates as a political unity in dealing with terrorism, the Balkans, the proliferation of weapons, the Middle East peace process, African development and many other issues.[21]

Against this optimism of Cameron, it is easy to find negative views. Take, for instance, the scathing judgment of his compatriot Charles Grant:

20 TEU, Art. 20.

21 Cameron (2007), p. 204.

> On many of the world's big security problems, such as Pakistan, the EU is close to irrelevant. Talk to Russian, Chinese or Indian policymakers about the EU, and they are often withering. They view it as a trade bloc that had pretensions to be a power but has failed to become one because it is divided, slow-moving and badly organised.[22]

It is not difficult to give Grant further ammunition by pointing to the European disagreement over, e.g., the recognition of Kosovo and Palestine as independent states.

Before jumping to negative conclusions about the international role of the EU as a whole, one should bear in mind that any judgment of the results achieved is strongly biased by expectations about the EU's possibilities to achieve a certain level of ambitions. If it is firmly believed that, in international relations, Member States (and particularly the larger ones) will hold on to a large measure of national autonomy no matter what, because they believe it affirms their own identity, the glass will be half full rather than half empty. However, if one takes the rational view that there is no sector where the economies of scale of European cooperation are as significant as in the field of foreign policy (and especially defence), the disappointment over past performance will of course be bigger. This will certainly also be the case if, at the same time, one is of the opinion that even the larger European countries acting alone can no longer make a difference in solving important international problems. Another important consideration concerns the context of EU actions. It makes a big difference whether issues are involved that fall within the Community framework or under the intergovernmental regime.

What is important is whether European objectives are closely intertwined with national interests and aspirations, or whether European action is mostly aimed at protecting global values, reinforcing the norms of international regimes and reforming the world organization structure. In general, the EU has been relatively successful in its external relations, that is, where the national interests or aspirations of individual Member States have *not* been interfered with or thwarted. This means that the EU has been able to play a significant role on issues relating to global governance, global public goods en global values. In other words: the EU has proven its value in exerting a positive influence on the organization of the international community as well as on the availability of material and immaterial resources that are important to all countries. It has also made itself useful in relation to issues where national interests strongly coincide with those of the other EU Member States and non-EU countries. This was particularly the case with a topic like the fight against terrorism.

Despite the existence of interconnections between the different levels of foreign relations, political leaders still make a sharp distinction between sovereignty-sensitive high politics issues (war and peace) and low politics issues, which are less

22 Grant, C. (2009). *Is Europe doomed to fail as a power?* London: Centre for European Reform, p. 1.

delicate from the viewpoint of national sovereignty. International trade is a clear example of the latter. To be sure, in international trade negotiations, major national interests may clash as well, but because of their more technical nature these much less affect the national identity, the essence of what makes a population a political community. The EU's exclusive competence in the field of trade relations with third countries is in sharp contrast with the fact that primary responsibility for the CFSP, even after the entry into force of the Lisbon Treaty, has remained with the Member States. This has far-reaching consequences for both the coherence and effectiveness of EU action. It need therefore not come as a surprise that the EU has managed to develop into a highly influential world player in the field of foreign economic relations.[23] The fact that the EU is the largest trading bloc in the world is not a sufficient explanation. It is just as essential that the European countries have transferred their national competences in the field of external trade policy to the European institutions. In the World Trade Organization, the EU speaks with one voice and the Commission conducts negotiations on behalf of all Member States. As Europe presents a united front in this organization, it can act on an equal footing with the other large trading powers of the world.

The picture is far less rosy in the case of those areas of foreign relations where the EU institutions' role is weak and EU policy clearly encroaches upon Member States' individual actions. Especially in relations with large countries such as China and Russia, this policy is clearly lacking in coherence. The effectiveness of the European efforts aimed at these countries has been undermined by governments of some Member States acting in the belief that they have more to gain by a national policy than an integrated EU approach. In the case of China, John Fox and François Godemont consider this as an outright illusion since "the concessions each of the 27 can extract from China on any major issue are usually so small as to be virtually meaningless".[24] Apart from the fact that Europe would need China more than vice versa, the discord between the EU Member States is seen as a significant cause of this disappointing outcome:

> China has learnt to exploit the divisions among EU Member States. It treats its relationship with the EU as a game of chess, with 27 opponents the other side of the board and squabbling about which piece to move. As irritating as Beijing finds this at times, there is no question about who is in a position to play the better game.[25]

23 *See* Meunier, S. & Nicolaidis, K. (2011). The European Union as a trade power. In C. Hill & M. Smith (Eds.), *International relations and the European Union* (2nd ed.). Oxford: Oxford University Press, Ch. 12.

24 Fox, J. & Godemont, F. (2009). *A power audit of EU-China relations*. London: European Council on Foreign Relations, p. 21.

25 Fox & Godemont (2009), p. 3.

Another expert, Jonathan Holslag, arrives at similar conclusions. He, moreover, points out that from the early 1990s, the EU tried to educate China in the spirit of its own postmodern values. However, this European policy of 'constructive engagement' was doomed to failure because no account was taken of the predominantly traditional views of power politics and the increased national awareness on the Chinese side.[26]

In the relations between the EU and Russia, comparable basic patterns can be seen. Despite the adoption of a common Russia strategy, here too, EU Member States that believe they can gain special benefits are often seen to act alone in regard to Moscow. As in the case of China, this allows Russian leaders to play the game of divide and rule. According to Mark Leonard and Nicu Popescu, the Russian pursuit of bilateralization of relations with EU Member States shows a clear trend, namely "to enter into friendly relationships with the bigger EU states whilst coercing smaller member states with political and economic pressure".[27] Particularly Germany and France have proved amenable to building a special relationship with Russia. And where the EU did manage to take joint action, the emphasis, again like in its relationship with China, was on spreading the values that the EU holds high. Here too, Europe's missionary zeal clashed with the 'realistic' power politics characterizing Russian foreign policy, which mainly defines international relations in 'zero-sum' terms. Moscow's willingness to listen to European sermons diminished as Russia, due to its abundant oil and gas revenues, recovered from the major economic downturn that occurred during Jeltsin's presidency, which many Russians felt was a time of national humiliation. Under Putin, Russian policy became more assertive; Russia sought confirmation of its status as a major power. During the negotiations over a new Partnership and Cooperation Agreement launched in July 2008, Russia thus strongly emphasized equality and reciprocity in its relationship with the EU.[28]

The EU's relations with the United States are of course of a different order from those with China and Russia, but this does not alter the fact that the EU has not been that successful in influencing the geo-strategic decisions of the United States either. True, both parties are rooted in common values and developed strong 'habits of collaboration' over successive decades. However, in view of its military weakness, Europe was heavily dependent on the United States in security matters; in this respect, therefore, their mutual relationship much resembled that between patron and client. Trade issues, not military strategic topics, have dominated the annual summits held between the EU and the United States over the

26 Holslag, J. (2010). The strategic dissonance between Europa and China. *The Chinese Journal of International Politics,* 1-21. doi:10.1093/cjip/poq012. *See also* by the same author (2011). The elusive axis: Assessing the EU-China strategic relationship. *Journal of Common Market Studies, 49*(2), 293-313.

27 Leonard, M. & Popescu, N. (2007). *A power audit of EU-Russia relations.* London: European Council on Foreign Relations, p. 14.

28 *See* in this respect the report of the Advisory Council on International Affairs. (2008). *Cooperation between the European Union and Russia: A matter of nutual interest.* The Hague.

past two decades. This explains why the EU has only had limited influence on the direction of America's foreign policy. Where it concerns security issues, most EU Member States primarily view the transatlantic relationship through the prism of NATO. Moreover, certain Member States believe to have a 'special relationship' with Washington and therefore prefer to discuss political matters bilaterally with the American government. Also in this case, action is determined by the conviction that taking the bilateral route brings more benefits than following the European path. This belief is not only found in the United Kingdom, but is also propagated by the Netherlands, Portugal and Denmark. Awe of Washington also comes into it. In this context, Jeremy Shapiro and Nick Witney point out, "The idea that the EU might collectively assert itself against the US seems somehow indecent".[29] Still, in the light of the United States' current strategic reorientation from Europe to – mostly – Asia, reproaches of Europe ganging up on the United States seem outdated.

3.4.1 *Summarizing*

It proves difficult to achieve good coherence between the political and economic aspects of the EU policy. A proper balance should in particular be struck between inherent tensions in economic relations and credibility in the field of democracy and human rights. But an even bigger problem is posed by the breakdowns between the common and Member State policies. Even though, under the Treaties, the Member States are bound by the common EU positions when determining their own views and subsequent actions (and are moreover obliged to inform their EU partners accordingly),[30] they repeatedly go it alone diplomatically. This is partly due to the difficulties the 27 EU countries experience in reaching mutual agreement, but it can also be ascribed to national ambition. Particularly the larger Member States use their relations with world powers to underline their own status and to play to their own audience ('grandstanding'). For instance, the diplomatic initiative in the European response to the Libyan crisis in spring 2011 lay initially entirely with France, which, together with the United Kingdom, also took the lead in the aerial operations against this country.[31] The performance of the High Representative of the EU, Lady Ashton, was outshone by, in particular, that of President Sarkozy and, to lesser extent, that of Prime Minister Cameron

29 Shapiro, J. &Witney, N. (2009). *Towards a post-American Europe: A power audit of EU-US relations.* London: European Council on Foreign Relations, p. 34.

30 This obligation is laid down in Art. 24 TEU.

31 After a short while, NATO took over command of these actions. The US kept a low military profile.

and other European government leaders.[32] Indeed, this pattern could not only be seen in the case of Libya; the European calls for Syrian President Bashar al-Assad to step down, which gained momentum over 2011, were also led by the leaders of the bigger nations (this time again including Germany).

3.5 Concluding Observations: Implications for the Dutch Policy

It has been nearly two decades now since Koen Koch posed the question of "whether the ongoing process of European integration should necessarily lead to the disappearance, or at least to a substantial metamorphosis of Dutch foreign policy in the strict sense".[33] At first glance, the answer to this question seemed to depend on whether the integration process would take a supranational or intergovernmental direction. If the latter route were followed, it would seem that the future of Dutch foreign policy was guaranteed, "exactly because in the intergovernmental framework maintaining national sovereignty in the field of foreign policy and defence is key".[34] But, added Koch wisely, despite the formal respect of national sovereignty and upholding of the unanimity requirement, an intergovernmental regime offers the smaller partners, like the Netherlands, little room for pursuing a foreign policy that can still be considered independent in more than a *declaratory* sense. His explanation for this rather paradoxical outcome was that such a regime would very likely lead to the creation of informal directorates and tête-à-têtes between the larger Member States, where they would in fact impose their will on the smaller Member States. True, the latter could use their veto, but that is only wise in exceptional cases. Whereas a bigger country can extract concessions through obstructive behaviour, a smaller country will be more likely to cause irritation by doing the same and provoke sanctions in other fields of cooperation. At the time, the quoted writer recommended that Dutch policy should focus more on the quality of the content of the national input in European policymaking and on increasing the visibility of Dutch positions within the European arena by actively lobbying the European partners.[35]

---

32 Andreas Isensee and Adriaan Schout endorse the view that the performance of duties by the High Representative has so far been disappointing. Nevertheless, they believe it is too early to write off Lady Ashton altogether. Both authors are of the opinion that she has had to perform her task under difficult circumstances. If she succeeds in better organizing her plans and presenting them more convincingly, opinions about her could take a positive turn. *See* their article (2011). Catherine Ashton: Hoge Vertegenwoordiger, matige resultaten [Catherine Ashton: High representative, poor results]. *Internationale Spectator, 65*(6), 310-313.

33 Koch, K. (1993). *Over staat en statenvorming* [On state and state building]. Leiden: DSWO Press, p. 197.

34 Koch (1993), p. 201.

35 Koch (1993), p. 206.

It should be evident that in the past 20 years the European CFSP has evolved mainly in an intergovernmental direction. Koch's analysis of the various resulting consequences for the position of the larger and smaller Member States seems to have been large confirmed by the de facto developments. In their mutual cooperation, France, the United Kingdom and Germany have undeniably been able to allow themselves more freedom than the other countries. Insofar as the EU was capable of decisive action, the initiative was usually taken by these larger Member States. The EU's response to the Libyan crisis of 2011 – mentioned above – is the most recent example. To be sure, in certain situations the smaller Member States have not been completely overruled. Examples are Greece's and Cyprus's resistance to the EU cooperating with Turkey in the field of security policy, Poland's and Lithuania's opposition to the negotiations with Russia on a new Partnership and Cooperation Agreement (leading to suspension of the negotiations) and the protracted refusal of the Netherlands to cooperate in ratifying the stabilization and association agreement which the EU had concluded with Serbia.[36] The Netherlands also attracted attention by allegedly blocking a joint EU position on human rights in Israel and the Palestinian Territories in the UN Human Rights Council in September 2011, because the text was supposedly too critical. Minister Rosenthal's defence was that the Dutch objections were shared by a number of other EU Member States, including Germany.[37] In any case, in all reported cases, it involved blocking unwanted developments, not instigating desired ones.

Koch's argument to invest more in internally influencing European policy and less in implementing national policy has lost none of its relevance. The introduction of the common EU foreign and security policy has, surprisingly, not caused a radical break in the extent and scope of the Dutch objectives. The WRR has been right in criticizing the fact that the Dutch policy consists of a broad range of general policy intentions that lack distinct strategic choices or clear priorities.[38] The question of which issues should preferably be dealt with at the European level and which by the Netherlands has hardly been seriously considered. As a result, there are two parallel policy circuits, a European and a national one, in which activities overlap. There are thus good reasons to believe that arriving at a specific division of tasks between Dutch and European policies should be considered a matter of urgency. For now, there is a long-standing practice of common policy and, recently, the launch of an EEAS. If, in the future, the Netherlands wants to put its intentions into practice, namely to help further develop the CFSP, a more reticent and subservient national position would be appropriate. At the same time, the Dutch diplomatic apparatus is being considerably

36 In June 2010, Minister Verhagen caved in following a positive report by ICTY Prosecutor Serge Brammertz on Serbia's cooperation with the Tribunal.

37 *See NRC Handelsblad*, 29 September 2011.

38 Wetenschappelijke Raad voor het Regeringsbeleid (2010), p. 47 *et seq.*

reduced in size due to ongoing cuts.[39] As a result, the requirement or wish that the Netherlands, as a small country with major international interests ('great power writ small'), should be visible on practically all diplomatic fronts where the larger countries are present as well, becomes untenable. In this context, a critical view should be taken of, for instance, the standard but useless visits that Dutch ministers pay to countries in the Middle East to support the peace process, or – in the recent past – the trips they made to countries in the Great Lakes Region in Central Africa and to Sudan to put a stop to the bloody conflicts there. The Netherlands is simply several sizes too small for such projects. The Dutch government can no longer ignore the fact that its pretence of being a medium-sized country meets with only little response abroad, especially now the door to the G20 also seems to be closed forever.

Where does the above analysis leave an autonomous Dutch foreign policy? Perhaps not surprisingly, the leading principle ought to be that this policy should remain limited to the promotion of specific Dutch interests, i.e., interests not shared with other countries. This will mostly concern support for the national economy, that is, promoting Dutch exports and encouraging direct foreign investment at home. It is a simple fact that in these areas the Netherlands is in a specific competitive relationship with other Member States. That is why trade promotion locally, unlike, for instance, the routine consular assistance to Dutch people abroad, cannot be left to the EEAS. The presence of Dutch diplomats in emerging countries, acting on behalf of the Dutch government, increases the chances of establishing fruitful contacts with bodies that are indispensable for obtaining orders and creating active interest for the Netherlands as a country of establishment. Maaike Okano and Huub Ruël again pointed out that embassies and consulates are closest to Dutch businesses abroad and know the local situation in target countries best. Perhaps even more important than supplying information on these countries is providing access to relevant, useful networks. Innovative international entrepreneurship especially needs contacts in niche markets.[40] It practically stands to reason that strengthening the Dutch position on the international markets in a time of global restructuring is an absolute necessity for future prosperity.

At the same time, Dutch efforts to protect human rights, fight poverty, stimulate economic development as well as strengthen the organization of global cooperation should gradually be diverted from the bilateral to the European framework. Such a shift should not be interpreted as some sort of sale of our ideals, since the

39 Nota modernisering Nederlandse diplomatie (2011). Memorandum on the modernization of Dutch diplomacy. The Hague: Ministry of Foreign Affairs.

40 Okano-Heijmans, M. & Ruël, H. (2011). Commerciële diplomatie en internationaal ondernemen. Koopman versus dominee in de nieuwe economische wereldorde [Commercial diplomacy and international business. Merchant versus vicar in the new economic world order]. *Internationale Spectator, 65*(9), 465-466.

limitations in the implementation of national actions should be accompanied by strongly increased efforts in all phases of European decision-making (including the preliminary stage where positions are explored). This implies taking initiatives and making proposals, rallying support and forming coalitions. If the Belgian minister Vanackere is right in saying that "a smaller country has sometimes more freedom to put certain items on the agenda and launch them",[41] this freedom should be used to its maximum extent. In line with that stated earlier, the focus must be on the quality of the Dutch input, also by putting forward the most talented persons for key positions in the Secretariat of the Council of the EU and the EEAS.

Of course, the pace and degree with which the Netherlands can step up the Europeanization of its policy will also be determined by the willingness of other European countries to make a similar effort. There is good reason to have doubts about this. However, we should not, as a result, lose sight of the desired prospect of 'more Europe', although bringing this prospect closer will inevitably be to the detriment of the recognizability and positioning of national views. The latter will be considered a great loss by, in particular, human rights and development organizations. The Netherlands might also be forced to accept, for instance, stronger condemnations of Israel's policy. However, the effectiveness of the efforts made should be of overriding importance. There are only few fields or topics where the Netherlands can initiate developments under its own steam. Of course, each Member State will be faced with the question of how many concessions it wants to make for the sake of a common position. But, in this respect, the position of the EU Member States is not much different from that of a political party having to choose between joining a broad government coalition and making do with a place in the opposition. The value of articulating one's own unadulterated message will have to be weighed against the chance to exert real influence as part of the group. In the case of the Dutch foreign policy, this basically amounts to choosing between pursuing a declaratory policy, characterized by mostly symbolic actions, and investing in a European policy which at least holds out the prospect of ultimately producing tangible results.

41 Vanackere, S. Roep om 'meer Europa' smoort stem van lidstaten niet: nationaal buitenlands beleid verrijkt extern optreden EU [Call for 'more Europe' fails to stifle voice of Member States: National foreign policy enriches EU external action]. *Internationale Spectator, (2011) 65*(5), 242.

4 The Netherlands – Europe or the United States?

W.F. van Eekelen

The year 1949 was crucial for the post-war orientation of our foreign policy: sovereignty was transferred to Indonesia, prompting an economic reorientation towards the European continent. That same year, the Netherlands became a member of the Council of Europe and NATO, after the Treaty of Brussels had already laid the foundations for broad Western European cooperation a year earlier. The Netherlands felt truly safe only when it could count on the United States in facing the Soviet threat. A small country with an open economy and global trade relations had more faith in the 'benevolent hegemon', the distant, friendly uncle, than in its nearby quarrelling cousins who constantly tried to impose their own views. Although we criticized Washington, quite severely at times, we often believed the US policy to be more consistent than that of our European partners. In addition, during the Cold War, it was not so much the United States as such that mattered, but rather the US leadership in NATO, in the belief that a free Western Europe was also of vital interest to the United States.

'Europe or the United States' was a choice we would rather not make. Why not both? But can we stick to this position now that collective defence is no longer an overriding priority, or is growing European integration making the balancing act between Europe and the United States too awkward? Successive governments kept believing that it was possible to stay on good terms with both Europe and the United States. Understandably so from a historical perspective, since we had close ties with the United States even before its independence. The Pilgrim Fathers had set off to Boston from Delftshaven. The young United States had been granted loans by the Dutch. The first salute to the republic was given by the Dutch from St Eustatius (for which the island was severely punished by the English). The second US President, John Adams, had been Ambassador in The Hague for some time and was close friends with the editor of the Leiden Gazette. But also later, this good image stayed with us – a reliable country with dependable and protestant hereditary stadtholders and, later, a monarchy. Windmills, tulips, polders and clogs proved unbeatable trademarks, and the tale of Hans Brinker putting his finger in the dyke was told worldwide. Not terribly exciting, but like-minded as well as open to the world with sea trade and free trade as idealistic mottos, and also acting out of enlightened self-interest.

Europe was nearby. We survived the combined attacks by our neighbours in the disastrous year 1672 thanks to water, mud and ice, but subsequent French and German domination had a less happy ending. After Napoleon, we became a buffer state, sandwiched between Germany and France under the watchful eye of the British, and with no natural boundaries except the sea. There was little left to do but keep our head down and focus on trade and manage our colonies. A small, content nation, conservative and looking to maintain the status quo.[1]

In World War I, we were able to stay neutral. This suited us and our neighbours just fine, although Belgium tried to take the Flanders part of Zeeland from us when the war was over. Meanwhile, our neutrality had, so we believed, given us an aura of benevolence and righteousness with which we had complacently adorned ourselves, comparable to the United States' 'exceptionalism' and championing of true democracy. At the beginning of the 20th century, we were involved in the peace conferences in The Hague and in establishing the International Court of Justice, but the famous Cornelis van Vollenhoven went a bit too far when he stated that the Netherlands was predestined to take the lead in enforcing the international rule of law.[2] Later, Article 90 of our Constitution stipulated – being virtually the only one in the world – that the government shall promote the development of the international rule of law. So this international law vocation was there to stay, and it is to the great credit of successive ministers of foreign affairs that they have managed to preserve this reputation (and have been willing to bear the associated costs), so that The Hague has indeed become the City of International Law.

Appreciation for the United States' role in our liberation in 1944-1945 has further fortified our ties with the United States. The annual ceremony at Margraten cemetery is still an imposing event, also thanks to the involvement of younger generations. During the war, President Roosevelt, having Dutch roots himself, formulated the 'Four Freedoms', which lay close to the heart of the Dutch: freedom of speech, of worship and freedom from want and fear. To this date, annual Four Freedom Awards are presented in both Middelburg and the United States, in alternate years. These freedoms continue to guide us in our foreign policy.

There was also appreciation on the side of the United States. Through Wikileaks, we learnt what departing ambassador Clifford Sobel thought of the Netherlands.[3]

1 Hellema, D. (2001). *Neutraliteit & Vrijhandel. De geschiedenis van de Nederlandse buitenlandse betrekkingen* [Neutrality & free trade. The history of Dutch foreign relations]. Houten: Het Spectrum, p. 293.

2 Boogman, J.C. (1978). Achtergronden, tendenties en tradities van het buitenlands beleid van Nederland (eind zestiende eeuw – 1940) [Backgrounds, tendencies and traditions of Dutch foreign policy (late sixteenth century – 1940)]. In *Nederlands buitenlandse politiek, heden en verleden* [Dutch foreign policy, then and now]. Baarn: In den Toren, p. 25.

3 US embassy cables: Why Holland is so important to US, cable of 22 August 2005, EO 12958, published at <www.guardian.co.uk>, 15 December 2010.

After stating that the myths about Dutch homogeneity, tolerance and pacifism no longer accurately reflected reality, he wrote,

> While the Dutch prefer to see themselves as 'balancing' between Europe and the US, this balance can shift due to domestic and international factors [...] Dutch pragmatism and our similar world views make the Netherlands fertile ground for initiatives others in Europe might be reluctant, at least initially, to embrace. [...] Coaxing the Dutch into the spotlight can take effort, but pays off royally

In 2011, his later colleague Fay Hartog-Levin, daughter of Dutch Jewish parents who fled the Netherlands, said, "The Netherlands underestimates itself, but does indeed make a difference in the world: third investor in the US, 1750 US head offices, leader in water management, as was again confirmed by the assistance provided after hurricane Katrina".[4] Some European ambassadors were less positive and were of the opinion that the Netherlands was too focused on its own affairs.

We grew less and less conservative. Following the 1968 Paris uprising, our society increasingly opened up. The turning point came with the post-war generation, progressive democratization, collapsing traditional social pillars, greatly improved provision of information via television, a near-cultural revolution with hippies, flower power and marihuana, and anti-establishment. The foolish glorification of Mao, Castro and Ho Chi Minh. The US military intervention in Vietnam put our sympathy for the United States to the test. President Carter's attempt to develop a 'neutron bomb' against the Soviet supremacy of tanks was fiercely opposed by the left wing of the Dutch political spectrum. The plan foundered when in Washington commentator Walter Pincus labelled it the ultimate capitalist weapon: killing people, but leaving property intact.

Gradually, our good relationship with the United States came under pressure. The 'US reflex', where it still existed, was diminishing, and we became more critical. We generally preferred Democratic to Republican presidents because of their international outlook and social engagement. Relations at governmental level continued to be good, but on both sides doubts arose about the future of our society. Like many European partners, the United States frowned upon our looser sexual morals, legalized prostitution, homosexual relations, and especially our tolerance of drugs use and euthanasia, even though similar developments were soon to follow elsewhere. We, on our part, did not understand the United States' religiousness bordering on hypocrisy and the low level of social awareness of the Tea Party, which is increasingly dividing the country and tarnishing the 'American dream'.

The Netherlands started wagging its finger again, but this time it was a political rather than a legal one. Ernst van der Beugel had already complained that time

4 *Algemeen Dagblad*, 14 September 2011, p. 10.

and again we managed to raise matters of practical policy by thundering them from the pulpit.[5] However, this would only be the beginning of a changing political game, more focused on making newspaper headlines and imparted in catchy one-liners, and of a parliament that would increasingly take the place of the government. It was a development which could also be observed elsewhere, but which in the Netherlands was reinforced by the special attention paid by Parliament to, e.g., security policy, non-proliferation and human rights, even though our ability to actually influence such matters on our own is limited.

4.1 What Europe?

Connecting with Europe was a slow process. It is true that the government declared war on Germany immediately after it had invaded the Netherlands on 10 May 1945 and that the governments-in-exile established the Benelux, but it took a long time for a real change to present itself. In 1948, we concluded the Treaty of Brussels with Belgium, Luxembourg, France and the United Kingdom, which encompassed a broad spectrum of cooperation and an automatic military assistance clause. However, this was mostly meant to enable Washington to continue the Marshall aid by proving that Europe was willing to cooperate. After the European Defence Community failed, this Treaty was transformed into the Western European Union (WEU), also including Germany and Italy. This enabled Germany to become an equal member of NATO, by controlling German rearmament in the WEU, but at the same time allowed inspections of the armed forces of the other Member States. The WEU became a reserve organization, doing useful work whenever things got bogged down elsewhere, for instance, when General de Gaulle vetoed the United Kingdom's accession to the EEC, or when, at the time of the Treaty of Maastricht, the European Union (EU) was not yet ready for a common defence policy.

The Netherlands played an important part in the first steps towards European integration, particularly at the Messina Conference, which was the breakthrough for the Treaty of Rome of 1957. It was obvious that we were unable to tackle most cross-border problems alone. Moreover, in the 1930s, we had experienced first-hand the major disadvantages of economic protectionism. But we were doubtful whether France, which put great emphasis on the role of the state, was that keen on free trade as well. To us, a powerful European Commission was essential, it being the only body able to rise above national interests and define European interests. The EU would have to become a community of law in which the Commission proposed, the Council of Ministers and the European Parliament

5 Van der Beugel, E.H. (1978). Atlantische samenwerking en Europese integratie [Atlantic cooperation and European integration]. In *Nederlands buitenlandse politiek, heden en verleden* [Dutch foreign policy, then and now]. Baarn: In den Toren, p. 54.

(EP) (through increasing co-decision) decided, and the Court guaranteed equal application of the law.

European integration was a dual process and therefore not always easy to understand: one the one hand, regulating mutual competition – the convincing argument being that one rule is better than 27 different ones – and, on the other, promoting cooperation, even solidarity, in many fields. Many Dutch people, even departmental ministers, were not sufficiently aware of the prosperity which the EU brought us. Only farmers felt its importance from the very beginning – not surprisingly, since the price mechanism favoured our high standard of agriculture. It took years for measures against overproduction to be taken, and it was not until a super levy on milk was imposed that a stop was put to it. Then, farmers, too, became less positive about Europe.

The attitude towards Europe grew less positive as painful and sometimes questionable measures were taken as well, where it could be argued that they need not be taken at the EU level, but might be left to the Member States. In certain areas, there was a tendency to over-regulate and national positions of departmental ministers became insufficiently coherent. More seriously, the debates were increasingly about money. We had become the largest net contributor and were told not to have been forceful enough in defending our national interests – a bitter reproach for all those promoting our interests in Brussels. Moreover, a difference of opinion had arisen about the figures: how should the 'Rotterdam effect' of own resources collected in the Netherlands, such as import duties, be calculated in relation to transit? Be that as it may, the Netherlands received a rebate of €1 billion on its contributions to the EU and is now doing everything to keep it.

The negative outcome of the referendum on the European Constitution in 2005 was an all-time low. It was badly prepared and hardly defended, carrying the dull slogan '*Europa, best belangrijk*' (Europe, rather important), the result being that the Netherlands lost its direction. The Left was in favour of a referendum, even though its outcome is usually conservative. There was a great deal of criticism from Ronald Plasterk – an outside commentator who later was to become minister – thus weakening support from the PvdA (Dutch labour party). As a result, the positive aspects of the Constitution and the later Treaty of Lisbon, such as greater cohesion between economic and foreign and security policy, a larger role for the EP and for the national parliaments, and the subsidiarity principle according to which problems are addressed at the most appropriate level, did not receive enough attention or were too complex for the average citizen. There were too many complaints about money being 'pumped around' in the structural funds (which, however, increased the visibility of the Union in the Member States) and about the Brussels-Strasbourg meeting circuit (which started off as a symbol of French-German reconciliation and can be changed only by offering France an international alternative).

Still, Europe is and will continue to be of vital importance. There is no point in saying that Europe is a means and not an end. It is an end, since we cannot manage without an internal market and cross-border cooperation. In 2011, the *Centraal Planbureau* (Netherlands Bureau for Economic Policy Analysis) calculated that, annually, our national income had been increasing by 6%-8% since 1970 thanks to the EU and the agreements concluded through the EU in the World Trade Organization (WTO). This amounts to an annual €1800 per inhabitant, against costs of €275 per capita minus €150 per capita in subsidies and reductions. Sixty per cent of our ever-increasing exports goes to eurozone countries, benefiting from 7% lower transaction costs.

4.2 Towards a European Foreign and Security Policy

Up until 1969, the Netherlands was against European cooperation in the field of foreign policy. Our influence would be limited too much by the intergovernmental set-up of the Fouchet Plan. Only when at the summit of The Hague it was decided to reopen accession negotiations with the United Kingdom did the Netherlands give in. Expectations were that, if Germany, France and the United Kingdom reached agreement on a common position, we could agree as well. Unfortunately, the United Kingdom would prove far less active than we hoped (also in view of its substantial military capabilities) and, under Prime Minister Thatcher, became a troublemaker that mainly wanted its money back. We had more affinity with the European position of Germany and France under Pompidou and Mitterrand.

The first steps towards a European security policy were taken in 1971 in the framework of European Political Cooperation, the chief elements being the Organization for Security and Cooperation in Europe (OSCE; a success), the Middle East (a fiasco) and joint positions in the United Nations (the problem being that the members of the Security Council wanted to determine their own positions despite agreements to coordinate them). Of the original six EC members, the Netherlands was the country most Atlantically oriented as well as most strongly opposed to a European role in the Israeli-Arab conflict. Our position was – and continues to be to this day – that only the United States had enough influence on both parties to be able to reach a solution. Unfortunately, this view would prove increasingly doubtful.

In the Den Uyl Cabinet of 1973-1977, Jan Pronk initially wanted a development policy independent of other countries. The motto was '*Nederland Gidsland*' (The Netherlands: Model Country), which later was adjusted to the reality that goals could be achieved only in cooperation with others. However, its outlines remained vague, since cooperation with 'like-minded countries' was not close and changed with the colour of their government coalitions. Pronk scaled down his ambitions and settled for an attempt to 'increase the margins' of policy. Max van der Stoel's aim was an active peace policy, but he made no bones about strongly disagreeing with the Soviets. Thanks to him, the Netherlands was able to play a part in drawing up the Final Act of Helsinki in 1975 and in establishing the resulting OSCE. This role was made possible thanks to European unity and to US willingness to give the OSCE a chance. Although Henry Kissinger was worried about too many European concessions to Moscow in exchange for hollow phrases, he had no objections as long as at the same time the 'Mutual and Balanced Force Reductions' would be seriously supported.

For Max van der Stoel, too, NATO continued to be "a constant, primary requirement of policy"[6] in the prevailing strategic and security situation. In addition, the 1973 oil crisis, during which the Netherlands received hardly any support from its European partners, made us even more dependent on the United States. To this day, other cabinets have kept considering NATO as a cornerstone of foreign policy, without, for that matter, bothering to explain this metaphor. What was new, however, was that security became more complex, with a domestic component and combined with other policy instruments that the EU did, but NATO did not, have.

Still, our preference remained transatlantic, and we saw no point in duplicating NATO structures at European level. This was different for a while when in 1987, during the war between Iran and Iraq, mines in the Persian Gulf and the Red Sea were posing a threat to free shipping. NATO was not yet allowed (by Germany) to act 'out of area', i.e., not outside the Treaty area, but the WEU was. Moreover, Belgium, the Netherlands and France had identical mine hunters, which the United States did not have. The WEU was also involved in enforcing the embargo against Serbia on the Danube and (together with NATO) in the Adriatic Sea.

Under the Treaty of Maastricht, the WEU was put in charge of preparing and implementing decisions with military implications, something which the new EU itself did not (yet) want to do. That would not change until the Treaty of Amsterdam, which transferred the WEU's tasks to the EU. It was agreed with NATO that the EU would be allowed to draw on 'NATO Assets', especially headquarters and communication systems, when the Alliance itself was not involved in an operation. However, this 'Berlin Plus' arrangement, which was implemented in Bosnia, where the EU took over the political lead but Deputy Saceur was put in command, has not been further extended due to the Cyprus problem which is paralysing NATO-EU relations. The initiatives to set up rapid-reaction units have not resulted in deployment either, neither by NATO nor by the EU.[7]

6 Heldring, J.L. (1978). De Nederlandse buitenlandse politiek na 1945 [Dutch foreign policy after 1945]. In *Nederlands buitenlandse politiek, heden en verleden* [Dutch foreign policy, then and now]. Baarn: In den Toren, p. 43.

7 The EU Helsinki Headline Goals for a force of 50-60,000 (1999), the NATO Response Force of 25,000 (2003) and the 19 EU Battlegroups of 1,500 from a small number of Member States (2007), modelled on Operation Artemis in Congo in 2003.

4.3 Nuclear Weapons

According to Heldring, the Euro-Atlantic contradiction was never more than a matter of nuance. This could well have been different, since the debate became quite heated at times, although more anti-US than pro-European. Prior to forming his cabinet in 1973, Den Uyl had earmarked non-proliferation as a top priority. This was still abstract enough, and besides, the Netherlands was only involved via Urenco's supplies of enriched uranium to Brazil. The fact that the nuclear option was kept open for a united Europe indeed contributed to establishing the Non-Proliferation Treaty (NPT), but received no support whatsoever from the Left. The debate on reducing the role of nuclear weapons in the security policy was more difficult because emotion and logic came into conflict. The role of nuclear weapons was to deter aggression from the conventionally superior Soviet Union. To be effective, possible use of these weapons should not be ruled out completely, despite the horrific consequences. Mutual deterrence relied on a rational assessment of risks, and for both parties these risks seemed unacceptably high or a first use of nuclear weapons. One could not be entirely sure, hence the claim that uncertainty was the best deterrent.

The nuclear debate had opened up since the decision by US Defence Secretary Robert McNamara in 1966 to involve the European allies in policy via the Nuclear Planning Group without letting them have a finger on the trigger. Times were turbulent, culminating in the decision in principle to station, in addition to the so-called dual-capable F-16 fighters already in place, 48 cruise missiles in the Netherlands against the Soviet threat of SS-20 missiles. Gorbachev's subsequent willingness to suspend the deployment of SS-20s brought a zero option within the range of possibilities. France was not too happy with this, arguing that the West gave up a chance to hit Soviet territory and was left with only short-range weapons to respond to a conventional attack. These would drop on the West's own territory and not reinforce deterrence.

In the light of the commotion of that time, it is quite remarkable that today, within NATO, arms control is hardly discussed any more. The US-Russian treaties on the reduction of strategic nuclear weapons were welcomed, but the debate on the Strategic Defence Initiative of President Reagan never really got off the ground and ended, for the time being, with the fall of the Soviet Union. In Europe, later initiatives concerning anti-missile defence against an Iranian threat were not considered that urgent. The Treaty on Conventional Armed Forces in Europe (CFE), involving a reduction of troops, is practically a dead letter after the Russian intervention in Georgia. Moreover, it had become unbalanced with the accession of so many Warsaw Pact members to NATO. Compared with the Cold War, there were fewer political consultations, and NATO increasingly became a military organization.

Initially, Washington handled the political transformation resulting from the fall of the Berlin Wall better than Western Europe did. President Bush Sr and Secretary of State James Baker took a more positive view of Germany's reunification (and the prevention of a neutral status) than most European partners, including the Netherlands. The Treaty of Maastricht, with its pillared structure, was not ideal, but still laid the foundation for further political and economic steps, including monetary union. It seemed a deal between Germany, which gave up its strong Deutschmark, and the French, who were willing to achieve 'political union', which was Helmut Kohl's wish. However, this concept did not develop in line with German expectations. Although the internal market and Jacques Delors' programme for Europe '92 became a success for all Member States, this largely excluded the integration of (macro)economic policy.

4.4 What United States?

Initially, the terrorist attacks of 11 September 2001, making the United States vulnerable, seemed to strengthen transatlantic solidarity: NATO established that it had been an external attack on the United States and applied Article V, although this had always been regarded as a US guarantee for Europe in case of Soviet aggression. *Le Monde* wrote, "*Nous sommes tous des Américains*" and AWACS reconnaissance aircraft were transferred to the western hemisphere. Unfortunately, the mood soon changed when, in response to the offer of assistance, Washington replied "Don't call us, we'll call you". The operation in Afghanistan was divided into the US-run Enduring Freedom and NATO's International Security Assistance Force, with a UN mandate and a range of national Provincial Reconstruction Teams, which came too late to keep the momentum against revival of the Taliban going.

More fundamental was the difference of opinion over Iraq: President Bush claimed Iraq had weapons of mass destruction (which, in the end, were not found), thus justifying a 'pre-emptive' attack. From a military perspective, this operation was a quick success, but it would be years before a civilian government could be formed in a country that consisted of three factions, of which the Iran-related Shi'ites were the biggest. Conceptually, the Pentagon made things even worse by claiming that now 'the mission determined the coalition', and the coalition did not determine the mission. This seriously undermined the consultation principle of NATO's Article IV and meant, in fact, that the United States would determine with whom they intended to operate in a 'coalition of the willing'. At the time, Germany, France, Belgium and Luxembourg explicitly distanced themselves, with the Netherlands taking a middle position, politically supporting the removal of Saddam Hussein, but not participating militarily. Military involvement started only when the UN issued a mandate for 'peacekeeping' in occupied Iraq.

Meanwhile, in the United States, serious doubts had arisen about Europe's willingness to embark on a military operation, especially when Germany only proved prepared to deploy a so-called stabilization mission in Afghanistan, which would involve no fighting, and, in 2011, did not participate in the bombing of Libya and even abstained on Security Council Resolution 1973 imposing a 'no-fly zone' to protect the population. The European 'battlegroups' were not deployed, but nor was NATO's Reaction Force.

Although NATO's 1999 Strategic Concept proved completely obsolete after 9/11, attempts to adapt it were only successful in November 2010, thanks to a new US president and a changed attitude of France, which, under Sarkozy, joined the military wing of NATO. In 2003, the EU did better with the so-called Solana strategy, i.e., the European Security Strategy. First of all, it couched the threat in the same terms as the United States: terrorism, weapons of mass destruction and failing states, together with organized crime, but at the same time placed explicit own emphases: conflicts could not be solved by military means alone and the aim should be effective multilateralism, the determining framework being the UN Charter.

The new NATO concept confirmed the traditional task of collective defence as stated in Article V of the Treaty, but at the same time underlined both the duty of consultation under Article IV and the wish to promote good relations with Russia. The result was a compromise between the old Member States which no longer regarded Russia as a threat and wanted a new NATO, focusing on, e.g., peacekeeping operations outside the Treaty area, and the new members which kept focusing on defence against possible aggression, read: by Russia. This was already a difficult combination in itself, especially when, according to the Baltic states, it should be accompanied by 'contingency planning' for a possible attack. The EU's priorities focused on failing states in combination with organized crime, for which it could deploy a wider range of instruments than NATO.

4.5 New Crises

During the crises in Libya and Ivory Coast, the UN's authority increased, but this period left a strange taste in Europe's mouth: first, without prior consultation at European level, President Sarkozy recognized the rebels in Benghazi, then Germany withheld its support for the 'no-fly zone' in the UN Security Council, and, finally, only a few countries joined in enforcing compliance with these zones. On the other hand, without quick action by the British/French, the uprising would have been nipped in the bud. Subsequently, it was openly acknowledged that the intervention had an ulterior motive: 'regime change', Gaddafi had to go. A remarkably broad interpretation of the UN Security Council's mandate to protect the population 'by all means necessary' made that happen.

The Netherlands again proved itself a headstrong ally. While taking a middle position on Iraq, in Afghanistan, we focused, for domestic political reasons, on a 'reconstruction mission', even though a basic security level had not yet been established. We tried to distinguish ourselves from the forceful actions of the United States by our three D concept: Defence, Diplomacy and Development. Attention for the 'hearts and minds' of the population was certainly the right approach and would be emulated later by US Secretary of Defence Gates, but the content of the three Ds did not stand out for its clarity. After all, it was not about defence, but about security, and not about diplomacy, but about establishing good governance. Moreover, the US military referred to a whole different trio: Disrupt, Degrade and Destroy the Taliban.[8] In Libya, although not involved in the bombing of Gaddafi's troops and headquarters, Dutch aircraft and a ship did join in reconnaissance flights and sea blockades. When fighting Somali pirates, we were part of both NATO and EU units, the latter proving to have a better mandate and more possibilities to punish the pirates in cooperation with the coastal states.

Still, the Netherlands has been commended for its professional military effort. We used quality equipment, and our personnel were well-trained and capable of doing more with less people than other countries. The percentage of GNP we were spending on defence was dropping steadily, but this mattered less as long as performance was good. What counts is how the money is spent, not on personnel costs but on an investment quota which should not drop below 20%. The armed forces, moreover, have a positive attitude: they want to be on the A Team. This particularly applies to the Royal Netherlands Air Force, which, in selecting its planes, prefers not only United States but also top-range aircraft. This is understandable for a country that has to make its equipment last a long time; in such case 'midlife modernization' is more useful. The Royal Netherlands Navy was mainly oriented towards the United Kingdom, where our frigates were being tested for readiness. The UK/NL Amphibious Force was a fine example of full integration, but has, unfortunately, never been deployed. Nor were attempts to get a joint frigate project off the ground any more successful. The Royal Netherlands Army relied more on Germany: the German/Dutch Army Corps in Münster offered us the opportunity to develop expertise at that level and operated effectively in Afghanistan. However, it no longer commands combat units. The new motto, both at NATO and in the EU, is Pooling and Sharing, which is certainly useful in enhancing effectiveness, but leaves the question, with whom and what will be the result?

Foreign policy, inevitably, remains selective, not only where participation in interventions is concerned, but also in choosing between stability and democracy in concrete cases. However, when perceptions of national interest are diverging that much, should we start considering, within the Alliance and the EU, deploying operations by a small number of Member States? The Treaty of Lisbon pro-

8 *See* Woodward, B. (2010). *Obama's wars, the inside story*. London: Simon & Schuster, where the President tries to define the threats of Al Qaeda and the Taliban and decides not to destroy the Taliban.

vided for this in the form of Permanent Structured Cooperation (PSC) between those countries that have the necessary military means and are willing to make stronger commitments towards each other. It is still unclear how decisions to launch such an operation are to be taken and how the costs will be distributed. In such cases, a joint strategic concept between the European participants will be essential.

The reality for now is that large military operations are not possible without US involvement, but even in the United States doubts are increasing as to whether ground troops should still be deployed on a large scale. The emphasis will be on 'Special Forces' and unmanned aircraft. In the Kosovo crisis, forcing Milosevic to withdraw without deploying ground troops proved very difficult. In Libya, however, the battle was won by air, with the rebels taking over ground duties. In the first phase, US cruise missiles took out air defence and then provided necessary assistance in target detection and air-to-air refuelling. The remainder of the battle was left to the European allies plus Qatar and the Arab Emirates, nine countries in all. With the death of Gaddafi, the emphasis shifted to the composition and power of the new leadership and to the country's reconstruction. Here certainly lies a bigger task for the EU than for NATO, since it is now a matter of carrying out administrative reforms, forming political parties and developing a system of transparency and accountability. This is even more true of Egypt, where the danger of Muslim fundamentalism is looming, even though there, like in Tunisia, the revolt started with high food prices and lack of jobs for young people.

Quite remarkable was the cautious attitude of President Obama, who after the loss of US prestige in the Middle East under his predecessor did not want a dominant role for the United States in the region.[9] But what does a different US leadership mean for the future of NATO? 'Leading from behind' is not a convincing notion. In addition, the United States, being a 'Pacific power', will give increasing priority to developments in Asia (the least organized continent) and relations with China. In that case, Europe will have to go it alone more often.

The EU has become active in export controls and in attempts to make Iran give up developing nuclear weapons. Iran continues to be a powder keg in the Middle East, which nobody wants to see exploding as long as the 'Arab Spring' offers opportunities for a democratic or, at least, anti-fundamentalist development. However, the question remains of whether Israel can tolerate a nuclear Iran, and if not, what the United States and Europe will do.

Unfortunately, the Israeli-Palestinian conflict is again threatening to disrupt Western relations with the Arab world. Israel has not responded adequately to the 'Arab awakening' and has fuelled incomprehension among its friends, particularly by continuing to expand its settlements and remaining vague about a two-state solution. For the previous cabinet (Rutte I), which, on taking office, wanted

9 In *Time* of 4 April 2011, Fareed Zakaria summarized his attitude as "not too much, not too little, not too unilateral, not too American. Call it the Goldilocks military plan".

to strengthen its ties with Israel, this was a problem that placed the Netherlands in a special position in EU consultations, more so than in its relations with Washington. Under Obama, the creation of a Palestinian state and the withdrawal of Israeli settlements on the West Bank were initially supported verbally, but due to the mounting election campaign, these issues did not become explicit policy. It is no surprise therefore that in these circumstances the call for a European role is gaining momentum.

4.6 Financial Disaster

The EU and the United States more or less agree on economic issues. Mutual trade and investment levels continue to be high, although dropping in relative terms. However, Washington no longer seems to conduct a trade policy and has become stuck in the Doha Round. Another problem concerns the environment, where the United States is resisting drastic CO_2 reductions in its energy-intensive society and ultimately cooperated with China to evade stiff international CO_2 reduction targets. At the conference in Copenhagen, during the negotiations on a new agreement on CO_2 reductions, the EU did not play the prominent role it had in mind. On the other hand, China and Germany presented a common front when the United States wanted to raise the issue of trade imbalances.

The most recent financial crisis, which started in the United States, has damaged confidence in the US economy. This crisis in a deeply divided country is also taxing the euro system. What started as a housing bubble and banking crisis in the United States soon became a transatlantic financial crisis which required intervention by national governments, resulting in rising public debt and further cuts. In this field, the European Commission had only limited powers, which meant that the talks mainly took place at intergovernmental level (also involving the ECB and IMF). The euro countries lacked decisiveness. Their main concern was to avoid risk of contagion by the Greek scenario by gaining time, thus enabling banks to restore their balance sheets before governments had to come up with the money. In addition, the euro countries were willing to pay up only if it was clearly established that Greece and Italy would implement effective reforms.

At the end of the day, these crises will make the European instruments stronger: supervision of banks and other sections of the financial sector, a proper alarm system when countries do not follow the rules of the Stability and Growth Pact and, ultimately, sanctions. The Netherlands reset its course in time and made a good impression when proposing to appoint a European commissioner for the euro. The EP played an important role with its 'six-pack', in particular with the amendment that proposals of the supervisor may only be rejected by a qualified majority. If this package is successful and the intergovernmental aspects do not gain the upper hand over the 'Community method', European integration will again have taken another step forward. In this respect, it is better not to aim for the vague concept of 'political union', but rather for measures needed to credibly implement actually agreed policy. Many other policy areas are better left to the Member States until there will be new impetus for joint action. The Lisbon Treaty was right in emphasizing the 'subsidiarity' principle: the EU should focus on those transnational aspects that cannot be dealt with by Member States individually without weakening the EU's inner consistency. In general, the EU is better served by framework directives than by highly detailed regulation. Key should be what is necessary for a 'level playing field' within the internal market.

Again we find that the development of European integration may be erratic but is making continuous progress. With the new European External Action Service (EEAS), dealing with all foreign policy aspects, the EU can develop into a more coherent player on the world stage, which, however, will require consensus on purpose and means. The United Kingdom continues to pose a problem in this respect, also for Europe's security policy, where, paradoxically, the country could play a major role. The British are struggling with inflation and a budget deficit which, percentage-wise, is as high as the Greek deficit. In addition, they are acting increasingly bilaterally instead of at European level. Whether, ultimately, they will be able to maintain their position as a service economy outside the eurozone has become a painful question.

4.7 Conclusion

'Europe or the United States' continues to be a difficult question for the Netherlands, especially where foreign policy is concerned. Preferably both, but sometimes the Dutch seem to want to say: neither. Still, with no other parts of the world do Europe as well as the United States have closer or larger comparable interests than with each other. But both are doing poorly, and Dutch influence on both sides has diminished with the enlargement of both NATO and the EU. Not too much should be expected of a role as 'balancer', except perhaps on a few specific issues where we can bring expertise and ensure proper preparation. There is not much left to balance anyway, now that the EU is developing in an increasingly wider area and has broader instruments than available under NATO's security dimension, which is limited to military aspects. The United States has growing internal problems with the system of 'checks and balances' and will need years to get out of the economic crisis, although in due course the country will bounce back thanks to its vitality and optimism, especially if it becomes independent of oil imports. However, the terrible ideological polarization has paralysed any solution. President Obama's re-election has been welcomed throughout Europe and augurs well for the continuation of the moderate foreign policy ably conducted by Hillary Clinton. Yet, as American attention shifts to Asia, and China in particular, the question remains whether our interests will continue to run more or less parallel in the future.

Things will also be difficult on the European side, especially with the United Kingdom staying on the sideline. Currently, Germany and France do not form a strong axis, but without their agreement nothing much happens. In 2003, Ben Knapen, later to become State Secretary of European Affairs in the Rutte I Cabinet, wrote that only a construction with federal features would offer scope for both globalization and some degree of social diversity, because the European nation state does not have sufficient assets 'to keep everything together'.[10] His message still applies. However, government and business are late in conveying it to a public that has come to see Europe as threatening. How can we continue earning our living in the future in the light of rising China and India? The answer is: only if our joint competitiveness stays strong enough, which is possible only through more Europe. The internal market is by no means complete yet, especially not the services sector, which is becoming increasingly important for the Netherlands. But also in the field of foreign and security policy the EU can become a 'global player' only if joint priorities are set and concerted action is taken. In that case, the United States, too, will stay interested in Europe.

10 *Gedogen is helaas van gisteren. Opgelegde democratie en Europees gewicht moeten Nederland bij elkaar houden* [Tolerance, alas, is a thing of the past. Imposed democracy and European weight should keep the Netherlands together], summary of the 2003 *Burgemeesterslezing* in *NRC Handelsblad* of 13 September 2003. Eight years later, Job Cohen, in his capacity of PvdA party leader, used these same words but may have been referring to something else.

5 The Shifting Sands of the Arab Spring: Can the European Union and Dutch Foreign Policies Make a Difference?

Dr Sarah Wolff

5.1 Introduction

The day 14 January 2011 will remain in the history books. During that night, Ben Ali, who had ruled Tunisia for 23 years, flew to Saudi Arabia like a criminal. The Jasmine Revolution tore down apolitical and mental iron curtain, urged on by the revolting Arab youth fighting for their freedom. The wind of revolution blowing over Tahrir Square led to the fall of Mubarak and to the overthrowing of the Gaddafi regime. In autumn 2011, Ennahda, the Tunisian Islamic party, won 40% of the votes and had to start looking for coalition partners. The first round of the Egyptian elections was marked by a landslide victory of the Muslim Brotherhood and a high rate of participation of 62%. Demonstrations on Tahrir Square show the continuing discontent among Egyptian citizens vis-à-vis the ruling military government. In the meantime, the Moroccan King Mohammed V nominated Abdelilah Benkiran, the leader of the Justice and Development Party (PJD), to become Prime Minister. New political forces with which Europeans had avoided establishing a dialogue are now in power.
The road to democratization will not be smooth. Even though democratization is the most desirable option, the political game of different domestic actors might provoke hiccups or even lead to a reversal of trends. In Egypt, the new President Mohamed Morsi, the winning candidate of the Muslim Brotherhood, will have to cope with the old military guard, which keeps its weather eye open. In July 2012, the first arm-wrestling took place, with the Highest Constitutional Court cancelling the decision of the new President to convoke the Parliament. The Parliament had been dissolved by the Court in June on the basis of irregularities in the legislative elections of 14 June 2012. In Libya, at the time this volume goes to press, the liberals organized in the 'National Forces Coalition', which led the rebellion against Gaddafi, took the lead after the elections of 7 July 2012. The Muslim Brotherhood, unlike its Egyptian counterpart, did not have a similar anchoring in the country, given its long exile abroad. With more than 150 political parties and discontent amongst the Amazigh minority and other tribes, the coalition led by Mahmoud Djibril will have to satisfy a wide variety of interests and reflect them in the future Constitution to be drafted by the new Assembly.

Democratization processes, learning the political game and finding the terms of a new social contract take time, sometimes generations. The role of the European Union (EU) and of the Netherlands is to support the steps towards democracy, to respect the choice of the Arab electorate, while at the same time promoting the normative ideals of democracy amidst competing local traditions.

One thing is certain: the rebels have disavowed the EU and the United States as efficient democracy promoters. The thirst for liberty has come from within. The people have felt the need to break away from corruption and authoritarianism and from monopolization of the oil, gas and tourism proceeds by a small and clientele elite. Especially young people want a better life with political freedom and jobs.

In turn, EU policy of the past 15 years has been characterized by a lack of a grand strategy for the region, an outdated government-to-government approach embodied by the Union for the Mediterranean, an inability to channel the money where Arab citizens most need it, slow progress towards free trade agreements and monopolization of the EU-Mediterranean agenda by the EU's internal security concerns regarding migration and counter-terrorism.

Compared with previous crises, such as in ex-Yugoslavia, it is fair to concede that Europe's answer has improved. Policy documents like the 'Partnership for Democracy and Shared Prosperity' and EU sanctions against Tunisian, Egyptian and Syrian leaders and businesses have been taken quite rapidly. Nevertheless, major challenges on the shifting sands of transition are still lying ahead.

Section 2 takes stock of the EU policies in the region so far, while the third section analyzes the EU answer to the Arab Spring. Section 4 investigates the added value of the Dutch foreign policy. Before drawing conclusions, Section 5 briefly looks at the new political actors with whom the EU and the Netherlands will have to engage.

5.2 From a Eurocentric Mediterranean Policy to a Pragmatic Policy?

In the wake of the 1993, Oslo Accords aimed at settling the Israeli-Palestinian conflict, the Barcelona Process was launched in 1995, gathering the EU and 14 countries around the Euro-Mediterranean Partnership.[1] Willing to spread democracy and the rule of law in the region, the Partnership also had the ambition to bring growth to the region, to establish a Euro-Mediterranean free trade area by

1 The Mediterranean countries also include Algeria, Egypt, Israel, Jordan, Lebanon, Morocco, Syria, Tunisia and Palestine, which took part in the Euro-Mediterranean Partnership launched in 1995. Libya has been an observer member since 1999. The Euro-Mediterranean Partnership has been extended to the Union for the Mediterranean, which now comprises 43 members, including Mauritania, the Western Balkans, Turkey and Monaco.

2010 and to foster cultural and educational exchange. The real innovation was that, next to the Arab countries bordering the Mediterranean (and Jordan), Israel was also a member. A Euro-Mediterranean Parliamentary Assembly was established in 2003, the Anna Lindh Foundation for Dialogue between Cultures was created in Alexandria in 2005, and the European Instrument for Democracy and Human Rights provided some aid to civil society in the region.[2]

However, the Partnership has encountered several pitfalls since 1995. First, the money did not reach those who needed it most or for whom it was intended. Tocci and Cassarino have shown that within the European Neighbourhood Policy (ENP)

> the south fares relatively well, receiving on average €13.9 percapita per year compared to the east's €6.9.
>
> However, if we remove the Occupied Palestinian Territory from these calculations, to which EU assistance per year stands at an astounding €350 million, the picture changes, and the average funds per capita per year to the south fall to €5.2 per capita.[3]

In addition, Bicchi has shown that, before 2007, support through the European Instrument for Democracy and Human Rights was channelled mostly to countries where such issues were less sensitive, and that there was a tendency to promote human rights rather than democracy.[4]

Second, the Mediterranean was subject to a multiplicity of policy frameworks, which collectively blurred the EU's visibility in and its view on the region. Next to the Barcelona Process, which had a strong regional and multilateral focus, the Mediterranean partners were integrated in the ENP. The ENP added a bilateral layer, but remained only a gentlemen's agreement since the legal basis for cooperation remained the Euro-Mediterranean Association Agreements. Later, President Sarkozy Europeanized French domestic interests in the region. He argued that functional cooperation in areas of 'low politics', such as solar energy or the de-pollution of the Mediterranean, would lead to significant cooperation in the field of 'high politics', where progress had stalled since the second intifada. In fact, the Union for the Mediterranean remained very much an intergovernmental framework strengthening relations between executives on both sides of the Mediterranean, while ignoring the socio-economic and political concerns of the citizens in the region and failing to facilitate transnational relations of businesses. The EU

2 The European Instrument for Democracy and Human Rights is one of the EU's external aid instruments to promote democratization and human rights through funding to civil society. It was established by Regulation No. 1889/2006 of 20 December 2006 of the European Parliament and the Council.

3 Tocci, N. & Cassarino, J-P. (2011, March). Rethinking the EU's Mediterranean policies post-1/11. *Istituto Affari Internazionali Working Papers*. Retrieved from <http://hdl.handle.net/1814/17154>.

4 Federica, B. (2009). Democracy assistance in the Mediterranean: An overview. *Mediterranean Politics, 14*(1), 61-78.

lost visibility and momentum for reform and became lost in the various layers of policy frameworks. Nor had an EU grand strategy for the region been developed yet.

Third, the EU policies towards the region suffered from a capability-expectation gap. While in their discourse the EU leaders claimed their normative ambitions for the region, in practice, Europeans were interested in working with authoritarian regimes. For Pace, the efforts of EU democratization can be typified as 'at best a very slow world in progress, at worst a regression', and external actors consider political transformation as a 'high-risk strategy'.[5] *Realpolitik* interests of the 'Club Med' EU Member States prevailed. They established privileged and sometimes friendly relationships with leaders in North Africa and the Middle East, which were crucial from an energy, economic and security perspective.

Finally, the EU also pursued its own interests. It needed the support of the regimes in the fight against illegal immigration and co-opted the southern neighbours in border control. The externalization of border control, the development of joint patrolling (EU Member States together with North African countries) and the return of migrants had become daily business in the Euro-Mediterranean relations. The signature of the Treaty of 'Friendship, Partnership and Cooperation' between Italy and Libya in August 2008 symbolizes this bilateral cooperation in border control. In exchange for Libyan cooperation in border control, Italy promised to fund the first half of the Libyan border control system, and the EU the second half.[6] This meant that EU leaders were ready to provide surveillance systems to a country that did not have international asylum and migration standards and fundamental rights. The need to externalize the EU's internal security nonetheless met with broad consensus amongst the Member States.[7]

The dilemma of preservation of EU stability versus its normative ambition to be a democracy promoter remained a constant characteristic of the EU's and its Member States' policies regarding the region. The fear of instability in the form of migrants or terrorism spilling over to Europe, led Europeans to cooperate with the authoritarian regimes and to accommodate their interests. Consensus on security brought the two rims of the Mediterranean together, in particular since 9/11. Europeans shelved the settlement of the Western Sahara conflict, and as a corollary, this conflict is still poisoning Northern African relations. Instead, an EU-Moroccan fisheries agreement was signed in 2005 that allowed European ves-

5 Michelle, P. (2010). Paradoxes and contradictions in EU democracy promotion in the Mediterranean: The limits of EU normative power. In M. Pace & P. Seeberg (Eds.), *The European Union's democratization agenda in the Mediterranean*. London: Routledge, p. 49.

6 Human Rights Watch. (2009, September). *Pushed back, pushed around. Italy's forced return of boat migrants and Asylum seekers, Libya's mistreatment of migrants and Asylum seekers*. Retrieved from <www.unhcr.org/refworld/docid/4ab87f022.html>.

7 Wolff, S. (2012). *The Mediterranean dimension of the European Union's internal security*. New York, NY: Palgrave Studies in European Politics.

sels to fish in Western Sahara territorial waters and thus denied the rightful sovereign claim of the Sarawis to those waters.
It is in this context that the Arab Spring took the European chancelleries by surprise. The EU's approach until 2011 can be characterized as a combination of pragmatism and a focus on 'intelligent conditionality'.

5.3 The Short-term Pragmatism and Conditionality of the EU's Policy Responses to the Arab Revolts

The Arab revolts have really tested the coherence and coordination of the Common Foreign and Security Policy and, hence, the leadership of Lady Ashton, the newly established European External Action Service. So far, the EU has taken a pragmatic approach by siding with the revolutionaries and congratulating the winners of the fair and democratic elections in the region, encouraging them to continue on the road towards democratization. However, most of these initiatives remain limited to a short term and selective vision. So far, no vision on the EU's interests and strategy in the region has been developed.
The proposals of the EU related to the new situation are contained in a series of policy documents. In March 2011, the Partnership for Democracy and Shared Prosperity with the Southern Mediterranean[8] was the first joint policy answer of Lady Ashton and Commission President Barroso to the Arab revolts. Later, a communication on migration in May 2011[9] and a revised ENP were issued.[10] These proposals focus mainly on short-term instruments and financial means to provide support to the democratic transitions, in particular to sustain economic and social reforms and post-conflict assistance for Libya.
The spirit of these documents promotes a 'smart conditionality' approach whereby the leaders in the field of political reform and democratization will receive more ('more for more') and those lagging behind less ('less for less'). The main focus is on Libya, Tunisia and Egypt. Here, it is important to recall that conditionality was already a keyword in the ENP, which put in place a thorough system of annual progress reports and which benchmarks the sectoral and overall progress towards reform among the ENP partners. With the benefit of hindsight, it is now evident that conditionality and its desired consequences should be defined more carefully.
It remains yet unclear how the EU would react if the newly elected governments were to breach the 'normative principles' that the EU claims to be promoting in

8 European Commission and High Representative. (2011, March 8). *Joint communication: A partnership for democracy and shared prosperity*. COM (2011) 200 final, Brussels.
9 European Commission. (2011, May 4). *Communication on Migration*. COM (2011) 248 final, Brussels.
10 European Commission and High Representative. (2011, May 25). *Joint communication: A new response to a changing neighbourhood*. Brussels, COM (2011) 303.

the region. However, scepticism seems justified given the EU's passive approach so far regarding the breaches of democracy and rule of law principles by Gaddafi, Mubarak and Ben Ali.

Can the EU be serious about implementing conditionality in the region? In the past, the EU's positive conditionality was rather limited. In the field of migration and border control, it co-opted authoritarian governments in the co-management of its internal security[11] in exchange for financial incentives and security equipment to control their borders. This conditionality was based on benefits in relation to the EU's security agenda and economic interests; it was not purely related to democratization in the region. It proved a false trade-off since security and democratization are part of the same conundrum. The EU can very well pursue its own security agenda, while conditioning financial incentives on the adoption of migration and asylum policies or security sector reform. In addition, the EU has not been able to deliver the long-awaited incentives of visa liberalization that would enhance the EU's positive conditionality. In the absence of economic prospects in their own countries, businessmen, students and other skilled migrants should be the first categories regarding which the EU could propose a liberalization of the visa regime.

Among the core proposals of the European Commissionare is the Mobility Partnerships. This instrument, now in force with Moldova, Cape Verde, Georgia and Armenia, is hoped to contribute to the democratic transitions. The idea is to provide mobility projects for young people, artists, researchers and students, and to improve the implementation of the Schengen Visa Code and the visa application process in the EU consulates in these countries. Twinning in higher education, exchange of good practices in labour recruitment, and other projects to facilitate circular migration or support have been identified as short-term EU actions. The European Asylum Support Office, operational since 2011, will also provide capacity building in the field of refugee protection and asylum regimes. The Mobility Partnerships also require strengthening of the partners' border control systems and, very often, the conclusion of readmission agreements.

The Mobility Partnerships, such as for Moldova or Cape Verde, have been criticized for their "conceptual overstretch, the (prevailing) overemphasis on security and curbing irregular migration and for primarily summarizing existing bilateral cooperation programmes between individual member states and third countries under a new heading".[12] Frustration has been mounting in the partner countries. "Indeed, Senegal, which started exploratory talks on a Mobility Partnership at the same time as Georgia in June 2008, abandoned the negotiations due to dissatis-

11 *See* Wolff (2012).

12 Roderick, P. (2009). EU mobility partnerships: A model for policy coordination? *European Journal of Migration and Law, 11*, 327-345; Sergio, C. & Raül, H. i S. (2009). *The externalisation of the EU's labour immigration policy: Towards mobility or insecurity partnerships?* (CEPS Working Document No. 321). Brussels: Centre for European Policy Studies.

faction with the offer the Commission was willing and able to provide on behalf of the member states".[13] It remains to be seen whether the new governments in Egypt, Tunisia and Libya will be willing to cooperate in the field of migration without the prospect of visa liberalization or substantial economic incentives.

Economic growth is one of the key elements of successful transition. Next to consolidating their rights and freedoms, North African citizens also want prosperity and growth. Labour markets in the region are in deep need of restructuring, notably to provide jobs for young people and women and to become competitive on a global scale. Growth had already slowed down before the Arab Spring due to the financial crisis, falling from 6.1% GDP to 2.2% GDP in 2009.[14] So far, the economic offer of the EU has been limited. The Euro-Mediterranean Free Trade Area did not see the light in 2010 and has been postponed. The trade imbalance between Mediterranean countries and Europe is perpetuated by asymmetrical tariff dismantling in disfavour of agricultural products and by higher EU technical and phytosanitary standards. Tourism or migrant transfers are not enough to compensate for this imbalance.[15]

Unemployment and poverty are key concerns in the region. Economists of the Euro-Mediterranean Forum of Economic Institutes (FEMISE) emphasize that revolts in the Arab world have always been linked to rising food prices, which seems to be the case here as well. Young people and women felt excluded, not only from the political system but also economically. Before the revolts, the rate of unemployment amongst young people oscillated between 18.8% and 24.1% of the active population, compared with 6.1% for adults.[16] As for the GDP per capita, the EU's GDP per capita is eight times higher than that of Tunisia, which had the highest GDP per capita of all countries in the region in 2009. The only exception was Libya, where the GDP per capita was only 3.5 times lower than that of the EU.

The EU has for the moment proposed the Support to Partnership, Reform and Inclusive Growth (SPRING) Programme in order to address these disparities. The SPRING programme is based on the 'more for more' principle and aims at committing €350 million before the end of 2012. In other words, the more a country progresses towards democratization, the more it will be rewarded through the programme. It takes a case-by-case approach, dependent on the pace of each

13 Sarah, W. & Florian, T. (2011), A European migration policy fit for future challenges. In S. Wolff, F. Goudappel & J. de Zwaan (Eds.), *Freedom, security and justice beyond Stockholm and Lisbon*. The Hague: T.M.C. Asser Press.

14 World Economic Forum. *Arab world competitiveness report 2010-2011*. Available from <www.weforum.org>.

15 FEMISE. (2011, October). *Report on the Euro-Mediterranean partnership towards a new med region: Achieving fundamental transitions*. FEMISE. www.femise.org.

16 Document of the International Labour Organisation. (2009, October19-21). *International labour migration and employment in the Arab region: Origins, consequences and the way forward*. Thematic Paper, Beirut, Lebanon: Arab Employment Forum.

country, and focuses on better business regulation, support to small and medium-sized enterprises and reduction of socio-economic inequalities. The latter were indeed additional reasons for the revolutions. Corruption and collusion of the elites with the authoritarian regime have led to deep inequalities in North African societies. The most significant disparities are visible in Morocco, Palestine and Jordan, if one compares the revenue of the 20% of the population with the highest income to that earned by the 20% of the population with the lowest income.[17] Such inequalities have been at the heart of the political campaign of the Islamist parties which are now in government in Egypt, Morocco and Tunisia. In Tunisia, Ennahda concentrated its campaign on the fight against poverty, combating inflation, and social justice. Such themes have also been at the heart of the campaign of the Justice and Development Party that has won the legislative elections in Morocco. These issues are shared by the EU, which wants to promote investment in the region and fight corruption.

In the coming years, the new democracies could actually turn to other economic partners, such as China, Turkey or the Gulf countries, and start to develop stronger economic relations with other parts of the world.Tunisia has already announced the diversification of its banking system and wants to include Islamic financial instruments. Of course, economic and energy interdependence between the two rims of the Mediterranean is high, but the EU is currently busy saving its own eurozone and may not be paying enough attention to potential rivals in its southern neighbourhood.

5.4 The Added Value of the Dutch Foreign Policy

The Netherlands has so far embedded its answer to the Arab Spring in a coordinated European policy. Smart conditionality, rationalization of development aid, economic diplomacy and support of human rights and internet freedoms are the main points where the Netherlands can make a difference. However, like the EU, the Netherlands still knows very little about the newly elected forces in Tunisia and Egypt and will need to engage with those new interlocutors if it wants its foreign and development policies to make a difference.

To start with, the EU's ambition to be more strategic while conciliating its normative ambitions of spreading liberal democratic values mirrors the Dutch concerns:

> The EU needs to make more strategic use of regular summits with such countries, first to put specific European interests on the agenda and second to address common European goals (e.g., on climate policy, combating protectionism and tackling piracy) and

17 Eurostat. (2011). *Pocketbook on Euro-Mediterranean statistics*. Luxembourg: Publications Office of the European Union.

> values (e.g., democracy, human rights and the rule of law). Europe should not be afraid to show its teeth. It has shown itself capable of imposing robust sanctions, such as those in the past year aimed at Iran, Libya and Syria.[18]

The EU approach to enforce 'smart conditionality' whereby the leaders of democratic transitions will be rewarded ('more for more') and those lagging behind sanctioned ('less for less') seems to also adequately match the Dutch goals in the field of development cooperation. The Netherlands has considerably reduced its list of beneficiary countries and insists on stopping aid to middle-income countries, focusing on fragile states and putting the 'emphasis on reciprocity', in particular in regard to readmission agreements.[19] However, in March 2011, the Dutch House of Representatives called on the government to revise its list of fragile states in order to include Arab countries. Libya could well be eligible.

The Dutch Parliament also strongly supported the Dutch participation in the intervention in Libya. The Netherlands deployed 200 troops, six F-16 aircraft and a mine hunter to the NATO mission. In addition, the Dutch government has also contributed one million euros to a UN mission that will analyze the post-reconstruction phase.[20]

Economic diplomacy is the new buzzword in the corridors of the Dutch Ministry of Foreign Affairs. It means strengthening the economic position of the Netherlands in the world, in particular anchoring Dutch interests in emerging economieswhile pursuing the completion of the EU internal market. Dutch employers have already made their interest known and prefer a more active stance in the Arab world and strongerinvolvement in the restructuring of these economies.[21] The acceleration of the conclusion of Deep and Comprehensive Free Trade Agreements and other initiatives in the field of trade and business exchange could be an approach by which the Netherlands can indeed make a difference. For this to be successful, it should be complemented by parallel efforts to create jobs and to help the new governments to restructure labour markets that are still mainly driven by the informal economy. The Dutch government has announced its ambition to make haste with opening up the European market to products from the region, especially because "improving the region's economic prospects is the best way to stem the flow of migrants heading to Europe".[22]

18 Dutch Ministry of Foreign Affairs. (2011). *The state of the European Union 2011-2012. The Netherlands in Europe and Europe in the world: Realistic and goal-oriented.* The Hague: Ministry of Foreign Affairs.

19 Ibid., at p. 10.

20 Dutch Ministry of Foreign Affairs. (2011, September 28). House of representatives supports extending Libya mission. *Newsflash.*

21 Wientjes, B. (2011, March 10). Arabische Lente. *Opinie VNO-NCW.* Available from <www.vno-ncw.nl/Publicaties/Forum/Pages/Arabische_lente_16078.aspx?source=%2fPages%2fZoek.aspx%3fk%3darabische>.

22 Dutch Ministry of Foreign Affairs (2011). *The state of the European Union 2011-2012.*

As regards support for democratic transition, the Netherlands has taken a couple of interesting initiatives. Dutch Foreign Minister Uri Rosenthalhas, together with his Swedish counterpart Carl Bildt, also promoted the initiative to prompt European Foreign Affairs Ministers to take action as regards online freedom of expression. This initiative has been taken on board by Lady Ashton and Commissioner Neelie Kroes (Digital Agenda), who have commissioned former German Federal Minister of Defence Karl-Theodor zu Guttenberg to come up with ideas on how to support cyber-activists censored by authoritarian regimes. This initiative is part of the 'no disconnect strategy' that aims at protecting online freedoms.[23] The Arab Spring has benefited widely from mobilization through social media. These social media and cyber-activism have also made it possible to learn of the political repression in, for instance, Syria. Asmaa Mahfouz, a young Egyptian blogger, received the Sakharov prize from the European Parliament for having posted YouTube videos that helped mobilize people to demonstrate on Tahrir Square.

However, one of the main drawbacks of the Dutch legacy in the region is the position it took in September 2011 on the resolution proposed by Palestine to acquire statehood. Even though, ultimately, the resolution was postponed, it ruined the possibilities of an EU common position within the UN, with the Dutch government deviating from the long-agreed EU common position on a two-state solution.[24] This weakened the potential for a coherent European approach, as well as the EU's credibility in the region.

So far, the Netherlands has been a rather erratic actor: on the one hand, adhering to the idea of 'smart conditionality' and support through its development policy, while, on the other hand, criticizing, with 11 other Member States, Lady Ashton and the European External Action Service for their lack of effectiveness and bureaucratization. What is most lacking at Dutch and EU level is a strategic vision on the region and, for the moment, knowledge of their future partners on the other side of the Mediterranean. The time has come to engage with the Islamist political parties in power and support them in consolidating democracy and economic growth. This takes more than blaming the EEAS for inaction or erratic initiatives.

5.5 Getting to Know the New Political and Geopolitical Actors

To be able to provide some support to the region, it is necessary to grasp the extent to which the rise of new domestic political forces in Tunisia, Morocco,

23 For more detail about the 'no disconnect strategy', *see* European Commission. (2011, December). Digital agenda: Karl-Theodor zu Guttenberg invited by Kroes to promote internet freedom globally. Press Release IP/11/1525.

24 Schult, C. (2011, September 28). Europe fails to agree on Palestinian question. *Der Spiegel*.

Libya and Egypt will impact on the relationship with the EU. Relations between the EU and these new governments will be marked by both continuity and change. Continuity, because European foreign direct investments are crucial for these governments to put in place the economic and social reforms they promised. For Morocco or Tunisia, trade interdependence with the EU is likely to continue, even though they would need to diversify their exports.

Change will also characterize the EU's relationship with the newly elected governments. The latter are the first democratically elected rulers after years of authoritarianism and can therefore be confident of their legitimacy. They are also seen as part of the historic opposition to authoritarianism, which applies in particular to Ennahda in Tunisia and to the Muslim Brotherhood, although the latter were not actually leading the revolution. These movements have been the result of the mobilization of civil society through social networks and with support of the liberals, the latter being the big losers of the elections in Tunisia and Egypt. The governing parties also have the benefit of the doubt, since they have never before been in power. Revolutions do not stop the old party class from coming back in new forms, as has been the case in Eastern Europe, or can lead to new types of authoritarianism, as happened with Meciar in Slovakia.

The case of the Justice and Development Party in Morocco is slightly different because it has to compromise with a monarchy that recently made some cosmetic changes to the Constitution. Some even qualify the PJD's victory as a 'moral guarantee' of the monarchy to citizens who have lost faith in politics.[25] The challenge is huge since the PJD will need to evolve between the constraints of compromising with the monarchy and delivering on its economic, social but also anti-corruption programme. As with the Muslim Brotherhood, observers have stressed that the PJD was nowhere to be seen in the streets during the demonstrations in Morocco and that it is mainly by 'opportunism' that Islamists claim affiliation with the revolutions.[26]

Getting to know the new political forces, establishing trusting relationships and working hand in hand with regional actors such as the African Union will be crucial factors in making EU and Dutch policies a success. This should help traditional government-to-government relations favoured so far by Europeans evolve into strategies that put local ownership at their heart. Strongly supporting independence and quickly setting up the European Endowment for Democracy in autumn 2012 would be a first step.

In addition, the EU and the Netherlands can count on other regional players as partners for the countries in transition. Turkey has developed its own neighbourhood policy, lifting visa requirements and concluding free trade agreements with

25 Seniguer, H. (2011, December). Au Maroc, les islamistes ont bien pour mission de relégitimer le roi. *Libération*.

26 Slimani, L. (2011, December 2). Amel Boubakeur. Si les Islamismes s'inscrivent dans la révolution c'est par opportunisme. *Jeune Afrique*.

many Arab countries.[27] The Gulf countries[28] are also looking for new economic opportunities. Admittedly, they did welcome the Ben Ali clan, but they have also opened the doors of the Gulf Cooperation Council to Morocco. Iran and Syria are striving to maintain their alliance by continuing the bloody repression of demonstrators. Palestine is spreading the seeds of its own revolution within international relations, bidding for statehood in the United Nations. China and Russia are also looking for new investments opportunities.

5.6 Conclusion: Evolution on the Shifting Sands of Democratic Transition?

Despite several policy frameworks embedded in a normative EU power conception, the old EU policy towards the region carries a number of weaknesses. It has been characterized by a lack of visibility, an inability to challenge authoritarian regimes on the grounds of democratic values, and a security and economic preference for cooperation with authoritarian regimes.

So far, the EU and the Netherlands have taken a short-term pragmatic and cautious approach towards the Arab Spring and the democratic transitions. On the EU side, no major strategy has yet been discussed and its approach has been rather incremental, focusing on 'smart conditionality'. EU internal security concerns such as migration have been prominent on the EU and Dutch agendas for the region. The Netherlands has been supportive of the EU initiatives while bringing into the debate initiatives in the field of internet freedoms. However, in order to make a real difference and promote Dutch economic interests, the Netherlands should contribute to an EU strategic long-term vision vis-à-vis the Arab countries. Rather than repackaging old policies, it is time for the EU to start thinking more profoundly about its own priorities in the region (economy, energy, migration, security) while remaining strategic about its normative values. Democratization and *Realpolitik* interests are not antonyms.

The road towards democratic transition is a very unpredictable and unstable one. Both the EU and the Netherlands will have to evolve their strategies on shifting sands.The first challenge is to establish contacts with the new political interlocutors on the other side of the Mediterranean. This can be done through more engagement, which is about establishing more transnational contacts with political leaders, parliamentarians, etc.

The second challenge is to evolve from a narrow security agenda that has traditionally focused on migration and counter-terrorism concerns, to a broad free-

27 Tocci, N. (2011, September 12). Turkey and the Arab Spring: Implications for Turkish foreign policy in transatlantic perspective [Commentary]. Washington, DC: Carnegie Endowment for International Peace.

28 Echagüe, A. (2011, October).*Don't forget the gulf* (FRIDE Policy Brief No. 98).

dom, security and justice agenda, embedded in support to democratic transitions. The EU will need to strike a delicate balance between promoting its own security and economic interests and remaining tough on conditionality. But drawing lines in the sand can only work if the EU is ready to propose the right economic and visa liberalization as a strong incentive. The EU and the Netherlands need to make the most of migration fluxes, which after all, in 2012, so far represents only 5% of the total number of migrants since the beginning of the Arab Spring.[29] Rather, Europeans should help countries in the region, which have been most affected by the migration influxes, in order to strengthen their migration and refugee policies and capacities.

Thirdly, a balance between security and development concerns needs to be struck. The EU's counter-terrorism concern will continue to prevail in North Africa and the Sahel region. The challenge is now to integrate this with the EU's development policy. The EU actually made a start in 2010 by drafting a security and development strategy for the Sahel. In this document, development is seen as the solution to security threats in the region.[30] The circulation of light weapons in the aftermath of the conflict in Libya and the fear that they will end up in the hands of Al-Qaeda in the Islamic Maghreb or organized crime currently attract a lot of attention from European security officials. It still remains to be seen to what extent a balance with development concerns will be struck. The ambition should be to put what is on paper into practice.

Both European and Dutch officials will be confronted with fragmentation in the region, and newly emerging democratic transitions will pose different challenges. Already the second wave of demonstrations on Tahrir Square shows that the Egyptian ruling military is not ready yet to give up its power that easily. Thus, the EU's conditionality as well as its ambitions for the region will soon be tested. By helping to consolidate democracy, the EU can make a difference compared to other players like China, Russia or the Gulf countries. To be successful, though, the EU and the Netherlands might have to pay more attention to the 'ownership' of those democratic values and understand that democratization means stability and security for the EU as well.

29 Fargues, P. (2011, May). Voice after exit: Revolution and migration in the Arab world. *Migration Information Source.*

30 European Union External Action Service. (2011). *Strategy for security and development in the Sahel.* Retrieved from <http://eeas.europa.eu/africa/docs/sahel_strategy_en.pdf>.

6 The Netherlands, Russia and the European Union

André Gerrits

6.1 Introduction[1]

The relationship between the European Union (EU) and Russia is subject to strong fluctuations. Following President Dmitri Medvedev's visit to Brussels in December 2010, the President of the European Commission, José Manuel Barroso, was pleased to note that the meeting which had just finished was "probably the best summit in which I have participated so far with Russia".[2] It was only two years ago, after Russia had invaded Georgia, that the relationship between Russia and the Union had hit rock bottom.[3] Relations between them had reached 'a crossroads', as the European Commission ominously put it.[4] But due to this volatility, we lose sight of the continuities in their interrelations. Although it is constantly argued that Europe is barely making any headway in its relations with Russia – symbolized by the authoritarian approach that Russia has adopted and a lacking ability, on both sides, to arrive at a new Partnership and Cooperation Agreement – there is, in fact, a stable undercurrent of practical contacts and of cooperation in many areas. The combination of volatility and continuity is chiefly determined by the special role of the EU Member States in the EU's Russia policy – a conspicuous omission in the literature on Europe and

1 This contribution has greatly benefited from interviews with officials of the ministries of Foreign Affairs and of Economic Affairs, Agriculture and Innovation, for which I am very grateful.

2 Barroso, J.M. (2010, December 7). Statement by President Barroso following the EU-Russia Summit Joint Press Conference with Herman Van Rompuy, President of the European Council and Dmitry Medvedev, President of Russia, Brussels. <http://europa.eu/rapid/pressReleasesAction.do?reference=SPEECH/10/734> (accessed 15 July 2011).

3 Prozorov, S. (2010). Beyond the paradigm of integration in EU-Russia relations. Sovereignty and the politics of resentment. In K. Engelbrekt & B. Nygren (Eds.), *Russia and Europe. Building bridges, digging trenches*. London: Routledge, p. 86.

4 European Council. (2008, September 1). Presidency conclusions. Extraordinary European Council, Brussels. <www.consilium.europa.eu/uedocs/cms_data/docs/pressdata/en/ec/102545.pdf>.

Russia.[5] The Member States of the EU are at the heart of the complex three-way relationship between Moscow, Brussels and the national capitals. This chapter on the role and significance of the EU in the Dutch Russia policy starts from the hypothesis that the Netherlands, just like the other EU Member States, is bilateralizing the results of the cooperation with the Russian Federation as much as possible, while it prefers to multilateralize the problems with Russia, i.e., passing them on to Brussels (the European Commission).[6]

6.2 The European Union and Russia

The relationship between Russia and Europe involves more than just *international* relations. Europe's alleged postmodern identity, based on shared sovereignty and normative power, exists by the grace of the traditional opposite, embodied to an important extent in the classical superpower Russia. The supposed 'value gap' between the EU and the Russian Federation, which is often mentioned as the chief obstacle to extensive cooperation, is rooted in a long tradition.

Despite repeated references to strong historical ties,[7] relations between the Kingdom of the Netherlands and Russia have hardly been close. The Netherlands was one of the last countries in Western Europe to recognize the Soviet Union (in 1943). Relations have since remained difficult and marred by incidents. Post-war Netherlands focused on relations with the United States, the European Community and parts of the Third World. Overall, there was little interest in Eastern Europe, including Russia. This changed only after the Berlin Wall fell and the Soviet Union collapsed.

Relations between the EU and Russia even date back not much further than the early 1990s. In the communist era, there was no institutional cooperation whatsoever between the European Community and its Eastern European counterpart, the Council for Mutual Economic Assistance (Comecon). Neither organization was prepared to recognize the other. They preferred relations with individual Member States – a political preference which exists even to this day, especially at Russian but also at European level.

5 Exceptions: Leonard, M. & Popescu, N. (2007). *A power audit of EU-Russia relations*. London: European Council on Foreign Relations; Schmidt-Felzmann, A. (2008). All for one? EU member states and the Union's common policy towards the Russian Federation. *Journal of Contemporary European Studies, 16*(2), 169-187. Important documents of the European Commission do not mention the essential role of the Member States either; *cf. Country Strategy Paper 2007-2013*, which still is the chief document of the Commission regarding Russia. (European Commission. (2007). *Country strategy paper 2007-2013. Russian Federation*. Brussels.)

6 What this contribution presents as a hypothesis is, according to Leonard & Popescu (2007), p. 16, a fact: "EU member states tend to 'Europeanise' their disputes with Russia while they bilateralize their 'sweet deals'".

7 Memorandum on Russia. (2008, February). DZO/OE-025/08. The Hague.

The EU's policy towards Russia in the 1990s can best be described as 'integration through change'. Russia's democratization and transition to a market economy was considered a condition for extensive cooperation (integration) with Russia. However, for Russia itself it was also, not coincidentally, a time of exceptional weakness and of uncertainty and disorientation. The EU's policy has always remained ambivalent, focused on practical cooperation *with* Russia, on the one hand, and on the transformation *of* Russia inspired by specific political values, on the other. Both aspects of the Russia policy experienced problems, but especially the Union's political reform agenda had little appeal to Russia. So, the mutual ambitions have never fully matched. A complex pattern of inclusion (cooperation, integration) and exclusion (sovereignty, exclusiveness[8]) by *both* parties has seriously hampered cooperation. Supply and demand in Russian-European relations are often not in balance.

Still, over the past decade, relations with Russia have developed considerably and changed drastically. There are few other countries with which the EU has built such an extensive network of joint plans, agreements and contacts. Relations with the Russian Federation concern nearly all areas of EU policy, at all levels, and involve practically all departments of the Commission and many other European institutions. In this context, the European Commission is responsible for the consistency and coherence of the Russia policy.[9]

Relations between the EU and Russia are governed by an elaborate and detailed Partnership and Cooperation Agreement, which was concluded in 1994 and entered into force three years later. It expired in 2007, but is continued by tacit mutual agreement until a new text will be decided.

Europe's relations with Russia have always been highly politicized on account of the initial intentions and ambitions of the EU (integration through change), the nature of the issues on the table (energy, human rights, relations with the common neighbours) and the political changes in Russia itself, in particular the re-establishment under Vladimir Putin of a quite effective, self-assured and authoritarian state power. This political dimension often overshadows the daily practical side of interactions between Russia and Europe. Quite often, 'high' and 'low' politics operate separately in the relations between the EU, the European Member States and the Russian Federation. Even at times of mounting political tension, Russia's gradual and selective adaptation to European standards (a condition for

8 (Self-)exclusion is evident in the case of Russia. Especially since the late 1990s, the Russian Federation has increasingly emphasized its political sovereignty and rejects any attempt at external influence on its political system. The EU's policy is also partly based on exclusion, both in practical terms (e.g., visa policy) and in a 'moral' sense (Brussels' constant tendency to present 'Europe' and 'European Union' as identical entities, thus actually placing countries that are not members of the Union outside the political and normative 'Europe' category). In this context, Sergei Prozorov (2010) refers to a 'pattern of mutual delimitation'.

9 European Commission (2007).

access to the common market) continued,[10] including consultations on sensitive issues such as visa liberalization and the return of illegal immigrants.[11]
Over the last years, the EU has considerably adjusted its policy towards Russia. The paradigm of integration through change has been largely abandoned. The normative agenda has been adapted and the rhetoric has been toned down. Cooperation focuses on Russia as it is, not as we want it to be. Still, this does not alter the pattern of selective (self-)exclusion in the relations between Europe and Russia. Developing a European common external energy policy proves difficult, and Russia persists in refusing to follow the rules of Europe's internal energy market. And while foreign investments in the Russian energy sector remain subject to political constraints, oil and gas production is slowing down and Europe is increasingly concerned about Russia's energy supply – not so much about its political will as about its physical ability to meet Europe's growing energy needs in the long run.

6.3 Moscow, Brussels and the Member States

According to the European Commission, no country is able to tackle today's complex problems on its own. Cooperation is expected to promote the consistency and effectiveness of foreign policy. Member States will be able to exert more influence if they work together. European cooperation is therefore considered to be in the interest of each Member State.[12]
The Treaty on EU (Maastricht, 1992) contains a number of provisions that remind the Member States of the foreign policy obligations they entered into. To enhance the EU's effectiveness in international politics, Member States are supposed to support common policy unreservedly and actively, "in a spirit of loyalty and mutual solidarity".[13] Member States shall inform and consult one another on "any matter of foreign and security policy of general interest"[14] and shall ensure that their national policies conform to the "common positions".[15] These are rules of conduct, not enforceable provisions. And in the relations with the Russian Fed-

10 Meloni, G. (2008, October). *Convergence, best-practice and Europeanization: A valuable way to rethink EU-Russian relations?* (Working Paper, Issue 33). Milan: Instituto per gli Studi di Politica Internazionale, Russia and Eastern Neighbours Program.

11 Zhecheva, M. (2011, July 7). *Changing the level: EU-Russia practical cooperation in the area of freedom.* MA thesis, European Union Studies, Leiden University.

12 European Commission. (2006, June 8). Communication from the Commission to the European Council of June 2006. *Europe in the orld – Some practical proposals for greater coherence, effectiveness and visibility.* COM (2006) 278 final. Brussels. <http://ec.europa.eu/councils/bx20060615/euw_com06_278_en.pdf>.

13 Treaty on European Union (TEU). (1992, July 29). Official Journal C 191, Title V, Art. J.1, 4.

14 TEU, Title V, Art. J.2, 1.

15 TEU, Title V, Art. J.2, 2.

eration they indeed proved to be no more than guidelines. Time and again, Member States have plotted their own course. Commonality was often hard to find. Internal division in the EU was therefore, as claimed until recently, the main challenge in the EU's Russia policy.[16] This division undermines the international authority and the influence of the EU and offers the Russian Federation a constant opportunity to play Member States off against each other. No country would so explicitly confront the EU with its lack of unity as Russia does.

Practically all aspects of the relations between individual Member States and the Russian Federation can be seen to have a national and a European dimension. But often they are difficult to separate. In many policy areas, responsibility is shared. Trade policy in the broad sense has been transferred to Brussels; trade promotion has remained a national responsibility. The EU defines the legal framework of the international trade relations; the Member States are chiefly responsible for their implementation. Negotiations on free movement of persons and visa facilitation and liberalization have been delegated to the EU, but the Member States remain responsible for implementing agreements and for issuing visas. Wide-ranging agreements have been reached regarding the European internal energy market, but the EU has no external energy policy. In this regard, Member States are largely free to act as they see fit, which they indeed do.

With a few exceptions (Poland, mainly under the presidency of Lech Kaczynski, Lithuania, and the United Kingdom, following the Litvinenko affair), relations between individual Member States and Russia have proved less 'cyclically sensitive' than those between the EU and the Russian Federation. The 'division of tasks' between Brussels and the national capitals seems partly responsible for this. The EU, in particular the European Commission, is, in a sense, doing the Member States' dirty work. In a number of fields, individual Member States implement agreements the outlines of which have been decided between the European Commission and Moscow, often after lengthy and difficult negotiations. This is simply a question of *realpolitik* – it is easier and more effective for Member States to make European agreements with Moscow in areas which are not seen as highly sensitive (investments, trade arrangements) than to try and do this at bilateral level. However, also on sensitive matters such as human rights, democratization and the controversial geopolitical relations between Russia and Europe in their common neighbourhood, the Member States tend to let the European Commission take the lead. The Commission, therefore, has a sharper profile in regard to human rights and democracy than most Member States. The latter consider Europeanization, i.e., cooperation within the EU, as an 'instrument' of political effectiveness and as a way to spread risk, or national *Schadenbegrenzung* – Moscow will be hesitant to tackle them individually on common European positions. The EU Member States are thus trying to maximize their gain from a combination of bilateral policy where possible (the primacy of national foreign

16 Leonard & Popescu (2007), p. i.

policy also prevails in the relations with Russia) and multilateral relations where necessary (i.e., where these serve the national interest).
The EU takes the view that serious problems between Member States and Russia are European problems as well, but also believes that issues between them should first be solved at Member State level. The Union's task in this regard is an advisory one at most. Indeed, bilateral issues are usually settled through direct negotiations, but in a number of cases Member States have deliberately taken their differences of opinion with Russia to the European level.[17] The general idea is that especially small(er) Member States would want to compensate their limited status and influence vis-à-vis the Russian Federation by uploading issues to Brussels. Common positions carry more weight than individual ones. Size, particularly of the population, is an important variable in countries' positions in the European negotiation process.[18] And this would certainly apply to relations with a superpower like Russia. The 'size' of a Member State largely determines when and in what matters it chooses to follow the path of the EU or to negotiate with Russia bilaterally, says Schmidt-Felzmann.[19] Also because of their generally limited administrative and diplomatic staff resources, small(er) countries would, as a rule, define their priorities more clearly than large Member States. They focus on matters which they expect to have explicitly positive or, on the contrary, negative consequences.[20] Moreover, smaller states would generally set greater store by formalized, common decision-making and supranational ties – as a strategy against possible marginalization as a result of coalition-building by larger Member States.[21]

17 Examples provided by Schmidt-Felzmann (2008), p. 174, are the tensions escalating between Russia and Estonia after a Russian war monument was moved from the town centre of Tallinn (April 2007), and the row between the Netherlands and Russia following the critical remarks made by Dutch Minister of Foreign Affairs Bernard Bot about the way the Russian authorities handled the Beslan hostage tragedy (September 2004). The Russian leaders were furious about the Dutch criticism and banned flower imports from the Netherlands. Restrictive measures against Shell and BP might also be linked to this incident. The problems between the Netherlands and Russia triggered a modest debate at European level about the policy strategy towards the Russian Federation.

18 Thorhallsson, B. (2000). *The role of small states in the European Union*. Aldershot: Ashgate, pp. 1-2; Thorhallsson, B. (2006). The size of states in the European Union: Theoretical and conceptual perspectives. *Journal of European Integration, 28*(1), 7-31.

19 Schmidt-Felzmann (2008), p. 172.

20 Thorhallsson (2000), pp. 69, 106, 239.

21 Rood, J. (2010). In a league of its own? The Netherlands as a middle-sized EU member. In R. Steinmetz & A. Wivel (Eds.), *Small states in Europe. Challenges and opportunities*. Aldershot: Ashgate, pp. 122-123. Of course, also in the relations with the Russian Federation, smaller Member States have a better chance to influence the agenda of the European Union once they hold the rotating presidency. This was the case with a number of European initiatives in the relations with Russia. The most recent example is the Eastern Partnership (2009), regarding which, besides Poland, Sweden, the country then holding the EU presidency, played a very important role.

However, the variety in the Russia policies of the (smaller) European Member States and the extent to which they choose a national or a European approach do not seem to confirm these general reasonings.
It is difficult to establish a hierarchy in the interests that Member States prefer to promote at bilateral or multilateral level. The difference between primary and secondary interests, respectively those that broadly affect national security and are thus chiefly promoted bilaterally, and ethical or normative interests that are preferably left to Brussels (the distinction is by Hyde-Price 2006), does not always hold good. As regards relations with Russia, Member States' strategies and positions are not so much determined by their size as by their geopolitical position, by specific economic interests and by historical and cultural 'sensitivities' – in short, by the specific political weight that national governments attach to certain issues.[22] What is of crucial importance to one country for material or immaterial reasons may be irrelevant for another.
Over the past years, the countries thus attempting to strengthen their positions in relation to Russia have mainly been the Central European Member States. The Netherlands has not or hardly done so, at least not in public. Apparently, neither the bilateral relations with Russia nor the positions of the EU have been enough reason for the Dutch government to try to significantly adjust the EU's Russia agenda.

6.4 The Dutch Interest

What do these special interests, position and preferences say about the EU's place in the Dutch Russia policy? I will confine myself to three key issues: energy relations, human rights, and relations with other former Soviet republics.

6.4.1 *Energy*

The Russian Federation accounts for 6% of European exports and 10% of its imports. European exports to Russia, chiefly industrial end products, amounted to €87 billion in 2010 (6.4% of total European exports). Imports from Russia, particularly energy, totalled €155 billion (10.4% of total EU imports). Compared to 2009, when Russia was hit hard by the financial crisis, trade volume in 2010 increased by 32%.
From a purely quantitative perspective, Europe is more important to Russia than vice versa. While the EU Member States are dependent on the Russian Federation

22 Panke, D. (2010). *Small states in the European Union. Coping with structural disadvantages.* Franham: Ashgate, pp. 201, 203-204.

for more than 25% of their oil and gas consumption, in 2010, 88% of Russian oil exports, 70% of its gas and 50% of its coal went to EU countries.[23]

Russia is an important trade partner of Europe in general and of the Netherlands in particular. It is the third largest trade destination of the EU, after the United States and China, and the second largest trade destination of the Netherlands (outside the EU), after the United States, but before the emerging markets China, Brazil, and India. In 2010, exports of goods to Russia amounted to €5.77 billion, or 1.6% of total Dutch exports. That same year, Dutch imports from Russia increased to €13.98 billion, i.e., 4.2% of total imports. The Netherlands is an important export destination for Russia, partly due, of course, to the transit port of Rotterdam.[24]

The EU Member States are important investors in Russia, and the Netherlands, that is, businesses established in the Netherlands, is one of the most significant European investors. In 2008, Europe invested €25 billion in Russia. This is a considerable amount, given that Russians invested only €2 billion in EU countries, but it is not enough to have a transforming effect on the Russian economy. Foreign direct investment in Russia, chiefly in the energy sector, accounts for about 20% of the Russian gross national product.[25]

Energy is at the heart of the political and economic relations between Russia and Europe. For the EU, the problem is not energy dependency as such, but rather the extent of diversity between the Member States – some Member States are almost fully dependent on the Russian Federation for their energy supply; others not at all. And while the internal energy market is largely subject to Brussels legislation, external energy relations are still primarily the responsibility of the Member States.

Energy relations with Russia form a prominent part of the so-called energy supply security policy of the Dutch government.[26] This policy is based on the assumption that energy supply will increasingly be an international affair. The Dutch government underlines Europe's growing significance in the Dutch energy supply, but also explicitly focuses on bilateral and multilateral contacts. To meet its growing energy needs, the Netherlands has selected four 'priority' countries: Algeria, Kazakhstan, Saudi Arabia and Russia.

---

23 EU-Russia Summit Nizhny Novgorod, 9-10 June 2011. MEMO/11/389. (2011, June 8). <http://europa.eu/rapid/pressReleasesAction.do?reference=MEMO/11/389&type=HTML>.

24 Figures on Europe (EU-Russia Summit, 2011). Figures on the Netherlands: Statline, Central Bureau of Statistics (<http://statline.cbs.nl/StatWeb/publication>).

25 Barysch, K. (2010). *Can and should the EU and Russia reset their relationship?* London: Centre for European Reform, p. 3; Jesien, L. (2011). Energy relations and trade. In K. Barysch, C. Coker & L. Jesien (Eds.), *EU-Russia relations. Time for a realist turnaround*. Brussels: Centre for European Studies, p. 28.

26 Policy plans have been set out in the report *Naar een nieuw kader voor internationale energierelaties* [Towards a new framework for international energy relations] of the ministries of Foreign Affairs and of Economic Affairs, Agriculture and Innovation (25 February 2011).

The frameworks for the national energy supply are mostly defined at European level, as are the energy relations with Russia. Also in its relationship with Russia, the Netherlands stresses the EU's importance for market forces, transparency and a good investment climate as regards energy, and raw materials in general. It supports the European energy policy, including the liberalization of the European energy market, such as the 'unbundling' of supply, and transport and sale of energy. In view of the European dimension of the Dutch energy supply, the Dutch government aims to influence policymaking in Brussels from the earliest stage possible and, if necessary, to steer it in a direction favourable to the Netherlands so as to strengthen its national position (gas hub) and bilateral contacts, including those with the Russian Federation, as much as possible. The European and the bilateral energy policy of the Netherlands, also in relation to the Russian Federation, seem be to largely complementary.

The Netherlands also approves of the recent Russian-European project, the 'Partnership for Modernisation'. The Dutch government and Dutch science and businesses will try to benefit from the Partnership insofar as it will be given concrete shape by the EU and the Russian authorities. The Dutch government tends to share the traditional but unproven 'European' belief that a more modern Russia will also be a more Western-oriented, more democratic Russia.[27] Internal documents of the Ministry of Foreign Affairs also indicate that, in general, the Netherlands preferred the somewhat more liberal approach advocated by Medvedev during his presidency, different from the state-centred, bottom-down approach which Vladimir Putin was said to favour.

6.4.2 Human Rights – Democracy – Rule of Law

The European Council on Foreign Relations describes the Netherlands as one of Europe's 'frosty pragmatists' in relation to Russia,[28] i.e., countries that focus primarily on their trade interests but are not afraid to tackle Russia about the violation of human rights. 'Pragmatic' is a correct description, but 'frosty' certainly is not. The addition 'frosty' seems mainly inspired by the Dutch reputation as a defender of human rights and democratization. However, there is less and less evidence of this in the Dutch policy towards Russia. Although in the past years Russia has hardly made any progress in the field of democracy and human rights, the rhetorical and practical significance of the human rights issue in the Dutch Russia policy has clearly diminished.

An important instrument of the Dutch human rights policy in Russia, the Matra Programme (in Dutch: *MAatschappelijke TRAnsformatie*/Social Transformation),

27 Internal documents of the Ministry of Foreign Affairs distinguish between political and economic modernization. One does not automatically follow from the other.

28 According to Leonard & Popescu (2007), this category also includes, besides the Netherlands, the Czech Republic, Denmark, Estonia, Ireland, Latvia, Romania, Sweden and the United Kingdom.

was adapted and its funding cut. Financial resources were reduced, the geographical focus was shifted from Eastern Europe to the pre-accession countries in the Western Balkans (later this decision was partially reversed at the request of the Dutch House of Representatives), and decision-making powers were partially transferred from the ministry to embassies. As of 2013, there will probably be no more Matra projects in Russia.

Although Russia's democratic development is still considered an essential Dutch (now mainly also *economic*) interest,[29] the actual significance of democratization and human rights appears to have diminished. This can be attributed to a combination of financial and political considerations: the need for budget cuts, the lack of results from democratization efforts[30] and, perhaps, though not mentioned in official papers, the possibly negative bilateral consequences of Dutch criticism of the state of democracy in Russia.[31] Although in Brussels, the Netherlands is still quite consistent in raising human rights issues (e.g., when preparing for summits between the Union and Russia),[32] for domestic policy reasons[33] and partly perhaps also because other Member States would be too disinclined to do so, the government does not consider the EU as the most suitable vehicle for promoting human rights in Russia. The Hague emphasizes in particular the significance of the Council of Europe, which is in line with the growing belief that an effective human rights policy should dovetail with agreements and organizations to which Russia itself is party. The Russian authorities should be tackled on international obligations they themselves entered into. Furthermore, the Netherlands, too, says to have shifted its focus from human rights and democratization to reinforcement of the rule of law. Alleged effectiveness plays a key role here as well. The government assumes that the Russian leaders themselves have a distinct

29 Ministry of Foreign Affairs. (2010). *Meerjarig Interdepartementaal Beleidskader Russische Federatie 2010-2014* [Multiannual Interdepartmental Policy Framework Russian Federation 2010-2014]. The Hague.

30 The European Commission (2007, p. 15) reported already in 2007 that, despite international efforts, the human rights situation in Russia was hardly improving, and arrived at the remarkable and unfounded conclusion that "Russian citizens in general are not sensitive to political or civic right issues".

31 The Russia Memorandum of early 2008 pointed out that economic relations between the Netherlands and the Russian Federation were progressing well, but that friction had arisen in the political and social field (Memorandum on Russia. (2008, February). DZO/OE-025/08. The Hague). The tête-à-tête between Putin and Balkenende in Moscow in November 2007, when the Russian President questioned the themes and project choice of the Matra Programme, will have contributed to this.

32 According to the officials involved in Brussels and The Hague.

33 In Dutch politics, just as at European level, the parliament generally tends to be more critical of the human rights situation than is the 'executive'. Minister of Foreign Affairs Rosenthal advised against a motion (June 2011) in which the Dutch House of Representatives asked for sanctions to be imposed against those who could be held responsible for the death of lawyer Sergej Magnitsky. He announced not to implement the motion. However, the Netherlands would continue to urge Russia to bring to trial those responsible for Magnitsky's death.

interest in strengthening the rule of law and that this is also more in line with the priorities of the Russian population.[34] In this respect, the Netherlands attaches great importance to a generation change in Russia, since a younger generation, raised in postcommunist Russia, will be more inclined to pursue "a rule of law based on equality and justice [...] where there is no room for arbitrariness and legal uncertainty".[35] Under this view, both Russian and Dutch (economic) interests are served by strengthening the rule of law in Russia.

The cautious reorientation of the Dutch Russia policy is in line with the new direction of human rights policy of the Netherlands Ministry of Foreign Affairs. In Dutch foreign policy, security, prosperity, and freedom are closely interconnected.[36] According to Minister of Foreign Affairs Rosenthal, foreign policy, including international efforts at democratization, should also, and much more explicitly, be a matter of domestic policy and national interest.[37] The economic diplomacy of the Netherlands can also be clearly seen in the relations with the Russian Federation.

Not only the Dutch but also the European Russia policy has changed gradually. The original paradigm – integration through change – has been abandoned for a less ambitious approach whereby the relationship with Russia is no longer defined by the (desired) development of Russia but by the *de facto* situation in the country. Although it is hard to imagine political and economic changes taking place in Russia from the mid-1980s without 'Europe' acting as a role model and making an active contribution, there is now a belief among Europeans that the practical impact of the Union on Russia's domestic policy development is limited. Throughout modern history, Russia has been too big, too powerful and too autonomous to let itself be ruled by the aspirations of the West. And Europe's frustration over the flawed transformation of postcommunist Russia (and, as a result, over the failure of the original integration-through-change strategy of the EU) should thus be seen mainly in the light of the Union's initial overestimation of its own powers. The adaptation of the Russia policy from change to modernization, from democracy to rule of law (ambitious enough in itself), constitutes an adjustment to the EU's limited real influence.

Leonard and Popescu characterize the European dimension of the Russia policy of the 'frosty pragmatists' as 'in many ways passive'. These countries do not seem genuinely interested in developing a European policy vis-à-vis the Russian Federation. This interpretation, too, seems only partly correct. The Netherlands, like the other Member States, is interested in a common EU strategy, but only as

34 *See*, for earlier suggestions along the same lines, the contributions in Gerrits, A.W.M. (Ed.). (2008). *The European Union and Russia: Perception and interest in the shaping of relations* (Clingendael European Papers No. 4). The Hague: Netherlands Institute of International Relations 'Clingendael'.

35 Ministry of Foreign Affairs (2010).

36 Ministry of Foreign Affairs. (2011). *Verantwoordelijk voor vrijheid. Mensenrechten in het buitenlands beleid* [Responsible for freedom. Human rights in foreign policy]. The Hague.

37 *See* <www.rijksoverheid.nl/regering/het-kabinet/bewindspersonen/uri-rosenthal>.

long as it is in the national interest, which is mostly the case. Being a country of limited size but with considerable economic significance, the Netherlands has a relatively strong bilateral position in relation to superpower Russia. They maintain excellent mutual relations. The Dutch passivity in Europe, if any, largely originates from the Netherlands being satisfied with the Russia policy of the EU, including the separate responsibilities of the Member States and the Commission.

6.4.3 *ENP/Eastern Partnership*

The European Neighbourhood Policy (2003) and its spin-off, the Eastern Partnership (2009), aim for far-reaching political cooperation and economic integration, without the prospect of membership, with Belarus, Ukraine, Moldova and Armenia, Georgia and Azerbaijan. Despite the fact that the EU (and, in its wake, many EU researchers) emphasized time and again that the neighbourhood policy would be in Europe's and Russia's *common* interest (a win-win strategy which should be seen separate from Russia's supposed *zero-sum* thinking), the Russian Federation regarded these initiatives with suspicion and wanted no part of them.[38] To the Russians, the ENP and Eastern Partnership embodied the EU's classic pursuit of influence. The Union's plan to create a 'ring of friends'[39] could only be interpreted by Moscow as a form of competition which ultimately, if the EU were to prove successful, would have negative consequences for the Russian Federation in terms of market separation, restricted freedom of movement of persons and undermining of regional cooperation. The neighbourhood policy was moreover developed at a time (2003-2004) when Russia felt forced on to the defensive in its nearby region, with 'colour revolutions' in Georgia, Ukraine and Kyrgyzstan. Much has changed since then. The European initiatives have proven less effective than expected, whereas Russia has strengthened its position, particularly in Ukraine, the most important state in the near abroad.

The Dutch government takes a conventional view of the neighbourhood policy, which is the same as that of the European Commission. Modernization of the Eastern Partnership countries would go hand in hand with 'Europeanization', that is, with a strong identification with Europe. Officials at the Ministry of Foreign Affairs underline that the Dutch interpretation of the Partnership is less politically inspired than that of some other Member States, especially in Eastern Europe. For the Netherlands, the accession prospect of the Eastern Partnership countries is not at issue. The Partnership is not about tearing these countries away

38 Haukkala, H. (2009, November). *From zero-sum to win-win? The Russian challenge to the EU's eastern neighbourhood policies* (European Policy Analysis, 12). Stockholm: Swedish Institute for European Policy Studies, p. 1.

39 European Commission. (2003). Communication from the Commission to the Council and the European Parliament. *Wider Europe – Neighbourhood. A new framework for relations with our eastern and southern neighbours*. COM (2003) 104 final, Brussels, 11.3, p. 4.

from Russia – so it is claimed – but about preparing them for extensive political cooperation and for economic integration with the EU. The possibility that far-reaching cooperation with Europe may imply looser ties with Russia will surely be understood by the Ministry as well.

6.5 Conclusions: the Netherlands, the European Union and Russia

The Dutch Russia policy is a slightly unbalanced combination of idealism and pragmatism, in which the 'idealism', insofar as the strategy focused on Russia's democratization can be characterized as such, is diminishing. The Netherlands believes that its national interest is served by 'good and pragmatic relations' with Russia's current regime. Reinforcement of the rule of law in Russia, as an alternative for the not very successful democratization strategy, is considered to be in the mutual interest of Russia and the Netherlands, and in this context the Dutch interest is increasingly defined in economic terms.[40]

In important policy areas, the political and legal frameworks of the relations between the Netherlands and Russia have been laid down in agreements concluded with allies in the EU, NATO and elsewhere. However, within these frameworks, the Netherlands has ample room for manoeuvre, which, like its allies, it uses as it sees fit in order to promote its alleged own interest.

The hypothesis posed at the start of this contribution – i.e., the Netherlands, and the same would apply, *mutatis mutandis,* to the other Member States, maximizes its gain from its bilateral relations with the Russian Federation, leaving the problematic, controversial aspects of the relationship with Russia to the European Commission – ultimately proves only partly correct. Essentially, it is not about a 'political' division of labour between the EU and the Member States but about a more functional separation of tasks.

This division of labour builds mainly on the belief that the Dutch economic interest is fundamentally served by agreements made between the EU and Russia. In spite of everything, Brussels still has more clout with Moscow than The Hague. In this context, one should mainly think of general agreements with the Russian Federation and the legal and political framework of the mutual economic ties. It is in the Dutch national interest that 'Europe' does the often difficult, sometimes problematic groundwork, the benefits of which can then be reaped by the Member States. It is an appealing, practical 'division of labour', from which all Member States – big, small *and* the Netherlands – benefit.

Does the Netherlands tend to pass on politically sensitive issues to the European Commission? It is, of course, in the Dutch interest if Russia's displeasure over interference with its domestic affairs is not directed against the Netherlands indi-

40 Ministry of Foreign Affairs (2010).

vidually but against the joint European effort. And this is often how it works in practice. Russia's criticism of 'Europe's' interference with the domestic state of affairs in Russia and in the common neighbours (ENP and Eastern Partnership) is levelled nearly exclusively at the EU, not at individual Member States. For Russia, too, this is a matter of political effectiveness. It is easier to criticize Brussels than denounce each single Member State. Russia's focus on the EU is also prompted by the fact, though, that Member States of the EU are indeed only too happy to leave the sensitive, normative, politico-ideological side of the relations with Russia to the Union, including the corresponding discourse and terminology. The Member States, Netherlands included, thus morally benefit from the European human rights policy, without having to pay a price for it in practical terms.

Still, the bilateral relations with Russia are strong and extensive enough to be able to tolerate differences of opinion over democracy and human rights. The Dutch economic interest hardly comes into play where it concerns promoting human rights in Russia. Effectiveness is another matter. Greater emphasis on strengthening the rule of law and less on promoting democracy (however fine the line between the two may ultimately be) seems a realistic approach. Besides, over the past years, not only the Netherlands but also the EU has considerably adjusted its ambitions and rhetoric. Europe's Russia policy, like that of the Netherlands, has become more practical and pragmatic. Its transformation strategy has not been abandoned completely (as is reflected by the partnership for *modernization*), but it has been substantially adapted. Success is no longer measured by the degree of democratic change in Russia, but by the extent and quality of cooperation with Russia. The basic assumptions of the Dutch and the European Russia policy are largely similar. For both the EU and the Netherlands, economic interests come first. The Dutch bilateral policy (including agreements with Gazprom on gas supplies, participation in the Nordstream project and the planned gas hub) is not hampered by European arrangements. Apparently, the Dutch government sees no discrepancy between the European and the national Russia policy. The role and significance of the EU in the Dutch policy vis-à-vis Russia are pragmatic, complementary and hardly controversial. Brussels, i.e., the European Commission and/or the European Council, does what Brussels does best (legal and political starting points and frameworks of the relations and, in exceptional cases, crisis management); the rest is a matter of bilateral policy and competition among Member States.

The smooth functional division of tasks between the Netherlands and Europe should not be taken for granted. Tensions between the Dutch and the European Russia policy are quite conceivable. For instance, the Dutch government did not care much for the confrontational approach to Russia taken by Central and Eastern European Member States a few years ago. The Netherlands welcomed the changing attitude of these countries. As regards Russia, the Dutch government advocates 'in general' "European positions that are as common as possible" but preferably in line with those of Member States that, like the Netherlands, "favour a pragmatic approach focused on the long term".[41]

The Dutch Russia policy is not without risk either. It forms no exception to the growing tendency among EU Member States to be able to blame the EU for unwelcome policy aspects while taking the credit for the attractive sides. In the long run, such a strategy could further undermine the legitimacy of European cooperation. Nor does the Dutch policy on Russia reduce the often suggested risk that Russia manages to play the Member States off against each other. The Netherlands and other EU Members are taking this risk, convinced that the national interest is best served by a combination of European and bilateral initiatives and agreements and by cooperation with and competition between Member States. Russia policy is an intricate set of national and shared European interests, levels and instruments – varying in topics and defined by the specific geopolitical and economic position of each individual Member State. So, the assumption that, in the end, the Member States will all lose by a continuation of the present disagreement within the Union and the diversity in Russia policies ignores the self-evident and healthy element of competition between the Member States and, based on past experience, does not seem to hold water.

41 Memorandum on Russia (2008).

7 Dutch Influence on Regulation of Migration in Europe: Goodbye Nation State or a Pioneer Country on the Wrong Track?

Kees Groenendijk

7.1 Introduction and Questions

Since nation states began to develop in Europe in the 19th century, guarding the territorial borders and deciding who are admitted to the country and to its more permanent population have been regarded as core tasks of the state. Over the past decades, the performance of these typical core tasks has been drastically restricted by European rules. According to some political parties in the Netherlands, the limit in terms of giving up sovereignty in this respect has been reached. A large portion of the chapter on immigration in the coalition agreement and the tolerance agreement (*gedoogakkoord*) which the conservative-liberal VVD and Christian-Democratic CDA concluded with the Freedom Party of Geert Wilders (PVV) in September 2010 could only be carried out after existing European rules that had recently been adopted unanimously had been amended to comply with the new Dutch wishes. This chapter is structured around three questions. First, the question to what extent and how the Netherlands has influenced the development of the European migration rules since World War II. The second question is in how far the Dutch position has changed over the past decade and what this means for the migration agenda of the first Rutte Cabinet (2010-2012). And the third, what dilemmas and questions will the European Union (EU) and the Netherlands face in this field in the coming years.

7.2 Migration Rules in Europe and the Dutch Influence: 1945-1970

In the first decades after World War II, the European rules on migration almost exclusively concerned workers migrating within Europe. Italy, in particular, put pressure on various European organizations to gain access to the labour markets in other countries for the large numbers of unemployed Italians. This Italian pressure, supported by the United States, stimulated the adoption of the Council Decision of the Organisation for European Economic Cooperation (OEEC) aimed at liberalizing labour migration in 1953, the negotiations in the Council of Europe on the European Convention on Establishment (1951-1955) and the incorporation of free movement of workers in the EEC Treaty of 1957.[1] The Dutch position in this respect was characterized by resistance and limited interest. Resistance derived from the emphasis in Dutch politics on emigration, fear of immigration, the wish to keep the low wages resulting from the restrictive wage policy and the housing shortage. The Netherlands only participated as observer in the negotiations on the OEEC Council Decision, which would later form the basis of the EEC rules on free movement of workers. Italy managed to ease initial British and French resistance.[2] Following the German example, the Netherlands gave up its opposition to the Decision only under pressure from the United States.

The negotiations on free labour migration within the Benelux, initiated by the three governments in London in 1944, continued until the three countries concluded the Labour Convention in 1956. The Netherlands was afraid that higher-educated people and skilled workers would leave for higher wages in Belgium. Belgium wanted to include labour migration among the subjects to be regulated in the EEC Treaty.[3] In 1960, the Benelux countries decided to abolish controls on persons at internal borders and rely on controls at the external borders of the Benelux. At the same time, the Benelux countries launched a uniform visa policy for nationals from third countries. Holders of a Benelux visa were allowed to travel freely in the three countries for a maximum period of three months. The agreement of 1982 to harmonize the rules governing admission of foreigners for a stay of more than three months was ratified by Belgium and Luxembourg, but not by the Netherlands. This agreement was superseded by the Schengen cooperation that began in 1985. Under pressure from the Dutch parliament, however, the Benelux policy in this field gradually became subject to more external controls: the Benelux migration rules were published, and the Benelux Court of Justice was authorized to give binding interpretations of these rules.

The European Coal and Steel Community provided for a limited form of free movement for skilled workers in the coal and steel sector only. In practice these rules had little effect. Dutch Minister Beyen's plan for what later would become

1 Goedings, S.A.W. (2005). *Labor migration in an integrating Europe. National migration politics and the free movement of workers, 1950-1968*. The Hague: SDU Uitgevers, pp. 74-84; Groenendijk, K. (2000). Long-term immigrants and the Council of Europe. *European Journal of Migration and Law, 1*, 275-292.

2 Lewin, K. (1964). The free movement of workers. *Common Market Law Review, 2*, 300-324.

3 Boekesteijn, A.J. (1990). The formulation of Dutch Benelux policy. In R.T. Griffiths (Ed.), *The Netherlands and the integration of Europe 1945-1957*. Amsterdam: NEHA, pp. 27-48; De Lange, T. (2007). *Staat, markt en migrant, De regulering van arbeidsmigratie naar Nederland 1945-2006* [State, market and migrant, the regulation of labour migration to the Netherlands 1945-2006]. The Hague: Boom Juridische Uitgevers, p. 30.

the EEC did not include free movement of workers.[4] The Belgian-Dutch initiative of Ministers Spaak and Beyen regarding the common market, which would form the basis of the negotiations on the EEC Treaty, only referred to a limited form of labour migration.[5] Again, Italy persistently argued for including free movement of workers and ultimately managed to convince the other five. Here too, the Dutch, partly under the influence of social-democratic prime minister Drees, took a defensive stance. In the end, it was decided to stop opposing the proposal because expectations were that the benefits the Netherlands would derive from free trade and services within the EEC would outweigh the possible negative effects of free movement of workers. Moreover, the Dutch arguments against labour migration became less convincing because of low unemployment rates in the Netherlands, declining emigration and increasing recruitment of workers from Mediterranean countries. The Netherlands, together with Germany, did manage to prevent binding rules on preferential treatment of labour migrants from other Member States from being included in the EEC Treaty. Governments and employers thus remained free to recruit workers from outside the EEC. The Netherlands managed to successfully defend this freedom during the negotiations on the three EEC regulations on freedom of movement for workers, in 1961, 1965 and 1968.

In the Dutch parliament, interest in these first European rules on labour migration was minimal. In both Houses of the Dutch parliament not the slightest mention was made of the OEEC Council Decision and the European Convention on Establishment. Of the 100 pages of Minutes of the Dutch House of Representatives regarding the Act approving the EEC Treaty, only one single page dealt with the provisions on free movement of workers. This mainly concerned problems of housing migrants, in view of the housing shortage at that time. This lack of interest was linked to the high demand for labour in the late 1950s and the 12-year transition period provided for in the Treaty in regard to free movement of workers. In the end, full freedom of movement was introduced as early as 1968. Nor was there much, if any, interest among Dutch politicians in implementing the rules adopted in the EEC at that time. However, due to the gradual enlargement of the EEC and the EU, these rules would gain increasing importance.

So, during the first postwar period, the Netherlands took few, if any, initiatives. Partly under pressure from employers, who wanted wages kept low, the overall aim was to limit commitments restricting the freedom of manoeuvre of the government and employers. Netherland buckled under pressure from other states, expecting to reap economic or political benefits in other areas, or gave in

4 Griffiths, R.T. (1990). The Beyen plan. In R.T. Griffiths (Ed.), *The Netherlands and the integration of Europe 1945-1957*. Amsterdam: NEHA, pp. 165-182.

5 Goedings (2005), pp. 107-138.

to liberal rules on labour migration when the number of vacancies far exceeded the number of registered unemployed people.

7.3 Migration Rules in Europe and the Dutch Influence: 1985-2002

In the two decades following 1970, no agreement was reached in the EEC on new migration rules. However, in that period the Court of Justice considerably increased the scope and practical significance of those rules through a number of judgements. Because lawyers and judges began to take these rulings seriously, immigration officials and politicians, too, saw themselves forced to take serious note of the Court's judgements and the European rules concerned. After the economic crisis of 1973, recruitment of labour from Mediterranean countries practically ground to a halt.

7.4 Internal Market, Intergovernmental Cooperation in Schengen, and the 'Third Pillar'

As part of the discussions on the creation of the Internal Market ('1992') and the Single European Act (1986), attention for European rules on migration picked up again. Now the discussions mainly concerned migration from outside the EC, focusing on the movement of those migrants within the Internal Market, on their admission for longer stays and on controls at the external border of the EU.

The United Kingdom doggedly opposed liberalizing free movement of persons between Member States. Germany and France, however, signed a bilateral agreement to reduce controls on their common borders in Saarbrücken in 1984. The Netherlands saw this as a threat to the position of Dutch exporters and mobilized the Benelux partners. The transport ministers of the Benelux first reached agreements with Germany and then joined the bilateral German-French agreement. The cooperation in the fields of customs, movement of persons, migration, police and justice decided by the five states in 1985 was based on a Benelux memorandum.[6] These Schengen countries abolished controls on persons at their internal borders, tightened their external border controls and adopted a common visa policy. In the Netherlands, the Ministry of Economic Affairs initially coordinated 'Schengen', but soon the Ministry of Justice took over.

In 1990, the Convention implementing the Schengen Agreement was signed. The Benelux rules served as a model particularly for the visa policy, the short-stay admission of persons from outside the EU and the rules on police and judicial

6 *See* the Recitals to the Schengen Agreement of 1985; van Es, A. (1991). *Schengen, of de nieuwe deling van Europa* [Schengen, or the new division of Europe]. Amsterdam: Van Gennep.

cooperation. However, it was not until 1995 that this agreement was approved by the parliaments of all Schengen countries. During the 1990s, first the Southern European Member States and then also the countries of the Nordic Union joined the Schengen cooperation.

In 1986, partly in reaction to the cooperation between the Schengen countries, and on the United Kingdom's initiative, the Ad Hoc Group on Immigration was established for consultation between the immigration ministers of the then 12 Member States. Just as with Schengen, it involved cooperation between Member States outside the EEC framework. The European Commission, the Court of Justice and the European Parliament (EP) were deliberately excluded from both this group and the Schengen cooperation. In Palma de Mallorca, in 1989, Member State officials drew up an elaborate document containing a whole range of new measures on migration and asylum to be taken in connection with the abolition of internal border controls. This intergovernmental cooperation produced many resolutions and recommendations, but few binding rules. The only binding arrangement was the Dublin agreement on the division of responsibilities for examining applications for asylum. This agreement was signed in 1990, but entered into force only six years later, after the last Member State had approved it.

In 1992, the Treaty of Maastricht brought cooperation in the field of migration and asylum largely under the Third Pillar of the EU, that is, deliberately outside the EC. Cooperation under the Third Pillar did not lead to binding rules on migration and asylum either, although the non-binding rules adopted under the Third Pillar on the basis of the Palma document did form the starting point for the binding rules that would be adopted later on the basis of the Treaty of Amsterdam. This also applies to the (binding) rules established by the Schengen countries. However, the Member States continued to make important decisions in this field without consulting their EC partners (e.g., the tightening of the asylum policy in Germany in 1992 or the amnesties and regularization campaigns in many Member States). The ever more intensive consultations at the frequent meetings of working groups in the EU led, however, to national policy officials becoming more familiar with the legal rules and instruments of other Member States. This learning process was often followed and imitated at informal level in Member States' national legislation.

When in 1995 the Schengen internal border controls were lifted, the limitations of the intergovernmental method became painfully clear. Drawing up and approving binding rules in treaties is a very time-consuming process. In addition, the lack of independent monitoring of compliance with those rules and of an effective dispute procedure was making itself felt. The conflict between France and the Netherlands about the Dutch drugs policy, resulting in the French refusal to lift controls on the borders with Belgium and Luxembourg, could be resolved via diplomatic channels or through pressure from other Member States. During the Dutch Council Presidency, the Dutch negotiator on the Treaty of Amsterdam, Michiel Patijn, used the fragile structure of the Schengen cooperation as an argu-

ment to incorporate Schengen into the EC: "[T]he whole Schengen operation [is] extremely light and vulnerable. It is being run by a small office within the Benelux secretariat, the chair rotates every six months and, in our view, the political, institutional and legal foundation has always been inadequate".[7]
In a protocol to the 1997 Treaty of Amsterdam the rules on migration and asylum adopted by the Schengen states were transformed into EC law. Moreover, under this Treaty, decision-making on these issues was transferred from the Third Pillar to the First. The new rules in this field would, from then on, be rules of Community law.

7.5 The Role of the Netherlands

What was the role of the Netherlands in this field during the last 15 years before the turn of the century? The Netherlands was active and influential in creating Schengen in 1985 due to early initiatives and its mobilization of support from the Benelux partners and because it took full advantage of the Benelux model and experience when elaborating the Convention implementing the Schengen Agreement. Remarkably enough, the Netherlands also instigated the termination of this intergovernmental experiment and initiated the integration of the rules that had meanwhile been adopted in the EU. This dovetailed with another institutional key priority: since 1991, the Netherlands has always argued in favour of giving the Court of Justice the power to interpret rules in this field and thus also strengthen compliance with these rules within the Member States.[8] At first, attempts to reach this goal were little successful. The opponents among the Member States initially accepted only the opt-in system proposed by the Netherlands: each Member State could decide for itself whether its courts would be allowed to ask the Court of Justice to give a preliminary ruling on the new rules. In the Treaty of Amsterdam, 12 of the 15 Member States agreed to their highest courts being able to refer cases regarding the interpretation of migration rules to the European Court of Justice.[9] Finally, the Treaty of Lisbon recognized the full powers of the Court of Justice, the Commission and the Parliament. The significance of this unrestricted application of the general EU law system of checks and balances in this field became very apparent following the agreement of the

7 Dutch House of Representatives, *Kamerstuk* 19 326, No. 167, p. 11. For other motives, *see* de Zwaan, J.W. (1998). Schengen and its incorporation into the New Treaty: The negotiating process. In M. den Boer (Ed.), *Schengen's final days? The incorporation of Schengen into the new TEU, external borders and information systems*. Maastricht, pp. 13-24.

8 The Netherlands presented concrete proposals to this end as early as in 1992, Dutch House of Representatives, *Vergaderjaar* 1991-1992, *Kamerstuk* 19 326, No. 53, and two memoranda during the Dutch Schengen Presidency in 1996, SCH/Tr-Rego (96) 5 and (96) 9.

9 Groenendijk, C.A. (1997). The European Court of Justice and the third pillar. In H. Meijers et al., *Democracy, migrants and police in the European Union: The 1996 IGC and beyond*. Utrecht: FORUM.

Rutte Cabinet with the PVV in 2010. Many new restrictive admission rules proposed in that agreement could now only be introduced with the approval and cooperation of the European Commission and the EP. The Netherlands will be corrected by the Court of Justice if it unilaterally takes restrictive measures that are contrary to Union law.

An issue championed by the Netherlands on various occasions during the 1990s involved strengthening the legal position of long-term resident immigrants from countries outside the EU with the aim to support their integration in the Member State of residence.[10] This issue was put on the agenda in various forms, e.g., through the secondment of an official to the Commission who wrote relevant policy documents (1991 and 1994) and the initiative to draw up a joint Benelux memorandum on this issue in preparation for the European Council on immigration in Tampere in 1999. Another constant but clearly less successful Dutch line of approach was the opposition to the reunification of Germany and the fear of migration from the former GDR, and the unwillingness to lift the visa requirements for Hungarian and Polish people in the early 1990s.[11] For political and economic reasons, Germany was strongly in favour of liberalization. The Netherlands kept up its resistance but, in the end, reluctantly agreed. The Dutch attitude was dominated by fear of migration and set little store by long-term political stability in Europe, all of which earned the Netherlands little credit. Here, we can see the analogy with the Netherlands being the only Member State that was against lifting the visa requirements for citizens of Albania and Bosnia Herzegovina in 2010 and against enlarging the Schengen area to include Bulgaria and Romania in 2011. The negative consequences of this attitude were ignored or taken for granted.

7.6 New EU Migration Rules, 2000-2011

In 1999, the Treaty of Amsterdam entered into force, empowering the EU Council of Ministers to adopt binding rules in the field of migration and asylum. In the decade following 1999, the Council of Ministers adopted directives and regulations on practically all aspects of migration law, based on proposals of the European Commission. As of 2005, regarding an increasing number of issues, the approval of the EP was required for the adoption of new EU legislation as well.

10 Strik, T. (2011). *Besluitvorming over asiel- en migratierichtlijnen. De wisselwerking tussen nationaal en Europees niveau* [Decision-making on asylum and migration directives. Interaction between the national and European level]. The Hague: Boom, p. 76.

11 Pool, C. (2011). *Migratie van Polen naar Nederland in een tijd van versoepeling van migratieregels* [Migration from Poland to the Netherlands at a time migration rules are relaxed]. The Hague: Boom, p. 55.

These measures restricted Member States' freedom to define their own immigration policy.

The first time the Netherlands came face-to-face with the reality of this restriction was when, in 2010, the Court of Justice ruled that the income requirement of 120% of the statutory minimum wage, introduced in 2004 under Minister Verdonk, was contrary to the Directive on family reunification. Only in regard to admission of workers from countries outside the EU do Member States still have practically unlimited freedom. But access to employment for third-country nationals (citizens from countries outside the EU) who were admitted for other reasons has been largely regulated under EU law.

In those 10 years, a total of nearly 30 binding EU regulations on border control, visa policy and illegal immigration were adopted. Negotiations on rules governing admission mostly took place during 2001-2005. In most cases, Member States were given two years to adapt their national legislation to these new EU rules. A German colleague called this rapid development, quite rightly, '*eine Europäisierung einer Kernfunction des Staates ohne Gleiches*'.

These new EU rules concern the legal position of third-country nationals, i.e., nationals of countries outside the EU, making up almost 60% of the non-Dutch nationals ('aliens') living in the Netherlands. The above-mentioned rules on free movement of EU citizens relate to the position of the remaining 40% (citizens from other Member States who have been registered because they have lived here for longer than six months). However, those rules also concern the hundreds of thousands of employees, students, businessmen and other citizens from other Member States who are staying in the Netherlands for a shorter period. Therefore, they are usually not registered in the population registers and, thus, are not counted in the population statistics. The government has very limited possibilities to regulate migration of EU citizens other than by support measures (such as tax advantages), whipping up public sentiment or in case of serious crime.

Developments in this field are clearly different from those relating to police cooperation.[12] For migration and asylum a great many detailed rules have been drawn up granting individuals concrete rights. On the one hand, these rules confirm existing powers of Member States, but on the other, they drastically limit the exercise of those powers as well as the freedom to adopt new national rules. In addition, over the past 10 years, actors like the Commission, the Court of Justice and the EP have come to play an increasing role in developing new rules in this field and in monitoring compliance by Member States with those rules, thus reducing Member States' competences and the exclusive lawmaking role of the Council of Ministers.

Developments in this field in other European organizations, such as the Council of Europe, the Nordic Union and the Benelux, are of marginal significance. Only the rulings of the European Court of Human Rights in Strasbourg, operating

12 Den Boer in this volume.

within the Council of Europe, play an important role in setting the minimum standards which, also in this field, are binding on all Member States. Two prime examples of such judgements are the Salah Sheekh judgement of 2007, correcting Dutch case law in asylum cases, and the judgement of 2011, in which the Court in Strasbourg ruled that the other EU Member States can no longer return asylum seekers to Greece on the basis of the Dublin regulation because Greece does not protect them from being sent back to the country they fled from, nor do the reception facilities in Greece meet the ECHR minimum requirements.[13]

7.7 The Role of the Netherlands, 2000-2011

What was the Dutch role in developing these new EU rules on the migration of nationals from countries outside the EU? The negotiations that were held in Brussels regarding five of these Directives have been studied in detail.[14] These studies show that during the negotiations the Netherlands, like other Member States, initially tried to copy important national rules into the EU rules. When this failed, it did everything to prevent that the national rules would have to be amended as a result of the EU rules. For the Netherlands this mainly meant defending the regime of the recently adopted Aliens Act of 2000. In certain respects, the Netherlands clearly continued its line of approach of the previous decade: strengthening the role of Community bodies (Court of Justice, Commission and Parliament) and promoting the integration of migrants from third countries by giving them a strong status.

In 2002, the Balkenende I Cabinet (CDA-VVD-LPF) brought a clear change in the position of the Dutch negotiators. At first, together with Sweden and sometimes Belgium and France, the Netherlands argued in favour of amending the Commission proposals with a view to strengthening the position of migrants. As of 2002, the vast majority of the Dutch amendment proposals were aimed at limiting the rights or the protection of migrants and increasing Member States' freedom to pursue their own policy. Moreover, other Member States were far more willing

13 ECHR 11 January 2007, No. 1948/04 (Salah Sheekh/Netherlands), and ECHR 21 January 2011, No. 30686/09 (M.S.S./Belgium and Greece).

14 Groenendijk, C.A. & Minderhoud, P.E. (2004). De Nederlandse invloed op nieuwe Europese regels betreffende migratie en asiel [The Dutch influence on new European rules in the field of migration and asylum]. In W. Asbeek Brusse et al. (Ed.), *Immigratie en asiel in Europa. Een lange weg naar gemeenschappelijkheid?* [Immigration and asylum in Europe. A long road to communality?]. Utrecht: Lemma, pp. 137-161; Ackers, D. (2005). The negotiations on the asylum procedures directive. *European Journal of Migration and Law, 7*, 1-33; Papagiani, G. (2006). *Institutional and policy dynamics of EU migration law*. Leiden: Martinus Nijhoff; Walter, A. (2009). *Familienzusammenführung in Europa: Völkerrecht, Gemeinschaftsrecht, Nationales Recht* [Family reunification in Europe: International law, community law, national law]. Baden-Baden: Nomos; Franssen, K. (2011). *Tijdelijke bescherming van asielzoekers in de EU* [Temporary protection of asylum seekers in the EU]. The Hague: Boom; and Strik (2011).

to support these latter Dutch proposals than those aimed at protecting migrants. In the case of the Directive on the reception of asylum seekers, the two Dutch proposals that aimed at strengthening the rights of these migrants foundered on Germany's wish to retain the freedom to make national rules. The same happened in the case of the Directive on temporary protection, the Directive on family reunification and the Directive on the asylum procedure. The Dutch proposals that focused on improving the position of migrants did not make it. During these negotiations, Dutch proposals to reduce the rights of individuals were often submitted together with Germany and the United Kingdom and would then be successful. In the case of the Directive on family reunification and the Directive on third-country nationals who are long-term residents, the Dutch negotiators succeeded, together with their German and Austrian colleagues, in getting amendments accepted that had to create room for the introduction of the integration policy agreed with the LPF in the 2002 coalition agreement. In her comprehensive analysis of the negotiations on the Family Reunification Directive and the Asylum Procedure Directive, Strik finds that proposals aimed at compliance with human rights treaties which, in the first phase, the Netherlands made together with Sweden were later replaced by restrictive proposals submitted together with Germany, which were successful far more often.

Large Member States like Germany, France and the United Kingdom managed to get much more of their proposals for amendments accepted than the relatively small Netherlands. However, Dutch negotiators made up for the lesser political weight by their language skills and expertise – recognized by their colleagues in the Council working groups – and by establishing timely coalitions with other Member States or strategic contacts with the Commission or the Presidency. Under the system of unanimity in the Council of Ministers in force at that time, the Netherlands, using its right of veto, sometimes succeeded in getting other Member States to accept Dutch wishes in the last phase of the negotiations. Another form of influence was to second a Dutch official to the Commission. The Commission proposal for the Asylum Procedure Directive was written by an official who previously worked at the Ministry of Justice in The Hague. He used his knowledge of the new Dutch asylum procedure for this task in Brussels. During the negotiations, he acted as representative of the Commission. In 2004, the Netherlands, moreover, used its presidency of the Council to ensure that a number of restrictive elements of the new Dutch policy were included in the policy programme on migration, police and justice for 2005-2010, the so-called Hague Programme.

7.8 Second Change in the Dutch Position in 2010 (First Rutte Cabinet)

In the run-up to the elections for the Dutch House of Representatives in 2010, it already became clear that, as regards migration, the programmes of many parties failed to respect the limits of EU law. Politicians of various parties argued in favour of following the Danish model, which is highly restrictive on family migration in particular. Denmark can take this approach because it is not bound by most new EU migration rules. However, the pleas of the VVD and PVV to still negotiate an opt-out, as Denmark had managed to do in the Treaty of Amsterdam in 1997, died down after the elections.[15] During the formation of the new government, it apparently dawned on the politicians concerned that this would be unacceptable to other Member States and that the Netherlands would, in any case, remain bound by the EU rules already agreed upon. The proposers were obviously not aware that, since 2007, successive Danish governments had been announcing that they wanted to give up this Danish opt-out because the disadvantages apparently outweigh the advantages.[16] However, the agreement of VVD, CDA and PVV did come to include a great many measures which can only be implemented following amendment of the EU Directives adopted by unanimity in 2003 and 2004 or after renegotiation of the 1963 Association Agreement between the EU and Turkey.

The fact that so many points of this agreement first have to be negotiated at EU level illustrates the limits EU law sets in this field. Most plans are aimed at restricting family migration and at providing for the possibility to subject Turkish or EU citizens to Dutch integration requirements, to deport EU citizens more often or to take Dutch nationality away from naturalized Dutch citizens in more cases.

In December 2010, Minister Leers presented his action plan ('Road Map') to rally support in the EU for these plans to the parliament. In March 2011, he arranged for an English, German and French translation of the plans to be distributed, together with a brief explanation in the form of a position paper.[17] Compared to the letter that Berlusconi and Sarkozy sent to the Commission a few months later,

15 P. de Krom (VVD) in Elsevier, 13 March 2010, and together with S. Blok (VVD) in NRC Handelsblad, 27 May 2010, M. Rutte (VVD) in Elsevier, 12 June 2010, and S. Fritsma (PVV) in a motion to the House of Representatives submitted and rejected on 20 May 2010, Dutch House of Representatives, *Kamerstuk* 19 637, No. 1343. G. Wilders (PVV) raised the idea again in autumn 2011, Parool, 29 November 2011.

16 Adler-Nissen, R. & Gammeltoft-Hansen, T. (2010). Straitjacket or sovereignty shield? The Danish opt-out on Justice and Home Affairs and prospects after the Treaty of Lisbon. In *Danish Foreign Policy Yearbook 2010*, pp. 137-161.

17 Letter of 22 December 2010, Dutch House of Representatives, *Kamerstuk* 30 573, No. 61, and Position Paper – The Dutch Standpoint on EU Migration Policy, website of the Ministry of the Interior, March 2011, B-8065.

following the conflict over Italian residence permits for Tunisian migrants and the temporary reintroduction of border controls by France, the position paper solely reflected the national Dutch policy perspective. The French-Italian letter used Brussels policy jargon and took its cue from the Brussels agenda. Within five months, this letter resulted in a Commission proposal to amend the Schengen Border Code. Minister Leers toured the capitals of a number of Member States to explain the plans and ask for support. On his return from Vienna, Prague and London, he was able to report that they supported his plans. In Rome, the Minister had received a warm welcome. No press statement was issued about his visit to Berlin.

In a first reaction to the Dutch plans, the European Commission dropped the Green Paper on family integration it had announced earlier from its 2011 work programme. It thus indicated not to want to offer a platform for a discussion on amending the Family Reunification Directive. Under pressure from the Netherlands, the Green Paper was re-included in the programme in spring 2011 and was published in November 2011. It particularly contains a range of questions about experiences with current rules, objectives and expected effects of any amendments, as well as an indication of the limits that Treaty rules set on any amendments.[18] It is a clear attempt to provide a rational basis for the discussion on the Directive and to put a stop to fact-free politics on this subject. The Netherlands invited representatives of other Member States to a meeting in Amsterdam in mid-December 2010 to discuss their reaction to the Green Paper. The fact that no press statement was issued afterwards did not indicate broad support for the Dutch wishes elsewhere in the EU. The Member States and any other interested party could react to the Green Paper until March 2012; 24 Member States and Turkey, three national parliaments, more than 20 international organizations and 65 NGOs and individual persons did so.[19] An analysis of the reactions showed that only a minority of Member States favoured changes of certain elements of the Directive. Some Member States were afraid that amendments would further limit the room for national policy; others feared unwelcome restrictive rules.[20] At a hearing in May 2012, the Commission made clear that it would not introduce a proposal to amend the Directive. Instead, it preferred to clarify ambiguities in the meaning of the Directive by drawing up legally non-binding 'guidelines', following consultation with the Member States, and to institute infringement proceedings against Member States flouting the applicable rules.[21]

18 COM (2011) 735 of 15 November 2011.

19 *See* <http://ec.europa.eu/home-affairs/news/consulting_public/consulting_0023_en.htm>.

20 European Commission, DG Home Affairs. (2012, May). *Summary of stakeholder responses to the Green Paper on the right to family reunification of third-country nationals.* Brussels. *See* the website of DG Home Affairs, under Consultations 2012.

21 Dutch House of Representatives, *Kamerstuk* 32 175, No. 36, pp. 10/11, where Minister Leers fails to refer to any infringement proceedings and paints a rather rosy picture of the reactions of the other Member States to the Dutch wishes.

7.9 Differences with Earlier Attempts to Exert Influence in this Field

The recent Dutch performance at EU level is quite different from earlier attempts to influence European migration rules. In terms of content, all proposals are aimed at restricting migration and reducing immigrants' rights. On earlier occasions, the Dutch position was far less one-sided. The present debate is about changing existing rules and not, as in the past decade, about making new arrangements. In fact, it mostly involves taking away or limiting rights granted to migrants in the form of European rules adopted a few years ago. The Dutch wish list of amendments regarding five different existing EU Directives was published without any prior consultation with other Member States or the Commission. Consultations only started after the plans had been published. Since all points were part of the 2010 coalition agreement, the Dutch position paper does not indicate any priorities. All points seem equally important. Some proposals, like amending the Association Agreement with Turkey, greater freedom to deport EU citizens or amending the European Convention on Nationality, were clearly doomed to fail.

To other Member States it is obvious that the Dutch wish list has been inspired by the agreement of the two coalition partners with the PVV. In Europe, Geert Wilders is known for his anti-migrant and especially anti-muslim opinions. This will affect the willingness to support wishes of a Dutch government that is politically dependent on that party, even in Member States that otherwise would be inclined to support such measures. This reticence also affects measures on the list that had already been proposed by CDA and PvdA ministers under the previous government. The opinions and actions of members of the first Rutte Cabinet regarding Polish migrant workers in the Netherlands, and the Dutch opposition to allowing Romania and Bulgaria to join the Schengen area, will not have made these three countries more willing to help realize Dutch wishes in this field. In addition, over recent years, the Dutch policy not to observe certain European migration rules as long as it is not forced to by a Dutch or European court has led to over 15 judgements of the European courts in Luxembourg and Strasbourg whose far-reaching effects often make themselves felt in other Member States as well. The Netherlands will not always be thanked for these products of this Dutch policy elsewhere in the EU.

Notably different is also the relationship with the European Commission. Ministers in previous governments – Cohen, Verdonk, and Albayrak – made deliberate efforts to win the Commission over to their plans early on, with the aim of using this support in the political debate at home, whereas the attitude now rather seems one of antagonism. Wilders' impolite disqualification of Commissioner Malmström and the failure to invite the Commission to the consultations in Amsterdam in December 2011 have not increased Brussels' sympathy for the Dutch wishes. The Commission's cooperation is essential in this case, since only the Commission can submit a proposal to amend the Directives in question. Only if the Netherlands manages to gain the support of a large number of Member States will the Council ask the Commission to submit a proposal to amend those Directives. The Netherlands is clearly taking a more intergovernmental approach as a result of its fixation with the national debate and the agreement with the PVV, focusing on support among Member States rather than on the Commission.

7.10 Conclusion: Choices in the Coming Years

In the coming years, the Netherlands will be facing three important choices in the field discussed. The first choice is how to deal with the *tension between Member States' pursuit of more cooperation and the wish not to give up even more national powers*. On the one hand, there is an increasing need for migration control and for more cooperation in this area between the Member States. On the other, Member States want to prevent further loss of powers or recover lost powers.

This tension is clearly visible in the construction of the so-called Common European Asylum System, the essence of which should be one uniform asylum status and a uniform asylum procedure. This system was supposed to be ready by the end of 2010, but should now be completed by late 2012. However, the very minor changes to the existing EU asylum regime that the Commission proposed in recent years met with a lot of resistance. During the negotiations, some Member States tried to regain room for national law and policy they had lost under the existing rules. In 2011, Greece's apparent non-compliance with the EU rules on the reception and protection of asylum seekers led the European Court of Human Rights to intervene. The basic principle of mutual trust of Member States in each other's legal systems no longer proved tenable. The prohibition to return asylum seekers to Greece imposed by the European Court of Human Rights illustrates the crisis in the EU Dublin System which resulted in fundamental rights of asylum seekers being violated. This crisis, like the euro crisis, will inevitably lead to more EU rules and more supervision of Member States, because there is no viable way back. A political solution to this dilemma has sometimes been to establish new agencies, like Frontex in 2004 and the European Asylum Support Office in 2010. But this is only a temporary solution and, in practice, leads to more and more powers being granted to those agencies. As with Schengen, cooperation between Member States is ultimately impossible without independent supervision of compliance with the common European rules and an independent court that settles conflicts between Member States and between Member States and individuals. Given the intensive and extensive cooperation in this field, the intergovernmental path is a dead end.

The second question is how to handle the *tension between the need for migrant workers and the wish to limit migration*. The number of school leavers wanting to enter the labour market will decline in many Member States over the coming years. The demand for labour will not drop accordingly. Part of, in particular, the low-skilled work (such as health care, cleaning and construction) is difficult to transfer elsewhere. As long as the objective of abandoning economic growth remains a taboo, labour migration from within or outside the EU, legal or illegal, will continue to meet the demand for labour. This tension is illustrated by the objective in the 2010 coalition agreement announcing a set of measures that 'will actually lead to a very substantial reduction of the influx'. This objective was formulated in the year when total immigration in the Netherlands was the highest since 1945, particularly as a result of very low unemployment rates.

The Dutch position within the EU concerning labour migration is not focused on a level playing field, but on competition with other Member States on the basis of national conditions in attracting desirable migrants and keeping out less desirable migrants, third-country nationals and Union citizens. During the negotiations on the Directive on the admission of highly qualified workers, the so-called Blue Card Directive, Germany and the Netherlands succeeded in amending this Directive such that both countries could maintain their own arrangements for knowledge migrants. For instance, by making this arrangement more attractive, they can try to outstrip other Member States in attracting highly qualified workers from countries outside the EU. The Netherlands is against the Commission proposal to include in the Reception Directive the rule that asylum seekers are allowed to work once the procedure has lasted six months. In the Netherlands, asylum seekers remain largely excluded from legal employment throughout the entire procedure, which may sometimes take years. The Netherlands thus hopes to stay less attractive to asylum seekers than other Member States. In both cases, it opposes a level playing field.

The third choice has to do with the tension between the wish to, on the one hand, control and restrict migration and, on the other, respect the fundamental rights of migrants, regardless of their nationality. These rights are enshrined in national constitutions and regional and global human rights treaties, and have recently, with the consent of the Netherlands, been extended in the EU Charter of Fundamental Rights. This Charter has been binding EU treaty law since the Treaty of Lisbon. The tension becomes painfully apparent in the large numbers of migrants who perish trying to enter the EU by crossing the Mediterranean: more than 7000 registered dead migrants on the EU's external borders in 1993-2006.[22] This tension is also clear from politicians' resistance to rulings of both European courts on the rights of family migrants or asylum seekers and the obligation to grant equal treatment to lawfully settled migrants. This resistance is particularly noteworthy in cases where, through prolonged or deliberate violation of European rules, the Dutch government let things come to a head and waited for the court to decide, thus passing the buck to the court. The criticism that is

22 Spijkerboer, T. (2007). The human cost of border control. *European Journal of Migration and Law, 9*, 127-139.

levelled at both European courts and that, since 2010, has been striking a chord in Dutch government circles as well is remarkable and risky. After all, the reinforcement of the position of independent European courts is very much in the interest of the Netherlands, being a small Member State with relatively little political weight, even if their rulings do not always suit the political majority of the day.

7.11 The Smaller Dutch Voice in Europe

There are two ways in which the enlargement of the EU from the original 6 to the present 27 Member States has drastically limited the possibilities of the Dutch government to regulate foreign migration. On the one hand, the entry and position of more than 40% of the non-Dutch nationals in the Netherlands are almost completely governed by the EU rules on free movement. The government is left with hardly any instruments to regulate the migration of Union citizens, who form a growing portion of the non-Dutch population. Even if all amendments proposed by the first Rutte Cabinet were accepted by the other Member States, this would only marginally change the scope for non-admission or deportation of Union citizens and their family members.

On the other hand, the possibilities for the Netherlands to influence the EU migration rules on the admission and legal position of migrants from outside the EU (60% of the non-Dutch population) are strongly restricted by a number of structural changes: due to the increased number of Member States, the Dutch vote in the Council of Ministers when the European legislation in question is to be adopted now carries far less weight. Moreover, the veto right in this field was abolished by the Treaty of Lisbon, and the more prominent role of the EP, the Commission and the Court of Justice in the field of migration has reduced the relative power of the Council of Ministers. Other factors having a similar effect are the disappearance of the Benelux as a 'natural' coalition and the disintegrating image of the Netherlands elsewhere in the EU as a country dealing, in a sensible way, with the integration of migrants from its former colonies and from the Mediterranean countries. This image may have been too rosy. Have the rigorous break with the Dutch policy pursued until 2002, the one-sided emphasis on restriction of immigration and the open insults to other Member States really increased the Dutch powers of persuasion in Europe?

8 Dutch Perspectives on European Police Cooperation

Monica den Boer

8.1 Introduction

In the European Union (EU), much has been achieved in the field of police cooperation as part of justice and home affairs (JHA) cooperation in a relatively short time. Faced with sweeping changes, like the fall of the Berlin Wall, the blending of internal and external security, and the emergence of transnational terrorist networks, the EU has gradually asserted itself as a security actor. Especially in matters of internal security, a great many policy initiatives have been taken in the EU framework, with themes varying from radicalization, organized (environmental) crime, to maintenance of public order, and based on instruments ranging from information systems to legal decisions and agencies such as Europol and Frontex. Under pressure from a politicized security agenda, many legal instruments have been adopted, such as a number of conventions and framework decisions which are binding on national laws and regulations.

Despite hundreds of legal instruments adopted since the Treaty of Maastricht, decision-making has been difficult. On account of the political, administrative and geographical diversity within and between Member States, international police cooperation proves to be a sovereignty-sensitive and complex policy area. In addition, instruments are not always implemented smoothly by the Member States. There are several reasons for this, such as lack of priorities and capacity in the field, and also the critical attitude of judicial authorities in the Member States. For instance, in the past the European Commission regularly complained about the lack of real progress in the Area of Freedom, Security and Justice (AFSJ), established in 1997 in the context of the EU.

This chapter discusses the significance of European police cooperation for the internal security policy and analyzes the role of the Netherlands in the dynamics of European police cooperation. First, an overview is provided of the treaties, instruments and agreements in the field of police cooperation. Next, the Dutch policy influence in this particular area of cooperation is dealt with. The Dutch reputation as a strategic actor in this field is mostly positive, although it may have suffered negative effects from recent developments in adjacent JHA fields, such as Schengen. However, the image of the Netherlands as *operational and implementing actor* in police cooperation as a whole is less favourable. This chapter discusses the factors obstructing the operational implementation of EU-wide agreements. These factors include the regional, complex organizational structure of the Dutch police organization, and also the lack of positioning, prioritization and profiling of the need for internationalization in the Dutch security policy. The chapter closes with concluding observations, which also look further ahead: what conditions should the Netherlands meet not only to promote European police cooperation as a policy area but also to actually integrate it into the key processes of the police and justice organization?

8.2 European Police Cooperation: the Policy Area

Throughout the years, the EU instruments for cross-border police cooperation have been considerably extended.[1] In the early 1990s, when the Treaty of Maastricht first established *formal* agreements on JHA, police cooperation was regarded as a joint policy area. In view of the sovereignty-sensitive nature of this field, it was decided to opt for intergovernmental decision-making so that the Member States could stay firmly in control. This meant that the national ministers were able to exercise their veto in the Justice and Home Affairs Council. The policy initiatives ranged from a (then still to be established) agency for European police cooperation (Europol) to legal instruments that had to promote European judicial cooperation in criminal matters (such as the Convention on Mutual Legal Assistance in Criminal Matters between the EU Member States).

In the mid-1990s, on the one hand, JHA was being deepened and institutionalized, while, on the other, the EU was rapidly expanding and much attention went to police and justice reforms in the then candidate countries. This was accompanied by training programmes with a view to incorporating the JHA acquis into national legislation and professionalizing the officials concerned in justice, police, customs and border control departments. The JHA acquis was gradually and increasingly extended with various new instruments that affected police work. For instance, a few instruments were adopted to fight international organized crime, drugs crime and human trafficking. International investigation and prosecution among the EU Member States was simplified, e.g., through the Convention on Mutual Legal Assistance. Strong emphasis was placed on information exchange via international databases such as the Schengen Information System (SIS), the football intelligence units and the unusual transactions hotlines.

1 Bruggeman, W. & den Boer, M. (2011). Policing and internal security in the post-Lisbon era: New challenges ahead. In S. Wolff, F.A.N.J. Goudappel & J.W. de Zwaan (Eds.), *Freedom, security and justice after Lisbon and Stockholm*. The Hague: T.M.C. Asser Press, p. 137; Block, L. (2011). *From politics to policing. The rationality gap in EU Council policy making*. The Hague: Eleven International Publishing.

Investments were also made in the establishment of Europol, Eurojust, CEPOL[2] and Frontex.[3]

The Treaty of Amsterdam, which entered into force on 1 May 1999, was dominated by the *communautarisation* of a number of JHA fields,[4] by the incorporation of the Schengen acquis into EU law and by the creation of the overarching AFSJ. Police cooperation continued to be one of the main pillars of cooperation and was reinforced by giving Europol the right of initiative and by encouraging multidisciplinary cooperation in the field of internal security. The Treaty of Lisbon, which entered into force on 1 December 2009, again further strengthened and extended police cooperation. The main modification concerns the decision-making process. For non-operational police cooperation, Council decisions are made according to the ordinary legislative procedure (co-decision by the EP and with qualified majority in the Council). This is a drastic change compared to intergovernmental decision-making and the unanimity rule. The ordinary legislative procedure now applies to coordination of and cooperation between police and judicial authorities (including information exchange, investigation techniques and training), the powers of Eurojust and Europol decisions, measures to fight crime and relating to racism and xenophobia, mutual recognition of judicial decisions in criminal matters, and approximation of laws. Another modification is that the European Commission may summon Member States before the European Court of Justice for poor implementation of agreements. Member States have thus given up part of their sovereignty.

However, ratification of the Treaty of Lisbon was difficult, partly due to growing anti-European sentiments in the Member States. Because of electoral pressure at home, government leaders of various Member States were inclined to negotiate exceptions to how the European Parliament (EP) should be consulted, such as in the field of operational police cooperation. Opinions of the EP are not binding. Also in the case of extension of EU powers in matters of criminal law and the transformation of Eurojust into a European public prosecutor Member States still decide by unanimity. They can also use the 'emergency brake clause': if a draft directive detracts from the *fundamental* aspects of a Member State's criminal justice system, the latter can ask for the legislative procedure to be suspended and for the draft to be submitted to the European Council. If no consensus is reached but at least nine Member States do support the draft directive at issue, they can enter into so-called enhanced cooperation in that specific area. These provisions in the Treaty of Lisbon underscore the sensitivities involved in transferring powers regarding security matters.

2 CEPOL stands for Collège européen de police (European Police College).

3 Frontex is the European agency for the management of operational cooperation at the external borders of the Member States of the European Union.

4 *See* the chapter by Kees Groenendijk in this volume.

In addition to the above, the internal security strategy of the EU[5] aims for mutual cooperation between regional, national and transnational levels (also advocated by the European Committee of the Regions) in matters of cross-border crime. This concerns issues such as terrorism, cybercrime, drugs trade, child pornography, financial crime, corruption and disasters. A further aim is more cooperation between various public and private security actors and sectors (e.g., health care). The efforts of police forces in the Member States must therefore explicitly be coordinated with judicial, border control, civil protection and disaster control authorities in the EU Member States.

After the conclusion of the Treaty of Maastricht, a number of specialized agencies were set up as well. In matters of police cooperation Europol has the biggest role to play. It has primarily a *strategic* intelligence and investigation task and is therefore not an operational service in that it exercises executive powers (such as arrest or house search). Through national units (ENUs), Europol collaborates with competent authorities in the 28 Member States. These, in their turn, liaise with local and regional police units. This means that Europol in no way *directly* intervenes in local, regional or national affairs. The Stockholm Programme agreed in 2009 does, however, state that in all large-scale cross-border investigations, Europol and Eurojust must be systematically informed and involved if a joint investigation team is set up. These joint investigation teams[6] are considered highly relevant by the police due to their practical significance in tackling organized crime and terrorism, and they are being used to an increasing extent.[7] Progress has also been made with the European arrest warrant.[8] What we are still waiting for is the full implementation of the mandatory European Evidence Warrant that will be binding on the Member States, and the draft Directive on the European Investigation Order.

The Intergovernmental Schengen Agreement, incorporated into EU law via the Treaty of Amsterdam in 1997, has had major consequences for European police cooperation as well. This Agreement has enabled the exercise of cross-border powers, such as in the field of information exchange, pursuit, controlled delivery and observation. European police cooperation has, moreover, impacted on the technological 'infrastructure', especially ICT. As a result of the SIS and besides a national facility (SIRENE), ICT links had to be established with the systems of the police, the border control authorities, customs and the immigration and naturalization service, thus creating a 'web' of ICT contacts within and outside the

5 *See* <http://register.consilium.europa.eu/pdf/en/10/st05/st05842-re02.en10.pdf> (5842/2/10).

6 In the Netherlands often referred to as JITs (Joint Investigation Teams); Council Act of 29 May 2000 establishing in accordance with Art. 34 of the Treaty on European Union the Convention on Mutual Assistance in Criminal Matters between the Member States of the European Union.

7 Sollie, H. & Kop, N. (2012). *Joint investigation teams. Lessons learned*. The Hague: Boom Lemma Uitgevers.

8 Council Framework Decision 2002/584/JBZ of 13 June 2002 on the European arrest warrant and the surrender procedures between Member States.

police. So the provision of data to foreign criminal investigation services in the EU and the interoperability between information systems like the SIS are in the course of development.

The Treaty of Prüm, which was negotiated as the successor to 'Schengen' by a small group of Member States and was largely incorporated in the EU in 2007, has led to considerable further extension of cross-border competences and information gathering.[9] Police forces in the Member States concerned are authorized to share vehicle data, fingerprints and DNA data, and to provide operational assistance during large-scale events and the maintenance of public order.

Finally, thanks to several other bilateral and multilateral treaties, the Netherlands is involved in various closer types of cooperation. Examples are the bilateral Treaty of Enschede with Germany, and the Treaty of Senningen with the other Benelux countries. Lighter forms of cooperation follow from agreements in the framework of the Meuse-Rhine Euregion and the Cross-Channel Intelligence Conference (with Belgium, France and the United Kingdom). Heerlen is home to the Euregional Police Information and Cooperation Centre (EPICC), where, on a daily basis, Belgian, Dutch and German police officers exchange police-related information. The Joint Hit Team on the Belgian-Dutch border is operationally active.[10] At global level, the Netherlands is a member of Interpol and is involved in various civilian peace missions and participates in the International Association of Chiefs of Police (IAPC).[11] So European and international police cooperation ranges from regional, bilateral, multilateral to European and global cooperation initiatives, which may be both policy and operationally oriented.

All in all, European police cooperation can be described as extensive, diverse and dynamic. Its development is strongly related to the political recognition in the Member States that international cooperation in security matters pays off. The terrorist attacks of 9/11 have increased interest in international security cooperation and have triggered a substantial expansion of the range of instruments. Especially in the field of international information and intelligence exchange, this can be of great benefit to police forces in Europe. The fact that all these instruments exist does not mean that Europe has become demonstrably safer; it does mean, however, that Europe is one of the safest regions in the world.

9 Trb. 2005, 197, signed on 27 May 2005 <http://wetten.overheid.nl/BWBV0002898/geldigheidsdatum_03-06-2010> (accessed 20 September 2011). For an analysis, *see also* den Boer, M. (2006, September). Schengen III: The show must go on. *SEW, Tijdschrift voor Sociaal en Economisch Recht*, pp. 316-322. <www.europa-nu.nl/id/vhu4eb6eg0y3/grensoverschrijdende_criminaliteit> (accessed 26 August 2011).

10 *See* <www.polfed-fedpol.be/pub/inforevue/inforevue4_05/JointHit_nl.pdf> (accessed 8 December 2011).

11 *See* <www.theiacp.org>; *see also* the 'Pearls in policing' project: <http://spl.politieacademie.nl/SubwebEnglish/PearlsinPolicing/PearlsinPolicing/tabid/222/Default.aspx> (accessed 8 December 2011).

Nevertheless, citizens feel far removed from the European efforts in the area of internal security and police cooperation. The subject is rarely discussed in national parliaments, and its legitimacy thus leaves a great deal to be desired, despite the recent strengthening of the powers of national parliaments and of the EP.[12] When rating how safe they feel (subjective safety), Europeans generally regard their own neighbourhood as safe (90%). They are somewhat less inclined to consider their country or region as safe. Still, a recent Eurobarometer survey shows that 81% of Europe's citizens believe that Europe is a safe place to live, 28% of whom fully agree with this statement. The Eurobarometer reports a difference in perception between the old (15) and new (12) Member States. Citizens of the old Member States are slightly more positive. Respondents from the Netherlands, together with Finnish, Danish and Austrian citizens, are most positive about their safety situation.[13] Member State citizens generally consider that institutions in the EU should cooperate more closely in tackling terrorism and organized crime. Just over half (52%) of Dutch respondents are of the opinion that Member States can counter the threat of terrorism and organized crime on their own.[14] This means that many Dutch citizens believe European police cooperation is not evidently an EU matter.

8.3 The Dutch Policy Influence on European Police Cooperation

Since the mid-1970s, the Netherlands, as a Member State, has played a role in putting issues on the police cooperation agenda. It supported the British initiative to establish TREVI[15] in 1976 in order to strengthen mutual legal assistance between EC Member States. This resulted in intensified cooperation and exchange of investigation methods.[16] Moreover, the Netherlands was one of the initiators of the Schengen Agreement, which enabled it to exert influence on the objectives, content and purport of the various legal instruments. In the early

12 Den Boer, M., Hillebrand, C. & Noelke, A. (2008). Legitimacy under pressure: The European web of counter-terrorism networks. *Journal of Common Market Studies, 46*(1), 101-124; Monar, J. (2007). The EU's approach post-September 11: Global terrorism as a multidimensional law enforcement challenge. *Cambridge review of international affairs, 20*(2), 267-283; Curtin, D.M. (2011). *Top secret Europe*. Amsterdam: University of Amsterdam Press.

13 Special Barometer 380: Awareness of home affairs. (2012, June), pp. 16/17 (Field work: December 2011). *See* <http://ec.europa.eu/public_opinion/archives/ebs/ebs_380_sum_en.pdf> (accessed 7 June 2012).

14 Special Barometer 380 (2012), p. 21.

15 Named after the first chairman, Mr. Fonteijn, at the first meeting in Rome, referring to the Trevi Fountain.

16 Anderson, M., den Boer, M., Cullen, P., Gilmore, W., Raab, C, and Walker, N.. (1995). *Policing the European Union: Theory, law and practice*. Oxford: Clarendon Press.

1990s, *communautarization* of police and judicial cooperation in the Treaty of Maastricht proved a step too far, e.g., during the negotiations on this Treaty.[17] The EU Presidency in 1997 offered a good opportunity to realize new goals in the area of police cooperation. For instance, in 1997 the Netherlands managed to get the fight against organized crime on the agenda – helped by the European Council in Dublin on 13 and 14 December 1996, which had decided to set up a High-Level Group to draw up a comprehensive action plan, including specific recommendations and timetables.[18] It was not long before this group had formulated 30 recommendations laying the foundations for the action plan to combat organized crime[19] and for the establishment of the Council Multidisciplinary Group (MDG) on Organized Crime.[20] Some elements of the action plan were incorporated into the Amsterdam Treaty, including the recommendation that the police should establish cooperation with customs and with immigration services, and that Europol should have a right of initiative, making cooperation more binding. Furthermore, the action plan emphasized the need for crime prevention, cooperation with the private sector and investigation of financial crime such as fraud and money laundering. To this day, this multidisciplinary approach to tackling organized crime and terrorism enjoys Europe-wide support. All this fits perfectly in the broader context of the AFSJ. The incorporation of the (intergovernmental) Schengen acquis into the EU Treaty and the pro-Community Dutch arguments were also in line with the Dutch position focused on further integration (see Schout and Rood in Chapter 1).[21]

During its EU Presidency [note:above with a capital] of 2004, the Netherlands headed the initiative to create 'Tampere II'. Later, this document was renamed the 'Hague Programme'. It advocated consolidation and implementation of exist-

17 Den Boer, M. (2011). Policing Schengen. In P. Burgess & S. Gutwirth (Eds.), *Europe under threat? Security, migration and integration*. Brussels: VUB Press, pp. 191-209. *See* <http://europa.eu/legislation_summaries/justice_freedom_security/free_movement_of_persons_asylum_immigration/l33020_nl.htm> (accessed 20 September 2011); Occhipinti, J. (2003). *The politics of EU police cooperation: Towards a European FBI?* London: Lynne Riener, p. 43; Beach, D. (2005). *The dynamics of European integration. Why and when European institutions matter.* Basingstoke: Palgrave MacMillan, pp. 69-71 and 110.

18 *See* <www.burojansen.nl/europol/plan_2.htm> (accessed 29 August 2011).

19 Action plan to combat organized crime, adopted by the Council on 28 April 1997, OJ C 251 of 15 August 1997, p. 1.

20 This Council working group studies proposed regulation submitted by the European Commission to the Council working group.
Source: <www.europa-nu.nl/id/vh7ej5swwyyt/multidisciplinaire_raadswerkgroep>. The MDG also evaluated the approach to tackling financial-economic crime and was positive about the Netherlands (see below).
See <www.rijksoverheid.nl/documenten-en-publicaties/persberichten/2010/10/14/eu-positief-over-nederlandse-aanpak-financieel-economische-criminaliteit.html> (accessed 29 August 2011).

21 Schout, J.A. & Vanhoonacker, S. (2006). Evaluating presidencies of the council of the EU. Revisiting Nice. *Journal of Common Market Studies, 44*(5), 1049-1075.

ing instruments, on the one hand, and argued in favour of a far-reaching approach to tackling terrorism and radicalization, on the other. In the field of police cooperation, few new legal instruments were proposed because a multitude of policy initiatives had already been taken after 9/11. The Hague Programme did, however, aim at improving exchange of information and intelligence between police forces, police integrity and concrete collaboration. The Programme was thus considered to provide incentives for further policy development in the field of European police cooperation.[22] Implementation of the Programme was found to lag behind in terms of police and judicial cooperation in criminal matters, crisis management, exchange of information and the fight against organized crime, but progress had been made in combating terrorism and in the field of migration and border control.[23] Meanwhile, the Hague Programme has been succeeded by the above-mentioned Stockholm Programme (2009)[24] and the Internal Security Strategy (2010),[25] including several new incentives for European police cooperation, such as promotion of interoperability of information systems and an exchange programme for police officers.

In 2004, the Dutch Presidency of the EU could boast an actual success: the Comprehensive Strategic Police Programme (COSPOL), which enabled the Task Force of European Chiefs of Police (TFCP) to align agreements and designate drivers for specific issues, such as cross-border human trafficking. Europol's strategic analyses would form the basis in this context. This was a difficult achievement compared with the other priorities of the then Dutch Presidency (such as fast information exchange between police forces based on availability and reinforced operational cooperation between judicial, police and security departments).[26] All

22 Sie Dhian Ho, M. & van Keulen, M. (2004, June). *The Dutch at the Helm – Navigating on a rough sea. The Netherlands 2004 presidency of the European Union.* Notre Europe, Research and European Issues, Number 34, pp. 27-28. *See* <www.notre-europe.eu/uploads/tx_publication/Etud34-en_01.pdf> (accessed 26 August 2011); Fijnaut, C. (2006). The Hague programme and police cooperation between the member states of the EU. In J.W. de Zwaan & F.A.N.J. Goudappel (Eds.), *Freedom, security and justice in the European Union. Implementation of the Hague programme.* The Hague: T.M. C. Asser Press, pp. 233-248.

23 Council and Commission Action Plan implementing the Hague Programme on strengthening freedom, security and justice in the European Union, OJ C 198 of 12 August 2005, <http://eur-lex.europa.eu/LexUriServ/LexUriServ.do?uri=CELEX:52005XG0812(01):EN:NOT> (accessed 26 August 2011).

24 *See* <http://eur-lex.europa.eu/LexUriServ/LexUriServ.do?uri=OJ:C:2010:115:0001:0038:en:PDF> (accessed 8 December 2011).

25 *See* <http://ec.europa.eu/commission_2010-2014/malmstrom/archive/internal_security_strategy_in_action_en.pdf> (accessed 8 December 2011).

26 Communication from the Commission to the EP and the Council – Enhancing police and customs cooperation in the European Union – I. Report on achievements since the entry into force of the Treaty of Amsterdam – II. Proposals for improvements, COM (2004) 0376 final. *See* <http://eur-lex.europa.eu/LexUriServ/LexUriServ.do?uri=CELEX:52004DC0376:NL:HTML> (accessed 26 August 2011).

in all, the Netherlands proved capable of achieving actual results at the European negotiating table.

Within the extensive European network that has emerged in this field, Dutch policymakers, being relevant actors, have to divide their attention between various Council working groups, such as the police cooperation working party, the Europol working party, the working group on terrorism, the working party on cooperation in criminal matters and the SIS/SIRENE working party. In addition, the Dutch police had to position themselves in the 'horizontal' Council working groups, including the MDG on organized crime, the working group on civil protection, and the Schengen evaluation working group. However, over the past years, direct input from police professionals has been considerably reduced in favour of official representation.[27] To compensate for the decline of influence,[28] the (former) *Korps Landelijke Politiediensten* (KLPD – National Police Services Agency) appointed, on 1 February 2011, an EU commissioner for executive European police cooperation 'in Brussels'.[29]

Relevant in this respect is the restructuring of a deconcentrated regional police organization into a national police force with 10 new regional units. A new police system, involving national coordination as well as information management, may result in more effective, efficient, coordinated and transparent cooperation with other EU Member States. A precondition for vision- and strategy-based international police cooperation is national prioritization, supported by budget, knowledge and leadership under the auspices of the Minister of Security and Justice. However, the reform of the Dutch police organization may result in reduced attention for strategic policy development in the EU, as the prime focus of the top-strategy officers of the new police force will be on internal organizational reform. It is not clear yet who will represent the Dutch police force in international bodies after it has been fully restructured, but there is only one national chief constable (*korpschef*). The ultimate intention is a better streamlining of Dutch police representation in EU bodies such as COSI and the Europol management board.

27 Van Keulen, M. & Mittendorff, F. (2011). Justice and home affairs 'at home': Shaping the AFSJ at the national level. In S. Wolff, F.A.N.J. Goudappel & J.W. de Zwaan (Eds.), *Freedom, security and justice after Lisbon and Stockholm*. The Hague: T.M.C. Asser Press, p. 42.

28 1According to former Chief Superintendent of Police Wiarda. <http://spl.politieacademie.nl/belang-european-chiefs-of-police-task-force-neemt-toe/tabid/607/Default.aspx>; *see also nota Beleidskader Internationale Politiesamenwerking (STIPS – 2002)* [Memorandum Policy Framework International Police Cooperation].

29 Source: <www.algemenebestuursdienst.nl/benoemingen/petra-bakker-ten-broek.html> (accessed 26 August 2011).

8.4 From Strategic Leadership to Policy Implementation

Having mapped the field of European police cooperation, it is time for a provisional assessment. On the one hand, the role of the Netherlands as a strategic, agenda-setting actor is seen as positive, but on the other, some evaluations point to the Netherlands struggling with the implementation of European obligations and expectations at EU level. As a participant, adviser, driver, negotiator and facilitator, the Netherlands has a visible presence in the field of European police cooperation. For instance, it was actively involved in a project under which, together with Belgium as president of the EU (autumn 2010), the United Kingdom and Europol, a new methodology was being developed to anticipate organized crime and to bring the control of serious transnational crime and terrorism in line with the strategic multi-annual planning of the EU in which strategic priorities are set in the field of crime control and to which various national and European agencies commit themselves (Harmony project).[30] Moreover, the Netherlands is a visible partner in police training and research in the framework of the European Police College (CEPOL). It is involved in many other forms of international police cooperation, ranging from education to criminal investigation. All police forces have a coordinator for international relations (a function which is embedded in several different ways); these coordinators will be retained in the 10 regional police forces that will form part of the national police force. The Netherlands has a few dozen police liaison officers abroad. In the meantime, however, it has been announced that their number will be reduced. In the framework of the Benelux, Schengen or the EU, liaison officers can be pooled with other Member States, but in practice this remains to be done on a full scale.[31] On the basis of recent policy, European liaison officers no longer exchange information bilaterally, but via Europol. All in all, this points to a reduction of the network model of Dutch police abroad and the prevalence of a more institutionalized environment.

The Treaty of Lisbon has paved the way for the establishment of a European public prosecutor from Eurojust, albeit with a limited mandate and only after the Member States have unanimously come out in favour of such potential further institutionalization. Many professionals from police circles would find it perfectly normal if a European criminal code were to be drawn up as well. However, at the moment, harmonization of penal and criminal procedures law is not an explicit objective in the EU. During the European Convention (2003-2004), the

30 Council of the European Union. (2010, November 8 and 9). *Council conclusions on the creation and implementation of an EU policy cycle for organised and serious international crime*. 3043rd Justice and Home Affairs Council meeting, Brussels. <www.consilium.europa.eu/uedocs/cms_data/docs/pressdata/en/jha/117583.pdf> (accessed 31 August 2011).

31 The Member States of the EU, Norway and Switzerland have stationed a total of 580 liaison officers in third countries (from police, customs and home affairs departments). *See* Bruggeman & Den Boer (2011), p. 139.

Dutch Minister of Justice still argued in favour of a joint European criminal-law enforcement area, with a European police service, a European public prosecutor, a European criminal court and a European rehabilitation service.[32] The guiding principle was the estimation that around 10% of all crime in Europe is cross-border. The proposal to create a European criminal justice system[33] was submitted to the European Convention in May 2003, but did not make it.[34]

For some years now, the Netherlands has gradually adopted a more pragmatic approach. This means, among other things, that it supports the mutual recognition of Member States' judicial systems. Importance is attached to the 'approximation' of substantive criminal law so as to facilitate mutual cooperation. Despite the tendency to emphasize national sovereignty in international criminal justice cooperation, the Netherlands decided to support the harmonization of penalization of members of, or participation in, a criminal organization and recognizes the added value of, for instance, the Framework Decision of 2005 ('Fight against organized crime') which harmonized criminal-law definitions between Member States.[35]

Indeed, the Netherlands has increasingly emphasized the preservation of national sovereignty. The reticent stance may be related to increased Euroscepticism, but certainly also with a more calculating attitude towards the costs and benefits of European police cooperation. At the time of the negotiations about the Single European Act, the Netherlands was still in favour of increasing the influence of the European Commission.[36] For some time, it has been able to milk negotiation successes in relevant areas, such as Schengen, Prüm, the Hague Programme and the administrative approach to tackling crime. Now that the EU has expanded considerably and cooperation in the field of JHA has become strongly institutionalized, the Netherlands finds itself in a different position. Moreover, the restructuring of the police organization demands an entirely new strategic approach.

As mentioned earlier in this chapter, the regional structure of the Dutch police system has been a challenge in jointly steering European police cooperation. The creation of the national police force offers an opportunity to reduce this fragmen-

---

32 Pijpers, A. (2003, June 4). Debat over de Europese Conventie is onnodig steriel [Debate on the European Convention is needlessly sterile]. *De Volkskrant*.

33 CONV 733/03, Contribution by Mr. Gijs de Vries, member of the Convention, 'The European Criminal Justice Area'.

34 De Zwaan, J., et al. (2009, October 30). *Justitie in de wereld. Op weg naar een interne balans. Evaluatie van het internationale beleid van het Ministerie van Justitie en DEIA in het bijzonder* [Justice in the world. Towards an internal balance. Evaluation of the international policy of the Ministry of Justice and DEIA in particular]. The Hague: Clingendael. <www.google.nl/search?q=evaluatie+nederlands+voorzitterschap+1997&hl=nl&rlz=1T4SUNA_enNL284NL293&prmd=ivns&ei=44dXTtWrI4ae-wbJiJmVDA&start=10&sa=N> (accessed 26 August 2011).

35 *Initieel standpunt Nederlandse regering* [Initial position of Dutch government]. <www.europa-nu.nl/id/vi8rm30037zz/com_2005_6_bestrijding_van#p2> (accessed 26 August 2011).

36 Beach (2005), p. 57.

tation and division, both nationally and internationally.[37] In the formation of the national police force, limited attention has been paid to steering on international police cooperation.[38] For the time being, it is assumed that regional international legal assistance centres meet EU requirements. The national information coordination unit (*Landelijke Informatiecoördinatie* – LIC) will act as a hub of the national Interpol, Europol and Schengen-SIRENE desks.

Over the past years, it has been difficult for Dutch police forces to efficiently deal with legal assistance requests from other countries. In 1999, the Netherlands was criticized by a European official expert group, because incoming legal assistance requests did not go further than the public prosecutor and executive police departments, or even got lost. Despite improvements to the organizational structure and the creation of the International Legal Assistance Centres (*Internationale Rechtshulpcentra* – IRCs) and the LIRC (*Landelijk Internationaal Rechtshulp Centrum* – National International Legal Assistance Centre), the position of the Netherlands is still referred to as "No priority and no capacity".[39] The Dutch criminal justice system rests on the opportunity principle, which means that prosecution may be waived. Under the direction of the public prosecutor, the police may set priorities on the basis of information. However, because international police cooperation is assuming an increasingly mandatory character, individual discretionary power may be diminishing. In the meantime, steps have been taken to improve the processing of legal assistance requests.[40] Now that the field of European police cooperation is also cautiously moving towards legal harmonization, coherence

37 Van den Bosch, M. & Zorko, P. (2008, November 1). Internationale politiesamenwerking: de normaalste zaak van de wereld? [International police cooperation: The most natural thing in the world?]. <www.websitevoordepolitie.nl/archief/internationale-politiesamenwerking-de-normaalste-zaak-van-de-wereld-416.html> (accessed 29 August 2011).

38 *Ontwerpplan Nationale Politie* [Draft Plan National Police], January 2012; den Boer, M. (2012, February). Is de Nationale Politie klaar voor Europa? [Are the national police ready for Europe?]. *Strafblad, 10*(1), anniversary issue, pp. 43-53.

39 Marchand, M. & Out, R. (2010). *Het Europees onderzoeksbevel. 'The next level' van wederzijds vertrouwen bij rechtshulpverzoeken?* [The European investigation order. 'The next level' of mutual trust in legal assistance requests?]. Politieacademie, p. 7. <http://spl.politieacademie.nl/Portals/0/docs/Internationaal/Columbus%20II%20Essay%20-%20Rob%20Out%20en%20Michiel%20Marchand.pdf> (accessed 26 August 2011); *see also* Spapens, T. (2011). Vertrouwen in internationale strafrechtelijke samenwerking [Trust in international judicial cooperation in criminal matters]. Strafrechtsdag 2011, mimeo; den Boer, M. (2002). Intelligence exchange and the control of organised crime: From Europeanisation via centralisation to dehydration?. In J. Apap & M. Anderson (Eds.), *Police and justice co-operation and the new European borders*. The Hague: Kluwer Law International, pp. 151-161; Van den Bosch & Zorko (2008).

40 *See* <www.websitevoordepolitie.nl/archief/internationale-politiesamenwerking-de-normaalste-zaak-van-de-wereld-416.html>. *See also* the column of Hoogenboom B. & Witjes L., for the Stichting Maatschappij, Veiligheid en Politie (SMVP – Dutch Foundation for Society, Safety and the Police). Inrichting nationale politie, maar welke richting (I)?: internationale politiesamenwerking [Organisation of national police, but which direction(I)?: international police cooperation] (<www.smvp.nl/column201103/>, accessed 20 September 2011).

between the various binding EU instruments will have to be established by subsumption under European framework legislation on the protection of personal data (e.g., in data retention). Since police work is largely based on collecting and storing data, these agreements will have far-reaching consequences for the national and international information exchange by the Dutch police.[41]

With regard to the control of financial-economic crime, the implementation of the EU's policy is proceeding well. According to the draft plan on the national police, the investigation of financial-economic crime is guaranteed at all levels of police work. The evaluation report on the fifth round of mutual evaluations 'Financial Crime and Financial Investigations'[42] already demonstrated that the relevant European legal acts have been 'duly' implemented. However, the evaluators had trouble getting a comprehensive picture due to the fragmented situation in the Netherlands and the different statistical methods used to, for instance, gain insight into the recovery of criminal assets and the seizure of goods. The Dutch police have in particular tried, through the FinEc Programme, to limit periods of inactivity and thus to proceed to confiscate more quickly and achieve a higher dispossession percentage. In addition, the Evaluation Report expressed appreciation for the dual approach to tackling financial crime, whereby specialist knowledge is combined with financial investigation work in the standard police processes. The programme-based approach according to which the police, together with the public prosecutor and other players, tackle financial crime was viewed positively. The administrative approach in regard to organized crime, where the Netherlands is taking the lead internationally, is considered an innovative strategy which can also be introduced as best practice elsewhere in Europe.

8.5 Concluding Remarks and Future Perspective

Since the formalization of police cooperation within the EU, the Netherlands has exerted *major* policy influence on the agenda and strategic policy papers. Insight into the wide range of relevant EU instruments is still lacking among police ranks. This is a problem, especially where international cooperation is required as a matter of urgency. It is, moreover, important that police force managers, such as team heads, understand what is going on across the borders. In general, European police cooperation is characterized by a high degree of 'proliferation' of legal instruments. The police organization does not have an overview of the

41 Council of the European Union. (2011, September 30). *Exchange of data within AFSJ and EU data retention and data protection standards: Need for further harmonisation/approximation.* Brussels (JAI 695).

42 Council of the European Union, Brussels. (2010, July 14). <www.rijksoverheid.nl/documenten-en-publicaties/verslagen/2010/10/15/evaluatieverslag-over-de-vijfde-ronde-van-wederzijdse-evaluaties-financiele-criminaliteit-en-financieel-rechercheren.html> (accessed 29 August 2011).

implementation of official policy initiatives in the Council working groups. At the moment, EU instruments are far from being fully integrated into police business processes (mainstreaming).[43] Due to the ongoing proliferation of EU policy in the field of police and judicial cooperation in criminal matters, implementation is not always on schedule. New legal instruments have succeeded each other too quickly, which may result in the practice that practitioners act "as they have always been used to acting instead of using the appropriate channel".[44] If this is correct, it means that relevant EU agencies and legal instruments may be underutilized.[45]

In the Netherlands, European police cooperation is rarely the subject of social debate. There seems to be little political-administrative attention for the effects of international cooperation on the security of citizens in the Netherlands. A sense of urgency seems to be lacking, in both politics and practice. However, in the military context, the urgency regarding more European cooperation has been recognized, also because of the austerity measures.[46] Still, there are frequent calls for closer European police cooperation in problem areas such as terrorism and organized crime.[47] The abolition of internal border controls in the EU is seen as one of the causes of insecurity and as an argument for European police cooperation. In certain (border) regions of the Netherlands, cooperation with foreign police forces is considered essential.

Despite difficult decision-making and faltering implementation, much has been achieved at EU level in the area of European police cooperation. The European Commission and the Member States now seem to be cautiously moving away from a hyperactive period of regulation. In the coming decade, the focus will be on consolidation and implementation. The Netherlands will have to forge coalitions in a strongly expanded EU in order to get issues off the ground, but this not only applies to police cooperation. This line of approach has already been launched, e.g., by adopting common positions with the other Benelux countries.

Police cooperation is situated more in the framework of globalization and the growth of interdependence, and is increasingly characterized by a system of

43 Beach (2005).

44 Guille, L. (2010). The proliferation of parallel tracks in police and judicial cooperation in Europe: The current 'chaos'. In A. Verhage, Terpstra, J.,, Deelman, P., Muylaert, E., and Van Parys, P. (Eds.), Policing in Europe. *Cahiers Politiestudies*, 2010-2013, 16, p. 63; *see also* den Boer, M. & Spapens, T. (2002). *Investigating organised crime in European border regions*. Tilburg: IVA/CRBI, University of Tilburg.

45 Block (2011); *see also* Neyroud, P. & Vassilas, P. (2010). The politics of partnership: Challenges to institution-building in European policing. *Cahiers Politiestudies,* 16, p. 76 ("[...] the gap between policy-makers and practitioners emerges as a key determinant of future shifts in policing.").

46 Advisory Council on International Affairs. (2012, January). *European defence cooperation* (Advice No. 78).

47 Eurobarometer survey on internal security: The economic crisis and terrorism on top of the agenda (2011, November 25). <http://europa.eu/rapid/pressReleasesAction.do?reference=-MEMO/11/829&type=HTML> (accessed 3 February 2012).

mutual obligations. While in the Netherlands a national police force is being formed, the realization is dawning that international police cooperation should be closely aligned with the public prosecutor, border management authorities,[48] special investigation services and other relevant security partners, such as the National Coordinator for Counterterrorism and Security. A condition for strong international cooperation is smooth exchange of information, both nationally and internationally. At the moment, international cooperation is still characterized by too much distrust. Education, work placements, exchanges and actual cooperation can deepen knowledge and understanding of each other's system and gradually dispel distrust.

A major challenge lies in the active use of the broad range of instruments which have thus far been developed at the EU level. National budgetary constraints offer new opportunities for more intensive cooperation in the EU framework, such as, for instance, the pooling of liaison officers between EU Member States and the semi-permanent staffing of joint investigation teams. The Netherlands can take a pragmatic approach by filing joint applications for financing of cross-border police cooperation, which should be supported by a broadly shared vision within the new national police force.[49]

In this context, the creation of the national police force provides an opportunity for international police cooperation, with better and clear-cut choices, as well as stronger and clearer motivation among all police staff. Other countries will keep a critical eye on the role of the national police in international police training, civilian missions and joint operational actions. It is of essential importance that the Netherlands actively collaborate with partners in the EU, the Council of Europe and the Organization of Security and Cooperation in Europe (OSCE), also where police reform is part of security sector reform. In this respect, the Netherlands can consolidate the role it has played on the international scene over the past decades, i.e., that of active champion of the democratic rule of law.[50] An internationally oriented police force is a key condition for realizing this international ambition.

For any police officer, knowledge about Europe is an elementary part of the curriculum. The Police Academy of the Netherlands has met this requirement in various police education programmes. International police cooperation can be integrated into the core tasks and key processes of the police. If Europe is actually

48 In the Dutch context, the Royal Military Police (*Koninklijke Marechaussee*) is responsible for border control.

49 Fijnaut, C. (2007). De komende politiereorganisatie: de voorlaatste halte op de weg naar het Korps Nederlandse Politie [The forthcoming police reorganization: The last but one stop on the way to the *Korps Nederlandse Politie*]. In C.J.C.F. Fijnaut, Muller, E., and Rosenthal, U. (Eds.), *Politie. Studies over haar werking en organisatie* [Police. Studies on functioning and organization]. Deventer: Kluwer, pp. 109-140, 163; Den Boer (2012).

50 Advisory Council on International Affairs. (2011). *The human rights policy of the European Union: Between ambition and ambivalence* (Advice No. 76).

considered as a matter of home affairs, it will automatically form part of mainstream policing. Apart from integrating operational and non-operational cooperation into the national police structure, it is time for a shared proactive Dutch strategy on international police cooperation which aligns priorities in terms of content, procedure and finance.

9 Security and Defence at EU Level: The Hague's Blind Spot?

Margriet Drent

9.1 Introduction

The intervention in Libya in 2011, led by France and the United Kingdom with the support of the US military capabilities that are indispensable for this type of conflict, seriously tarnished the image of the non-deployed Common Security and Defence Policy (CSDP) of the European Union (EU). The European countries had managed to arrive at a common position in response to the developments in Tunisia and Egypt, but military action by the EU in Libya was a bridge too far, both politically and in terms of available military resources. While during Operation Unified Protector, NATO acted as some sort of service provider for the coalition partners, the EU prepared itself rather half-heartedly for a humanitarian-military support mission and launched a post-Gaddafi plan that focused on "money, market access and mobility".[1] The question that arises is whether this division of roles has been an incident or is characteristic of how security and defence policy in Europe is taking shape. Libya again demonstrated that disunity and lack of relevant military capabilities stand in the way of the CSDP becoming a mature policy.

Meanwhile, the Netherlands had grown averse to intervention because of the political and military complications of the Uruzgan mission, and the brand-new minority coalition wanted the Dutch involvement in Afghanistan to be low-profile. For a moment, it seemed that this low profile would be short-lived: it was exactly at this time that the Netherlands was heading an EU Battlegroup, and the Libya crisis seemed the ideal occasion to deploy it. But when a possible humanitarian CSDP mission in Libya was made dependent on a request from the UN Office for the Coordination of Humanitarian Affairs (OCHA), this mission became very unlikely. Since the cabinet had already announced major cuts in the defence budget, a costly deployment of the Dutch/German Battlegroup (90% of the costs are borne by the countries that take part in the operation) would have upset these plans.

Libya did again prove, however, that the Battlegroup concept does not work in its current form, but that a bigger issue is at stake as well: what is the purpose

1 Ashton, C. (2011, March 18). What next in North-Africa?. *International Herald Tribune*.

of the CSDP, and how does the Netherlands wish to proceed with it? This chapter discusses the priorities regarding the EU's CSDP in the medium term and what this means for the Dutch policy agenda for security and defence at EU level. First, a concise overview will be given of developments in this field since 1999 and the Dutch position on the matter. Subsequently, some of the major outstanding questions regarding an effective CSDP will be discussed.

9.2 Development of the Common Security and Defence Policy

The expectations prevailing at the time the EU took its first steps in the area of security and defence have only partly materialized. The initiators – France and the United Kingdom – had very different expectations when they provided the decisive impetus to the (then) European Security and Defence Policy (ESDP) in St Malo in 1998. But neither the British hope of strengthening the European military capabilities nor the French wish to play an important part in world politics via a militarily strong Europe has come true.

In the short history of the CSDP, the focus in the first years, influenced by internal and external factors, was on the CSDP's military aspects – despite a less visible deployment of civilian missions. This then shifted towards the civilian-military sphere, while recently, in relative terms, the 'hard' military side of the security policy has gained prominence again. This fluctuating movement follows developments in the field of international conflict management, European threat perceptions and the CSDP's position in relation to NATO.

The changing threat perception after the end of the Cold War chiefly resulted in European countries collecting the peace dividend, but led only to a partial adaptation of the armed forces to the new threat analyses. The establishment of a large EU reaction force, as agreed in the Helsinki Headline Goal, soon proved to be too high an aim. Many gaps remained that could not, or only insufficiently, be filled by the EU Member States. And although realization of a large, rapid reaction force continues to be an EU aim, in 2004, the Battlegroups concept led to the level of ambition being shifted towards several small mobile, rapidly deployable units of 1500 to 2500 strong.[2]

Already during the negotiations on the British-French proposal for an ESDP, its highly military character was a source of dispute. Especially under the influence of neutral countries and countries with a less assertive strategic culture, the ESDP was given a second arm for civilian crisis management. As of 2003, an impressive array of crisis management operations were carried out under the CSDP flag; so far, 7 of these 24 operations have been military. During this period, the CSDP's focus shifted towards 'civilian security tasks', whereby the recon-

2 The Battlegroups concept is often viewed as a lowering of ambitions, but considering the rapid response time (5-10 days), this is a matter of debate.

struction of a post-conflict country in terms of good governance, rule of law, democracy and reform of the security chain (police, justice, border control, armed forces) gained increasing importance. So far, the Battlegroups that have been operational since 2007, two of which are on standby each half year to rapidly intervene in acute crisis situations, have not been deployed. However, in 2008/2009 a robust EU operation was deployed in Chad and the Central African Republic, and in 2008 the EU Atlanta operation, the anti-piracy mission off the coast of Somalia, was launched and is still running.[3] Time and again, the urgency of deploying a Battlegroup was not considered high enough, which to an important extent was determined by the different views within the EU on the use of violence and the high cost for the Member States participating in the Battlegroup.[4]

Unanticipated by the British and French initiators, after 2003, the 'comprehensive security approach' became the main feature of the EU as a security actor. The European Security Strategy of that year codified what in the initial years of the ESDP had emerged as a middle path between the different security cultures of the Member States, whereby the use of military violence is only one of the EU's instruments to deal with security threats.[5] This comprehensive approach reflects the many dimensions which the EU has available to promote security in the broad sense. Besides the CSDP military and civilian crisis management instrument, the EU also has instruments in the fields of humanitarian aid, disaster relief, development cooperation, international trade and diplomacy. One of the main challenges for the Union is to be able to effectively deploy this large potential also in a joint context.

The choice for a comprehensive approach went hand in hand with emerging security threats to Europe. The interventions in Bosnia, Kosovo, Iraq and Afghanistan demonstrated that stabilizing a country is an even greater challenge than winning a war. Over the past eight years, the EU has chiefly emphasized its added value in the first phase after military intervention and in stabilizing and rebuilding a country. Looking back, the EU has so far opted for missions and operations that were small-scale or of short duration or had a low level of ambition or took place in a less hazardous phase of the conflict.

After more than 10 years of CSDP, criticism of this reactive type of action has been mounting, and the question increasingly arises how the CSDP can be used more forcefully as a strategic instrument of EU foreign policy. In addition, the development of the CSDP will continue to depend on the volume of military

3 For a proper overview of CSDP missions, *see* <www.isis-europe.org>. The EU military Operation Althea in Bosnia Herzegovina is also still running. There are another 10 EU civilian missions in operation and 1 civilian-military mission in Uganda to train the Somalian army.

4 Major, C. & Mölling, C. (2011, June). *EU battlegroups: What contribution to European defence?* Berlin: Stiftung Wissenschaft und Politik, p. 22.

5 *A safer Europe in a better world. European security strategy.* (2003, December 12). Brussels, <www.consilium.europa.eu/uedocs/cmsUpload/78367.pdf>.

and civilian capabilities and resources that the Member States make available for deployment. For years, the CSDP planners in the EU military staff (EUMS) have identified the same military shortcomings, and under the influence of the financial crisis, a change in thinking about military capability in the European context is becoming increasingly essential. At the same time, the EU is still insufficiently able to make optimal use of its potential as a comprehensive security actor. These themes are discussed later in this chapter.

These challenges should also be of interest to the Netherlands. In a complex security situation where Dutch interests strongly depend on stability and a properly functioning international legal order, an influential EU is of great significance. As a result of the shifting international power constellations, the United States wants to further reduce its direct involvement in conflicts in the European environment. The Europeans are therefore increasingly left to their own devices, the result being that the 'work in progress', which the CSDP still is, will have to be strengthened further.

9.3 The Dutch Attitude Regarding the CSDP

In 2011, the Netherlands opted for consolidation of the CSDP agenda, which means no new initiatives, but implementing and executing what was initiated in the past.[6] This is not an unwise attitude, because a number of important provisions on the CSDP in the Lisbon Treaty still need to be implemented, such as the far-reaching articles on a Mutual Assistance Clause and Permanent Structured Cooperation in the field of defence, which were decided already over eight years ago at the time the Constitutional Treaty was established.[7] However, this attitude forces the Netherlands into a passive role, where it mainly has to react to initiatives taken by others. In this regard, the ministries involved strongly focus on the United Kingdom and Germany. In this light, it may be stated that the CSDP is not a priority for the relevant departments of the Ministries of Foreign Affairs and (to a lesser extent) Defence, because the EU does not seem to be regarded as a serious security player next to NATO. Furthermore, the EU's role as security actor is still pretty unknown, and unknown is unloved. As if time has stood still, Dutch cabinet members still strongly focus on the transatlantic context and go by what the Americans can dictate in Europe.

Still, in the Netherlands, the CSDP as a policy priority has also known better times. The Netherlands managed to play a quite active part in the development

6 Interview with Foreign Affairs official, 22 June 2011.

7 *See*, in this context, Mengelberg, S.N. & Drent, M. (2010). Een effectievere Europese Unie? De gevolgen van het Verdrag van Lissabon voor het Europees Veiligheids- en Defensiebeleid [A more effective European Union? The consequences of the Treaty of Lisbon for the European Security and Defence Policy]. *Militaire Spectator, 179*(11), 544-557.

of the ESDP in 1999-2005. Following the example of the British, the Netherlands mainly focused on military capacity building and initiated the European Capability Action Plan (ECAP) in 2001 and cooperation between the EU and NATO.[8] During its active EU presidency in the second half of 2004, the Netherlands made big strides forward in the implementation of the Headline Goal 2010, the Battlegroups, the creation of the European Defence Agency (EDA) and the preparation of the EU operation in Bosnia. However, the referendum on the Constitutional Treaty of 2005 turned the tide. The political leaders in the ministries hesitated to continue playing an active role on this issue and reverted to the reflex of putting their money on NATO.

In 2008, Minister of Foreign Affairs Maxime Verhagen announced a change of policy. According to him, the focus of the Dutch foreign policy should shift to Europe: "a necessary condition for the Netherlands to be able to promote its interests in the world". Verhagen stated that the Netherlands had to invest in the ESDP since Europe would also have to be able to take autonomous military action, independently of NATO.[9] By that time, the United States had already expressed its support for the ESDP, and the Netherlands was increasingly looking to Germany instead of the blocking British. However, this change of policy did not result in the Netherlands taking the lead in this matter, even though it might have been expected to do so, as an unsuspected transatlantic country with a reputation of being militarily capable.

Formally, lip service is paid to the CSDP. A progressively orientated document from 2010 under former ministers of Foreign Affairs and Defence Verhagen and Van Middelkoop stated that "the Netherlands have an interest in a more effective and efficient CSDP. This will benefit our national security. This is a message that the Netherlands has been spreading for some years now".[10] However, CSDP practice takes its cue from the position expressed by Minister of Defence Hans Hillen: "I will consider all initiatives from a pragmatic viewpoint, with interest, but not rejecting them before seeing them".[11] A cautious 'no, unless' and not a

8 Venema, A. & Zandee, D. (2005). Europese Defensie: het Nederlandse EU-voorzitterschap [European Defence: the Dutch EU presidency]. *Atlantisch Perspectief, 29*(1), 15-20.

9 Verhagen, M. (2008). *Veranderende wereld, vaste waarden: buitenlands beleid in de 21e eeuw* [A changing world, fixed values: foreign policy in the 21st century]. *Internationale Spectator, 62*(10), 507-512. Verhagen, M. (2008, September 25). Maak eindelijk werk van een Europese interventiemacht [Finally start working on a European intervention force!]. *de Volkskrant*.

10 Letter from the ministers of Defence and Foreign Affairs. Toezegging notitie Gemeenschappelijk Veiligheids en Defensiebeleid onder Verdrag van Lissabon – Raad Algemene Zaken en Raad Buitenlandse Zaken [Commitment document Common Security and Defence Policy under the Treaty of Lisbon – General Affairs Council and Foreign Affairs Council], 16 June 2010.

11 Minister of Defence Hans Hillen. In *Ongecorrigeerd verslag van een algemeen overleg van de vaste kamercommissies buitenlandse zaken en defensie over de informele defensieraad* [Uncorrected report of general consultations of the standing parliamentary foreign affairs and defence committees on the informal Defence Council], 15 September 2011. Hans Hillen was Minister of Defence from 2010 to 2012 (November).

more positive 'yes, on condition that' attitude characterizes the Dutch policy on the CSDP. Despite some well-written documents, the Netherlands does not have its own, proactive agenda on defence and security in the EU. Due to this positioning, the Netherlands is a follower (with the United Kingdom and Germany leading the way): pragmatism (cost and direct output) and the condition that transatlantic relations will not be harmed, count.

However, in view of the level of Dutch defence spending, its active role in crisis management operations and the Dutch interests involved in an effective CSDP, the Netherlands should take a more active stance. In the field of security, economy, trade, migration, justice, the environment, and many other issues, the Netherlands shares far more interests with its European partners than with its traditional ally the United States. The emphasis on NATO as the cornerstone of our security policy is therefore, to a certain extent, outdated. NATO is dominated by the United States, which also constitutes the added value of this military alliance. But it is becoming increasingly clear that US interest in Europe and the willingness of the present political elite to do Europe's dirty work have strongly decreased. NATO is retaining its value as a forum where Europeans and Americans can meet, but when facing the complex security threats of the 21st century, the Europeans have to turn to the EU. The CSDP is a very important instrument in this respect and essential for the EU to retain its influence in the world. As Nick Witney so concisely put it, 'It's CSDP – or live in a world run by others'.[12]

The Netherlands has the position and reputation to be able to play an important part in the CSDP. It is a medium-sized country with a solid military image, but also has a good track record in the field of development cooperation. The Netherlands is moreover one of the pioneers in international defence cooperation. In addition, it maintains good relations with the United States, the United Kingdom and Germany. Due to its small size, it cannot be suspected of imposing a diktat, as happens quite often with the big EU countries. The Netherlands has credibility with the Member States prepared to take more robust military action as well as with countries that focus more on civilian crisis management. However, in recent years, this legitimacy has not been translated often enough into actual influence to further develop the CSDP.

There is no shortage of issues where this would be possible. The tricky points standing in the way of an effective CSDP and determining the medium-term agenda are developing a joint strategy, arriving at a comprehensive approach to security and crisis management, and generating the necessary civilian and military capabilities.

12 Witney, N. (2011, September). It's CSDP – or live in a world run by others. European Council on Foreign Relations. <http://ecfr.eu/content/entry/commentary_its_csdp_or_a_world_run_by_others> (accessed 15 May 2012).

9.4 Developing a Common Strategy

The international interests of the 27 Member States of the EU are largely similar. They all have much to gain by a strong EU in a multipolar world where Europe's relative weight is decreasing. It is evident that none of the EU Member States, not even the big three – United Kingdom, Germany and France – can optimally deploy their influence without united European action. The EU acts as a power multiplier which can operate effectively only if countries are prepared to weigh non-vital, national interests against long-term, shared European interests. This applies in the first place to the EU's foreign policy, but, as a corollary, also holds for the Union's security and defence policy.

In this context, the European Security Strategy of 2003 is an excellent example of diplomacy of the then High Representative for Common Foreign and Security Policy, Javier Solana.[13] He managed to get the then 15 Member States to endorse a joint threat analysis, which is still relevant today: terrorism, proliferation of weapons of mass destruction, regional conflicts, failing states and organized crime. In 2008, climate change, energy security and cyber security were added.[14] However, since the European Security Strategy only states what constitutes a threat to the EU, it remains unclear what actors are involved, what interests are to be defended and with what means and at what level of ambition the EU wants to defend these interests. The Strategy states this ambition only at a rather abstract level (need for effective multilateralism and a comprehensive approach) without specifying the capacities required.

The actual level of ambition of the EU is stated in the Headline Goals (Civilian and Military) and in the Petersberg Tasks, but these are outdated or hardly based on identified threats.[15] In 2006, the EDA presented an Initial Long-Term Vision for European Defence Capability and Capacity Needs, stating the qualitative requirements for the capacities needed for ESDP operations. ESDP operations should typically be expeditionary, multinational and comprehensive, thus increasing the importance of synergy between armed forces divisions and non-military actors in the field of capacities. The requirements regarding military capabilities such as rapid reaction capacity and continuation are also gaining significance.[16] The EDA has rightly inferred this from the experience gained so far in ESDP missions. But how far these kinds of missions also reflect the EU's strategic priorities is a question that still remains unanswered. The reason is that interests

13 *A Safer Europe in a Better World. European Security Strategy* (2003).

14 *Report on the Implementation of the European Security Strategy – Providing Security in a Changing World.* (2008, December 11). Brussels. <www.consilium.europa.eu/ueDocs/cms_Data/docs/pressdata/EN/reports/104630.pdf>.

15 Biscop, S. & Coelmont, J. (Eds.). (2011, June). *Europe deploys. Towards a civil-military strategy for CSDP* (Egmont Paper 49). Royal Institute for International Relations. Brussels: Academia Press.

16 European Defence Agency. (2006, October 3). *Long-term vision for European defence capability and capacity needs.*

have not been prioritized on the basis of a security strategy. As a result, the ESDP/CSDP has remained *ad hoc* and demand-driven, or has even been deployed to substitute for a strategic vision,[17] instead of becoming an important and indispensable instrument to strengthen the EU's foreign and security policy. That is why initiatives should be taken to develop such a strategic vision. Because of its coordinating and comprehensive character, the new European External Action Service is pre-eminently suitable to develop a strategy for the CSDP. High Representative Catherine Ashton should be put in charge of this project, which should have an open and inclusive character. To generate as many ideas and as much legitimacy and exchange as possible, such a strategy project should be set up as a kind of Strategic Defence Review process, offering room for a structured dialogue, such as in the European Convention in 2002/2003, and where extensive output will be provided by experts from outside the EU institutions. To streamline this project, it would be advisable to appoint a group of wise men, modelled after the Albright group which drafted the NATO strategic concept. In 2013, 10 years after the adoption of the European Security Strategy, a new strategic document should be ready, identifying the EU's vital interests (i.e., interests to be defended), priority regions and how these are translated into scenarios and capacities. However, an external security strategy would not suffice, since in the meantime, in 2009, an internal security strategy of the EU was established as well,[18] and integrating both documents into a comprehensive security strategy would be a big step forward. Such a comprehensive security strategy does justice to the broad nature of the EU as a security actor, which for years has been operating in the Area of Freedom, Security and Justice, both externally and internally, and where internal security is increasingly externalized.[19]
An often heard argument against such a strategy development is the fear that a new security strategy will reflect the lowest common denominator and will thus mean a step backwards compared to the current concept. However, this argument does not seem to hold up when taking into account the circumstances and timing of Solana's document. In 2003, Europe was more divided than ever around an 'old' and a 'new' Europe. At the time, there appeared to be a great need for a 'cleansing' project which would give the EU Member States the chance to pull themselves together and focus on what they had in common. Seen in this light, the chances of a new strategy project even seem better now: the United States is no longer interested in a 'divide and rule' policy in relation to the EU, but explicitly stimulates an independent European role. In addition, such a strat-

17 Gnesotto, N. (2009). The need for a more strategic EU. In A. De Vasconcelos (Ed.), *What ambitions for European defence in 2020?* (2nd ed.). Paris: EU Institute for Security Studies, pp. 29-38.

18 Internal security strategy for the European Union: 'Towards a European security model' [Draft]. (2010, February 23). <www.consilium.europa.eu/eeas/security-defence/european-security-strategy.aspx?lang=enl>.

19 *See, e.g.*, Rees, W. (2008). Inside out: The external face of EU internal security policy. *Journal of European Integration, 30*(1), 97-111.

egy project could be therapeutic in itself because it would raise Europeans' awareness of their common interests and of the EU's role in this respect, and could incite them to adopt a more strategic discourse in a rapidly changing world.

9.5 Realizing the Comprehensive Approach of the CSDP

The EU is a perfect example of an organization that has the many instruments at its disposal which can be deployed in conflict situations. To date, the Union has been unable to make sufficient use of this potential. One reason is the compartmentalization resulting from the Treaty of Maastricht, with, on the one hand, a supranational form of decision-making in the field of the Community's external relations (strong role of the Commission) and, on the other hand, an intergovernmental CSDP (with the Council being the dominant institution) and, in addition, within the CSDP itself, a division between civilian and military operations. For instance, decisions regarding the CSDP are made in the Council of Ministers of Foreign Affairs (or Defence), acting unanimously. The CSDP's design is therefore intergovernmental in nature in an otherwise supranationally organized Union. Moreover, from the beginning, the development of the CSDP has generated a separate military and civilian arm with distinct institutions, financing structures and planning.

Security and defence policy played an important role in the Convention on the Future of Europe where, in 2002/2003, the new Constitutional Treaty of 2004 was being prepared. In the end, the ESDP provisions in this Treaty were taken over, practically unchanged, in the subsequent Treaty of Lisbon.[20] The amendments aimed at increasing flexibility in decision-making, broadening and deepening the EU as a security actor and improving coherence in regard to the common foreign, security and defence policy. Lack of coherence was seen as the biggest obstacle to comprehensive action in which all available EU instruments would be used to their full potential. To overcome this obstacle, a new type of institution was set up in the EU structures: the European External Action Service (EEAS). The position of high representative for the Common Foreign and Security Policy (CFSP) was merged with that of commissioner for External Relations into a new high representative heading the EEAS as well as coordinating the actions of all commissioners with an external dimension in their portfolio. The institutions of the CSDP, such as the EUMS, the Crisis Management and Planning Directorate (CMPD) and the Civilian Planning and Conduct Capability (CPCC), have also been brought under the EEAS.

20 Missiroli, A. (2011). The new EU 'foreign policy' system after Lisbon: A work in progress. *European Foreign Affairs Review, 15*(4), 427-428.

Bringing all these foreign and defence policy instruments under one roof and under the control of one person will, in due course (consolidation of the EEAS is expected to take three more years), lead to more coherence and enhanced effectiveness of the CSDP.[21] This will require a change of culture within the structures, where thinking in comprehensive terms and coordination should be an automatic reflex. However, in the bureaucratic arena, the Commission has so far managed to retain much of its original competences (e.g., in the crucial area of development cooperation), resulting in a sort of 'nick' in policy: programming takes place in the EEAS, but subsequent implementation and most funds remain in the hands of the Commission. It seems that opportunities offered by the creation of the EEAS have in particular been missed in the field of 'early warning'[22] and in regard to a comprehensive conflict prevention policy. The effectiveness of EU crisis management should however be a first priority, and theological discussions on retaining competences in the field of Community decision-making should be secondary to this.
Despite these measures aimed at more coherence in foreign and defence policy, civilian and military strategic and operational planning under the CSDP still seems to take place in separate worlds. In 2008, this problem was partially solved. The CMPD was to take on the strategic planning of civilian-military missions, following which the CPCC would provide the operational planning and direct the missions. But military operations are still being prepared within the EUMS, and there are no less than seven possible operational headquarters, none of which are optimal for carrying out military operations. Therefore, general rationalization of the separate civilian-military planning and control and of this proliferation of headquarters is necessary.

9.6 Permanent EU Civilian-Military Operational Headquarters

As stated above, the EU can currently choose between seven headquarters for military operations. There are five national headquarters, which can be multinationalized *ad hoc* if used for EU operations. These are the headquarters in Northwood, Paris, Potsdam, Rome and Larissa. Regular exercises take place to enable conversion to an EU operational headquarters, resulting in a quintupling of infrastructure, connections, staff deployment and, of course, costs. From an operational perspective, the biggest drawback is the distance to the Brussels institu-

21 According to the Chief Executive Officer of the EEAS in a speech: O'Sullivan, D. (2011, January 14). Setting up the EEAS. <www.eeas.europa.eu/speeches/2011_1201_dos_iiea_en.pdf> (accessed 15 May 2012).

22 For recommendations in this respect, *see* Montenaro, L. & Schünemann, J. (2011, February 28). *Walk the talk: The EU needs an effective early warning system to prevent conflict and promote peace.* Madrid: FRIDE.

tions. Due to this distance, the comprehensive approach of EU operations does not really come into its own, while such an approach should precisely be one of the biggest added values of crisis management by the EU.

However, there are more drawbacks to the use of national headquarters. For instance, it took over three months before the French operational headquarters for the EU-Chad mission could be used. During this operation, 200 officers from other EU Member States stayed in Paris, which was reflected in the costs. Furthermore, for each operation, a country has to be found that is willing to run the financial, military and political risks of providing the headquarters. This was one of the reasons why the Netherlands advocated the use of national headquarters: guaranteed participation of a large EU country. However, past experience has shown that such extra risks for the country providing the operational headquarters impede and/or complicate the realization of operations. Lack of continuity is another major disadvantage. When an operation is terminated, the trained troops go back home, taking with them their experience and thus large parts of the institutional memory for EU operations. For the next mission, this has to be rebuilt from scratch.[23]

Another option for the EU is to borrow NATO headquarters capacities in Mons via the Berlin-Plus Agreement of 2003. However, experience with this during EU operation Althea in Bosnia-Herzegovina was not positive. The complex and slow decision-making proved to be a particular problem, and the different memberships of the EU and NATO led to complications in terms of access to military information (Cyprus and Malta are not Partnership for Peace members). In the event of the EU taking over NATO operations, Berlin-Plus could, with adaptations, still work, but is not a good alternative to a permanent, own command structure. In rudimentary terms, the EU already has such a structure, i.e., the Operations Centre in the EUMS in Brussels. But this is not a permanent structure and has core staffing only; when deployed, it would have to be 'beefed up' into a civilian-military operational headquarters.

It is proposed that this proliferation of headquarters should be rationalized into one permanent, well-staffed civilian-military operational headquarters in Brussels. In July 2011, High Representative Catherine Ashton issued an evaluation of the CSDP. Unfortunately, this evaluation is not publicly available by order of the United Kingdom. Meanwhile, it is clear that one of the spearheads of her report was the proposal for a permanent civilian-military planning and conduct capability, i.e., an operational headquarters.[24] A permanent civilian-military operational

23 Drent, M. & Zandee, D. (2010, January). *Breaking pillars. Towards a civil-military security approach for the European Union* (Clingendael Security Paper, No. 13). The Hague: Netherlands Institute of International Relations 'Clingendael'.

24 Britain blocks EU plans for 'operational military headquarters'. (2011, July 18). *Telegraph*. Ashton avoids using the term Operational Headquarters by order of the UK.

headquarters would not be another structure[25] but would replace existing structures such as the EU Operations Centre, the CMPD and the CPCC, and would also obviate the need to use the five national headquarters designated for EU operations. An EU headquarters would facilitate willingness to take part in EU operations. Guidance, planning and the guarantee of confidentiality can be better regulated. Having a permanent headquarters would moreover ensure more continuity in strategic planning, operational planning and command. In this proposed set-up, it will not be necessary to transfer all information to NATO or to a national headquarters after the planning process. In addition, an EU headquarters and the command and control system can be aligned with the specific civilian-military and comprehensive approach to crises, thus putting an end to separate planning for civilian and military missions. The proximity of the EEAS and the Commission in Brussels is important in this context. The reasoning that the 250 staff members of such an operational headquarters would duplicate the 11,000-strong NATO command structure is increasingly becoming a mantra of the British, who are becoming more and more isolated in this matter, rather than a credible argument.

Frustrated by London blocking progress on a permanent operational headquarters, the countries of the Weimar triangle (France, Germany and Poland) and Spain and Italy sent a support letter to Ashton. This letter is not public, but has been leaked via the media.[26] The letter suggests creating a permanent headquarters with a leading group of countries, without the United Kingdom. This would require using the Permanent Structured Cooperation (PSC) instrument introduced by the Treaty of Lisbon.[27] The letter should also be seen as a strong diplomatic signal to London to abandon the taboo of a Brussels EU headquarters. In this regard, the Netherlands stands a good chance of acting as a bridge between London and the other countries. Late 2011, it became clear that a temporary compromise was reached between the positions of the British and the Weimar group. From January 2012, a new civilian mission with military elements to strengthen maritime capacities in the Horn of Africa and the West-Indian Ocean (EUCAP HOA/WIO) will be led from the EU Operations Centre in Brussels. Thus, the EU returns to the headquarters compromise which had already been reached in 2004 but which so far has not been put into practice. Activation of the EU Operations Centre instead of the operational headquarters in Northwood, United King-

25 A condition for the Netherlands, which was in favour of setting up permanent civilian-military headquarters.

26 'Big five' tell Baroness Ashton to bypass Britain over EU Military Headquarters. (2011, September 8). *Telegraph*.

27 Art. 28 TEU: This Article allows a group of countries to work together more closely in the field of defence. Participation in PSC is for those countries that are prepared to meet military criteria attached in a protocol to the Treaty. However, disagreement exists over the advisability of PSC, and to date no agreement has been reached on the interpretation of the criteria of the protocol. *See* Mengelberg & Drent (2010).

dom, from which Operation Atalanta in the same area is being led, clearly constitutes an olive branch offered by the British. The small and non-permanent Operations Centre is, in its current form, no alternative to a permanent operational headquarters for the CSDP, but may indeed be the basis of a growth model for which perhaps the first step has been taken with this mission in the Horn of Africa.

An often heard argument is that the EU should first and foremost focus on building capacities for the CSDP. However, a sound headquarters capacity is an indispensable part of this. The current structure of controlling operations is needlessly cumbersome, slow, costly, ineffective and not civilian-military. The fact remains, though, that one of the CSDP's biggest problems is lack of military and civilian capabilities.

9.7 Building Capacities for the CSDP: Military, Civilian and Civilian-Military

9.7.1 *Military*

It is illustrative of the pressing situation of the EU's defence capacities that several 'force generation' conferences and months of negotiation are necessary to be able to find sufficient military equipment and troops for crisis management operations. For years, we have seen that the European countries lack certain capacities.[28] Since the CSDP is dependent on the capacities that Member States are willing to provide for EU operations on an *ad hoc* basis, this is a problem that keeps coming back. NATO, for that matter, has practically the same problems. Both organizations have tried to solve this by creating semi-permanent, rapidly deployable military units: the NATO Response Force and the EU Battlegroups.

So far, the EU Battlegroups have mainly been a useful exercise in multinational mobilization, acting as an education and training entity for militarily less advanced countries and as a capacities generator. But that is not enough. The Battlegroups were meant to intervene in conflicts and have never been deployed as such. The concept is criticized because the units would be too small (around 1500-2500), they would be less suitable for the most obvious tasks (such as humanitarian assistance, evacuation of EU citizens) and too much of the costs of mobilization and activation would have to be borne by the participating countries alone. Analogous to the proposals of the Polish EU presidency (second half of 2011), a number of measures could reduce the mobilization effort. This involves

28 European shortages still exist in the field of helicopters, protection against CBNR weapons, information, surveillance possibilities, air-to-air refuelling, precision ammunition and command and control systems.

extending the standby phase (from 6 to 12 months) in a more fixed, rotating composition with like-minded partners. Recurring, longer-term and fixed partnering in Battlegroups (such as the Netherlands with the United Kingdom and Germany) strengthens European military cooperation and is cost-efficient. In this context, the countries of the Weimar triangle have decided to set up a more structural Battlegroup and put it at the EU's disposal.
Deployability can be further enhanced by adding a civilian-military element and by increasing the speed with which parts of the Battlegroup are deployed (now: 5-10 days). The financing structure of the Battlegroups also needs urgent reforming. At the moment, the ATHENA mechanism for common financing covers only 10% of the costs of deployment, and the CSDP start-up fund, being a new article in the Treaty of Lisbon, has not yet been elaborated. The deployment itself is covered fully by the participating Member States.[29] In addition, in the event of activation, the ATHENA mechanism covers only the costs of transport by air, not by sea. Greater flexibility in this mechanism would enhance its applicability.
Over the past 20 years, the budgetary pressure on defence organizations in Europe has been considerable. The Netherlands is one of the countries that are prepared to mitigate the effects of cuts on the deployment potential of the armed forces by working together with other countries. A policy paper of April 2011 entitled 'Defence after the credit crisis: a smaller army in a turbulent world'[30] again strongly focuses on the possibilities of international cooperation. Apparently, due to the credit, crisis initiatives that used to be considered impossible have been taken in Europe. For instance, even the British and the French were forced to closely cooperate in the field of, e.g., nuclear capabilities, aircraft carriers, special combat units and unmanned reconnaissance aircraft. On account of constant cuts and rising costs per soldier, on the one hand, and the fact that European countries (can) no longer act alone, on the other, intensive cooperation is more necessary and logical than ever.
The wave of cuts in the defence budgets in Europe in 2010 (5%-10% on average[31]) also explains the new momentum at the informal meeting of EU defence ministers in Ghent in September of that year. There was only one item on the agenda of that informal gathering: how to bridge the gap between what is asked of the European armed forces and what they can actually provide. The ministers decided to take stock of the military resources suitable for cooperation. This so-called Ghent Initiative aims to maintain and increase national operational capaci-

29 For an interesting idea to calculate material contributions by Member States as 'in kind' contributions, *see* Wouters, P. (2008, June). *Balancing defence and security efforts with a permanently structured scorecard* (Egmont Papers, No. 23). Royal Institute for International Relations. Brussels: Academia Press.

30 Ministry of Defence. (2011, April 8). *Defensie na de kredietcrisis: een kleinere krijgsmacht in een onrustige wereld.*

31 EDA Defence Data – <www.eda.europa.eu/DefenceData>. The aggregate defence expenditure of the 26 EDA countries dropped from €201 billion in 2008 to €193 billion in 2010.

ties. These capacities should be more effective and more interoperable and, if that is not enough, more cost-effective as well.[32] The intention is that, by saving costs, the released funds will be invested to fill the shortages shared by the European countries. Thanks to this Ghent Initiative, 300 projects suitable for cooperation were identified. As a result, in late November 2011, the EDA issued a list of 11 concrete projects.[33]

These projects partly reflect what the EDA was already doing in terms of multinational projects, but also the shortages which the European countries turned out to have during the operation in Libya.[34] For instance, the development of precision ammunition and of air-to-air refuelling were again designated as priorities. The helicopter training programme, which has already been successful so far, will be extended and has been complemented by the training of pilots of transport aircraft. By pooling the determination of needs for satellite communication, an important strategic shortcoming can be tackled and considerable costs saved as well. The lack of Dutch interest in these projects is striking, although the Netherlands does participate in a network for maritime surveillance and the European Air Transport Fleet (EATF).

Dutch Minister of Defence Hillen proposed organizing an extraordinary ministerial conference to pool the initiatives at EU level and the various bilateral and multinational initiatives outside the EU framework.[35] The Netherlands thus chooses, quite rightly, to act as a facilitator of initiatives, but should also be more emphatic in demonstrating that the new momentum among the European Member States to work together at military level is supported by more active Dutch participation in new projects.

NATO also came with an initiative to spur on cooperation in defence matters, the so-called Smart Defence initiative of Secretary General Anders Fog Rasmussen. Both initiatives threatened to strongly overlap each other, but via informal coordination between the EU and NATO, complementary projects were proposed.[36]

The need for an extraordinary ministerial conference as proposed by the Dutch indicates that the different multinational and binational cooperation projects and

32 German-Swedish paper Food for thought. European imperative. Intensifying military cooperation in Europe. 'Ghent initiative'. (2010, November). <www.europarl.europa.eu/meetdocs/2009_2014/documents/sede/dv/sede260511deseinitiative_/sede260511deseinitiative_en.pdf>.

33 Helicopter Pilot Training; Maritime Surveillance Network; Naval Training and Logistics; Medical Field Hospitals; Air-to-Air Refuelling (AAR); European Satellite Communications Procurement Cell (ESCPC); Future Military Satellite Communication; Intelligence, Reconnaissance, Surveillance (ISR); Pilot Training; European Air Transport Fleet (EATF); Smart Munitions.

34 With thanks to Dick Zandee.

35 Minister of Defence. (2011, September 22-23). *Geannoteerde Agenda informele bijeenkomst EU Ministers van Defensie te Wroclaw* [Annotated Agenda informal meeting EU Ministers of Defence in Wroclaw]. Despite this initiative having been included in Ashton's CSDP report, no date has been fixed yet.

36 Minister of Defence. (2011, October 5-6). *Verslag van de NAVO-ministeriële te Brussel* [Report of the NATO ministerial meeting in Brussels].

initiatives lack a coordination mechanism that monitors 'top down' the overall deployment capability of the European armed forces. The EU offers opportunities as a facilitator of military cooperation, the aim being to achieve the highest output with scarce resources.[37] The EU Member States, including the Netherlands, have so far not exploited these opportunities to their full potential. This mainly concerns the EDA established in 2004, and also the role which the European Commission can play in research and stimulation of market forces in the defence industry. The EDA's task is to promote cooperation between Member States in the field of military capabilities. Particular priorities in this regard are harmonization of capacity requirements and breaking protectionism towards national defence industries. A voluntary Code of Conduct agreed in 2006, which offers companies from other Member States the opportunity to compete for defence orders, is a small step forward in this regard. The EDA, moreover, manages a small number of projects, for example, the 'Force Protection Programme', in which 20 countries develop, amongst others, joint technology for the protection of troops in urban environments. However, for the moment, the EDA's potential is being insufficiently exploited because the Agency is understaffed and underfinanced and many EU Member States still prefer to plan, to develop and to buy equipment at national level. To counter this tendency, the EDA should be given more influence in coordinating planning, standardizing and ensuring interoperability, harmonizing the determination of requirements and creating civilian-military synergy.

The EDA's activities relating to the 'dual use' development of equipment should also be stimulated. It may be worthwhile to seek more intensive cooperation with civil-technological companies and find synergies with developments in this field. Under market circumstances, capacities can be developed better and at lower cost (e.g., satellites and sensors). The EDA can also be given a coordinating and guiding role in preventing duplication of equipment, resources and tasks. In this respect, it is crucial that, already in the planning phase, coordination with co-planners from other European countries takes place. The EDA can facilitate this.

In addition, the opportunities offered by the Treaty of Lisbon (Article 179.1 TFEU) for pooling Research and Technology funds should be exploited. In this way, defence research can be covered by the EU's research budget. This would lead to a better use of the still highly fragmented, shrinking, nationally financed budgets and would do much to boost the European armed forces.

The European armed forces (and not least the European taxpayer) need an efficient European defence economy. The European Commission has a strong position when it comes to liberalizing the defence industry in Europe, where protec-

---

37 *See also* Drent, M., Homan, C. & Hagemeijer, W. (2011, September). *Internationale militaire samenwerking: knelpunten en kansen* [International military cooperation: problems and opportunities] (Clingendael Policy Brief No. 6). The Hague: Netherlands Institute of International Relations, Clingendael.

tionism and inefficiency are still rife. The Commission's Defence Procurement Directive of 2009, providing for partial application of internal market rules also to the defence industry, has been in force since 21 August 2011. Transposition into national law is still lagging behind. The Netherlands ought to set an example in this regard, as well as advocate strict enforcement of competition rules.
For European countries to optimize their cooperation on military issues, a number of internationally agreed conditions will have to be met. For this, the Netherlands and the other European states will have to be prepared to take a broader, European view of their national armed forces, considering them as part of a combined European defence capability. Although, in this respect, the Netherlands can only exercise limited influence in the EU and NATO, it could play a significant role as a front runner. The Dutch have built a sound reputation as pioneers in the field of defence cooperation and, as a result, are relatively well placed to encourage other countries to join them in exploiting existing mechanisms and in developing new initiatives.

9.7.2 *Civilian*

The EU is increasingly called upon to deploy ever more intensive and longer civilian missions. However, mobilizing civilian capabilities for missions carries problems of its own. At the moment, the mandates of the joint civilian missions would comprise about 2950 staff members. However, only 2400 civilian staff positions are actually occupied. This means that 550 positions remain unfilled, with all the resulting consequences for the effectiveness of these missions. The EU Member States are responsible for supplying staff to the missions which they themselves decided to deploy. Recruiting civilian staff with the right expertise and experience proves a bottleneck. Such staff include judges, public prosecutors, penitentiary staff, election observers, police staff and experts in good governance. It partly concerns experts who are also hard to find in the Member States themselves. Good employment conditions and career prospects are lacking as well. In many countries, recruitment is not systematic, nor are good preparation and training programmes in place. To improve this, all Member States are expected to develop a national strategy for civilian crisis management, indicating what capabilities will be made available and how the staff involved will be prepared.[38]
Despite this push in the right direction, the Council decisions drafted by the Member States themselves are not, or not adequately, complied with. This also applies to the Netherlands, where attempts at coordination of the Dutch contribution to civilian crisis management made by the Ministry of Foreign Affairs encounter resistance from the 'supplying' ministries, such as Security and Justice.

38 Drent, M. (2010). Tien jaar het EVDB: Problemen en Prioriteiten [Ten years of ESDP: Problems and priorities]. *Internationale Spectator, 64*(1), 16-20.

If in this decentralized manner insufficient civilian capabilities are generated, the EU needs to take the initiative itself and create permanent pools of sufficient civilian staff. These should be properly trained and be deployable on short notice. Civilian units such as the Crisis Response Team pool, the pool of Security Sector Reform Experts and the Integrated Police Units do exist, but mainly on paper only. These units should be better staffed, trained and be on standby, thus constituting actually available capacities. Moreover, a permanent pool of potential heads of mission should be created. It is quicker and more effective to, from the very beginning, involve the intended head of mission (and his direct team) in the planning and preparatory phase of a mission. The EU also has a role to play in providing a framework for the highly fragmented and qualitatively varied training landscape for civilian staff in the Member States themselves. A coordinating body within the EEAS that brings together training supply and demand and monitors the comprehensive civilian-military approach would be a solution.[39]

9.7.3 *Civilian-Military*

To a certain extent, military and civilian missions need the same material capabilities. Overlap can especially be seen in the areas of communication, information, protection, transport and logistics. This should be taken into account in the determination of needs for and development of these capabilities, which will greatly improve civilian-military cooperation in the field as well as save costs due to upscaling. At the same time, over the past few years, the CSDP has acquired a new dimension besides its strictly external nature. When the EU is referred to as security actor, this increasingly also means providing security against risks and threats at *national* level, i.e., within the EU Member States. This is clearly reflected by the Solidarity Clause in the Treaty of Lisbon (Article 222). The Union and the Member States have agreed to take joint action if a Member State is hit by a terrorist attack or a natural or man-made disaster. According to this clause, such action may also involve military means.[40] Here too, there is an overlap with the military side in terms of resources. The internal security organizations Frontex, Cepol, Eurojust and Europol also make use of satellite communication and surveillance and detection capacities, and where, for instance, unmanned airplanes are developed for military purposes, these will also be of interest to this sector.[41] The Maritime Surveillance Network that is being developed in the framework of

39 Jacob, G. (2011, September). *EU training for civilian CSDP – Which coherence?* (Security Policy Brief, No. 28). Brussels: Egmont Institute.

40 In this respect it should be remembered that if EU action under the solidarity clause has a military character, the Council must still decide unanimously. But in the event of measures without such military dimension, a qualified majority will suffice.

41 Zandee, D. (2010). Europa moet, ook voor defensie! [Europe is a must, also for defence!]. *Atlantisch Perspectief, 34*(6).

the Ghent Initiative is a good example of a capacity where civilian and military interests coincide.

9.8 Conclusion

On many fronts, the CSDP of the EU needs to be further elaborated. The Treaty of Lisbon provides excellent scope for this. It is especially the implementation and exploitation of the possibilities offered by the Treaty that may make a difference. In the coming years, the following key items will be on the agenda: strategy development, further implementation of the comprehensive security approach and the development of military, civilian and civilian-military capabilities. Strategy development is a first requirement to identify what military and civilian capacities are necessary for what tasks, which suggests that this should be the main priority on the European agenda. However, this is not completely true: the need for an effective European headquarters has now become so urgent that this matter has now become separate from strategy development. Furthermore, the shortages in military and civilian capabilities were already relevant eight years ago and have still not been tackled.

A European Security Strategy '2.0' presupposes solidarity in security between the European countries. At the moment, under pressure of the financial and euro crisis, short-term interests prevail, while it is precisely in times of crisis that big steps can be taken. Is the Netherlands too small to act as a pioneer? When the ESDP was first launched, the Finnish and Swedes were not too small to provide the French-British military initiative with a civilian arm. Since the Netherlands has good relations with the British and Germans and has an appealing military track record, also in the field of multinational, military cooperation, it is relatively well placed to head initiatives.

10 Limits to the Enlargement of the European Union

Jan Marinus Wiersma

The fall of the Berlin Wall and the collapse of the communist system are far behind us. They were at the root of the ambition to unite Europe under the roof of the European Union (EU). By 2012, this goal has only partly been achieved. The Union may have been considerably enlarged, but an important group of countries is still in the waiting room. The most notable among these is Turkey, which has already been working together with the Union for dozens of years, for instance, in a customs union. Most countries of the Western Balkans have not made much progress in the accession process either. 'The hour of Europe has come', exclaimed Luxembourg's Minister of Foreign Affairs Jacques Poos in 1991. What he actually meant was that the EU had to take former Yugoslavia under its wing and end the conflict flaring up in the region. The fact that nothing came of this was something that the population of these countries learnt the hard way. In the end, it was NATO that enforced peace twice. By way of compensation and for the sake of stability in the region, all countries of the Western Balkans were offered the prospect of EU membership at a European summit in Thessaloniki (June 2003). However, the only Balkan state that actually succeeded in becoming a member was Slovenia. Negotiations with Iceland are continuing, and considering that this country is already largely integrated, membership will not be a problem, at least not for the EU. Many inhabitants of the country itself are sceptical. Nevertheless, it was with a fair amount of optimism that, in October 2011 (which was repeated in 2012), the European Commission presented the annual progress report on the countries of the Western Balkans, Turkey and Iceland. According to Stefan Füle, the responsible European Commissioner, 2011 was a good year for European enlargement.[1] The question is, however, to what extent his optimism is justified. To answer this question, this chapter provides a critical analysis of the accession process so far. Special attention is paid to the shifts in the position of the Netherlands in particular and of the EU in general, which took shape after the enlargement rounds of 2004 and 2007. Of course, this is partly a snapshot in time – the EU but also the candidate Member States are

1 Melin, A.S. (2011, November 13). *De EU breidt uit, koste wat het kost* [The EU is expanding whatever the cost]. <www.presseurop.eu/nl/content/ article/1053661-de-eu-breidt-uit-koste-wat-het-kost> (accessed 11-11-2011).

moving targets – but a clear trend can nevertheless be discerned: a less enthusiastic one. The boundaries of the EU are not so much geographical – in principle any European country can become a member – as determined by politics, by the EU's absorption capacity. They are therefore time-bound and flexible.[2] The EU and the Member States say they are keeping their promises made to Southeast Europe and Turkey. New Eastern neighbours such as Ukraine and Moldavia might as well, for the time being, forget about their European ambitions. The EU is said to have reached its limits for now. But this has more to do with the nature of these countries than with a decision in principle. Should Switzerland and Norway decide to knock on the door tomorrow, the boundaries will suddenly prove flexible again.

10.1 Enlargement in 2012

Where does the enlargement process stand in 2012? Negotiations with Turkey have practically come to a halt. In 2006, talks about a number of negotiation chapters were suspended by the EU because of Turkey's refusal to extend the association treaty with the EU to include Cyprus, something which it did in the case of the other new Member States. Ankara argues that the Greek Cypriots are blocking direct trade in the Turkish northern part of the island. France has moreover stipulated that the EU should not discuss chapters directly related to membership with Turkey. The former government in Paris was an outspoken opponent of Turkish accession and wanted a privileged partnership with the country. Relations between both countries are also under pressure because of the Armenian question.

The credibility of the negotiations is suffering severely from this situation. Both sides no longer seem to take these talks seriously, which has quite a negative impact on public opinion in Turkey. Opposition to the EU is voiced more and more often and increasingly overtly. The country's current economic success is being compared with the EU's euro troubles. In the field of foreign policy, Ankara is increasingly acting on its own: it is much more critical of Israel than before and strongly focused on enhancing Turkish influence in the region. This goes against the agreement that candidate Member States align their external activity with that of the EU. Turkey is becoming less tolerant of criticism of its domestic policy, and, somewhat provocatively, froze relations with the EU during Cyprus' half-year Presidency of the EU. However, Turkey has not completely abandoned its European ambitions, as is evident from the creation of a separate Europe ministry. Also, the Turkish government regularly points to the intrinsic

2 Lagendijk, J. & Wiersma, J.M. (2001). *Brussel-Warschau-Kiev. Op zoek naar de grenzen van de Europese Unie* [Brussels-Warsaw-Kiev. Pushing the boundaries of the European Union] Amsterdam, The Netherlands: Uitgeverij Balans, pp. 163-166.

value of operating on the basis of EU standards. But it is in no hurry to open non-taboo negotiation chapters like competition, social policy and procurement. Reforms that might result from such negotiations meet with resistance in Turkey itself. Why make concessions without knowing what will be offered in return? The situation being as it is, Ankara and Brussels aim to intensify their relations in areas that lie outside the scope of the negotiations but do support the process, e.g., visa policy, migration, and energy policy. The European Council of December 2011 endorsed this approach.[3] However, many EU Member States are hesitant to support visa liberalization for Turkey, which has high priority in Ankara.

In the 1990s, the Western Balkans missed the enlargement boat, even though the liberal nature of the former communist regime had given Yugoslavia a headstart over many other Eastern Bloc countries. After a period of ostensible peace, Yugoslavia violently fell apart after 1991. The aftermath of the bloody conflict and the unresolved simmering tensions hinder the region's development. The leaders of that time opted for a hard nationalistic line which is still reverberating today. The sanctions imposed on Serbia stimulated the emergence of criminal networks which still exist and are active throughout the region. The international community enforced peace through the Dayton Agreements and UN Resolution 1244/99 for Kosovo, but its implementation encountered all kinds of obstacles, causing regional and ethnic disputes to persist. Furthermore, the attraction of EU membership – the transforming potential of the membership prospect – seems to be less strong in this region than in the countries that acceded to the Union in 2004 and 2007. There, agreement was unanimous, which is far less the case in the Western Balkans.

This background is one of the reasons why Croatia only reached the finishing line in 2011. Negotiations were concluded in June of that year and the accession treaty was signed in December 2011. The country is expected to accede in 2013. However, it took a lot more time to meet Brussels' – strict – requirements than originally envisaged. Besides, Croatia has been given a *provisional* green light. It will still need to put some of its affairs in order by 2013, particularly its judiciary and the enforcement of fundamental rights.[4] The European Commission will, partly on Dutch request, monitor Croatia's continued implementation of the necessary reforms. Should the half-yearly reports of the Commission indicate the country's failure to comply, 'appropriate measures' may be taken. By this, the Netherlands also means the possibility to postpone Croatia's actual accession.[5]

At the same time, Zagreb was worried about the outcome of the referendum on accession. After all, over the past years the EU has been given varying scores in the media. The population was outraged over the extradition of former general Gotovina to the Tribunal in The Hague. It is feared that employment will suffer

3 European Council Conclusions, 9 December 2011, EUCO 139/11.

4 Dutch House of Representatives. *Vergaderjaar* 2011-2012, 23 987, No. 120, p. 5.

5 Dutch House of Representatives. *Vergaderjaar* 2010-2011, 23 987, No. 117, p. 3.

as a result of EU membership. But the concerns proved groundless: in January 2012, two thirds of the Croatian electorate voted in favour of accession.

In the case of Montenegro – candidate member since December 2010 – the Commission proposed, in 2011, to start negotiations on membership. Here too, the Netherlands remained on the fence, because it was not convinced that Montenegro had a credible track record.[6] For instance, a large number of new laws and reforms were adopted only very recently and, consequently, Montenegro has not yet been able to show that they are actually being implemented. In addition, according to the Dutch government, the country has provided insufficient proof that corruption and organized crime are being adequately dealt with. However, it does agree with Brussels that, in possible negotiations, the most difficult issues should be raised first: rule of law, fundamental rights, justice, freedom and security.[7] This is a lesson learnt from the accession negotiations with Croatia, during which these topics were only brought up at a later stage and the Commission was unable to take interim measures in this regard.[8] Negotiation Chapters 23 and 24 (judiciary and fundamental freedoms; justice, freedom and security) have been given absolute priority. The Dutch criticism was taken on board at the December summit of 2011. The European Council decided not to set a date yet for the start of the negotiations. Eventually, this was done in spring 2012, following new Commission reports about the above mentioned subjects.

"Macedonia is ready to start accession negotiations", repeats the European Commission in its 2011 and 2012 reports. This time the Netherlands agrees with the Commission. For instance, a broad package of legislation has been drawn up to strengthen the judiciary, and the elections held in Macedonia in June 2011 proceeded successfully. Nevertheless, the Netherlands points out that Macedonia must ensure that the reforms and adopted legislation are implemented.[6] For example, in the field of human rights and protection of minorities, little progress has been made – despite increased European involvement in Macedonia since 2001.[9] The Netherlands therefore states that the country must continue working on cooperation with and the integration and socio-economic position of various ethnic minorities.[6] Macedonia's accession process is moreover slowed down by a lingering name dispute with Greece. According to Athens, the name of its neighbour implies a claim on Greek territory because it refers to the Greek province of Macedonia. Both countries have to find a joint solution, says The Hague.[10] However, this may still take a long time, also considering that the Greek government

6 Dutch House of Representatives. *Vergaderjaar* 2011-2012, 23 987, No. 120, p. 9.

7 Ibid., pp. 9-10.

8 European Commission. Enlargement strategy and main challenges 2011-2012, p. 23.

9 Koinova, M. (2011). Challenging assumptions of the enlargement literature: The impact of the EU on human and minority rights in Macedonia. *Europe-Asia Studies, 63*(5), 808 and 822.

10 Ibid.

is now mainly focusing on the debt crisis.[11] In the current Greek political context, there is no room for a political gesture to Macedonia; the issue is still too sensitive. To soften up the authorities in Skopje, the European Commission has started a High Level Accession Dialogue as a kind of surrogate for real negotiations.

10.2 Major Political Obstacles

As for the other countries of the Western Balkans, it would be more accurate for the Commission to refer to stagnation than progress reports, not so much because of a total lack of progress but because of political instability and regional conflicts that seem impossible to resolve. Albania, Bosnia-Herzegovina, Serbia and Kosovo, as (potential) candidate Member States, must not only meet the stringent EU requirements, but are also struggling with some major political obstacles. Having learnt its lesson, the Netherlands does not want to import these political problems into the EU. It is not alone in this view, and a new element has actually been added to the concept of absorption capacity: these (potential) candidate Member States must have settled their mutual conflicts and internal political problems before they can accede to the EU. Such a political conflict was in fact imported when the divided island of Cyprus acceded to the Union in 2004. Despite the many objections, Cyprus became a member because Greece exerted a great deal of pressure by threatening to veto the accession of the Central and East European countries. The EU moreover expected that the partition of the island was coming to an end.[12] Nearly 10 years after this decision, however, an agreement between the Greek and Turkish Cypriots is still not in sight. It is believed that this situation is not likely to arise a second time. Regional cooperation is therefore a must. It is unlikely for one Member State to again put that much pressure on the rest as around 2004, because new Member States are now admitted one by one.

What are the (political) obstacles? First of all, Albania is at risk of becoming the laughing stock of the enlargement process because of the ongoing political polarization and the resulting impasse in the country. The Netherlands shares the Commission's criticism about the lack of progress in the country and, in 2011, spoke of a lost year for Albania.[13] This situation did not actually change in 2012. The then Dutch government expressed reservations when, in October of that year, the European Commission proposed to grant the country conditional candidate status. In addition, the accession process of Bosnia-Herzegovina has reached a deadlock, on account of continuing disagreement between three ethnic religious

11 Pop, V. (2011, November 9). Greek government collapse not helping Macedonia. *EuObserver*. <http://euobserver.com/15/114224> (accessed 20 November 2011).

12 Müftüler-Bac, M. (1999). The Cyprus debacle: What the future holds. *Futures, 31*(6), 571.

13 Dutch House of Representatives. *Vergaderjaar* 2011-2012, 23 987, No. 120, p. 11.

groups: the Bosniaks (Muslims), the Croats (Roman Catholic) and the Serbs (Orthodox). After the October 2010 elections, the political leaders took a very long time forming a central government, the result being that the badly needed reforms as yet fail to materialize.[14] In Serbia, on the other hand, a major obstacle has been removed by the arrest and transfer of the last two war criminals – Ratko Mladic and Goran Hadzic – to the Yugoslavia Tribunal in The Hague. The European Commission is satisfied with the pace of reforms in the country. Yet, in 2011, the Kosovo issue threatened to become the next serious impediment to Serbia acquiring the status of candidate Member State of the EU.[15]
The European Commission, supported in this by the Netherlands, demanded that the candidate status be preceded by Serbia and Kosovo engaging in a positive dialogue.[16] In December 2011, the European Council considered that this demand had been insufficiently met and postponed a decision on Serbia's status. At the very end of the summit of March 2012, Belgrade and Pristina reached agreement on technical cooperation and on Kosovo's participation in regional conferences. This cleared the last obstacle to Serbia's candidacy, but has not solved the Kosovo issue. Despite 22 European Member States having recognized Kosovo's independence, Serbia keeps considering the country as an (autonomous) province, its original status.[17] An example is the hard-won compromise on Kosovo's participation in regional conferences. The name of the country may be used, but reference must be made to the fact that this should not be regarded as official recognition. However, it is inconceivable that negotiations between Belgrade and Pristina can lead to restoration of the *status quo ante*. The Albanian Kosovars will never voluntarily agree to this and a violent solution is out of the question because of the presence of international forces. An impasse has arisen, leading to distressing situations in North Kosovo. On the one hand, Belgrade wants to support the Serbian Kosovars in the North who refuse to accept the central government in Pristina. Serbia, on the other hand, also wants to meet the European Commission's requirements so as to start official membership negotiations.[18] Since the EU is internally divided over the Kosovo policy and the Serbian government claims to have too little influence in North Kosovo, it seems unlikely that either party, Serbia or EULEX, will be prepared to intervene and restore order in and around the city of Mitrovica. At the moment, there is a power vacuum in the northern part of this city, leading to all kinds of excesses.

14 European Commission. Enlargement strategy and main challenges 2011-2012, p. 16.

15 The pull of Brussels. At least the Western Balkans is still starry-eyed about the European Union. (2011, October 15). *The Economist*. <www.economist.com/node/21532306> (accessed 20 November 2011).

16 Dutch House of Representatives. *Vergaderjaar* 2011-2012, 23 987, No. 120, p. 11.

17 Ministry of Foreign Affairs in Kosovo. Countries that have recognized the Republic of Kosova. <www.mfa-ks.net/?page=2,33> (accessed 20 November 2011).

18 The pull of Brussels (2011).

This situation is being cleverly exploited by local corrupt politicians. Matters can only improve if Serbia and Kosovo – supported by the UN, NATO and the EU – demonstrate that through practical cooperation certain problems can be solved, e. g., in the field of mutual recognition of diplomas and customs agreements. Belgrade must be prepared to restore law and order in North Kosovo together with EULEX, the 'rule of law' operation of the EU. In 2012, parliamentary elections were held in Serbia. The polarized debate on Kosovo left the outgoing pro-European government little room for concessions. Its place was taken by a more nationalist-oriented coalition that, nevertheless, has so far respected the policy adopted by its predecessor. Serbia will not be able to accede to the EU without an agreement on Kosovo's status. In this regard, the country has two options: to recognize Kosovo as an independent state, or to adopt another construction of international law. The first option is invariably rejected and the latter will be vetoed by Pristina. Ironically, the EU leaves both possibilities open. Within the EU, 22 Member States want Kosovo recognized and some will certainly block Serbia's membership of the EU should this fail to occur. The remaining five will try to prevent the EU from making such a demand. So, it is not only Serbia that has to make a choice which will open the door to the EU. The same goes for the Union. As long as this does not happen, the bookmakers will give the country little chance of success. In the meantime, the European Commission wants to strengthen relations with Kosovo by starting a feasibility study about a Stabilisation and Association Agreement with the country.

10.3 Low in Ambition

The above analysis does not justify the Commission's optimism about progress in the Western Balkans and Turkey. Even in the most positive case – Croatia – the EU has made a reservation. In addition, the multiannual financial framework for 2014-2020, as proposed by the European Commission, shows that the EU neither expects the accession process to speed up, nor sees any chance of stimulating it through extra investments.[19] Proposals by candidate Member States to allot more money have been ignored.

At a meeting with the Dutch House of Representatives, Serbian Deputy Prime Minister Bozidar Djelic referred to a joint proposal by the countries of the Western Balkans about financing the enlargement of the EU in 2014-2020.[20] Two points in his argument stand out. There is a big difference between the amounts that candidate Member States receive through the Instrument for Pre-Accession Assistance (IPA) and what they, as new Member States, will subsequently be

19 COM (2011) 500/1 final.

20 Address by H.E. Bozidar Djelic, 10 November 2011, European Affairs Committee of the Dutch House of Representatives.

able to claim from the EU structural and cohesion funds. So, before accession they may well receive less money than they can spend and after accession too much. They may even, for lack of absorption capacity, become net contributors, which happened before. The region thinks to have found a solution to this by offering candidates, before accession, the opportunity to draw from the major EU funds, with the additional advantage that they will have time to learn how to apply the complex financial rules of the EU. This would of course involve an increase in pre-accession assistance, which can however be recovered later – after accession – by reducing amounts from the funds. Apparently, Serbia's proposal has fallen on stony ground. It is not mentioned in the draft multiannual financial framework which the Commission presented in Brussels in June 2011. The draft does not go beyond the proposal to dress up assistance to candidate Member States as support they may later receive from the EU funds. Brussels wants to keep its purse strings tight, and advancing expenditure implies increasing expenditure now, without it being clear when this can be recovered since it is uncertain when the countries of the Western Balkans will become members.

However, the second plan also seems interesting: to offer the candidate Member States the chance to take part in the so-called European semester. This is a new EU arrangement – a result of the euro crisis – enabling the European Commission to annually scrutinize the financial operations and economic policies of the Member States, propose corrections where necessary and even impose sanctions. Participating candidate Member States could thus prove that their policies are fiscally and economically sound. In exchange, the EU would have to help develop a guarantee scheme for the Western Balkans that would make it easier and cheaper for the region to borrow on the financial markets. The guarantees should be limited in size. The current EU arrangement for macroeconomic support to the region can serve as a basis. In this way, the candidate Member State would kill two birds with one stone: a sound financial and economic policy 'certified' by Brussels, and cheaper loans. However, the response has been less than enthusiastic. The eurozone (and thus the EU) is up to its ears in the euro crisis and has already issued enough guarantees to the debtor countries within the eurozone. Guarantees – even if they need not be recovered – are entered in the accounts and thus become, de facto, an item of expenditure, something Brussels can apparently do without.

In June 2010, a report came out about the future financing of the enlargement, commissioned by the European Commission to an evaluation consortium led by GHK and Technopolis.[21] The report examines four options, the most drastic one being a zero option whereby IPA is discontinued and the candidate Member States fall back on the financial programme for the EU's neighbouring countries. The second option is based on continuation of the present policy with more or

21 *Evaluation to support the preparation of pre-accession financial instruments beyond 2013.* (2011, June 13). Brussels: European Policy Evaluation Consortium.

less the same amounts. Option three involves only allocating funds for assistance if the accession conditions are met and nothing for socio-economic development. The variant most attractive to the candidates involves an increase in funds for socio-economic development. The writers of the report consider the cheaper options undesirable and the more costly policy unfeasible, due to predictable resistance from the countries that are net contributors to the EU. Therefore, the preferred option is continuation of the existing policy.

The European Commission has arrived at the same conclusion and has reserved roughly the same amounts for 2014-2020 as in the current multiannual framework. A sum of €100 billion will be earmarked for external policy as a whole, more than €12.5 billion of which for enlargement covering a period of seven years.

The Dutch government's reaction to the first proposals of the European Commission does not mention the costs of enlargement,[22] presumably because it agrees with the approach taken. However, the government is critical of the foreign policy expenditure as a whole – not enough choices are made. The Netherlands wants priorities set: neighbourhood policy, poverty reduction and stability, security and crisis management.

Perhaps other Member States will take up the cause of the candidate Member States; however, the negotiations on the multiannual framework are expected to focus on other matters. How big may the EU budget be? Should it target new priorities such as innovation? Can agricultural expenditure be reduced in this context? May the EU start imposing levies of its own, e.g., in the form of a financial transaction tax? And – last but not least – what will happen with the rebates some Member States are receiving now? In the tough fight that this will entail, little attention will go to the interests of the candidate Member States. The European Commission has already taken this into account. It is too bad for the creativity of Djelic *cum suis*.

With the position it has adopted, the European Commission in fact endorses the Dutch government's stance of 2011: "The road to actual membership is long, very long".[23]

10.4 Deadlock

The present deadlock in the European accession process is much like the situation in 2000, when negotiations with the 12 candidates could be seen to progress only slowly. However, the response at the time was completely different. Around the turn of the century, the Dutch government stated that the accession process should keep its momentum, allowing all candidates to hold on to the concrete

22 Dutch House of Representatives. *Vergaderjaar* 2010-2011, 21 501-20, No. 53.

23 Dutch House of Representatives. *Vergaderjaar* 2011-2012, 23 987, No. 120, p. 3.

prospect of European integration and ensuring they would not lag behind an ever-developing EU.[24] Structuring the accession process via a 'roadmap' and 'timetable' was considered a good idea to be able to wrap up the first negotiations by late 2002. "A so-called 'hold-up' situation should be avoided, where owing to a lack of visible progress both parties lose their motivation for the process as a whole", wrote the then Dutch government.[25] So, at the time, clear political guidance as well as support for those lagging behind was needed to keep the train going.[26]

How different the situation is now. In 2011, the Dutch government considers itself strict and fair, the guiding motto being 'first the red lines, then the red carpet', meaning that the Netherlands

> will only be able to approve the accession of new Member States if they meet the strict criteria, in particular the Copenhagen criteria, including the EU's absorption capacity and the tightened enlargement criteria of 2006.[27]

In addition, the Netherlands closely monitors whether the new legislation and reforms are actually being implemented. Of course, this is an implicit criticism of how the earlier enlargements of 2004 and 2007 were handled. This was said to have been a matter of just ticking off the list of laws without sufficient attention being paid to implementation and 'track records'.[28]

However, the change in the political climate surrounding enlargement is not recent. The enlargement of 2004 and particularly that of 2007 also met with a lot of incomprehension and criticism from public opinion. Possible membership of Turkey did not go down well with many people either. Opposition to further expansion of the EU was one of the reasons why a majority of the Dutch population voted against the Constitutional Treaty in 2005.[29] This 'no' put a resolute end to people's tacit agreement with the widening and deepening of European integration. And this happened not only in the Netherlands. Growing objections among voters forced many governments to be more critical of the enlargement process. At the 2006 Madrid Summit, it was therefore agreed, also on Dutch request, to tighten the accession criteria. This implied a far greater emphasis on the candidate's capacity to implement the *acquis* – particularly in the field of justice and home affairs. Furthermore, new criteria were formulated, namely, public opinion support (in the EU and the acceding Member State) and the absorption

24 Dutch House of Representatives. *Vergaderjaar* 2000-2001, 23 987, No. 3, p. 4.

25 Ibid., p. 5.

26 Ibid., p. 6.

27 Dutch House of Representatives. *Vergaderjaar* 2011-2012, 23 987, No. 120, p. 3.

28 Ibid., p. 4.

29 Van Grinsven, P., van Keulen, M. & Rood, J. (2006). *Over verkiezingen, politisering en het Nederlands Europa-beleid* [On elections, politicisation and the Dutch Europe policy]. The Hague: Netherlands Institute of International Relations Clingendael, p. 6.

capacity of the EU (to admit new members). Absorption capacity, however, is a vague concept: it concerns the EU's capacity to integrate new Member States, for instance, at institutional (broadening and deepening of cooperation should go together), financial (would it not be too expensive?) and social level (e.g., unwanted labour migration), or it is linked to public acceptance of enlargement. The current EU Member States place different emphases when putting the concept into practice. The criterion has as yet never been used to block accession, nor did it come up in regard to the newest prospective member, Croatia. This may be different in the case of Turkey, since possible accession of this (much bigger) country may indeed have consequences in various fields. Public opinion, however, has far more substantial influence than before, and is mostly appeased through far stricter enforcement of the accession conditions. After 2006, new steps in the rapprochement process were only taken if the Council unanimously agreed that the set criteria had been met. By placing greater emphasis on the objective application of accession criteria, the EU tried to depoliticize the process. Moral and political arguments were thus relegated to the background and replaced by economic considerations: what do we get out of enlargement?

The evolution of the Dutch position is also well illustrated by the government programmes of the last 20 years. In 1994, the new government announced that it wanted to concentrate on creating a larger EU. Four years later, it stated that the EU's policy on Eastern Europe should be open and focused on integration. The first Balkenende Cabinet (2002) adopted, for the first time, a more critical tone by stressing that the accession conditions should be strictly adhered to. This government was concerned about society's lacking interest in issues such as EU enlargement. One year later, the government programme mainly spoke of safeguard clauses and the fulfilment of obligations entered into by the candidates. In 2007, the programme stated: "The European Union is facing a new stage in its development. Further enlargement and deepening are not obvious driving forces of European cooperation in the next decades".[30] In 2010,

> [a]ccession of new Member States to the EU will take place if they meet the stringent criteria, in particular the Copenhagen criteria, including the absorption capacity of the EU, and the 2006 enlargement strategy. There is however a limit to the European Union's capacity to enlarge.[31]

The VVD-PvdA government, which was formed in November 2012, devotes only a short sentence to enlargement in its coalition agreement. The (potential) candidate countries can join the EU if they fulfil the criteria. Looking back, we can say that the Dutch Presidency in the second half of 2004 was the last effective Dutch contribution to the enlargement process. Led by then Prime Minister

30 Coalition Agreement 2007.

31 Coalition Agreement 2010.

Balkenende, the EU adopted the negotiating framework for Turkey. At the same time, the Dutch policy of recent years cannot be called a failure. The European Commission has listened carefully to critical Member States and adjusted its policy by placing more emphasis on implementation and enforcement and on the credibility of the process. That is why, in October 2012, the Dutch government was able give a positive opinion about the Commission's work.[32]

10.5 The 100% Union

So, the Dutch approach to the EU's enlargement shows a remarkable trend. While, in 2000, the Dutch government was still reaching out to the applicant Member States, 10 years later the ball was mainly put in the (potential) candidates' court. "The European Union should not appropriate problems that are primarily the responsibility of the enlargement countries themselves", is now the prevailing view of the Dutch government.[33] The tone of the debate has hardened as well. For instance, in 2000, the Dutch cabinet still aimed for a target date for actual accession so as to "maintain the momentum on both sides".[34] The Rutte I cabinet was strongly opposed to prematurely setting target dates and was moreover highly critical of the European Commission's view that, in the course of the process, the candidates should be offered tangible results such as visa liberalization. "We do not owe them any presents", said The Hague.[33] The new Dutch government, which took office in November 2012, might change its tone but is unlikely to alter its basic attitude towards enlargement. In reply to questions from the House of Representatives, the new Minister of Foreign Affairs, Frans Timmermans, stated that he aims for high-quality enlargement of the EU as a shared interest.[35]

The enlargement process in the Western Balkans is thus gradually starting to resemble a long-distance race which lacks the dynamics of earlier laps. Once, the region's ambition was for all countries to simultaneously accede to the EU around 2015. Nothing has come of this, not only through its own fault but also for lack of political ambition on the part of the EU. Consequently, the Netherlands is among those countries that are okay with the much slower pace of enlargement. This position seems justified insofar as it is the result of a stricter application of accession conditions. The EU is a community based on rules, and applicant countries just have to get used to this. The emphasis has been too much on

32 Letter from the Dutch House of Representatives regarding the cabinet assessment of the EU enlargement package, 26 October 2012.

33 Dutch House of Representatives. *Vergaderjaar* 2010-2011. 23 987, No. 112, p. 7.

34 Dutch House of Representatives. *Vergaderjaar* 2000-2001, 23 987, No. 3, p. 8.

35 Reply to questions from the Dutch House of Representatives regarding the statement: "EU commissaris. EU Verder uitbreiden" [EU Commissioner. Further enlarge the EU]. 8 November 2012.

becoming a member and not on *being* a member. At the same time, the EU must abide by its own rules. Whether everyone will be able to do so for 100% is doubtful, as the euro crisis has made clear. Some modesty when presenting the Dutch policy is therefore in order: it is not only the accession countries that have to be able to keep to the rules.

For a long time, the Nederland was seen as a pillar of the EU's enlargement policy. Through its active bilateral approach, financed through the MATRA programme, our country gave it an extra dimension. That is history now. The critical and at times unyielding stance of the past few years has marred its positive image in the Western Balkans. The unilateral position of the Netherlands on Schengen – blocking the accession of Bulgaria and Romania – does not help the Dutch reputation in the region either. The Netherlands is accused of dragging its feet on the enlargement process because of national policy reasons. Of course, this may be the perception of those involved, but it is also the result of an awkward presentation of the 'strict but fair' policy of The Hague. The government should make greater efforts to dispel the impression that, although it believes the EU should keep its promises to the region, it does too little to live up to them itself. The Netherlands could improve its reputation by, for instance, becoming more active in helping to find a solution to the regional conflicts that are seriously hampering the enlargement process.

11 The Internal Market

Jacques Pelkmans

11.1 The Internal Market: Foundation of the European Union

The internal market constitutes the hard core of European integration. The founding fathers of the Rome Treaty based their report (Spaak et al., 1956) on the novel idea of a 'common market', and 55 years later it is far better understood how ambitious this idea really is. Nowadays the single market has become economically, politically, legally and institutionally indispensable for the Union. In good times, the internal market tends to be largely ignored by the European political leadership. Therefore, it is difficult to assemble highly dispersed and splintered initiatives in this huge domain and package them in a coherent strategy which deserves political priority on the overloaded European agenda. In bad times, like the crisis that began in the autumn of 2008, one observes that the internal market regime is robust and gives short shrift to protectionist electoral campaigns or sneaky restrictions of Member States.

Before discussing the status quo of the single market and options for further deepening, it is useful to first sketch what the internal market is exactly. The European Union (EU) internal market is a combination of what is called 'negative' and 'positive' market integration. Negative integration consists of the removal of barriers to free movement (of goods, services, persons/workers, capital and codified technology [like intellectual property rights – IPRs]) across intra-EU borders and to unhindered establishment of firms and independents in other Member States, including any form of discrimination as to (intra-EU) origin or nationality. Member States legally commit *not* to raise any barriers anymore; in fact, EU countries lose, step by step, the right to take this type of national measures. This goes very far indeed. In lots of laws and decrees in all EU countries, countless restrictions and forms of discrimination turned out to be hidden in domains relevant to all the free movements and the right of establishment for reasons of market failures or on numerous other grounds.

The more one zooms in on details, and the more one realizes which vested interests (everywhere) had to be overcome, the better one begins to appreciate why it has taken four to five decades before truly 'deep' market integration could be accomplished. Nevertheless, it is not conceivable that merely and solely going for negative integration will lead to fully free movement and unhindered establishment. Quite the contrary, the logic of the EU internal market also requires 'positive' integration in all those cases – which are very many – where initial national regulation or other market intervention is justified, at least in principle, due to market failures. The EU internal market is no different; it can fail as well, and this ought to be prevented, for example, by means of common regulation[1] or common policies. Without such positive integration, Member States would not agree to free movement or unhindered establishment as it would reintroduce market failures.

After 55 years of market integration since the Treaty of Rome, it is positive integration that attracts the attention of politics, the press and often European business, too. This is understandable, but one should never forget that the driving force of welfare gains from market integration is negative integration, the free movements and establishment. The latter induce more intense competition in the entire EU market by facilitating new entrants, export opportunities and import competition. In the longer run, this is likely (and has proven) to lead to Europeanization of markets, to genuine European companies, to greater efficiency, to new corporate methods and business models (think of Ryan Air and EasyJet versus the traditional carriers), to more variation in supply, to a wider variety in quality, to more innovation (as innovation reacts positively to market size) and altogether to a higher level of prosperity. The common competition policy strengthens this promotion of intra-EU competition. Other instances of common policies largely boil down to EU regulation (*e.g.*, the six modes of transport, environment policy, consumer protection). In two common policies it turns out to be more complicated. EU trade policy is legally laid down in regulations (given the WTO framework conditions), but it is undeniable that international negotiations and commercial diplomacy play a major role. And the Common Agricultural Policy (CAP) is an exception to the general idea that the EU is about 'rules', not 'money', because farmers receive an annual income per farm (dependent on particular criteria). To some degree this constitutes a redistributive policy, which is usually a prerogative of national governments, if only because that is where taxation takes place. The EU is typically focused on the proper functioning of markets, as elements of the internal market, and – except for funds for hard and soft infrastructure of poor regions, with a view to improving their capacity to compete in the internal market – the EU is not tasked to redistribute. In agriculture, the EU history has remained exceptional. Initially, national agro-interventionism was so intrusive and distortive that an internal market for agro-products would be feasible only if such interventions were to take place at EU level. After many reforms since the early 1990s, EU agricultural interventionism has become much less damaging economically, but its removal at EU level (and

1 When regulatory requirements based on risk assessment are relatively light and national objectives are 'equivalent', mutual recognition (*i.e.*, without EU regulation) is a better option. *See* Pelkmans (2007, 2012).

partial, EU-controlled substitution at national level geared to national standards of living and social policies) is not to be expected soon.

Few people seem to realize the depth and wide policy scope of the internal market as the hard core of European integration. Far too many aspects are quite specialized or technical, and such issues hardly ever reach the evening TV news or the front pages of the newspapers. No less than 13 directorates-general (DGs) in the European Commission are working on the internal market in various ways. Given that positive integration is part and parcel of the internal market logic, these DGs do include domains like environment, transport and consumer protection. The single market logic, together with the subsidiarity principle (Ederveen, Gelauff & Pelkmans, 2008; Pelkmans, 2005), is the principal reason that there is so much EU policy in so many fields. For the very same reason, there is 'so much' EU regulation. Pushing 'rules' to the EU level requires the passing of a serious, functional subsidiary test, asking the question whether the shift to the EU level is justified. If yes, the next question is whether the cost of such centralization as well as the cost of this EU regulation can be minimized without undermining the unity and coherence (*e.g.*, no distortions) of the single market. Cost minimization can be achieved by means of RIAs (regulatory impact analyses) which has gradually become more elaborate at EU level[2] and on the basis of 'Better Regulation' strategies.[3] The economic approach to 'good regulation', whether at EU or national level, together with the proportionality principle, can reduce regulatory costs and raise common benefits. At EU level, there are many examples.[4]

11.2 What Has Been Achieved? Deepening, Widening and Enlargement of the Internal Market

In 1982, the Internal Market Council was initiated by Member States at a suggestion of Commissioner Karl-Heinz Narjes. There were good reasons for this initiative. Taking stock after 25 years since the Rome Treaty, the European Economic Community turned out to have come no further than a 'customs-union-plus'.[5]

2 *See, e.g.*, Fritsch, Radaelli, Schrefler & Renda (2012), Renda (2011), EU Court of Auditors (2010).

3 European Commission (2010) [smart reg. COM (2010) 543 8 October], Baldwin (2010), Pelkmans (2006), Ch. 4.

4 Pelkmans (2006), p. 77, Figure 4.3, provides six major new approaches which all have the effect of systematically disciplining EU regulation. Another significant example is Commission Memo 10/654 of 7 December 2010, with the results of the EU red tape reduction exercise over three years, in 13 domains of EU regulation, with a total cost reduction of €40 billion.

5 *See,* for elaborate analysis, Pelkmans (1985). The 'plus' consisted of the CAP, an incomplete (un) common trade policy, an EEC competition policy predominantly for goods markets, without merger control and too weak and somewhat politicized state aid control, and with scattered and often partial EEC regulation of high-risk goods. Putting it differently, negative integration was seriously incomplete in goods markets, and largely absent in services (even transport!), capital and labour. Nothing was foreseen, let alone accomplished, for IPRs.

The economic misery (stagflation, with high unemployment and large budget deficits) at the time was often attributed to 'Eurosclerosis'. This term referred to a combination of aspects throttling the good functioning of markets, with detrimental effects to adjustment and economic growth: rigidities in (national and EU) regulation, slow adaptation of real wages to productivity developments, shielding of sectors against competition, an emphasis on redistribution at the cost of growth and trade protectionism. When it came to voting on internal market dossiers in Brussels, this Eurosclerosis provoked more, and more frequently, vetoes and blockages. The Internal Market Council was expected to attempt to break through this behaviour by consistently following an agreed agenda of 'deepening'. Eventually, this led to the first internal market strategy. Subsequently, the internal market has been transformed radically from a modest customs-union-plus into a deep, wide (in scope) and far larger internal market.

11.2.1 What Has EC1992 Brought?

Figure 11.1 summarizes the EC1992 programme. This programme has been entirely executed and 95% of it even before the end of 1992. This is remarkable, to say the least, as this period of 7½ years witnessed two successive Commissions, two periods of the European Parliament and many national elections, with changes in national governments, not to mention numerous powerful lobbies of affected goods and service sectors[6] resisting the implied new rivalries in markets. Notwithstanding the impressive programme (shown in Figure 11.1), EC1992 went far beyond the original 1985 programme by beginning to tackle the network industries (broadcasting and airlines first), terminating national (!) quotas against third countries (like Japan for cars and many developing countries for clothing) and removing intra-EU border controls (with all the implications involved). What makes Figure 11.1 so impressive is that significant progress was accomplished with respect to all five free movements (including codified technology), usually with ambitious common regulation. Only in the case of capital movements were exchange controls (in 1986 still present in 6 of 12 EEC countries) removed without any further common rules.

6 *E.g.*, insurance and banking, automotive industry, textiles and clothing, airlines, etc.

Figure 11.1 Summary of the EC-1992 Programme.

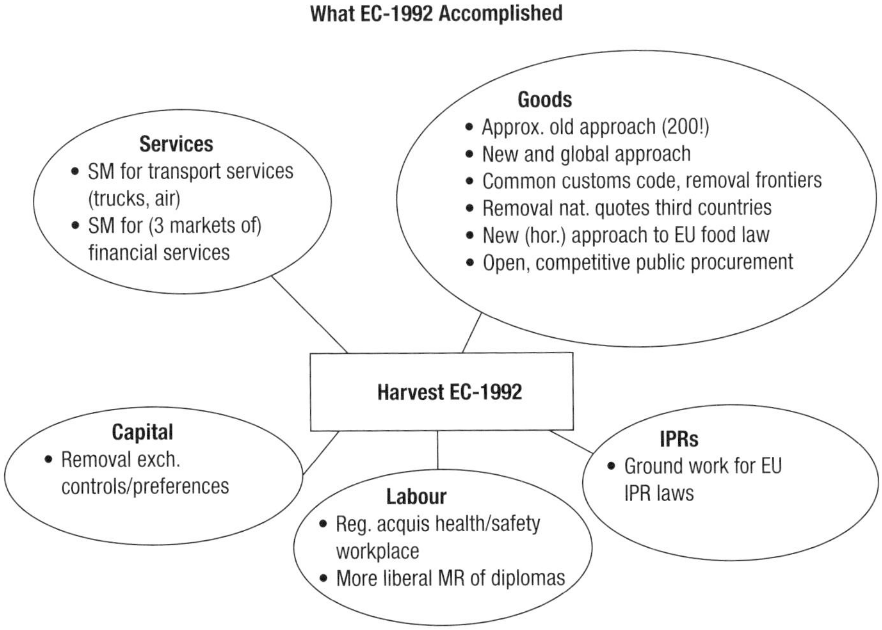

Notes: (1) CJEU case law promoted M.R.; (2) Preventing new barriers in SM via 83/189; (3) Network industries not in White Paper (exc. broadcasting); began early 1990s

The EC1992 ambition, as expressed in total volume and degree of difficulty of common regulation (in goods, selected services and, *e.g.*, regulation of occupational health and safety), contrasts sharply with the excessively slow and cumbersome EEC decision-making before the Single European Act of 1985 (in force in 1987). In those days, say, the 1970s and early 1980s, entire policy domains were avoided or seen as taboo, and EEC regulation was, more often than not, too rigid, partial and of bad quality (disproportional and/or too costly, frequently with exceptions). Of the near-300 measures listed in the EC1992 programme, some 160 amounted to what nowadays would be called SPS-type directives,[7] an absolute taboo before 1985. Sensitive sectors with considerable political powers in many Member States were liberalized (e.g., the monopolized and cartelized air transport sector, insurance [after a courageous judgment of the CJEU, the European Court in Luxembourg in 1986], banking and investment services).

In transport, with liberalization having stagnated for 20 years even in road haulage, a common transport policy was agreed and executed in just a few years in all six modes (with rail trailing for deep-seated reasons). As noted, third coun-

7 Sanitary, veterinary and phyto-sanitary measures and their tight controls on animals, meat and plants.

tries' quotas were abolished and customs controls at intra-EU borders disappeared, although this radical provision can be found neither in the Treaty[8] nor in the EC1992 programme. It is interesting to notice how rapidly EU business and citizens have become used to these 'deep' accomplishments, as if they were entitlements and 'obvious' attributes of the Union. At first, nothing was further from the truth. The Single Act ensured that qualified majorities were sufficient for legislation of a stream of EEC regulation on the internal market, which, in turn, drastically altered the conduct of Member States in the Council: communitarian thinking became more habitual and respectable, whilst alternative solutions would be tabled in order to pre-empt blocking minorities. In addition, the internal market grew more interesting because of the Iberian enlargement. Moreover, the combination of ambitious deepening, widening of the scope of policy domains and enlargement of the number of EEC countries prompted EFTA countries to rethink their European integration strategies, so far confined to EFTA and those countries' free trade areas with the EEC. EFTA countries were confronted with new choices: either stick to the accomplished market access for industrial products (in the free trade areas), or participate in the deeper and wider EU internal market but then according to the EU-driven integration model (what later would become the EEA, the European Economic Area), or EU membership. Three EFTA countries opted for EU membership, and three went into the EEA (Norway, Iceland and Liechtenstein). After a negative referendum on the EEA in 1992, Switzerland opted for a bilateral 'salami' model of more than 100 negotiated sectoral agreements, mimicking the EEA (with its ambitious negative and positive integration) only selectively – and without its central institutions – so as to prevent another negative referendum, which might have blocked participation in the internal market, so crucial for Swiss business.

11.2.2 *The Rich Harvest of 18 Years of 'Muddling Through' until 2010*

After 1992, no consistent and widely supported priority programme on the single market was designed. Instead, an incredible number of splintered initiatives, often highly specialized, have been pursued, with little or only token top-level political support. Figure 11.2 summarizes the more important elements of deepening and widening of the EU internal market from 1993 up until the 2010 Monti report. Figure 11.2 shows clearly that it is wrong to assert that the internal market was not deepened and widened. On the contrary, a lot was achieved, even though the process was somewhat fragmented and piecemeal.

8 Unless one reads the Single Act's Art. 8A defining the internal market 'without internal frontiers' as literally meaning this. Art. 26/2 of TFEU still contains the same text. This literal interpretation came up only after several years of successfully pursuing EC1992 and was at first highly controversial.

Figure 11.2 Elements of Deepening and Widening of the EU Internal Market, 1993-2010.

IM Harvest 1993-2010

Services	**(selective)**	**Goods**
• Third generation EU regulation financial services (FSAP) • Fourth generation (id.) [since 2008] • Opening up of 6 network industries (in stages) • EU Agencies (Safety, Air, Maritime, Rail; Air Traffic) • Horizontal services dir. 2006/123		• 2008 Goods package (+ MR) • Reach (chemicals) • Adaption old approach (+ simplif.n food specific dir.) • EU Medicinal, Chemical, Food Agencies • EU emission trading system & climate policy • Prudent liberalization of EU SM in defence goods
	More single market	
Labour • MR for professionals • Minimum labour market reg; + 300 sectoral agreements Social Dialogue	**Capital** • Stock exchanges; more competitive and standarised cross-border securities trade	**IPRs** • EU trademarks regulation and EU Agency • Other EU IPR (copyright, design)

Notes: (1) Modernization of EU policy; (2) RIAs (since 2003) and Better regulation;
(3) Better inter-MS horizontal/adm. cooperation; (4) Public procurement, 2nd generation

Sometimes, the term 'strategy' was employed (Commissioner Bolkestein in 1999 and again in 2003), sometimes the single market agenda was combined with the one on 'competitiveness' (the Delors initiative in 1993), sometimes initiatives were *ad hoc*, and sometimes 'cumulative logic' played a role (building on earlier initiatives, subsequently deepened). For goods markets, EU regulation was refined or improved drastically[9] and EU Agencies were established. At long last, an EU system of intellectual property rights was created for trademarks, designs, copyright and, in 2012 finally, for the EU patent (valid in 25 EU countries). Most of the progress since 1993, however, can be found in services markets in three principal policy domains: financial markets, network industries and the horizontal liberalization of services.

9 Major examples: in 2008, the so-called goods package, meanwhile known as the New Legislative Framework (for goods), plus a solid framework supporting mutual recognition in goods markets; in 2006, the REACH regulation on chemicals (despite high start-up costs, a far better and coherent regulatory regime than before); since around 2003, the cap-and-trade system (ETS) creating a market price for carbon emissions.

Knowing that the second generation of financial services regulation (in Figure 11.1) was incomplete and technically weak, a third generation of more than 40 directives, regulations and recommendations was enacted under the Financial Services Action Plan (2000-2006), technically an improvement and also with greater coverage of market activities. Nevertheless, notwithstanding all the technical refinement, the essence of financial regulation was, is and will always remain the trust and confidence that savers, consumers and investors can have in financial institutions and their risk management. And this is critical for individual banks but, in the final analysis, just as much for the financial system as a whole (financial stability). Much of the FSAP was based on rather 'light' regulatory requirements, and the national provisions deviated from the EU rules in numerous instances. Had supervision been tough on the risks assumed, this might have been less of a problem, but this toughness was pre-empted by a fear that national disadvantages for 'their' banks would be costly. Neither EU rulemakers nor national supervisors were sufficiently conscious of the weak risk management of financial institutions, and the further risk of contagion amongst European banks at large. Worse still, the cooperation between national supervisors at EU level left much to be desired, and crucial information remained hidden. And there was no EU body paying careful attention to the 'systemic risk' of European contagion and financial instability. The sensible notion of truly common supervision of transnationally operating banks in Europe (some 55), say, with a lead supervisor doing the technical inspection and controls, was taboo because of the ultimate consequence of such supervision, namely, the so-called fiscal capacity. The latter remained firmly in the hands of the Member States, as only Member States[10] could raise taxes or borrow large sums to rescue a failing financial institution. The simple solution of creating special EU funds for this purpose did not even enter the discussion. The carving up of Fortis Bank, operating in three Benelux countries, according to national lines, went against all the basic internal market principles. After the De Larosière report had revealed the shortcomings, gaps, omissions and mazes in the third generation of EU regulation of financial markets and suggested solutions, widespread political support emerged to propose a fourth generation of EU regulation and greater Europeanization of supervision. The fourth generation of EU financial markets regulation has been enacted with high speed since the end of 2008 and is in the final stages at the time this chapter is being drafted. For all its weaknesses, the second (EC1992) and third generations of EU financial markets regulation did facilitate a forceful deepening of financial market integration (ECB, 2011). In the long run, 'deep' and very liquid financial markets are beneficial for investment and growth in the Union. At the moment, however, this might work against the Union interest because the strongly increased interdependence of the transnational banks with

10 Note that the EU has a very small budget (1% of EU GDP), has no right to tax and can borrow only under very strict conditions. Its budget must always be in balance.

each other and with markets of sovereign bonds can weaken financial stability in times of very high state debt. Turbulence in these swiftly responding markets can, surely when there is a lack of trust, lead to self-fulfilling prophecies, which, in turn, can force ever more extreme interventions to restore calm.

Second, progress was made in the network industries. It is often forgotten that these sectors were not even mentioned in the 1985 White Paper. There are seven network sectors relevant to actual or potential cross-border transactions and hence falling under the internal market[11]: broadcasting (audiovisual), gas, electricity, telecoms (now, e-communications), postal services, air and rail (freight) transport. The EU has never designed an overall EU strategy for network industries, although it is not easy to comprehend the logic of not including them in the internal market from the beginning.[12] Until the late 1980s, however, this was politically impossible since Member States regarded their 'public utilities' as a national instrument. In the meantime, all seven sectors have been liberalized, be it with varying success.[13] In several sectors, market integration requires large and sustained infrastructural investments (*e.g.*, interconnectors in gas and electricity), special European corridors for freight rail transport (with numerous obligations and required investments) and a European rather than primarily national approach to competition policy.[14] Furthermore, all these sectors in all OECD and many other countries have a powerful 'regulator', with competences for competition, regulation and, if indispensable, immediate intervention. Curiously, the EU does not have a single regulator for such sectors, with all the problems that this might entail for the proper functioning of the single market in such sectors. Indeed, for legal and political reasons, the EU has to live with a peculiar blend of splintered competences between who regulates (at two levels of government) and who executes competition policy (at two levels), which prevents a single market from coming into being and functioning properly. The Safety Agencies mentioned in Figure 11.2 are an improvement, but they do not have economic powers. This 'blend' is the consequence of the prohibition of independent EU agencies at EU level (Meroni doctrine). Unfortunately, an attempt in the Euro-

11 Thus, local or regional transport or, for instance, water supply falls outside the internal market, except if FDI is undertaken (*e.g.*, French water companies in South England).

12 The legal and regulatory logic in the Treaty is based on what are called 'services of general economic interest', in Art. 106, TFEU, for which Member States ought to have considerable discretion. This is a complex issue which has also witnessed a shifting interpretation over time. *See* Sauter (2009). For the development of the fragmented network policies after the later 1990s, *see* Pelkmans (2001), Geradin (2006).

13 The single market in telecoms appears to be simply non-existent (*see* Pelkmans & Renda, 2011). Liberalization has been 'national', though based on EU rules and (largely) on EU competition policy principles. For in-depth surveys of the single market for network industries, see European Commission (2013) and Pelkmans & Luchetta (2013).

14 *See, for example,* COM (2010) 474 of 17 September 2010, Communication concerning the development of a Single European Railway Area; COM (2011) 144 of 28 March 2011, White Paper – Roadmap to a single European Transport Area; *see also* Kapff & Pelkmans (2010).

pean Convention of 2003 to insert in the Treaty a simple legal basis (with unanimity) to be able to set up an independent EU agency, where necessary for the proper functioning of the internal market, did not obtain a majority, almost certainly due to a lack of preparation and understanding.
Third, the Horizontal Services Directive 2006/123 has been enacted and incorporated in national and regional law with special efforts. Thus, all national and regional legislation was 'screened' on incompatibilities with the Directive (an unprecedented and laborious undertaking), and a unique process of 'mutual evaluation' between Member States with respect to each other's implementation further improved compliance whilst also helping convergence between national services laws. Around 1000 new national laws have been enacted in order to render the Services Directive effective at national level.[15]
Finally, one should not forget that, in 1995, Sweden, Finland and Austria joined the Union, enlarging the internal market.[16] This has rendered the internal market more attractive to European business and, in some respects, will facilitate competitiveness as well. Another two waves of enlargement took place in 2004 and 2007, resulting in a huge internal market of 500 million consumers and 27 Member States. It should be noted that the Eastern enlargements have raised economic growth in *all* EU-27 countries until the crisis.[17]

11.3 The Economic Significance of the Internal Market

The economic significance of the EU internal market has gradually increased due to steady deepening, widening (of the scope of policy areas covered) and six enlargements. Although the attractiveness of the EU for third (European) countries is certainly also determined by political and security considerations, participation in the internal market has remained a constant and strong preference of candidate countries and others. The latter include countries which explicitly do not wish to become a member of the Union (like Switzerland and Norway) because their prosperity is dependent, in no small measure, on *de facto* participation in the EU internal market.
When participating in the internal market as member or via the EEA, there are two kinds of effects which reflect its economic significance. In the first place, one finds the economic effects of the introduction of the entire complex of market

15 *See* the reports in COM (2011) 20 of 27 January 2011 and the extensive and detailed summaries in Commission Staff Paper SEC (2011) 102 of 27 January 2011.

16 Note that the European Economic Area (EEA) extends the internal market (other than fish and agriculture) to Norway, Iceland and Liechtenstein. For an accessible overview, EFTA Bulletin, September 2012, The EEA and the single market 20 years on, Brussels, <www.efta.int>. For a detailed review of the EEA, see Pelkmans & Boehler (2013).

17 The empirical evidence is in European Commission. (2009). Five years of an enlarged EU, European Economy, 2009/1, Ch. II, 2.

institutions which has enabled the build-up of EU 'positive' market integration. Market institutions consist of general but highly pervasive principles (such as non-discrimination as to nationality, and proportionality), besides substantive EU regulation preventing market failures (with respect to safety, health, environment and the protection of consumers, savers and investors). The quality of EU market institutions has gradually improved.[18] The introduction of EU market institutions is especially attractive for countries with a communist past or legacy, or for countries having lagged behind for other reasons (Turkey, for reasons of development and/or corruption, at first; Spain, due to long isolation in Western Europe). For Switzerland (with its many bilaterals), Norway (EEA) or Finland (now a member), such effects are at best marginal. In the case of Central European countries, there is a strong correlation between the increase of real economic growth rates in the mid- and late-1990s and the rapid introduction of the EU *acquis* even before EU membership (Fischer, 1998). This correlation is absent for former communist countries having no prospect of membership.

In the second place, there are the economic effects of (mutual) market access to the ever 'deeper' and larger EU internal market. In Straathof, Linders, Lejour and Moehlmann (2008), an unique attempt is undertaken to estimate the economic benefit over four decades, rather than 'only' for deepening like 'EC1992'. The authors find conspicuously larger long-run economic effects of the EU – which is mainly the single market – than can so far be traced in the economic literature (which always focuses on more limited periods and events). Indeed, the empirical studies on economic effects of the internal market, especially on GDP, have always been disappointing. With the old customs union of the EEC-6, the empirical methods were still quite simple (many effects were not included), and the economic welfare effects were often thought not to exceed 0.5% of GDP, or at most 1%. In today's empirical economic work, many more effects are incorporated, such as economies of scale, productive efficiency improvements due to greater import competition as well as a prerequisite to enter other EU country markets, product variety and greater choice, deeper specialization in goods and services, and incentives for innovation (Pelkmans, 2012 for a survey). Moreover, the customs union is all about goods, and nowadays also services markets and (intra-EU) foreign direct investments (FDI) are studied. The first breakthrough

18 Behind this assertion lies the fascinating question whether and, if so, why, nowadays EU market institutions are an improvement over the past (for its members) and why they are *grosso modo* superior (with respect to the better functioning of markets) to the market institutions of candidate countries. For the Central European countries, the intensive process of pre-accession and the early incorporation of the EU *acquis* has proven, without a trace of doubt, that EU market institutions are far superior to institutions these countries had at the time. For other candidate countries, this is much harder to show (e.g., Sweden, Austria and Finland before entry in 1995, perhaps only for the absence of competition policy; before 1986, Spain and Portugal were found to be heavily (over)regulated, relatively protectionist and quite weak in terms of administrative capacity for properly implementing the *acquis*, and rapid modernization followed). *See also* footnote 4.

comes from the Cecchini report (Emerson, Aujean, Catinat, Goybet & Jacquemin, 1988), simulating a 4.5% GDP increase from the full implementation of EC1992. However, the Monti report (1996), based on an incomplete implementation, only found a 1½% increase in EU GDP; this was updated by Roeger and Sekkat (2002, as in Ilzkovitz, Dierx, Kovacs & Sousa, 2007) to an additional 2.2% GDP. Straathof et al. (2008) get around the direct measurement of the effects of negative and positive integration by means of gravity analysis. The authors conclude that the economic effects for the EU at large are 3% (and 6% for the Netherlands), without incorporating FDI. However, the long-run economic impact is much larger due to slow but crucial adjustment processes like the reallocation of production factors, further productivity increases and innovation, leading to 10% increase for the EU and no less than 17% for the Netherlands. Interestingly, services markets contribute very little (which might well be a limitation of the model used). A serious deepening of the internal market for services would bring appreciable additional gains (Mustilli & Pelkmans, 2012). Also, the FDI effects would ultimately generate additional GDP.

11.4 The Quest for an Internal Market Strategy

Twenty years after the end of EC1992, one has to acknowledge that the lack of an internal market strategy in the period since has not been reflected in a lack of progress (see Figure 11.2). In fact, what was held impossible in the mid-1990s can actually be observed with hindsight: the internal market has deepened, widened in scope of policy domains and has been enlarged with no less than 12 countries, and all this at the same time. Nevertheless, certain coalitions in the European Parliament, European business[19] and think tanks call incessantly for a credible and ambitious 'internal market strategy'. This call was hardly listened to in the Brussels cacophony, where numerous policy themes compete for the attention of the European Council, not to mention the little short-term fires to be extinguished by the prime ministers despite overloaded Council agendas with carefully prepared new initiatives. Commissioner Bolkestein launched two successive 'internal market strategies' in 1999 and 2003, although the unrelated ragbag of initiatives without much of a vision hardly deserves these labels. Still, they were pursued with gusto, piecemeal or not, and included what would later become the Horizontal Services Directive proposal. In November 2007, Commissioner McCreevy published an 'internal market review' which did not include new EU regulation at all, focusing mainly on 'consolidation' by means of improved enforcement in much closer cooperation with the Member States and

19 *See*, for instance, the booklet *It Is the Internal Market, Stupid* of UNICE (now, BusinessEurope) (2004), which received too little attention.

other technical initiatives.[20] In fact, McCreevy had little choice after three years of political turmoil about two of the most important EU regulatory initiatives ever, namely, Horizontal Services Directive 2006/123 and REACH Regulation 1907/2006, and the negative referenda on the EU draft constitution in France and the Netherlands in 2005.

The financial crisis, which started late September 2008, immediately changed this. Suddenly, political leaders in Europe began to speak about the natural shielding the single market offered against the negative and perhaps protectionist fallout of the crisis elsewhere in the world. Sarkozy's electoral speech early October 2008 in which he went as far as summoning French car assembly investors in the Czech Republic to return to France prompted a very powerful awareness also at top level in the Union that the internal market had to remain the unassailable hard core of the Union. This awareness led to a firm stance by political leaders backing the firm stance of the Commission as the 'guardian of the treaty' and, hence, of the accomplishments within the internal market. Sarkozy's list of protectionist suggestions to support the (French) car industry (including subsidies and job protection under restrictive conditions) was reduced to a far shorter list of initiatives which all fell under the established EU state aid regime or other EU measures already decided, no more.[21] When Barroso had finally been reappointed in the late summer of 2009, he requested Mario Monti to write a report about the internal market. Although the term 'strategy' is not explicitly mentioned in Barroso's letter (although it does say "[...] to relaunch the Single Market as a key strategic objective [...]"), it was clear that "[...] a report containing options and recommendations" had to constitute the basis for a new internal market strategy. The Monti report (2010) is surely strategic in nature and also interesting for other reasons.

In the late autumn of 2012, one can discern a more strategic approach to the single market. However, it took the European Commission quite some time to respond proactively to the Monti report, and once it did, the report was made less prominent than it could have been by adopting a tactic of successive but relatively modest stages. One explanation is the crisis and in particular the overly dominant problems of sovereign debt in the eurozone.[22] Another reason for a slow and tactical rather than a strategic approach is, at first, found within the

20 For a detailed and critical analysis of initiatives since 1993, and in particular the Internal Market Review of November 2007, *see* Pelkmans (2010). Meanwhile, it has become clear that this consolidation did increase the effectiveness of implementation and enforcement in the single market, as shown empirically in Pelkmans & Correia de Brito (2012).

21 For details, *see* Commission Memo 09/90 of 28 February 2009 on the French aid programme for the car industry.

22 The date the Monti report was issued (Schuman Day, 9 May 2010) unfortunately happened to coincide with the first emergency aid package for Greece after much panic and huge attention from the world press. The announcement effect of Monti's well-argued call for 'more Single Market' got lost and little was heard from the Commission for a number of months.

Commission. The internal market is splintered over no less than 13 directorates-general in the Commission, and Barnier, as the lead commissioner, cannot be expected to control and fully integrate all of the many aspects in a single, integrated and coherent 'strategy'. Thus, 10 days after the Monti report had come out, Commissioner Kroes launched the EU Digital Agenda,[23] surely one of the most important building blocks of any new internal market strategy because the 'Agenda' is really about a Single Digital Market. Only in late October 2010 did the Commission announce that it would come with a Single Market Act in the spring of 2013, based on a consultation about 50 ideas for proposals[24] which were not embedded in a strategy. The asserted potential of an additional 4% EU GDP was not even underpinned by economic analysis or a respected external source. Indeed, the Digital Single Market has been said to possibly generate this GDP increment (Copenhagen Economics, 2010) on its own account.

Subsequently, two successive Single Market Acts[25] were launched with a strong emphasis on the potential for additional growth, so welcome in the Great Recession (and not claiming budgetary resources!). The first Single Market Act is said to be strategic, but there is little evidence from the paper itself. It blends lingering initiatives from the 2007 Review (see above), already existing initiatives (like the Digital Single Market, the follow-up to the Services Directive, a renewed determination to conclude the never-ending saga of the EU patent[26] and some tax proposals) and some new ones (like tightening mutual recognition of professional qualifications, alternative dispute settlement for consumers, a new package on European standardization and simplifying public procurement directives).[27] Perhaps surprisingly, the (low key) better implementation and enforcement initiatives of November 2007 have quietly yielded good results due to greater 'ownership' by Member States responsible for implementation, in close cooperation (and not with endless litigation) with the Commission. Together with several new and informal methods of enforcement, the landscape of compliance efforts has drastically improved, and this can be empirically substantiated (Pelkmans & Correia de

23 COM (2010) 245 of 19 May 2010, A Digital Agenda for Europe.

24 COM (2010) 608 of 27 October 2010, Towards a Single Market Act.

25 The term 'act' should not be understood in the legal meaning of a 'law', rather a firm commitment. *See* COM (2010) 206 of 13 April 2011, Single Market Act, twelve levers to boost growth and strengthen confidence, and COM (2012) 573 of 30 October 2012, Single Market Act II, Together for new growth.

26 This time, 'enhanced cooperation' between 25 of 27 EU countries seems likely to result not only in an EU patent regulation but also in a single patent enforcement structure (which was long controversial). The CJEU has objected to some legal details but these can probably be accommodated. The lack of a (cheap and single) EU patent is a huge hindrance to innovation in the single market, and overcoming it would be a major success.

27 In addition, the Commission made many proposals to address long-standing complaints by citizens about cross-border intra-EU conflicts of law causing hardship for individual citizens or couples (divorce, inheritance problems, etc.). *See* COM (2010) 603 of 27 October 2010, EU Citizenship Report 2010, dismantling the obstacles to EU citizens' rights.

Brito, 2012). With the lingering crisis, the strategic nature of the Single Market to generate growth and higher productivity has begun to be exploited much better by the Commission and, indeed, the European Council. Besides active reporting and pressing EU institutions to move quickly,[28] a letter by 12 prime ministers listing eight EU dossiers for more growth started with the Single Market and a range of recent EMU decisions insist on the internal market as essential for a good functioning economic union.

The second Single Market Act of October 2012 is probably more modest, depending on the elaboration of the specifics. The headings promise more than the details; for example, the label 'developing fully integrated networks in the Single Markets' in rail, maritime transport, air and energy is in fact about highly specific initiatives. Two illustrations clarify this: (1) maritime transport has been effectively liberalized in the EU for years, but customs handling in ports does not distinguish intra-EU (*e.g.*, coastal) shipping from vessels arriving from the rest of the world – this will be improved, which is helpful, but to advertise this as 'developing fully integrated networks' is pretty exaggerated; (2) the initiative in rail is in passenger rail, which again is useful but far less important and less promising in terms of welfare gains than the deeper integration in freight rail, which remains the least integrated network industry. Truly strategic is the intention of the Commission, stimulated by the European Council, to incorporate national obligations under the two Single Market Acts into the so-called European Semester of economic coordination, with national recommendations as well. This process links what national parliaments do with what the EU (and the eurozone) requires for integration issues and the overall EU growth strategy, and plays in an interactive way between the EU and national level during the first five months of each calendar year. The Annual Growth Survey 2013[29] has indeed strengthened its attention for the Single Market. Moreover, it is accompanied by the first Single Market Integration report,[30] which, fortunately, takes a more strategic perspective and moves far beyond Single Market Act II, including energy, transport and digital markets and their functioning. When this manuscript was finalized, the promised report on the 'untapped potential' of the Single Market had not yet been published, but this is surely the kind of economic analysis that can provide a strategic perspective to Single Market policies (which are always splintered over many technical details). The more the Single Market returns to the heart of EU economic policy thinking, the greater the probability that the economic union (or EMU) will serve as a sound and solid foundation of the monetary union.

28 *See*, for instance, the Commission report 'Making the single market deliver, annual governance check-up, November 2011', and the stock-taking in SWD (2012) 21 of 15 February 2012, Delivering the Single Market Act: state of play.

29 COM (2012) 750 of 28 November 2012, Annual Growth Survey 2013, esp. pp. 8-9.

30 COM (2012) 752 of 28 November 2012, State of the Single Market Integration 2013.

11.5 More Internal Market and Obstacles on the Way

The plea for 'more internal market' has been heard regularly since the early 1980s. And every time, the further deepening and widening of scope that is sought clarifies that achieving 'the' internal market is an incredibly demanding project, with many ramifications and some profound institutional implications for the Union. In 2012, it is once again necessary. It is incorrect to think, though often held, that the internal market is more or less 'completed' – after all, was not the title of the 1985 White paper 'Completing the Internal Market' and was not EC1992 a success? Of course, EC1992 was a success, but the programme merely constituted one major step towards a genuine and properly functioning internal market, as shown in Figure 11.2 and Section 2.2.

Making the case for 'more internal market' in 2012 cannot be disentangled from the lingering sovereign debt crisis in the EU. Deepening and widening the internal market is a non-budgetary instrument, better, a broad range of such instruments, to pursue higher productivity and growth in the medium and longer run. It is therefore attractive in an era that budgetary stimulus is out of the question. I shall summarize a recent plea for 'more internal market' (Pelkmans, 2011) as space constraints allow no more. The plea revolves five EU public interest arguments. First, 'more of the internal market for services', which the Treaty (and increasingly CJEU case law) has set out for 55 years, should urgently be pursued; it is likely to generate growth – after a delay, of course – and interact positively with other reforms.[31] Second, many other shortcomings or bottlenecks in the internal market still hinder all kinds of cross-border activities or lessen the menace of cross-border competition to local incumbents. Examples can be found in Single Market Acts I and II, including in particular the Digital Single Market (difficult due to complexity and private law issues, not normally the competence of the EU), energy and transport. Gains from the latter two mainly hinge on huge infrastructural investments over the coming decades. It is exceedingly hard to give reliable impact figures here, but several per cents of extra GDP over the period until 2030 seems feasible, if not more. Third, a properly functioning single market is in and by itself helpful for the 'lubrication' of adjustment patterns in the eurozone. Without internal exchange rates facilitating adjustment, the eurozone needs flexible and highly responsive markets throughout the entire area so as to absorb economic shocks, and the internal market (and even more so, domestic reforms in its wake) improves performance in this respect.[32] Fourth, a deeper internal market has a positive effect on the competitiveness of EU firms

31 *See* Monteagudo, Rutkowski & Lorenzani (2012) for empirical estimates of the impact on EU GDP of the Services Directive; Mustilli & Pelkmans (2012) for the growth potential of wider reforms in services markets.

32 For an empirical demonstration at sectoral and Member States level, *see* Pelkmans, Acedo Montoya & Maravalle (2008).

in Europe and globally, and this, in turn, tends to help growth. Fifth, as shown several times in EU history, a genuine deepening of the internal market generates 'inner dynamics' in the EU, stimulating other activities or initiatives which are complementary or indeed pre-conditional, both substantively and institutionally. Every case for more internal market ought to start with the Monti report (2010), giving a fascinating presentation of the problems with the sociopolitical legitimacy of the combination of 'more market' (surely, after the dramatic failure of some of the financial markets) and 'more Europe' (ill understood by the electorate, to say the least), followed by a long list of proposals. The cautious remarks by Mario Monti and other reflections add up to five types of 'obstacles' which might stand in the way of 'more internal market'. These are as follows: (1) some omissions in the TFEU (including, *e.g.*, vetos for tax issues), (2) resistance from vested interests (which can be fierce, *e.g.*, when reducing the restrictiveness of professional regulation and national codes of conduct), (3) invoking national policy autonomy in some areas as non-negotiable ('red lines' as Tony Blair called them), (4) the lack of political legitimacy of many EU measures with certain voters or workers, and (5) the permanent overburdening of the European Council agenda, causing the internal market (so central to the EU, yet splintered in numerous dossiers over so many years) to compete with many other concerns and making it easier for blocking minorities in ordinary Councils to frustrate progress.

11.6 The EU Internal Market and the Dutch Interest

11.6.1 The Netherlands as an Advocate and Frontrunner

The Netherlands is an articulate and long-standing advocate of a deep and properly functioning internal market. The point of view is not dependent on the nature or composition of the government. This is not surprising. The Dutch economy has always been oriented towards the world economy, and that is no different today, be it that the internal market has meanwhile led to a very high share of the EU in Dutch foreign economic activities (some 75% in goods flows and 60% for services; somewhat less for FDI).[33] The EU internal market is the life blood of the Dutch economy. The empirical study by Straathof et al. (2008) once again shows, in much detail, that the internal market raises Dutch income, in the past, recently and in future without additional deepening (due to long-run effects) and even more so when assuming further deepening.

33 Within the EU, trade and FDI are less often substitutes than vis-à-vis other continents. Excluding financial transfers via Dutch head offices (a huge sum), outgoing FDI stocks amount to $950 billion and incoming stocks to some $650 billion. *See DNB Bulletin*, 9 August 2011. About half is with EU countries.

In 'The State of the Union 2010-2012',[34] the central role of the internal market is emphasized. Indeed, "Dutch prosperity is largely based on it. An optimally functioning internal market is the 'engine block' for economic growth and employment in Europe. The Netherlands has therefore a great interest in strengthening and perfecting the internal market". No wonder the Single Market Act I has been well received.[35] In the 12 proposals, the Dutch government discerns five priorities in 2011: the EU patent, the digital internal market, 'more' services market, essential infrastructural investments for network industries and the emphasis on smart and 'better' EU regulation. These priorities make sense. The Dutch support for the single market remained just as strong in the autumn of 2012 when a new government came into power. The initial government declaration about its four-year programme says, "The internal market will be strengthened further. Effective measures to underpin necessary growth in Europe will be pursued and supported. Protectionism is inconsistent with the basic philosophy of Europe".[36] With the Single Market Act II, again very much welcomed, the new government has slightly altered its five priorities because the EU patent is about to be accomplished. Its priorities are now as follows: again the EU digital market; 'more' services market; an emphasis on better integrated goods transport (with a social component as well); given the huge Dutch interest in intra-EU road haulage, the completion of the internal energy market; and, again, smart EU regulation.[37] Conspicuous is the emphasis on better implementation and enforcement of the Services Directive. The Netherlands has been leading in the domestic screening exercises and the 'mutual evaluation' between Member States in 2010, and this is noticeable in the Dutch positioning. The Services Directive has been implemented much better than expected, thanks to this intensive domestic screening and 'ownership' by many Member States. There has been a lot of abolition and reduction of restrictiveness of services regulation in EU countries.[38] The Commission's follow-up initiatives for services are wholeheartedly supported by the Dutch government.

11.6.2 Some Sensitive Aspects of Dutch Single Market Policies

At times, the Netherlands may have problems with internal market policies which are rather intrusive with respect to national competences. This has been the case in the semi-public sector, such as social housing (where subsidized and non-subsidized segments are not always clearly separated, which is seen as dis-

34 Dutch House of Representatives, *Kamerstuk* 33001, No. 1, of 20 September 2011.

35 Dutch House of Representatives, *Kamerstuk* 22112, No. 1170 of 16 May 2011, p. 4, New Commission proposals and initiatives of the EU, letter from the State Secretary for EU Affairs.

36 *Regeringsverklaring*, The Hague, 30 October 2012.

37 Dutch House of Representatives, *Kamerstuk* 22112, No. 1507, 2012.

38 A good overview can be found in COM (2011) 20 of 27 January 2011: Towards a better functioning Single Market for services – building on the results of the mutual evaluation process of the Services Directive; and the detailed SWD of the Commission of the same date.

tortive by the EU regime for state aids) and corporate taxation. As to the latter, a formal letter to the Dutch House of Representatives from State Secretary for EU Affairs Ben Knapen[39] rejects the Commission proposal for a common consolidated corporate tax base (CCCTB) because of the expected negative effects for the Netherlands. The Dutch government recognizes that the lack of a common tax base can lead to double taxation and greater administrative burdens, but considers that the disadvantages for the country are too large. However, it is widely known that it is precisely the Netherlands (perhaps with Belgium, Ireland and Estonia) which causes significant distortions in the internal market due to a highly beneficial tax (base) regime for multinationals. The Netherlands is especially popular for the discretion to shift corporate earnings across borders in the EU. This is the source of a series of distortions, of incentives to engage in a race-to-the-bottom between Member States, a bias to shift tax burdens away from capital to labour – and, in doing so, towards personal income tax up to about a quarter of the loss (De Mooij & Nicodeme, 2008) – the allocation of capital in the single market (by artificial flows of direct investments and attracting headquarters of such firms), besides complications and transfers with respect to transfer pricing within multinationals. Many multinationals hardly pay corporate tax in countries such as the Netherlands (or, indeed Belgium). The Netherlands is thus the very source of the problem that the Commission proposes to overcome. It cannot be a surprise that the Netherlands will lose when these distortions are rectified at EU level. The Dutch preference, seemingly a concession, to choose to 'opt in' on a voluntary basis goes against the general EU interest (and probably also the Dutch public interest) because the voluntary approach has been proven to lead to great losses, whereas the loss resulting from a compulsory approach is drastically less and can even yield a gain.[40] The loss for the Netherlands can be minimized by various options. Besides, the EU as a whole will enjoy a significant welfare gain, and gladly add the elimination of large (and wasted) compliance costs.[41] The letter makes no reference whatsoever to the significant distortions in the internal market caused by the mere fact that Member States maintain widely divergent corporate tax bases. The 1992 Ruding report already pointed to this in no uncertain terms.[42] The Netherlands also has a problem with free movement of workers. In a letter from Minister Kamp[43] a range of measures are announced. They include a more

39 Dutch House of Representatives, *Kamerstuk* 32 728, No. 2 of 11 April 2012 about the proposed CCCTB (EU corporate tax base). The technicalities of this proposal go far beyond the purpose of the present contribution and will not be discussed.

40 *See, for instance,* the survey in McLure (2008) and Van der Horst, Bettendorf & Rojas-Romagosa (2007).

41 Bettendorf, Devereux, van der Horst, Loretz & de Mooij (2009) find only small positive welfare effects (not counting compliance costs) and fear huge discrepancies between Member States.

42 *See* Ruding et al. (1992) (CEPS, Brussels).

43 Letter 'Measures labour migration from Central and Eastern Europe', ref. AV/SDA/2011/4711, Ministry of Social Affairs and Employment.

effective regime of penalties for illegal workers (especially for employers) and exploitation (including substandard housing) and a number of administrative measures. Some measures do, however, require amendment of EU secondary legislation and imply both administrative and political choices which sit uncomfortably with free movement of workers.

11.6.3 *The Social Partners as 'Co-owners' of Dutch EU Policy*

Decades of Dutch internal market policy are reflected in the views and arguments of the social partners. Since the beginning of the old EEC, the Socio-Economic Council (SER), very important in the Netherlands, has been consistent in supporting the construction of the EU internal market and has taken numerous initiatives to promote the deepening and widening of the internal market. The Council has never been afraid to consult and coordinate as long as it took to come to consensus (which was nearly always achieved) and to go into specific and highly technical details to facilitate solutions. A high point in this long history is undoubtedly the very detailed 2005 SER report on the Horizontal Services Directive, a thorough and unanimous (!) advice which could have served EP rapporteur Evelyne Gebhardt's work much better had it been duly incorporated into the Brussels negotiations. Nevertheless, the internal market has generated some sensitivities. The labour unions are broadly in favour, but show sensitivities as to the labour side of services liberalization, including posted workers supplying temporary cross-border services, misuse of EU law (exemplified by splitting up contracts in construction between 'independents' without personnel, although *de facto* the workers operate as a group; in contracting this way, they can bypass minimum wage laws) and a few cases of minimum clauses in labour markets (*e.g.*, Working Time Directive).
Dutch business is enthusiastic about the internal market for reasons of potential growth, transport (a Dutch stronghold), direct investments and the great scope for trade in goods and services. In Brussels, the two business associations (VNO-NCW and MKB) work closely together[44] for specific Dutch interests and for effective lobbying work via BusinessEurope. In VNO-NCW and MKB (2008) many examples are provided where the internal market still has shortcomings. Dutch business is often more European than the government: it has pleaded for EU supervision of banks for years already (the government only yielded in late 2011, if not later) and in network industries, where the government is still hesitant or plainly resisting (*e.g.*, in telecoms, the new body BEREC is very weak, which is partly due to Dutch resistance). Had EU (rather than purely national) supervision of banks existed much earlier, Fortis Bank would not have been split up over the three Benelux countries, at tremendous costs and losses for many small (Belgian) shareholders whose pensions were based on those shares. A

44 For example, the half-yearly 'Rondje Europa' publication is a solid status report from a business point of view.

deep frustration for Dutch transporters is the uncontrolled proliferation of weekend bans and other restrictions at regional or national level throughout the Union. All these restrictions differ in terms of timing, weight (on axles), distance, load and exceptions for some shipments. Altogether, some 150 days a year are affected this way – a clear case of individual autonomy on a relatively small scale adding up to a collective throttling of freight mobility throughout Europe, with great sensitivity at political level.

11.7 Conclusions

The internal market is and remains the hard and comprehensive core of European integration. The public and politicians do not always realize this. There are many reasons for this lack of awareness, and these are not easy to address. First, the publicity about the internal market is far below its importance in the economy or to many aspects of daily life. Second, and not unrelated to the first reason, much of the legislation is highly technical, although the broader aims (often SHEC objectives) tend to be widely supported. Third, the lack of general politicization, both domestic and European, which can make the main decisions more intelligible to voters, does not help either (what politicization there is, is frequently based on more narrow interests). Fourth, the confusing messages by some leading politicians have suggested to voters that the single (mind the word) market is more or less completed, which is anything but correct – even though much has been accomplished. Fifth, the gradual but unmistaken shift of ever more decision-making on single market issues towards Brussels (where national voices are also heard but these are all specialists, the national voters or the press being too remote for the many internal dossiers to reach domestic politics) risks alienation of domestic politics vis-à-vis the EU unless the Europeanization of national parliaments and the power of the subsidiarity test that national parliaments now possess are fully exploited. Kester and van Keulen (2011) suggest that this Europeanization and the occasional reservation of parliament to impose a kind of mandate for EU negotiations before the minister agrees to anything in Brussels have only selectively strengthened domestic politics on Europe.[45]

The internal market has developed in an amazing way, knowing where the EU stood after 25 years of its existence (1983), and the dynamism is far from petering out. The erstwhile conviction that deepening and widening of the scope of areas and enlargement of the number of countries could not all take place at the same time has been proven wrong. Since the early 1990s, the EU has just done that.

45 Their analysis shows that, regarding 700 Commission initiatives, the Dutch House of Representatives decided to impose 10 reservations; both Houses of the Dutch Parliament decided only once to reject a proposal on the basis of subsidiarity. However, even these conspicuous cases hardly found their way to the Dutch media.

The late-1992 status was far better than when the EC1992 programme started in late 1985. Today's internal market is much deeper and wider (and with 27 rather than 12 countries) than in 1993. The 2010 Monti report shows convincingly that it ought to be a combination of new strategic aims and lists of new initiatives, on the one hand, and assurance of sociopolitical legitimacy of the proper functioning of such a deeper and broader internal market, intrusive and at times far-reaching as it tends to be, on the other. This legitimacy must be acquired at both EU and national levels.

Furthermore, the single market is now so advanced that it has become inevitable that so-called national competences are questioned with respect to their exact boundaries. Sometimes, it has to do with private or penal law, normally the domains of the Member States, other times with the blurring of these boundaries (*e.g.*, in public health, where are the 'red lines' when patients want to exercise their rights of cross-border mobility when seeking quicker or 'better' or cheaper health care?). Sometimes, the Treaty is insufficiently tuned to the modern internal market, which is so much deeper than expected when the Rome Treaty was drafted, such that the internal market fails to work well due to these rigidities. The Meroni doctrine constitutes a prominent case as it prohibits independent EU regulatory agencies, but in some network sectors (those with physical infrastructures) and in banking, such EU agencies are indispensable to make the single market work properly. Member States have nonetheless also become more cooperative once their power was ceded to the EU level: since 2002, many new EU regulations rather than directives have been enacted for the single market, which avoid troublesome implementation problems and guarantee homogeneity where Member States have equivalent objectives anyway.

The Netherlands continues to regard the internal market as the hard core of its EU policies. Occasionally, governments have some misgivings or even resist, but such instances are relatively few. The Netherlands has benefitted a great deal from the single market and still does. The sensitivities are found in the themes Monti (2010) brings up in his report as well (labour migration; labour markets; rarely, certain services; also some border cases of services which are 'non-economic' but which involve improper practices so that distortions might still arise; and of course, corporate taxation). Major controversies about the single market are absent in the Netherlands, even with the infamous Bolkestein Draft Services Directive. The Dutch remain faithful to their centuries-old habit: good in commerce.

References

Baldwin, R. (2010). Better regulation: The search and the struggle. In R. Baldwin, M. Cave & M. Lodge (Eds.), *The Oxford handbook on regulation*. Oxford: Oxford University Press.

Bettendorf, L., Devereux, M., van der Horst, A., Loretz, S. & de Mooij, R. (2009, November). *Corporate tax harmonisation in the EU* (CPB Discussion Paper No. 133).

Copenhagen Economics (2010), The economic impact of a European Digital Single Market, March, study for the EPC, http://www.epc.eu/dsm/2/Study_by_Copenhagen.pdf.

De Mooij, R. & Nicodeme, G. (2008). How corporate tax competition reduces personal tax revenue. *CESifi Dice Report, 6*(1), 27-31.

ECB. (2011, April). *Financial integration in Europe*. Frankfurt: ECB.

Ederveen, S., Gelauff, G. & Pelkmans, J. (2008). Assessing subsidiarity. In G. Gelauff, I. Grilo & A. Lejour (Eds.), *Subsidiarity and economic reform in Europe*. Berlin: Springer.

Emerson, M., Aujean, M., Catinat, M., Goybet, P. & Jacquemin, A. (1988, March). *The economics of 1992*. (European Economy, No. 35).

EU Court of Auditors. (2010). *Impact assessments in the EU institutions: Do they support decision-making?* (Special Report No. 3). Luxembourg: European Union. Retrieved from <http://eca.europa.eu/portal/pls/portal/docs/1/7912856.PDF>.

European Commission (2013), Market functioning in network Industries – electronic communications, energy and transport, *European Economy*, Occasional Papers 129, February 2013.

Fischer, S. (1998). *How far is Eastern Europe from Brussels?* (IMF Working Paper 98/53).

Fritsch, O., Radaelli, C., Schrefler, L. & Renda, A. (2012, January). *Regulatory quality in the European Commission and the UK: Old questions and new findings* (CEPS Working Document No. 362).

Geradin, D. (2006), *Twenty years of liberization of network industries in the EU : where do we go now?* Inaugural lecture Tilburg University, November 3, 2006

Ilzkovitz, F., Dierx, A., Kovacs, V. & Sousa, N. (2007). *Steps towards a deeper economic integration: The internal market in the 21st century* (Economic Papers No. 271). DG EcFin, European Commission.

Kapff, L. & Pelkmans, J. (2010). *Interconnector investment for a well-functioning internal market – What EU regime of regulatory incentives?* (BEER Papers No. 18). Bruges, College of Europe. Retrieved from <www.coleurope.eu/ECO>.

Kester, J. & van Keulen, M. (2011). *De Tweede Kamermethode: versterkte parlementaire invloed op Europese besluitvorming*. Unpublished.

McLure, C. (2008). Harmonising corporate income taxes in the US and in the EU: Legislative, judicial, soft law and cooperative approaches. *CESifo Forum, 9*(2), 46-52.

Monteagudo, J., Rutkowski, A. & Lorenzani, D. (2012, June). *The economic impact of the services directive: A first assessment following implementation* (Economic Papers No. 456). DG EcFin, European Commission.

Monti, M. (2010, May 9). *A new strategy for the single market at the service of Europe's economy and society*. Retrieved from <www.ec.europa.eu/bepa/pdf/monti_report_final_10_05_2010_en.pdf>.

Monti, M., Spachis, A., Farnell, J. & Buiges, P. (1996). *The single market and tomorrow's Europe*. Luxembourg: Office for Official Publications of the EC.

Mustilli, F. & Pelkmans, J. (2012, November). *Securing EU growth from services* (CEPS Special Report No. 72). Brussels: CEPS. Retrieved from <www.ceps.eu>.

Pelkmans, J. (1985). The institutional economics of European integration. In M. Cappelletti, J. Weiler & M. Seccombe (Eds.), *Integration through law – Europe and the American federal experience* (Vol. 1, Book 1). New York, NY: Walther de Gruyter.

Pelkmans, J. (2001), Making EU network markets more competitive, Oxford Review of Economic Policy, autumn, Vol. 17, 3

Pelkmans, J. (2005). Testing for subsidiarity. In T. Bruha & C. Nowak (Eds.), *Die Europaeische Union: Innere verfasstheit und globale Handlungsfaehigkeit*. Baden-Baden: Nomos. BEEP Briefing No. 13, College of Europe. Retrieved from <www.coleurope.eu/ECO>.

Pelkmans, J. (2006). *European integration, methods and economic analysis* (3rd ed.). Essex: Pearson Education.

Pelkmans, J. (2007). Mutual recognition in goods, on promises and illusions. *Journal of European Public Policy, 14*(5), 699-716.

Pelkmans, J. (2010). More internal market without strategy? In M. Guimaraes & A. Faria (Eds.), *Product market integration: A multi-faceted approach*. Bingley, UK: Emerald Publishers.

Pelkmans, J. (2011). EU single market: Economic impact. In *The new Palgrave dictionary of economics*. Retrieved from <www.dictionaryofeconomics.com>.

Pelkmans, J. (2012). Mutual recognition: Economic and regulatory logic in goods and services. In T. Eger & B. Schaefer (Eds.), *Research handbook on the economics of EU law*. Cheltenham, UK: Edward Elgar.

Pelkmans, J., Acedo Montoya, L. & Maravalle, A. (2008, October). How product market reforms lubricate shock adjustment in the euro area (Economic Papers No. 341). DG Ecfin, European Economy. (Also published in: M. Buti, et al. (Eds.), *The EURO, the first decade*. Cambridge: Cambridge University Press.)

Pelkmans, J. & Correia de Brito, A. (2012). *Enforcement in the EU single market*. Brussels: CEPS. Retrieved from <www.ceps.eu>. (Also as eBook, pp. 143).

Pelkmans, J. & G. Luchetta (2013), *Enjoying a single market for network industries?* Paris, Notre Europe, Studies & Reports no. 95, February.

Pelkmans, J. & Renda, A. (2011). Single eComms market? No such thing .... *Communications & Strategies, 82*, 21-42.

Renda, A. (2011). *Law and economics in the RIA world*. Antwerp: Intersentia.

Ruding, O., et al. (1992). Conclusions and recommendations of the Committee of Independent Experts on company taxation. Luxembourg: Office of Official Publications of the EC.

Sauter, W. (2009). Services of general economic interest and universal service in EU law. *European Law Review, 33*(2), 167-193.

SER. (2005, June). *The services directive in the EU internal market* [in Dutch, extensive summaries in English and French]. The Hague: SER, Advies 2005/07.

Spaak, P.H., et al. (1956, April). *Report of the heads of delegation of the foreign affairs ministers*[in French], Brussels. Unpublished.

Straathof, B., Linders, G., Lejour, A. & Moehlmann, J. (2008). *The internal market and the Dutch economy, implications for trade and economic growth* (CPB Document No. 168).

UNICE. (2004). *It's the internal market, stupid*! Brussels [now BusinessEurope].

Van der Horst, A., Bettendorf, L. & Rojas-Romagosa, H. (2007, March). *Will corporate tax consolidation improve efficiency in the EU?* (CPB Document No. 141).

VNO-NCW & MKB. (2008). *When is EC1992 really coming? Concrete proposals to complete the internal market (in Dutch)*. The Hague & Brussels.

12 The Stability Pact: an Eternal Promise

*Amy Verdun**

12.1 Introduction

The Stability and Growth Pact (SGP, or the 'Pact') was established to ensure that governments of the Member States of the European Union (EU) would keep their respective budgetary deficits and public debt under control. The Pact applies to all 27 countries of the EU. The purpose of the rules was to impose the necessary discipline on countries (government and – indirectly – citizens). Since the irrevocable fixing of exchange rates in Economic and Monetary Union (EMU) in 1999, which was followed by the introduction of euro coins and banknotes (on 1 January 2002), the SGP was supposed to enforce this discipline. However, it soon became clear that the SGP was too much of a 'fair weather' pact: in economic good times, governments more or less stuck to the rules, but in economic bad times, they were all too easily overlooked. In 2003, the French and German governments ignored the rules, resulting in a temporary suspension of the Pact and in a reformed SGP in 2005 (see below). The global financial and economic crisis had such a major impact on the economies of the Member States that many governments have allowed their deficits and debt to rise, thus bringing them into conflict with the SGP. Of the 27 Member States, only 4 more or less stay within the so-called 3% budgetary deficit rule stipulated in the Pact; 23 are in the so-called excessive deficit procedure for exceeding this norm.[1]

In this chapter I examine what the SGP has managed to achieve. In the context of the current crisis, I seek to analyze what lessons may be learned from the first 10 years of EMU so as to inform us about what decisions need to be taken now.[2]

This contribution focuses particularly on the role that the Netherlands has played in developing the euro, and, what role is it playing in addressing the current

* The author would like to thank the Social Science and Humanities Research Council of Canada (SSHRC) for its financial support (Grant: 410-2011-0405 'Europe's Sovereign Debt Crisis: Lessons for European Integration'). She is also grateful to Prof. Dr. Adriaan Schout (editor), Prof. Dr. Adri Smaling and H.C. Verdun for comments on earlier versions of this chapter.

1 *See* the website of the European Commission: <http://ec.europa.eu/economy_finance/economic_-governance/sgp/deficit/index_en.htm> (accessed 25 March 2012).

2 *See also* Verdun, A. (2010). Ten years EMU: An assessment of ten critical claims. *International Journal of Economics and Business Research*, 2(1/2), 144-163.

financial crisis and the sovereign debt crisis. In the past, the Netherlands usually acted as gatekeeper,[3] championed strict and binding rules and strived hard for a proper monitoring of their enforcement. What could be the role of the Netherlands in the next stages of the integration process? I also address whether the Netherlands can, for instance, evade the stipulated 3% rule and whether it should continue to support countries in trouble.

This chapter starts by describing the background and reforms of the Pact (Section 2). Then, I go into the effects of the global financial and economic crisis on public finances, European integration in regard to EMU and the debt crisis (Section 3). Section 4 deals with the role of the Netherlands in developing and reforming the SGP, its role in fighting the negative effects of the crisis as well as its influence on the European responses to the debt crisis. Finally, in the conclusion, I discuss what the Dutch contribution could be in shaping the future of economic and monetary integration in Europe.

12.2 Background

The euro was introduced in three steps following the blueprint set out in the Delors Report (1989). The first phase was to liberalize the capital markets (1990). Step two involved setting up the European Monetary Institute (in 1994) – forerunner of the European Central Bank (ECB). As already stipulated in the Treaty of Maastricht (1992), each Member State that wanted to participate in the so-called third phase of EMU (irrevocably fixing exchange rates, followed by the introduction of the single currency) had to meet the following four convergence criteria: (1) *Low inflation*. The average annual inflation rate in a Member States must not exceed the average of the three best performing Member States by more than 1.5%; (2) *Sound government finances*. The budget deficit of the Member State must not be more than 3% of gross domestic product (GDP) (also known as the '3% rule') and government debt must not exceed 60% of GDP, unless this debt had been sufficiently diminishing and approaching the reference value; (3) *Exchange rate stability*. For at least two years, the Member State must have observed the normal fluctuation margins (±15%) of the exchange rate mechanism of the European Monetary System (EMS); (4) *Low interest rates*. The average long-term interest rate must not exceed 2% of that of the three best performing Member States in terms of price stability.

As Germany was concerned about the way the euro countries would behave after joining the euro, there were calls to create a 'stability pact' (to which later the 'growth' element was added by the French, see below). Under pressure from then German Minister of Finance Theo Waigel, the SGP was finally established in 1997.

3 Maes, I. & Verdun, A. (2005). The role of medium-sized countries in the creation of EMU: The cases of Belgium and the Netherlands. *Journal of Common Market Studies, 43*(2), 327-348.

Waigel feared the prospect of EMU starting with a large number of (southern) countries, whose performance in terms of exchange rate stability and sound public finances had so far been less than satisfactory. He wondered how adequate the rules would be in enforcing discipline on budget deficits and public debt once Member States had introduced the euro. Indeed, the Treaty of Maastricht had provided for more or less clear convergence criteria to be met by countries before being allowed to participate in the euro. The Treaty was, however, much vaguer about how discipline would be enforced after that. Therefore, in November 1995, Waigel proposed safeguarding price stability through an intergovernmental treaty after the third EMU phase would have started. The fact that Waigel made such a proposal, and at that moment, should be seen against the background of the domestic political situation in Germany.[4] At that time, regional elections were being held, and moreover, in Waigel's party (the CSU) a leadership struggle was taking place. It was important for Waigel to appear as the guardian of price stability. In the end, no new intergovernmental treaty was signed, but the same idea was simply couched in a regular European framework: in 1997, two Regulations[5] were adopted which further explained Articles 99 and 104 of the Maastricht Treaty. In addition, the European Council adopted a resolution which clarified the application of the Protocol on the so-called excessive deficit procedure.

Once the euro was firmly established, in 1999, and the euro coins and banknotes began circulating in the 12 Member States in 2002, it was hoped that the SGP rules would ensure that Member States would keep their public finances under control. In accordance with the SGP, it was the task of the European Commission to assess whether countries were complying with the Pact. Already in the first years, some Member States had difficulty staying within the so-called 3% limit. In 2003, this was a problem even for Germany and France, which was all the more remarkable since Germany and France in particular had urged for the creation of the SGP. For instance, in 1997, the French had single-handedly ensured that the Pact would not just be called 'Stability Pact' but 'SGP'. It therefore came as a surprise to most countries that in November 2003 Germany and France, of all countries, were practically flouting the Pact.[6] Following a vote in the Council of Ministers of Economic Affairs and Finance on 25 November 2003, it appeared that not enough Member States were prepared to reprimand Germany and France in line with the SGP rules. The fact was that Germany's and France's budget deficits had been too high for three years in a row and, according to the rules of the SGP, these countries now had to be reprimanded. However, Germany and France were able to round up just enough support to prevent a vote in the Council. In 2003, a qualified majority had to be found to go through the next phase of the

4 Heipertz, M. & Verdun, A. (2010). *Ruling Europe: Theory and politics of the stability and growth pact.* Cambridge, UK: Cambridge University Press, pp. 50-51.

5 1466/97 and 1467/97.

6 Heipertz & Verdun (2010), pp. 140-149.

EDP. Germany and France made sure that a few loyal allies (such as Luxembourg) voted against, only just managing to prevent the required qualified majority. Instead, the Council adopted 'conclusions' in which Germany and France indicated how they would fight the deficits. Later, in July 2004, the adoption of 'conclusions' of this type instead of following the normal procedure would be declared null and void by the European Court of Justice in Luxembourg. However, the damage had already been done. As a result, it was assumed that the November 2003 vote and the Council conclusions had been the final blow to the SGP.[7] In the end, this whole episode triggered the realization that the SGP would have to be revised.[8]

Finally, after many rounds of negotiations, the SGP was reformed in 2005.[9] The modified Pact was more flexible in that it broadened the economic basis of the budget rules. In addition, more account could be taken of the type of reforms a government was carrying through (for instance, pension reforms might involve high short-term costs but could consolidate the debt in the long run). Furthermore, the medium term had to be considered as well, and, in particular, better use should be made of periods of growth beyond the trend to consolidate budgets so as to minimize problems in times of low growth. Finally, it was decided that in monitoring the budgetary position, more account would be taken of the level and sustainability of the debt.

During the time following the reform of the Pact, Member States' budgetary positions greatly improved, benefiting especially from the incoming economic tide. However, this soon came to end when in September 2008 the global financial crisis hit us with full force.[10]

Throughout this genesis of the Pact, the Netherlands remained convinced of the importance of clear rules. Already when the SGP was first planned, at the time of Minister Waigel's initiatives, the Netherlands, through Minister of Finance Gerrit Zalm, supported his ideas. When the rules were further elaborated, the Netherlands persisted in its opinion that they should be clear and unambiguous and must be adhered to according to the letter of the law – and not fluctuate with the political whims of the day.[11] When the crisis broke out in 2003, the Netherlands believed that Germany and France ought to be presented with the consequences of their lax behaviour regarding their public finances. The Dutch

7 For a more detailed description and analysis of this period, *see* Heipertz & Verdun (2010), pp. 128-153.

8 The Six-Pack has now reversed the rules. Should a similar situation occur, a qualified majority will be required to stop the procedure.

9 Regulations 1055/2005 and 1056/2005.

10 As mentioned earlier, the financial crisis began in 2007, when banks became increasingly reluctant to lend to each other and several banks ran into financial problems; *see also* Verdun, A. (2007). Economic developments in the Euro area [Annual Review]. *Journal of Common Market Studies, 45*(S1), 213-230.

11 Schure, P. & Verdun, A. (2008). Legislative bargaining in the European Union: The divide between large and small member states. *European Union Politics, 9*(4), 459-486.

stance was all the more remarkable since the Netherlands itself would soon also run an excessive deficit. So, in the long run, the rules would also pose similar difficulties to the Netherlands. The Dutch attitude vis-à-vis the SGP during 2003-2005 was rooted in the principle that the rules should be enforced and not be applied flexibly whenever politicians so wished.[12] Thus, in 2004-2005 the Netherlands was part of the minority that preferred maintaining the strict SGP rules and not allowing them to become too flexible.

Returning to the questions posed at the beginning of this chapter, what has the SGP achieved in the EU? The Maastricht Treaty was vague about the enforcement of the convergence criteria after the launch of the euro. The SGP changed that. The rules were too strict, on the one hand, and too lenient, on the other. Germany and France had been able to circumvent them. The renewed Pact is somewhat better targeted to the needs of the day, but it is still more or less the same Pact.

In my view, the first phase of the SGP has shown us that the Pact does not work if one or more countries do not stick to the rules. This jeopardizes not only solidarity, but also the very nature of the EU – a Union built on laws and rules. If there is to be a different type of governance, the rules should be changed first. Moreover, it was obvious that in the absence of an economic government, governance by rules was necessary instead.

12.3 The Financial and Economic Crisis and the Debt Crisis

The situation took a dramatic turn in 2008. As a result of the global financial crisis that held the world in its grip in the last quarter of 2008, economic relations were completely disrupted, the banking industry came under great pressure, companies had big problems getting credit, and the financial system came to a halt, or worse, was at risk of collapsing. Due to this turmoil, the economy shrank, the result being that in 2009 most EU Member States went into economic recession. That year, the euro countries' GDP decreased by 4%.[13]

The governments of most member countries of the Organisation for Economic Cooperation and Development (OECD) initially chose to tackle this financial crisis by spending money. Governments – e.g., of the Netherlands, the United Kingdom and the United States – tried all sorts of things to keep the economy going, for instance, stimulating demand via investments, in the hope to thus revive the economy. The same path was followed by EU-level authorities.[14] They chose to

12 Schure & Verdun (2008).

13 IMF. (2011, April). *World economic outlook: Tensions from the two-speed recovery. Unemployment, commodities, and capital Flows*. Washington, DC: IMF.

14 Verdun, A. (2012a, October 26). Small states and the global economic crisis: An assessment. *European Political Science*. Advance online publication. doi:10.1057/eps.2012.34.

spend money, even if they did not really have any. Also, governments had to step in to support banks. In the Netherlands, the rescue of ABN AMRO cost €30 billion besides another 200 billion in guarantees for banks. This stimulation and bank support resulted in ballooning budget deficits and public debt, not only in the Member States of the EU but also in the United States.

The EU responded by announcing that the Pact was still in force. In fact, the SGP contains a clause stating that if in a crisis a Member State's economy shrinks by more than 2% and its excessive budget deficit is exceeding the reference value but close to it, and the excess is temporary, normal sanctions may be suspended for as long as the Member State in question is struggling with this crisis. An international financial crisis resulting in the economy shrinking by 2% is an example of such a situation. Admittedly, many countries immediately reported a much bigger budget deficit than one which would be considered 'close to the reference value'. Indeed, in an early stage the EU said that the rules would be strictly enforced. It thus happened that in 2009 and 2010 the European Commission was still issuing convergence reports reprimanding governments of Member States for allowing their national budget deficits to go well beyond the 3% limit.[15]

However, the debt crisis that started in the autumn of 2010 cannot directly and solely be attributed to the problems surrounding those countries that had an excessive deficit of several per cent above the three per cent limit. The origins of the crisis can be traced back to the economic problems in countries struggling with the effects of the financial and economic crisis: Greece, Portugal, Spain and Ireland. But other countries have been a factor as well, such as Italy. Even the domestic policy of a country like Germany has contributed to the debt crisis.

In Greece, a new government took office in autumn 2009 and immediately had to admit that the budget deficit was much higher than reported by the previous government. In October 2009, it announced that the deficit was 12.8% instead of the 3.6% of GDP reported earlier. This announcement was the beginning of a long period of problems that grew worse over time. The credit rating agencies kept downgrading Greece's status. It thus became more difficult for Greece to further extend its debts, the result being an ever-increasing risk that repayment would no longer be possible – and that the Greek government would go bankrupt.[16] This situation plunged the eurozone into crisis.[17]

What is striking about this crisis is that a relatively small country, Greece, has posed a European – and almost global – risk to financial stability. One of the rea-

15 European Commission. (2010). *Convergence report 2010*. European Economy No. 3. DG Economic and Financial Affairs. <http://ec.europa.eu/economy_finance/publications/european_economy/2010/pdf/ee-2010-3_en.pdf>.

16 For a discussion of the Greek crisis, *see* Featherstone, K. (2010). The JCMS annual lecture: The Greek sovereign debt crisis and EMU: A failing state in a skewed regime. *Journal of Common Market Studies, 49*(2), 193-217.

17 *See also* Verdun, A. (2012b). Introduction to the symposium: Economic and Monetary Union and the crisis of the Eurozone. *Journal of Common Market Studies, 50*(6), 863-865.

sons is that the EMU rules provide for a 'no-bailout clause'.[18] When EMU was created, the Member States wanted to be sure that each of them would keep its own public finances in check. The convergence criteria had even been especially developed to ensure that interest rates would not suddenly go up when a Member State's debt would be (far) higher than that of the other Member States and it would thus be more expensive for that Member State to attract money. Demand from that country would be too high, thus triggering higher interest rates and inflation. Initially, the possibility that the creation of the euro might lead to government bankruptcies was not taken into consideration.

Of course, throughout 1992-2007, hardly anyone doubted that the 'no-bailout clause' was something other than a purely political statement. Everyone assumed that in case of a real crisis the Member States would help each other anyway. The most remarkable signal came from the financial markets, which during the SGP crisis of November 2003 had barely reacted to the crisis.

However, legally speaking, the 'no-bailout clause' did make it very difficult for Germany to act quickly and decisively with regard to the Greek problem in autumn 2009 and spring 2010. It was difficult for the Germans to provide funds to Greece, not only on account of the size of the amount, but also and particularly because of the existence of this 'no-bailout clause'. In addition, for Germany it was necessary to give off the right signals. So, if funds were to be made available, it would have to be clear that there would be rules on how the funds, public finances, tax collection and public expenditure would be dealt with in the future. In other words, how can the problems underlying the government debt crisis be tackled in the future?

Germany, like the Netherlands for that matter, found it very important to prevent what economic literature calls 'moral hazard'. If banks and governments are not held accountable for their behaviour, they will never be able to make a sound assessment of the risks. In other words, if the Greeks are given money to pay off their debts or to buy out banks but the underlying problems are not addressed, how can the problems be prevented from recurring in the future? In addition, dealing with the Greek debt problem was a politically very sensitive issue, particularly in Merkel's own political party, the CDU. As a result of these political and legal considerations, the Germans have had great difficulty making swift decisions since the start of the crisis. Consequently, the problems became bigger and bigger as the deadlock persisted. In May 2010, a decision had to be taken to support Greece. In the end, a coalition was formed consisting of the International Monetary Fund (IMF), the European Commission, the ECB and the euro Member States, which together promised to help Greece with an amount of €110 billion.

18 Art. 125 of the Treaty on the Functioning of the European Union, in short 'EU Functioning Treaty' (formerly: Art. 103 Treaty of Maastricht).

The banking industry, but also the rest of the economy, suffered major losses as a result of the financial crisis, and, in the end, the fear of the 'double dip' became reality. Governments responded by spending money, thus incurring huge government debt and budget deficits.

After Greece was first helped out in May 2010, the problems were not over yet. Between May 2010 and March 2012, further rounds of support were provided to Greece, as well as to Ireland and Portugal. So, the solutions had to be found at European level. First of all, the European Financial Stability Facility (EFSF) was set up. The EFSF is a transitional body, a temporary organization helping Member States and to be succeeded by the ESM. The EFSF is a temporary emergency facility that was not even allowed to carry the name 'fund' in order to emphasize that it is not a permanent bailout fund. Thanks to Member State guarantees, the EFSF can raise funds on the market and grant loans to problem countries. The tighter European rules, such as the 2011 Six-Pack, made it politically possible to go a step further and set up the permanent European Stability Mechanism (ESM). With this financing mechanism, debt, restructuring and loans can be handled in a European context. The ESM's capacity will probably be around €700 billion. In December 2011, it was decided to speed up its launch, i.e., as of July 2012. After the decision of the German Constitutional Court in Karlsruhe, the ESM entered into force on 27 September 2012, with the inaugural meeting on 8 October of that year.

In addition, the 'Euro Plus Pact' was adopted (on 11 March 2011) by the eurozone countries and a number of other Member States[19] (hence the name 'Euro *Plus* Pact'). France and Germany were the driving forces behind this Pact, which had to strengthen the SGP and Member States' competitiveness. Moreover, objectives were set regarding employment and financial stability, albeit, in early 2011, still through the – soft – open coordination method (OCM). With open coordination, countries have far more freedom to decide how to go about achieving objectives.

In the course of 2011, this non-committal arrangement was replaced by the 'Six-Pack' (five Regulations and one Directive).[20] The Six-Pack, which entered into force in December 2011, has tightened the rules governing the Stability Pact. It has sharpened the SGP's teeth and thus forces Member States to keep their public finances under control. For example, in November 2003, Germany and France could quite easily circumvent the SGP because they 'only' needed a blocking minority to be able to ignore the recommendations of the European Commission. The Six-Pack has reversed the roles. If a Member State's deficit continues to be too high, the Commission will propose recommendations that the European Council can block only by a *qualified majority*. Frustrating the SGP procedure will thus be much more difficult. Another issue is the role of government debt. In the

19 Bulgaria, Denmark, Latvia, Lithuania, Poland and Romania.

20 Negotiations on the Six-Pack already started in autumn 2010; it was approved by the European Parliament in September 2011 and entered into force in December 2011.

past, both debt and deficit were important, but the SGP particularly focused on the budget deficit. With the Six-Pack, the significance of government debt has increased. A Member State whose debt exceeds 60% of GDP will now automatically enter the 'excessive deficit procedure' and must reduce its debt annually by at least one twentieth. Also, a ceiling is imposed on the growth of government expenditure, which may not exceed a certain percentage based on average medium-term economic growth. Lastly, some new elements have been added, such as rules on correcting macroeconomic imbalances (e.g., as regards balance of payments deficit, increase in house prices and labour productivity).

Finally, on 30 January 2012, 26 countries agreed to sign a new fiscal treaty – the United Kingdom did not join.[21] This legal framework offers in particular Germany more certainty that the euro rules have been reinforced. Together with the ESM (with more funds) it offers more guarantees, thus paving the way for a larger – and potentially riskier – role of the ECB and for the IMF to expand its activities in the euro crisis.

12.4 The Role of the Netherlands in Europe

Over the past 20 years, the role of the Netherlands in the SGP has been quite consistent. From the very beginning of EMU and the SGP, the Dutch have insisted on clear rules and strict enforcement.[22] The Netherlands played a leading role in creating the SGP, in preventing the SGP from being reformed in 2003 (together with countries like Finland and Austria), and in tightening control in 2011.

When the sovereign debt crisis broke out in full force in Greece, later followed by similar problems in Ireland and Portugal, there were those in the Netherlands – not only in parties like the PVV and the SP, but also in the government parties CDA and VVD – who did not want to help solve the problems. As alluded to in Section 3 above, the Netherlands, like Germany, faced a dilemma: either helping the weaker countries and running the risk of undermining the EMU architecture, or not helping but with the resulting danger of the entire euro edifice collapsing like a house of cards. The past period has shown that it is important to adapt the European governance rules so that there are clear rules on how to address the risks of moral hazard. The Netherlands has always been consistent in pointing this out.

21 On 1 March 2012, 25 government leaders signed the new treaty (the Czech Republic and the UK have not yet joined).

22 Verdun, A. (2002). The Netherlands and EMU: A small open economy in search of prosperity. In K. Dyson (Ed.), *European states and the Euro: Playing the semi-sovereignty game*. Oxford, UK: Oxford University Press, pp. 238-254; Verdun, A. (2008). The Netherlands: A turning point in Dutch-EU relations? In Kenneth Dyson (Ed.), *The Euro at ten: Europeanization, convergence and power*. Oxford, UK: Oxford University Press, pp. 222-240; Maes & Verdun (2005); Schure & Verdun (2008); Heipertz & Verdun (2010).

The decision to conclude a new fiscal treaty is quite remarkable – even though not all Member States have signed it. The signatories hope that this treaty will be incorporated into the EU Treaty within five years.
In September 2011, Prime Minister Rutte launched the idea of an independent EU commissioner in charge of budgetary discipline – which was soon supported by Finland, Germany, France and also by Commission President Barroso.[23] Furthermore, over the past few years, the Netherlands has constantly argued in favour of clear rules and their consistent application. Many of the Dutch demands have now been met. The hard line taken by Minister De Jager managed to win the Netherlands some, initially dubious, points, such as involvement of the IMF, a stronger role of the European Commission, and the so-called haircut for financial institutions (public sector involvement).[24]
During the euro crisis, the Netherlands – that is, Minister of Finance De Jager and Prime Minister Rutte – has always stayed closely in touch with Germany. However, on repeated occasions, Germany (traditionally a very important partner and a driving force in European integration) appeared not to be that keen on, or even need, support from the Dutch. The all-time low for the Netherlands proved to be the bilateral French-German talks in Deauville (October 2010) where 'Merkozy' (Federal Chancellor Angela Merkel and President Nicolas Sarkozy) decided to exchange the strict line agreed between Germany and the Netherlands for less binding budgetary rules.[25] This begs the question of the Dutch role and influence. Considering the ultimate results, the Netherlands has managed to achieve a great deal by sticking to its guns.
In spring 2012, the Netherlands threatened to run into problems and break the 3% rule. As a result, a debate emerged in the Netherlands about the strict applications of the European rules on government finances.[26] As we have seen in the

23 Barroso steunt Nederlands plan begrotingscommissaris [Barroso supports Dutch plan budget commissioner]. (2011, October 11). *Trouw.* <www.trouw.nl/tr/nl/7964/Schuldencrisis/article/detail/2963661/2011/10/11/Barroso-steunt-Nederlands-plan-begrotingscommissaris.dhtml> (accessed 24 May 2012).

24 Visser, M. (2012). *De Eurocrisis. Onthullend verslag van politiek falen* [The euro crisis. A revealing report of political failure]. Amsterdam, The Netherlands: Atlas-Contact.

25 Schout, A. & van der Tas, R. (2012). Van Rompuy als oliemannetje van de Europese Raad: opereren in de schaduw van Merkozy [Van Rompuy oiling the wheels of the European Council: Operating in Merkozy's shadow]. *Internationale Spectator, 66*(4), 191-195.

26 In March 2012, the Netherlands Bureau for Economic Policy Analysis (Centraal Planbureau – CPB) calculated that the Netherlands would have problems complying with the European budgetary rules. In early March, the government stated that the party chairmen of the tolerance parties would exceed the 3% mark: 'Gedoogcoalitie laat 3-procentsnorm los' [Tolerance coalition abandons 3-per cent mark]. (2012, March 1). *Trouw.* <www.trouw.nl/tr/nl/4500/Politiek/article/detail/3210885/2012/03/01/Wilders-9-miljard-bezuinigen-wellicht-niet-verstandig.dhtml> (accessed 24 May 2012). Mid-March 2012, neither the PVV nor the PvdA supported the proposal to keep to Europe's budgetary rules: <www.joop.nl/politiek/detail/artikel/pvda_zegt_nee_tegen_-europese_begrotingsregels>.

case of Germany and France in 2003, and in subsequent years, it is inadvisable to ignore the SGP rules in a European context for the purpose of gaining short-term domestic advantage. Such actions undermine solidarity in the EU and the foundation for regulating government finances in the EU, which is based on the SGP rules. In most liberal democracies there is more room for political debate because these countries have a government that has been democratically elected and a parliament that may send the government home if government policies lose the necessary support. At the European level, democracy is more indirect and in light of the absence of democratic processes, the SGP rules play a larger role in coordinating public finances.

With the new SGP regime, the rules have become stricter, thus making it more difficult to break or fail to comply with them. In the Netherlands, members of parliament frequently raise the question whether rules that are clearer and easier to comply with should be seen as further political integration and thus as a limitation of sovereignty (see, for instance, the Slob motion of 17 February 2011[27]). However, European integration cannot be regarded as a so-called zero-sum game. Better enforcement of 'European' rules does not imply a limitation of a Member State's sovereignty. I believe that if Member States set objectives at European level and certain rules are found to be less effective in pursuing those objectives, a logical next step is to review and possibly tighten these rules. An important question in this context is whether there is agreement on the objectives and, if so, how they can best be achieved. In my view, there is no point in immediately raising the issue of sovereignty in that case. For years, the Netherlands basically wanted clear rules that are easy to comply with. Now that they are here, this goal has been met. In that sense it is bizarre that many Dutch do not want to comply with these rules now, after politicians had been asking for them for such a long time.

12.5 Conclusion: the Role of the Netherlands in the Future of Europe

Being a medium-sized country, the Netherlands generally benefits from a stricter interpretation of the role of budgetary rules in the EU and from an independent position of the Commission.[28] In this respect, it often failed to rally the specific support it had hoped for. The Netherlands has traditionally been in favour of deeper integration and wants the rules to be clear and easy to enforce.[29] It has

27 Dutch House of Representatives, *Vergaderjaar* 2010-2011, 21 501-07, No. 779, Council of Economic and Financial Affairs, motion by Member of Parliament Slob et al., 17 February.

28 Schure & Verdun (2008).

29 *See* the '100%' Union aspired by the Netherlands, Schout, A. & Wiersma, J.M. (2012, April 21). Rob de Wijk zit ernaast: Nederland is in EU geen paria [Rob de Wijk is wrong: the Netherlands not a pariah in EU]. *Trouw*.

acted as pioneer and has wanted to make Member States aware of the fact that it is impossible to continue managing national public finances on too weak a basis. The most recent developments at European level – the fiscal treaty – indicate that, finally, the rest of Europe also realizes the importance of saving the euro and appreciates that it is first and foremost the responsibility of the euro countries themselves to keep their accounts in order. For a long time, the aim was to prevent stringent rules, but now such stricter rules seem to become the new standard.

As has become apparent now, the Netherlands would be well-advised simply to keep insisting on good governance and enforcement of the rules, thus underlining that it is taking European integration to the next level. On account of the domestic political vicissitudes, Germany has had difficulty consistently taking the lead. The Netherlands, in its own special way, has always kept the dialogue open, entering into discussions and debates. It seems that this Dutch approach has paid off quite well in the long run.

At national level, too, it is vitally important to keep explaining what is at stake. In my view, it is essential for the Dutch political leaders to continue to explain to the Dutch people, other Europeans, and political elites why it is important to opt for deeper European integration in response to the economic crisis in Europe. After all, political inaction often leads to political crisis.

13 The Paradox of the Netherlands: Why a Successful Economy Is Struggling?

*Arjen van Witteloostuijn en Corina Hendriks**

13.1 The Paradox

Though relatively speaking, the Netherlands is still doing well, public debate seems to suggest quite otherwise. For a country in recession, unemployment is exceptionally low and there is very little sign of more poverty. Of course, the Dutch Railways frequently grind to a halt, the housing market has collapsed, health care is becoming too expensive, housing corporations' speculations are hitting the roof and the public deficit threatens to run out of control. To be sure, all these problems demand attention, but what is rankling is that these lamentations are hiding the fact that, globally speaking, the Dutch population is by and large remarkably rich and happy. In this chapter, an attempt is made to explain this paradox. Is there really an apparent contradiction? Or is reality not what it seems? Is the Netherlands doing well or badly? Or is it doing both well and badly? And why is that? In the sections below, we will try to find out whether the Netherlands is not doing well (Section 2), where it is perhaps doing quite well (Section 3) and why it should do better (Section 4). This analysis will lead to more lamentation: where is the political courage that Europe and the Netherlands need for bringing about the necessary changes and reforms (Section 5)?

13.2 The Netherlands Is Not Doing Well

For a few decades now, a curious group of mostly leftish economists/politicians and rightish economists/politicians have been worrying about the Dutch economy. From time to time, this group sounds the alarm, pointing out that the Dutch economy should soon and drastically be reformed to keep up in a rapidly changing Europe and world. Depending on the messenger's political preference, two different categories of indicators are used. Leftish economists/politicians see the low spending on education and research and development as a sign of creep-

---

* Arjen van Witteloostuijn is Professor of Economics and Management at the Universities of Antwerp and Tilburg. Corina Hendriks works at the *Mr. Hans van Mierlo Stichting*.

ing decline.[1] International rankings demonstrate time and again that in these three areas the Dutch economy is among those at the bottom of the class of rich economies. This means, in their eyes, that not much is done in the way of achieving the necessary strengthening of the knowledge economy. Sure enough, the European rankings in Table 13.1 show that Dutch performance is certainly not among the best.

Table 13.1 Investment in Research, Development and Education as a Percentage of GNP in 2003 and 2008

	Investment in research and development		Investment in education	
	2003	2008	2003	2008
Belgium	1.87	1.97	6.38	6.83
Bulgaria	0.48	0.47	4.90	5.19
Cyprus	0.35	0.43	8.64	8.76
Denmark	2.58	2.85	8.65	8.30
Germany	2.54	2.69	5.62	5.25
Estonia	0.77	1.28	–	–
Finland	3.44	3.70	6.57	6.28
France	2.18	2.12	6.46	6.18
Greece	0.57	–	3.76	–
Hungary	0.94	1.00	6.45	5.64
Ireland	1.16	1.45	4.69	5.96
Italy	1.11	1.21	5.14	4.99
Latvia	0.38	0.62	5.15	6.31
Lithuania	0.67	0.79	5.59	5.43
Luxembourg	1.65	1.57	3.77	3.15
The Netherlands	1.92	1.77	5.73	6.38
Malta	0.25	0.65	6.10	6.32
Austria	2.24	2.67	5.88	5.96
Poland	0.54	0.60	6.01	5.77
Portugal	0.71	1.50	5.66	5.38
Romania	0.39	0.57	3.45	5.25
Slovakia	0.57	0.46	4.75	4.29
Slovenia	1.27	1.65	5.65	4.29
Spain	1.05	1.35	4.90	5.28
Czech Republic	1.20	1.41	4.88	4.65
Sweden	3.80	3.70	7.49	6.91
Switzerland	2.90	3.00	6.62	5.93

1 Of course, this is not the only thing leftish (or rightish, for that matter) economists/politicians worry about. For instance, a more equal distribution of wealth and the protection of the 'underclass' are permanent items on their agenda. However, not everything can be addressed in this chapter. Hence, we focus on a few key issues we believe are critical to understanding the Dutch paradox.

	Investment in research and development		Investment in education	
	2003	2008	2003	2008
UK	1.75	1.79	6.19	7.08
EU-27	1.76	1.77	5.78	7.21

Source: Eurostat. Investment in education (public and private) as a percentage of GNP. Figures on Luxembourg and Romania only relate to public investment.

With a meagre percentage of 1.77% of gross national product (GNP) spent on investments in research and development in 2008, the Netherlands ranks 10th, far behind countries such as Finland and Sweden (both ranking first with 3.70%), as well as Switzerland, Denmark and Germany (in third, fourth and fifth place, with 3.00%, 2.85%, and 2.69%, respectively). Unlike that of many other countries, the Dutch percentage has continued to drop after 2003. Investments in education are doing slightly better, the percentage being 6.38 in 2008 – a rise compared with the 5.73% in 2003. This puts the Netherlands sixth in Europe in 2008.

Rightish economists/politicians often come up with two further observations: the lack of entrepreneurship and the enormous burden of the public sector on the national economy. On the one hand, fast-growing businesses in the Netherlands are as rare as the *Elfstedentocht*. Nearly all large Dutch firms are either very old or were established when they split from an ancient dinosaur. On the other hand, people break out in a sweat each month they receive their payslip. Even allowing for employers' costs, a large percentage of the gross salary disappears to some public fund or arrangement. Some illustrative indicators are listed in Tables 13.2a, b and Figures 13.1a, b.

Table 13.2a Self-employment (% of the Working Population)

	2001	2002	2003	2004	2005	2006	2007	2008	% 2001-2008
Belgium	11.5	11.6	11.3	10.7	11.1	11.1	11.5	11.1	– 3
Denmark	6.4	6.7	6.5	6.3	6.4	6.9	6.9	7.0	9
Germany	8.6	8.6	8.8	9.3	9.6	9.7	9.7	9.7	13
Finland	7.8	7.9	8.1	8.2	8.3	8.6	8.5	8.8	13
France	8.2	8.1	8.1	8.2	8.4	8.6	8.7	8.8	7
Ireland	11.4	11.4	11.4	11.8	11.5	11.0	11.6	11.6	2
The Netherlands	10.4	10.3	10.5	10.7	11.0	11.5	11.9	12.1	16
UK	10.4	10.4	11.0	11.2	11.1	11.2	11.4	11.4	10
EU-15	11.5	11.5	11.6	11.8	12	12.1	12.2	12.1	5
Japan	9.3	9.2	9.1	9.1	9.0	8.8	8.6	8.4	–10
US	10.0	9.8	10.0	10.1	10.1	10.1	10.1	9.8	– 2

Source: EIM (Benchmark Entrepreneurship) in: van Praag, M. & Stevens, L. (2010). Ondernemerschap na de crisis [Entrepreneurship after the crisis]. In A. van Witteloostuijn (Ed.), *Nederland na de crisis: Preadviezen van de Koninklijke Vereniging voor de Staathuishoudkunde 2010 [The Netherlands after the crisis: Pre-advice of the Royal Association for Political Economy 2010]*. The Hague: Sdu Uitgevers.

Table 13.2b Entry Percentages (New Businesses as a % of Existing Businesses)

	2001	2002	2003	2004	2005	2006	2007	2008
Belgium	6.5	6.5	6.5	7.3	7.7	8.4	9.3	9
Denmark	10.1	9.2	10.8	10.8	12.5	13.3	12.7	NA
Germany	9	8.8	9.7	10.3	8.8	8.1	7	6.6
Finland	8.4	8.6	9.4	10.2	10.8	11.5	11.8	11.1
France	6.8	6.7	7.8	6.5	6.4	6.6	6.9	7.1
Ireland	12.6	11.9	12.5	13.3	13.9	14.5	11.6	8.8
Italy	7.9	7.7	7.3	7.7	7.6	7.6	7.9	7.1
Japan	4.1	4.3	5.4	5.4	NA	4.1	NA	NA
The Netherlands	9.7	8.1	8	8.8	9.9	10.5	11.6	12.8
UK	12.7	12.6	13.2	12.7	12.1	12.1	13.2	13
US	9.5	9.5	9.2	9.7	10	9.9	9.9	9.6

Source: EIM (Benchmark Entrepreneurship) in: van Praag, M. & Stevens, L. (2010). Ondernemerschap na de crisis [Entrepreneurship after the crisis]. In A. van Witteloostuijn (Ed.), *Nederland na de crisis: Preadviezen van de Koninklijke Vereniging voor de Staathuishoudkunde 2010 [The Netherlands after the crisis: Pre-advice of the Royal Association for Political Economy 2010]*. The Hague: Sdu Uitgevers.

Figure 13.1a

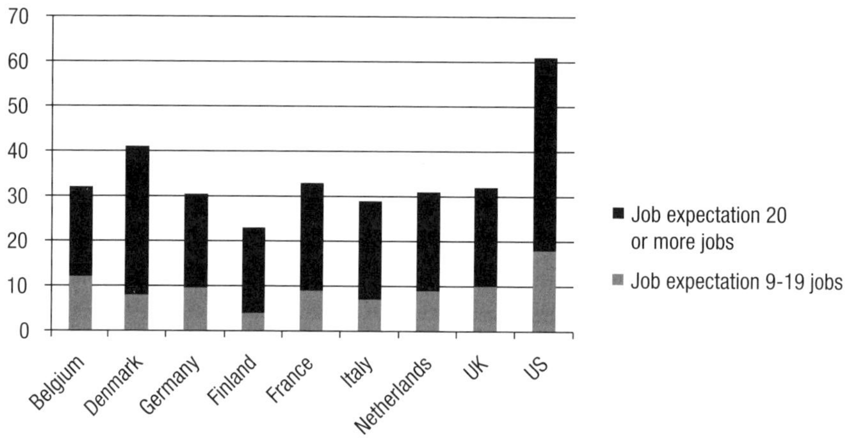

Figure 13.1b

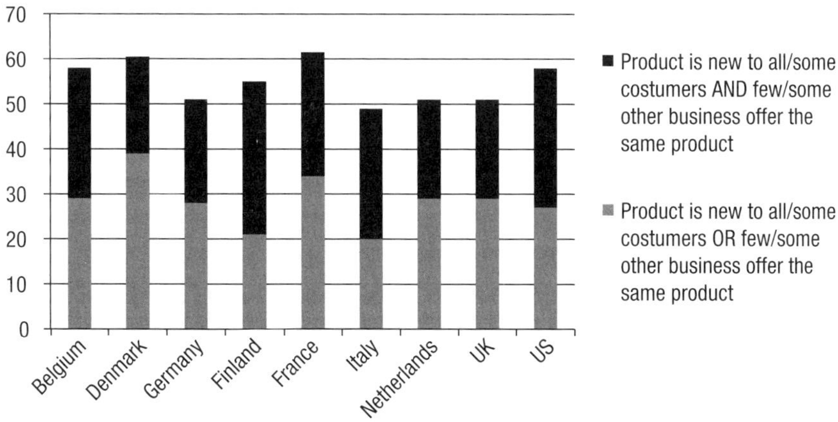

Comparative data of the Global Entrepreneurship Monitor (GEM) confirm the assumption that there are two sides to business activities in the Netherlands. On the one hand, the number of self-employed persons is strongly increasing, i.e., by 16% from 2001 to 2008 – an achievement that is reflected in, for instance, the proportionately high percentage of 12.8 new businesses in 2008. This puts the Netherlands in the lead globally. The result is that self-employed people represent 12.1% of the working population – a percentage not even reached in Anglo-Saxon countries like the United Kingdom (11.4%) and the United States (9.8%) in 2008. On the other hand, these businesses are doing far worse when it comes to growth expectations and innovations. Compared with eight other developed economies, Dutch performance in 2008-2012 is disappointing in that respect: in terms of growth expectations, only Finland and Italy are doing worse; and as regards innovations in starting businesses, the only country doing worse is Italy. At the same time, Tables 13.3a, b shows that with a public spending level of 51.2% of gross domestic product (GDP), the Dutch (semi-)public sector has returned to the level of the Den Uyl cabinet of the mid-1970s demonized by the right. The Netherlands thus joins the large group of European economies wrestling with the same phenomenon. This high percentage is also reflected in the proportionately high tax rates and social security contributions: in this respect, the Netherlands outstrips nearly all other OECD countries with a rate of 32.8%.

Table 13.3a Total Government Revenue and Expenditure as a Percentage of GNP

	Total revenue			Total expenditure		
	2000	2005	2010	2000	2005	2010
Belgium	49.0	49.3	48.8	49.1	52.1	52.9
Bulgaria	40.1	38.3	34.9	43.3	37.3	38.1
Cyprus	34.7	40.7	41.0	37.1	43.1	46.4
Denmark	55.8	57.8	55.7	53.7	52.8	58.8
Germany	46.2	43.6	43.6	45.1	46.9	47.9
Estonia	35.9	35.2	40.0	36.1	33.6	40.6
Finland	55.4	53.0	52.5	48.4	50.4	55.3
France	50.2	50.6	49.5	51.7	53.6	56.6
Hungary	44.7	42.2	45.2	47.8	50.1	49.5
Ireland	35.9	35.5	35.5	31.2	33.8	66.8
Italy	45.0	43.4	45.8	45.9	47.9	50.3
Greece	43.0	39.0	39.5	46.7	44.6	50.2
Latvia	34.8	35.4	36.1	37.6	35.8	44.4
Lithuania	35.7	32.7	33.8	38.9	33.2	40.9
Luxembourg	43.6	41.5	41.4	37.6	41.5	42.5
The Netherlands	46.1	44.5	46.2	44.2	44.8	51.2
Malta	34.5	41.7	39.3	40.3	44.6	42.9
Austria	50.1	48.2	48.1	51.9	50.0	52.5
Poland	38.1	39.4	37.5	41.1	43.4	45.4
Portugal	38.2	39.9	41.6	41.1	45.8	51.3
Romania	33.9	32.4	34.0	38.6	33.6	40.9
Slovenia	42.8	43.8	44.3	46.5	45.3	50.1
Slovakia	39.9	35.2	32.3	52.1	38.0	40.0
Spain	38.2	39.7	36.3	39.2	38.4	45.6
Czech Republic	38.0	39.8	39.3	41.6	43.0	44.1
UK	40.4	40.7	40.3	36.8	44.1	50.4
Sweden	58.7	55.8	52.8	55.1	53.9	52.9
EU-27	45.3	44.4	44.1	44.8	46.9	50.6

Source: Eurostat.

Table 13.3b Income Tax and Social Security Contribution

	2000	2005	2010
Belgium	43.0	41.9	42.1
Canada	25.4	23.9	22.2
Denmark	44.2	40.9	38.6
Germany	43.2	42.2	39.2
Finland	34.2	31.3	29.1
France	28.7	28.9	27.8
Ireland	27.4	24.5	21.8
Italy	28.8	27.8	29.8
Greece	17.1	17.0	18.8
Luxembourg	28.8	25.9	26.4
The Netherlands	33.2	32.5	32.0
Norway	30.7	29.0	28.7
Austria	31.0	32.8	32.8
Portugal	22.4	21.8	21.5
Spain	19.9	20.3	21.6
UK	25.8	26.9	25.4
US	24.9	24.3	22.9
Sweden	33.7	31.2	24.7
Switzerland	16.5	16.2	16.0
OECD total	25.9	25.3	25.4

Source: OECD.

Leftish and rightish economists/politicians are therefore all more or less right. Year after year, investment in education and R&D has been poor, large new businesses are exceptionally rare and the size of the public sector has returned to the high level of the 1970s. With this many disastrous figures, it is quite remarkable however, that the Dutch economy is still among the world's best. In terms of gross domestic product per capita in the European Union (EU), only Luxembourg is doing better, as shown by the macroeconomic indicators listed in Table 13.4.

Table 13.4 Some Macroeconomic Indicators, 2010

	GNP per capita of the population	Unemployment
Australia	40,791	5.3
Belgium	37,676	8.4
Canada	39,070	8.1
Denmark	40,170	7.6
Germany	37,411	7.2
Estonia	20,383	17.2
Finland	36,585	8.5
France	34,148	9.3
Greece	28,246	12.7
Hungary	20,545	11.2
Ireland	35,642	13.9
Italy	31,962	8.5
Japan	33,751	5.3
Luxembourg	86,226	4.4
The Netherlands	42,175	4.5
Norway	57,231	3.7
Austria	40,017	4.5
Poland	19,833	9.7
Portugal	25,451	11.4
Slovakia	23,307	14.4
Spain	32,229	20.2
Czech Republic	25,245	7.4
Sweden	39,024	8.5
Switzerland	46,622	4.4
UK	35,512	7.9
US	46,588	9.8
OECD	33,967	8.5

Source: OECD; GNP per capita of the population, current prices in US dollars; unemployment as a percentage of the working population; percentage of people living below 50% of the median income of a country.

Furthermore, it is a fact that Dutch unemployment is and continues to be exceptionally low[2] – global crisis or not: in this respect, again, only Luxembourg is doing better in theEU. Dutch public debt is much lower than that of nearly all other Western economies.[3] Year after year, the Dutch balance of payments shows a splendid surplus. Dutch people are among the happiest in the world. How can it be

2 Comparing unemployment figures across countries is notoriously difficult, given the fuzziness of definitions and the plethora of alternative arrangements. For instance, Dutch society includes a remarkably high number of people in arrangements for the disabled, handicapped or ill.

3 As yet another recession has set in; public debt will rapidly increase in the coming years if nothing is done. The cabinet is therefore forced to take substantial extra austerity measures.

that a society where not enough is invested in education and R&D, where entrepreneurship is ailing and where the public sector dominates the private domain, is managing to hold its own among the world's most successful economies?

13.3 Where the Netherlands Is Doing Well

This monthly sum of taxes and social security contributions on people's payslip is not lying, nor are the large numbers of civil servants and semi-civil servants figuring in the annual national employment statistics. The Dutch (semi-)public domain is exceptionally large. However, measuring the size of the public sector is not an easy task, nor is measuring entrepreneurship and spending on education and R&D. For instance, it cannot be ruled out that in large businesses, entrepreneurial behaviour is very common, and that all sorts of impressive expenditure on research, development and training is hidden in other balance sheet items in the annual reports; that 'intrapreneurship' in the Meuse-Rhine delta is far more important than 'entrepreneurship', but that such activity occurs in the shadow of official statistics. This is all possible, but not very likely. Why would such measurement noise be worse in the Netherlands than elsewhere in the world?
Two alternative explanations are worth serious consideration. The first is that the Netherlands excels in sectors that require less entrepreneurship and lower investment in education and R&D to still be successful. The overview in Table 13.5 provides insight into the Dutch sector structure compared with the EU15.

Table 13.5 Sector Structure and Innovation

	Share in GDP in 2007 (%)		R&D expenditure as % of value added 2007 (basic prices)	
	NL	EU15	NL	EU15
Industry	13.5	16.9	6.1	6.5
Food	2.5	1.9	2.2	1.3
Chemistry	2.2	1.8	12.2	14.5
Mechanical engineering	1.4	2.0	8.7	5.9
Electrical engineering	0.7	2.0	40.9	13.7
Transport equipment	0.7	1.8	5.5	17.8
Services	73.7	72.0	0.3	0.3
Trade and repair	12.9	11.0	0.3	0.1
Financial institutions	6.0	5.6	0.2	0.2
Mining and quarrying	3.3	0.8	0.6	1.1
Agriculture	2.1	1.8	0.7	0.6
Other	7.4	8.5	0.1	0.2
Total economy	100.0	100.0	1.1	1.4

Source: Letter of 23 May 2011 from Minister Maxime Verhagen to the Dutch House of Representatives.

The sector structure operates to the disadvantage of the Netherlands, which has a relatively small industrial sector that moreover invests less in R&D compared with the EU15. The transport sector, with, e.g., the port of Rotterdam and Schiphol airport, plays a key role in the Dutch economy without high investments in education and R&D. The port industry and air traffic are dominated by a few large parties, without many enterprises entering or leaving the sector. Even in absolute terms, the Netherlands is the second world exporter of agricultural products, after the United States. The agricultural sector is not known for its 'sexy' high-tech reputation either. The Dutch corporate services sector has acquired a prominent place in the economic structure, but never makes the headlines because of its impressive budgets for research and development. Still, within these sectors that are somewhat lacking in education and R&D, Dutch productivity, seen from an international perspective, is high.[4] This offers comparative advantages in the international arena, generating a high level of prosperity and healthy economic growth.

The second alternative explanation is that the Netherlands has an exceptionally efficient and effective (semi-)public sector. Where organizations such as municipalities, ministries, schools, universities and hospitals make up such a large part of the Dutch economy, the economic performance of those organizations will also enter the national statistics. This direct contribution to the gross domestic product by the (semi-)public sector is impressive. In addition, the indirect contribution to the economy should not be underestimated. Efficient government departments are the lubricant of the economy. Universities supply high-quality human capital. Hospitals make sure employees are healthy. The traditional grumbling about a (semi-)public sector that is supposedly mainly obstructing the enterprising business sector may largely be based on misconception. A case in point concerns the Dutch universities. According to the prestigious *Times* Higher Education World University Rankings 2011–2012, eight Dutch universities are in the global top 200. The top 10 and the position of the Dutch universities are shown in Table 13.6. This puts the small Netherlands in third place behind the much bigger United States and the far larger United Kingdom, which dominate the top 10.[5]

---

4 This second paradox needs to be analyzed separately: how can a country without above-par investment in education and R&D still score high on productivity year after year? One of the possible reasons is discussed below: an exceptionally efficient and effective (semi-)public sector makes a very productive contribution to economic operations, also as regards education and research.

5 That is not to say that the Netherlands can be content with this, and can now sit back and relax. On the contrary: not only should the 16th economy in the world also be represented in the top 20, but it should also be realised that higher education in other parts of the world is progressing. While in the Netherlands – again – cuts are being made in the field of higher education and research, many other countries instead use the recession argument to invest *more* in the knowledge economy. So, if the Netherlands does not change course, Dutch universities will slowly disappear from the top 200 – making a mockery of cabinets which keep beating the knowledge economy drum. Here, rhetoric is far removed from reality.

Table 13.6 ***Times*** **Higher Education World University Ranking 2011**

	University	Country
1	Harvard	United States
2	California Institute of Technology	United States
3	Massachusetts Institute of Technology	United States
4	Stanford University	United States
5	Princeton University	United States
6	University of Cambridge	United Kingdom
7	University of Oxford	United Kingdom
8	University of California, Berkeley	United States
9	Imperial College London	United Kingdom
10	Yale University	United States
114	Eindhoven University of Technology	The Netherlands
124	Leiden University	The Netherlands
139	VU University Amsterdam	The Netherlands
143	Utrecht University	The Netherlands
144	Wageningen University	The Netherlands
151	Delft University of Technology	The Netherlands
165	University of Amsterdam	The Netherlands
170	University of Groningen	The Netherlands

Source: Financial Times.

Unfortunately, valid measurements of qualities of the (semi-)public sector are hard to find. Figure 13.2 shows a few indicators based on World Bank indicators. In terms of government effectiveness, regulatory quality and control of corruption, the Netherlands ranks among the global top performers together with Finland, Sweden and Switzerland. The role of public sector quality should not be underestimated. It is though exactly in regard to the stimulation of the quality of the (semi-)public sector that the EU is invisible. This is regrettable: in many EU countries – particularly in the East and South – the quality of the (semi-)public sector leaves much to be desired. The example of Greece speaks volumes. We will return to this below.

Figure 13.2

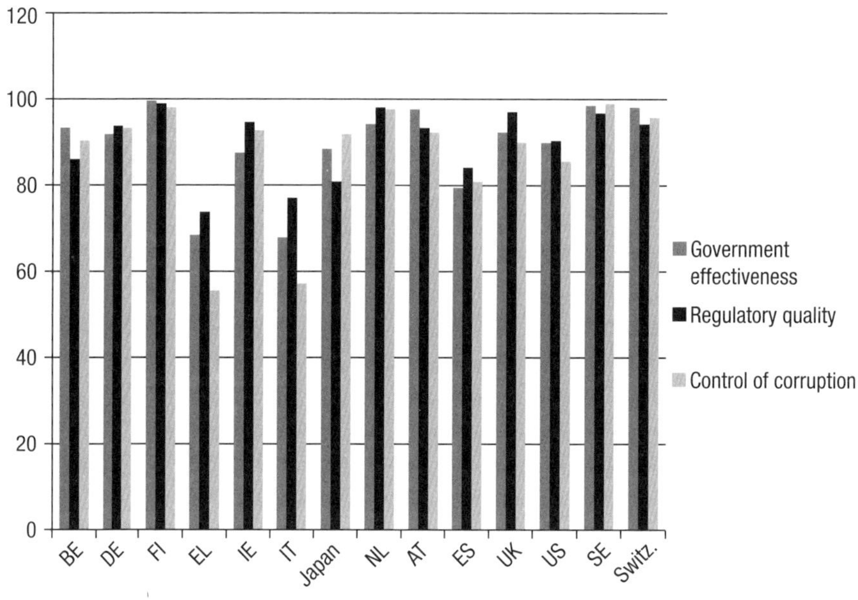

13.4 Why the Netherlands Should Do Better

13.4.1 *What Everyone Knows*

The fact that the Dutch economy is doing well does not mean it cannot and/or should not do better. In two areas, the need for improvement is so evident that it requires little explanation. First, the financial-economic crisis has made clear that the Dutch, European and global system is in need of a thorough overhaul. The neoliberal form of capitalism shows some fatal flaws.[6] Much has already been said and written about the nature of the desired reforms, so only a few observations suffice here.[7] The crux is that neoliberal shareholder capitalism – through far-reaching liberalization of financial markets, also within the EU – has dug its own grave in the form of huge debt accumulation, reckless speculative behaviour, a shocking lack of transparency, and financial arbitration constructions gone wild.[8] Unfortunately, much-needed reforms are (long) overdue.

6 Van Witteloostuijn, A. (1999). *De anorexiastrategie: over de gevolgen van saneren* [The anorexia strategy: on the effects of downsizing]. Amsterdam: De Arbeiderspers; VanWitteloostuijn, A. (2007, April 7 and 8). De naam van het virus is aandeelhouderswaarde [The name of the virus is shareholder value]. *NRC Handelsblad*, 15.

7 Van Witteloostuijn, A. (2008). Eenvoudige kleinschaligheid [Simple small scale]. *Economisch statistische berichten*, 93, 774-777.

8 *See also* Pelkmans in this volume.

It is to be hoped that the necessary measures will still be taken. This requires international political coordination, certainly also within theEU, which demands drive and courage.[9]

This brings us to the second area where the need for change is obvious. The current provincial and xenophobic[10] attitude should again become one of openness and tolerance. This certainly holds true for the Netherlands, which is flouting European directives in all kinds of sensitive areas. The example of free movement of persons speaks volumes. Such freedom of movement is an essential pillar supporting the European internal market. Ongoing efforts to restrict this freedom because "the Poles are stealing our jobs" are counterproductive, as demonstrated by the discussion on the Bolkestein Directive, the commotion about the hotline Central and Eastern Europeans and the fruitless European anti-immigrants mission of Minister Gerd Leers. In any case, no effective socio-economic policy can be built on fear of the unknown at home and abroad; this applies in particular to the small and open Dutch economy, which runs almost completely on European fuel.[11] On the contrary, instead of less, more Europe is urgently needed[12]: monitoring, broadening and deepening the European internal market need ongoing attention[13]; but the floundering approach to tackling the festering euro crisis also makes it patently obvious that the existing financial-economic institutions need radical Europeanization. A monetary union cannot survive without effective – and in times of crisis: decisive – political coordination of economic policy within and between the Member States, a view that can be found in any textbook on international economics.

An example of an institutional flaw is the inadequate mandate of the European Central Bank (ECB). Since the ECB cannot actively intervene in the market for government bonds other than in half-decent, roundabout ways, the euro countries are almost completely at the mercy of the financial markets. Another example is that national supervision of what are de facto European banks and markets leads to ineffective fragmentation. The realization that something should be done about this has resulted in the EU Semester, which provides for a procedure of prior consultation of Member States in the context of policy in line with the Stabi-

9 *See also* Verdun in this volume.

10 Of course, the majority in the Netherlands are not xenophobic. However, this is a nuance that is irrelevant for the reputation of the Netherlands abroad. The fact, for instance, that it was the PVV that set up a hotline for complaints about 'the Poles', and not the cabinet that was officially tolerated by that same PVV, is a fig-leaf argument which fails to impress abroad.

11 Van Witteloostuijn, A., Sanders, M. & Hendriks, C. (2011). *Ordening op orde* [Governing Governance]. The Hague: Mr. Hans van Mierlo Stichting.

12 Van Wegberg, M. & van Witteloostuijn, A. (2006, 23 March). Kies voor meer in plaats van minder Europa [Opt for more instead of less Europe]. *NRC Handelsblad*, 9 (reprinted in: Gelauff, G., et al. (Ed.), *Jaarboek 2006/2007* of the *Koninklijke Vereniging voor Staathuishoudkunde* [Dutch Royal Association for Economics], 102-104).

13 *See* below, and *see* Pelkmans in this volume.

lity and Growth Pact. This prior consultation should operate in tandem with ex post sanctions, based on the 3% rule. Such initiatives towards enhanced coordination of (macro) economic policy at EU level are to be applauded, and, in due course, will also benefit the Dutch economy. However, such initiatives do not mean the job is done. A single currency can only survive if all relevant institutions are Europeanized. Without some form of political union, a monetary union cannot survive. However, the single currency is a means, not an end. The aim is to strengthen the European economy in a sustainable way, within and outside the eurozone, such that Europe can look forward to a sunny future in a world of rapidly shifting power relations. In this context, it is high time to also start focusing on elaborating deeper structural reforms.

13.4.2 What Everyone Should Know

To anyone who understands economics it is clear that the reforms proposed above are necessary. In the context of this observation, it is, however, more important to emphasize that mere renovation of the Dutch, European and global financial-economic structure, in combination with a re-establishment of openness and tolerance, will not be sufficient. Other reforms are needed as well, and not because the Dutch economy has not done well over the past decades, which is simply not true – on the contrary. The question is rather whether past performance offers guarantees of future results, which is not the case either – alas. The ageing of society and declining birth rates, together with shifts in the global balance of power, pose challenges to any Western economy, including the Netherlands. Ultimately, a too large (semi-)public sector will go too far in the way of pushing out private dynamics. In addition, energy, climate and food crises are looming, stealthily undermining the sustainability of the present economic system. An effective response to these challenges demands a flexible and adaptive economy. In a rapidly changing world, it is impossible to predict how Dutch businesses will be able to earn their money in the future. The economic structure should therefore be flexible in adapting to shifting opportunities and threats. Businesses entering and leaving the market in combination with growing and shrinking enterprises are the other side of this adaptation coin.

Such adaptive capacity requires a subtle combination of economic contestability and social safety.[14] A citizen or organization should feel socially safe. Not only is this a sign of civilization, social safety[15] is also the platform on which risky entrepreneurship can flourish. Contestability implies that positions can always be challenged. This stimulates innovation and selection, thus preventing abuse of power. Power is the enemy of contestability (and of social safety). The EU has

14 Van Witteloostuijn, Sanders & Hendriks (2011).

15 We refrain from using the term 'security', because 'social security' has a connotation that is too limited to cover what we mean here. For lack of a better word, we rather use 'safety'.

made great progress in the field of competition policy, the aim being to safeguard economic contestability. Contestability can be further increased by strengthening and deepening the internal market[16] (see Pelkmans, this volume). Resistance to further Europeanization of trade is therefore to be regretted. Free movement of goods, services and people is essential to contestable markets. However, an important observation is in order here: businesses benefit by *in*contestability, which is why an alert government is needed to prevent markets from sliding toward incontestability. This requires a razor-sharp competition policy, combined with active prevention of excessive scale expansion (see also below).

However, this keeps about half of the European economy out of range. How can contestability in the (semi-)public domain be promoted? The difficult discussions about and experiences with reforms in (semi-)public areas such as education and health care clearly prove that we still have far to go here. Complex and ever-expanding regulation in these and other sectors stand in the way of contestability.[17] Complex regulation not only hampers entrepreneurial flexibility, but also protects existing power positions against competition and challenge. Adaptability and flexibility are preconditions for the entrepreneurship that is needed to rise to the modern challenges in a world that is in constant flux; a government that is too big and too interfering is an obstacle in this respect. The challenge mostly lies in combining a simple system of social security with stimulation of innovative entrepreneurship in all sectors of society, including the (semi-)public sector. This comes at a price: in the (semi-)public sector protected positions should be made contestable as well; this means that there, too, mechanisms must be introduced which ensure that failing organizations do not survive.[18,19]

The question is what role the EU can play in fortifying these pillars of an adaptive and flexible economy. On the one hand, it may be stated that guaranteeing social safety is, by and large, a key task of the individual Member States themselves. TheEU's influence is limited in that context. The Netherlands will have to reform its social security system on its own; simplicity should be the guiding principle. The current system has organically grown into a jungle of detailed regulation standing in the way of contestability. On the other hand, in terms of pro-

16 *See* Pelkmans in this volume.

17 It is not possible to analyse these and related questions regarding the causes and effects of overregulation here. For first analyses in this field, the reader is referred to van Witteloostuijn, A. & de Jong, G. (2010). An ecology of national rule birth: A longitudinal study of Dutch higher educational law, 1960-2004. *Journal of Public Administration Research and Theory, 20*(1), 187-213, and Kaufmann, W. & van Witteloostuijn, A. (2012). European and national rules as potential red tape drivers: An ecological analysis of Europeanization of Dutch competition law, 1962-2010, forthcoming in the *International Public Management Journal.*

18 Van der Mandele, H. & van Witteloostuijn, A. (2012). *Free to fail: Why all organizations will always (have to) fail, ultimately*. Cheltenham, UK: Edward Elgar (forthcoming).

19 This would mean that, for instance, poorly functioning schools and hospitals should be closed in favour of their better functioning counterparts.

moting and safeguarding economic contestability, it may be concluded that the EU is a key player, the European internal market being the heart of the EU. The internal market is far from being completed. This will require more hard work, with an alert government that prevents or dismantles any form of objectionable concentration of power – in all sectors of society, private and public. Power is positively correlated to size. The movement towards ongoing economies of scale in organisational life should therefore be reversed. Such scale expansion thwarts contestability. Overestimation of economies of scale and underestimation of diseconomies of scale are endemic, also at EU level. It is too easily assumed that big would be beautiful, whereas diseconomies of scale are disregarded.[20] Not only do these economies of scale often fail to live up to expectations in practice, as, for instance, reflected in the large percentage of failed acquisitions and mergers, but they also – which is even more important – thwart economic contestability.[21]

13.5 Political Courage

The Dutch economy is still doing relatively well. This may, for a large part, well be due to an efficient and effective (semi-)public sector. It stands to reason that efficiently and effectively operating authorities are crucial for efficient and effective economies. However, the EU generally steers well clear from trying to influence the public sector in the Member States, which would regard this as an objectionable infringement of their sovereignty. This is not expected to change any time soon – on the contrary. Nevertheless, a great deal can be achieved by improving the functioning of the (semi-)public sector in the Member States. Many Eastern and Southern European countries, in particular, are struggling with a dysfunctional (semi-)public sector. Huge economic gains can be made in this field, considering that in 2010 total government revenue and expenditure for the EU27 amounted to 50.6% of GNP (see Table 13.3a). Within theEU, an effort could at least be made to collect reliable and valid comparative indicators that give an idea of the level of efficiency and effectiveness of (semi-)public sectors. In addition, dissemination of best practices can be stimulated. In this respect, it is crucial to look for ways to promote contestability also in the (semi-)public sector. This requires unorthodox reforms which will make (the threat of) closure of failing organizations a normal occurrence also within the (semi-)public sector.

However, that is not enough. In a world where economic (and political) power relations are rapidly shifting, the European economy must hold its own through entrepreneurial flexibility. It is doubtful whether much will come of this if the public sector burden on the economy stays at this high percentage of around

20 Williamson, O.E. (1967). Hierarchical control and optimum firm size. *Journal of Political Economy, 75*(2),123-138.

21 Van Witteloostuijn (1999).

50% of GNP. In that respect, it can even be stated that the current 3% budget deficit limit is still far too high. From a Keynesian perspective, temporarily allowing such public deficits in times of economic recession can be justified. In the longer term, however, advantage will have to be taken of periods of economic prosperity by using surpluses to downsize the (semi-)public sector. In that context, cuts alone will not be enough. Such downsizing demands well thought-out reforms which will return a larger part of the economy to private initiative. This will also require deregulation, stimulating entrepreneurial dynamics *and* economic contestability.[22]

The EU and Dutch society are facing a range of serious challenges. Little is to be expected from stopgap measures. The fact that everything went well for a long time offers no guarantees for the future. The changes taking place within and outside the Netherlands are so fundamental that reforms are needed today to keep performing well tomorrow. Reform is difficult. Reforms have losers – always. Losers are visible; losers make themselves heard in no uncertain terms. That is why reform is hard; and that is why reform takes political courage, which, unfortunately, is hard to come by. It cannot be denied that the call for strong leadership sounds standard. But what sounds standard does not have to be wrong.

22 Such an argument is nearly always associated with right-wingers – with neoconservatism and neoliberalism, which is not right. A small government may also be a left-wing one: van Witteloostuijn, A. (2012). Een kleine maar linkse overheid? [A small but left-wing government?]. *Socialisme & Democratie, 69/6*, 26-32.

14 The European Budget: Consolidation or Modernization?

Frans van Nispen en Richard Blankenstein[*]

14.1 Introduction

The draft of Janusz Lewandowski, European Commissioner responsible for the European budget 2013, caused quite some debate. The proposal included a 6.8% increase in expenditure, which, according to many government leaders, could hardly be justified at a time when they had to make cuts 'at home'. However, the debate on the European budget was largely a rearguard fight, because most expenditure is fixed in the Multiannual Financial Framework (MFF) 2006-2013. Here and there, marginal changes are possible but, by and large, the general outlines are fixed. The disputes over the European Union (EU) budget for next year were therefore, as such, more a prelude to the negotiations on the MFF 2014-2020. The opening move for the negotiations on the MFF was Lewandowski's proposal to invest today in tomorrow's growth (see Annex 1), leaning on the proposals for *modernization* of the European budget. In this, he is supported by the Netherlands, which is backing the modernization of the European budget. The aim of the Dutch government is, moreover, to secure the rebate received earlier on its EU contribution and to reduce the level of EU expenditure. This chapter addresses the question of whether the Dutch interest is best served by a strategy focused on thinking in terms of '*juste retour*' – i.e., retaining the rebate and limiting European expenditure – or whether the government is best guided by what Alexis de Tocqueville called 'self-interest rightly understood', which, in this case, is based on reallocation of expenditure with a view to stimulating economic growth and thus tackling in the EU of today the sovereign debt crisis.
This chapter first focuses on the *unique* character of the European budget (Section 2). We then look back on the Dutch position during the negotiations on the Financial Perspectives 2007-2013 (Section 3).[1] The subsequent sections respectively address the opening position of the European Commission (Section 4) and the Dutch position (Section 5) in the negotiations on the MFF 2014-2020. The

* The authors would like to thank three persons directly involved for the background information they provided.

1 Until recently, the multiannual agreements on European finances were called Financial Perspectives. Today, they are referred to as Multiannual Financial Framework (MFF).

Netherlands aims for modernization of the budget, in which case the current rebate on the Dutch contribution to the EU could be dropped. The chapter ends with some concluding observations cumulating in a plea for compensation on the expenditure side instead of on the revenue side of the budget.

14.2 The European Budget: a Budget '*Sui Generis*'

The budget of the EU can best be characterized as a budget '*sui generis*'. A large part of the revenue (74%) comes from payments by the Member States, which is dependent on the level of their gross national income (GNI). The remainder is collected in the form of, amongst other things, Member States' levies on agricultural products and imports of goods (a country may keep 25% of the yield). Legally, import levies are a source of income for the European budget, but are considered by the Dutch government as payment to the EU. Finally, the Member States have to transfer a percentage of their VAT revenue to the EU.

Figure 14.1 Development of the European Budget by Income Category (1958-2008)

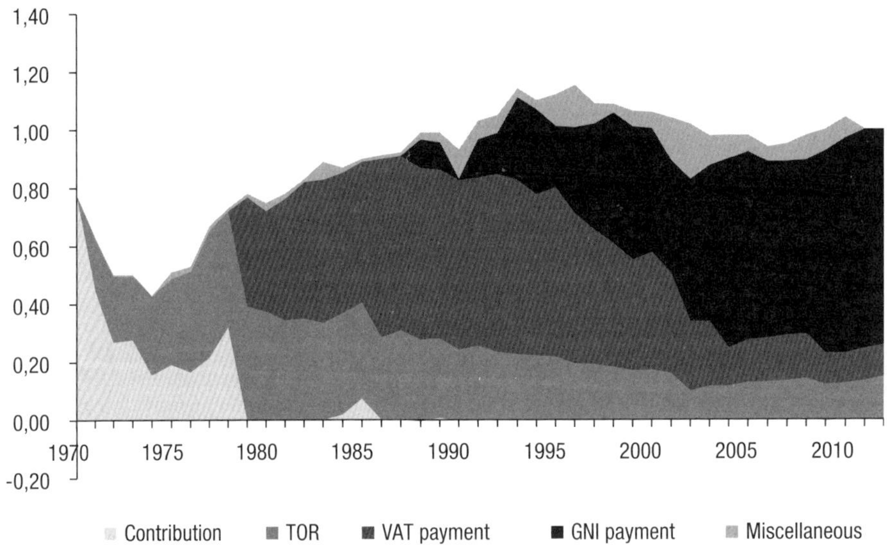

Data provided by DG Budget.

The EU budget is relatively small compared with the budgets of the Member States. Total expenditure is set at about 1% of the common gross domestic product (EU GDP) of the European Member States, as a result of which entire spending categories, which national budgets do include, are left out of consideration, irrespective of political or economic considerations in favour of centralization.[2] Moreover, according to critics, the budget is not up to date, does not meet the demands of the day, and is locked in path dependency, thus seriously limiting possible or desirable changes.[3] These same critics claim that the potential impact of the EU budget is, as such, negligible.[4] The question is whether this criticism is justified. First, the EU's policy is, to a considerable extent, shaped by *non-financial* instruments, in this case regulation and coordination. The budget is often not the most important instrument.[5] Secondly, implementation largely takes place at national level, the costs of which are borne by the Member States. These therefore impact on the national instead of on the European budget. Moreover, *financial* instruments often involve co-financing, such as in the case of cohesion policy and structural funds. The EU budget, as such, thus portrays a somewhat distorted picture of the level of European expenditure. The size of the budget may be relatively small, but the interests are considerable, judging by the heated debates over reallocation of available resources.[6]

2 Begg, I. (2009). *Fiscal federalism, subsidiarity and the EU budget review*. Stockholm: SIEPS, p. 51.

3 Begg (2009), p. 11.

4 Begg, I., Sapir, A. & Eriksson, J. (2008). *The purse of the European Union: Setting priorities for the future*. Stockholm: SIEPS, p. 9; Lejour, A. & Molle, W. (2011). *The value added of the EU budget: Subsidiarity and effectiveness*. The Hague: Centraal Planbureau [CPB – Netherlands Bureau for Economic Policy Analysis]. Presentation at the joint CEPS-SIEPS seminar 'The Next Long-Term Budget: What Should Go In? What Should Go Out?', Brussels, 9 March.

5 Pisani-Ferry, J. (2008, April 4). *Comments on Begg and Molle*. Paper delivered at the BEPA Conference on Public Finances in the EU, under the auspices of the European Commission, Brussels; Tarschys, D. (Ed.). (2011). *The EU budget. What should go in/what should go out?* Stockholm: SIEPS, p. 13.

6 The discussion on [the content of] the EU budget largely takes place in terms of 'public goods'. To what extent does it involve 'public goods': what is the added value? (Heineman, F. (2011). European added value for the EU budget. In D. Tarschys (Ed.), *The EU budget. What should go in/what should go out?* Stockholm: SIEPS). A problem is that it is not exactly clear what is to be understood by 'public goods', let alone European 'public goods'. The arguments that can be derived from the theory of 'fiscal federalism' regarding centralization and decentralization do not provide enough support. The same applies to the subsidiarity principle, according to which, for reasons of efficiency, services are best provided at national level.

Figure 14.2 Development of the European Budget by Spending Category (1958-2008)

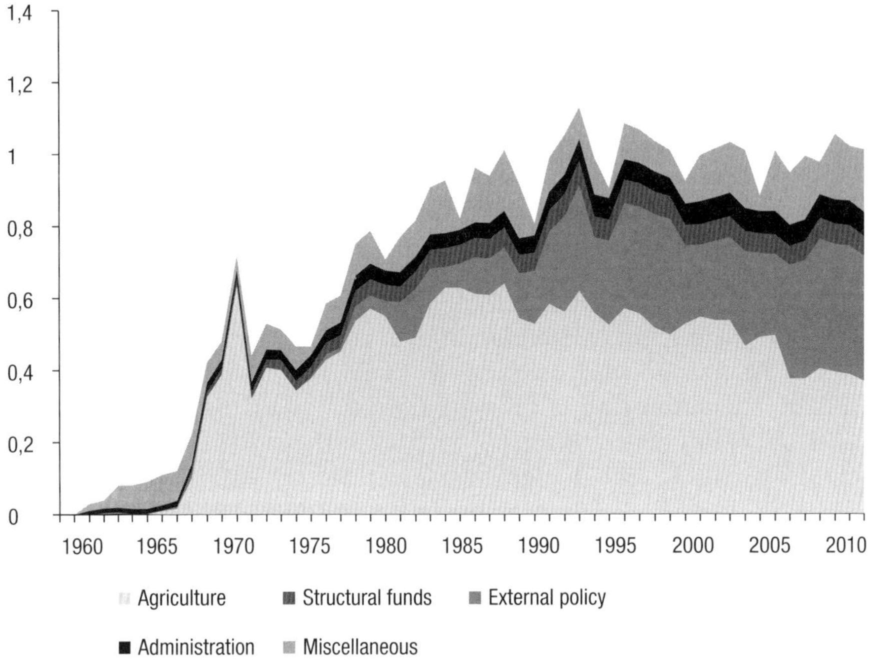

Data provided by DG Budget.

The European budget is mainly characterized by redistribution of funds. The main part of the European budget goes to agricultural policy, which is considered as a barely disguised form of income support to farmers (42.5%), and to the structural funds (35.6%), which are largely characterized by money that is being pumped around. In this context, mention should be made of underspending of the structural funds because Member States have insufficient absorption capacity.[7] The actual effect of the expenditure under this heading is moreover difficult to determine.[8]

The annual budget is 'dictated' to a considerable extent by the so-called MFF (previously Financial Perspectives), which covers a period of seven years. It is therefore important for a Member States to seize its chance during the negotiations on the MFF before the annual budget is adopted. The annual budget should subsequently remain below the stipulated MFF ceilings. In practice, it often stays below the established spending caps because a number of programmes are not realized, or are not fully spent because the Member States do not have enough funds for co-financing. For instance, the amount of commitments of 1.00% of EU

7 Bos, M. & van Riel, B. (2011, September 16). Naar een nieuw begrotingskader voor de EU [Towards a new budget framework for the EU]. *Economisch Statistische Berichten, 96*(4618), p. 540.

8 ECORYS, CPB & IFO. (2008). *A study on EU spending*. Rotterdam; Lejour & Molle (2011), p. 107.

GDP corresponds with actual spending of around 0.94 of EU GDP.[9] Unlike the annual budget – which is adopted by qualified majority – the MFF requires unanimity.[10]

14.3 Financial Perspectives, 2007-2013

In the run-up to the negotiations on the multiannual budget for 2006-2013, the Dutch cabinet had already achieved a significant result as regards future spending within the framework of the European agricultural policy. In autumn 2002, it was agreed that the agricultural budget would remain constant in real terms until the end of 2013 (i.e., would only be adjusted for inflation). As a result, the negotiations on the largest spending category of the EU budget only dealt with the question of whether the ceiling should also apply to new Member States (i.e., Bulgaria and Romania) and with the development of expenditure on rural development.
Together with his colleagues, the then President of the European Commission, Romano Prodi, had reviewed all 'necessary' expenditure. The result was an expansive opening move (between 1.14% and 1.21% of EU GNI) made by the European Commission to the Member States. The proposal was rejected as too ambitious and unrealistic by the Dutch Council Presidency (second half of 2004), after which a round of consultations was held. In consultation with the Ministry of Foreign Affairs, the Dutch Ministry of Finance then developed the 'building blocks' method, whereby information had to be provided by Member States about both the total amount of money and the allocation of resources per spending category.[11] A couple of countries – Belgium and Luxembourg – were not inclined to cooperate, because they were satisfied with the European Commission's review. The consultations showed that most Member States preferred a lower instead of the higher multiannual budget as provided by the Prodi package. Thus, it soon became clear that the demand of the European Commission

9 Peet, J. (2005). *The EU budget. A way forward*. London: Centre for European Reform, p. 2.

10 In his annual New Year's message, the former Secretary-General of the Ministry of Economic Affairs proposed to abolish the veto on the European multiannual budget after a solution has been found for the net contributor position, so that funds can quickly be transferred from 'old to new' (Oosterwijk, J.W. (2007, January 12). Maatwerk en modernisering in Europa [Customization and modernization in Europe]. *Economisch Statistische Berichten*, p. 7).

11 Zalm, G. (2009). *De romantische boekhouder* [The romantic bookkeeper]. Amsterdam: Uitgeverij Balans. The 'building blocks' method is an effective way of changing the playing field. During the negotiations on the financial perspectives of 2000-2006 [Agenda 2000], the net contributing Member States had put the so-called Table C on the agenda, with ceilings for each category of expenditure. This determined the room of negotiation between both proposals. The Commission proposal was not the centrepiece of the negotiations.

was quite different from the Member States' preference. The Commission proposal therefore hardly came into play during the negotiations.[12]
The Dutch position during the negotiations initially focused on the following:

- The Dutch contribution to the EU should be proportionate to that of Member States with a similar level of prosperity.
- The general expenditure framework of the EU does not exceed 1% of EU GNI.
- The agricultural budget should not be increased for new Member States.
- The cohesion funds should be limited to the poor regions in the poorest Member States.

In the course of the negotiations, the Dutch position increasingly concentrated on a 1-billion rebate on the EU contribution. This focus on a rebate on the Dutch EU contribution– in line with the British rebate – thus marks an important turning point in Dutch thinking on European integration, defining the Dutch position to this day.
In his memoirs *De romantische boekhouder* (The romantic bookkeeper) Gerrit Zalm (the then Dutch Minister of Finance) puts forward the following arguments for this strategy[13]:

- A euro less paid to Europe is a euro that the Netherlands can spend entirely in line with its own priorities.
- A euro of the European budget for the benefit of the Netherlands is not part of the national budget and reflects, as such, the European priorities and requirements for subsidy.
- The rules and regulations for subsidy are complicated and contain many administrative conditions that must be met. Consequently, the money is often not spent.
- The money has to be paid back, possibly with a fine, when it turns out afterwards that not all conditions have been met.

However, he adds that his arguments have never been narrow-nationalist. He had always accepted that the Netherlands, being a prosperous country, would be a net payer rather than a net recipient. The Dutch stance was geared to a general rebate arrangement instead of separate treatment for the Netherlands only.[14]
Subsequently, during the Luxembourg Presidency, the 'building blocks' method was replaced by the 'negotiation boxes' approach, which involved ever-increasing fine-tuning: first, the principles of the policy were defined, and then the parameters were set for further allocation of available resources. Finally, an overview

12 The same applies to the role of the European Parliament (EP), which, by the EP's own account, had hardly any influence on the outcome of the negotiations due to a combination of limited competences and internal division (de Lange, E. (2011, March 30). *Financial perspectives after 2013*. Presentation for the IMP programme, European Parliament, Brussels.

13 Zalm (2009), pp. 334-335.

14 Zalm (2009), p. 342.

was made of the consequences for the Member States.[15] The proposals contained, in principle, all negotiation points, thus preventing agreements on separate issues. In the last phase, the level of expenditure could thus be brought in line with the proposals concerning the allocation of available resources.

The negotiation boxes method failed to produce an agreement because three countries– the Netherlands, Sweden and the United Kingdom – did not accept the individual rebate on payments, which, in their view, was too low. In the subsequent negotiations during the Council Presidency of the United Kingdom, which shared the Dutch view on the rebate on the contribution, agreement was finally reached. The expenditure framework and thus the contribution of the Member States were reduced, and, as a result, the Netherlands received a 1-billion rebate on its EU contribution. In exchange, the key for the allocation of resources was revised to also make the agreement profitable for net recipients. Negotiators regarded the common interest of the Netherlands and the United Kingdom as an important success factor.[16]

Finally, during the negotiations on the financial perspectives, a few Member States, including the Netherlands, stipulated that there be a fundamental debate on the modernization of the European budget. One of the things they objected to was the incremental nature of the European budget, due to which the purpose and necessity of whole spending categories are not or only marginally scrutinized once the MFF has been adopted. Therefore, the heads of state and government of the Member States commissioned a Budget Review, involving a comprehensive reassessment of the European public finances.[17]

14.4 The Multiannual Financial Framework, 2014-2020

14.4.1 *The Proposal of the European Commission*

Already in autumn 2010, the European Commission published a first communication on the possibilities to modernize the MFF.[18] The final outlines of the pro-

15 Bachtler, J. & Wishlade, F. (2005). *From building blocks to negotiating boxes: The reform of EU cohesion policy*. Glasgow: European Policies Research Centre.

16 Zalm (2009), pp. 336-337.

17 Cipriani, G. (2007). *Rethinking the EU budget. Three unavoidable reforms*. Brussels: Centre for European Reform, pp. 19, 130. The so-called Budget Review was carried out by the European Commission through a public consultation in 2007/2008. Member States as well as civil society organizations published their views on a website launched by the European Commission (European Commission. (2011a). For contributions to the public consultation, *see* <http://ec.europa.eu/budget/reform2008/issues/read_en.htm>, accessed April 2011). Due to a reshuffle of the European Commission, the debate on the European budget mainly took place in academia (Laffan, B. & Lindner, J. (2010). The budget: Who gets what, when and how. In H. Wallace, W. Wallace & M. Pollack (Eds.), *Policy-making in the European Union*. Oxford: Oxford University Press).

18 European Commission. (2010). *Budget review: Lessons learnt for tomorrow's budget*. Brussels.

posal were adopted in May 2011, after, on a tour of the capitals, Lewandowski had consulted the individual Member States on the question of whether either ambitious goals should be set so as to have some room to manoeuvre during the negotiations, or the opposite should be done to avoid that the proposal, like last time, would not be taken seriously. The result is a proposal for modernization of the budget, which, as such, is in line with the new priorities set in the framework of Europe 2020, which aims for smart, sustainable and inclusive growth with high levels of employment within the EU. In this context, Lewandowski commissioned a consortium, led by the ECORYS research agency, to study the extent to which the subsidiarity principle applies to spending in the context of the European budget. To this end, a large number of policy fields were examined in terms of efficiency and feasibility. One of the conclusions of the study is that a large part of the agricultural policy can be decentralized, while at the same time centralization of environmental policy and security policy is justified.[19] Transferring these policy areas to the EU need not affect the budget, since in these areas regulation and coordination is largely sufficient and large funds are not required.[20]

In total, the multiannual budget represents 1.05% of GNI, which is in line with the call of 9 of the 27 Member States to limit the increase in the budget to inflation correction. However, the percentage rises to 1.11% of GNI if 'off budget' expenditure is taken into account as well; in this way Lewandowski follows the view of the European Parliament (EP) that "[...] freezing the next MFF at the 2013 level [...] is not a viable option [...] [and that] at least a 5% increase of resources is needed for the next MFF".[21] The *consolidated* budget, i.e., the sum of 'on budget' and 'off budget' expenditure thus provides for an increase of the expenditure ceiling.[22]

The Commission proposal contained a number of controversial and drastic measures. For instance, on the revenue side of the budget it wanted to include a new own resource, financial transaction tax (FTT), which would reduce contributions by Member States by 50%. In addition, the Commission wished to introduce a generic correction mechanism. The amount that Member States are allowed to keep for collecting traditional own resources will be further reduced (from 25% to 10%), which will have major consequences for the Dutch position given the import levies collected at the port of Rotterdam. Unlike last time, Lewandowski has tabled a 1.050-million rebate on the Dutch contribution. The proposal concerning the expenditure side of the budget is lower than that pro-

19 ECORYS, CPB & IFO (2008), p. 248.

20 Molle, W. (2008, April 4). *Assessing the structure of EU expenditures*. Paper delivered at the BEPA Conference on Public Finances in the EU, under the auspices of the European Commission, Brussels.

21 European Parliament. (2011b). *Resolution of 8 June 2011 on investing in the future: A new multiannual financial framework (MFF) for a competitive, sustainable and inclusive Europe*. Strasbourg.

22 Mijs, A. & Schout, A. (2012). *Views on the commission's draft EU budget. Excessively ambitious or overly rimid?* (EPIN Working Paper, No. 32), p. 9.

posed during the previous negotiations. However, a number of budget items, such as the Globalization Fund and the Solidarity Fund, are placed off budget, thus distorting the overall picture of actual spending. The proposal also provided for a reform of the agricultural policy (reducing the difference in acreage price which is used as a basis for income support) and of the structural funds by introducing the category of transition regions (regions that are making the transition from subsidy to no subsidy).

14.5 The Dutch Position

The cabinet decided to follow a pro-active strategy and did not wait for Lewandowski's proposal. It announced the Dutch position as early as 28 March 2011.[23] The primary aim was *modernization* of the European budget, namely, the following:

- A frugal and effective budget, i.e., limitation of the increase in expenditure, staying below inflation.
- A future-proof budget, i.e., one that reflects the priorities of the Europe 2020 strategy. The funds for these priorities should be generated by exchanging 'old for new'.[24]
- Balanced burden-sharing by replacing the current patchwork of own resources by a system fully based on GNI.[25]

The payment correction served as a bargaining chip and could be dropped if sufficient progress was made on the above-mentioned points. The question is whether it is wise to show the Dutch hand already at this stage. In any case, it makes clear what the Dutch position is.

The Dutch position, as such, is similar to that at the time of the Financial Perspectives 2007-2013,[26] although it should be noted that circumstances have since changed drastically, thus making it more difficult for the Netherlands to attain its goals[27]:

23 Letter from the cabinet to the chairperson of the Dutch House of Representatives regarding the EU Multiannual Framework as of 2014, dated 28 March 2011 (TwK 2011a).

24 To this end, the common agricultural policy and administrative expenditure would have to be nominally frozen and the cohesion policy limited to the least prosperous regions in the least prosperous countries.

25 Introducing a generic system based on GNI also means abolishing the traditional own resources, thus relieving us in one go from the accounting discussion on the payment of part of the levy on imports. As a result, the rebate on the Dutch contribution could even turn out higher.

26 Mijs & Schout (2012), p. 10. However, some aspects of the Dutch position have altered. For instance, the Netherlands is in favour of nominal instead of real growth of the budget. In addition, the government is more relaxed about increasing flexibility within the European budget.

27 Unlike during the negotiations on the Financial Perspectives 2006-2013, the Netherlands is unable to exert influence by using the rotating presidency.

- The influence of the new Member States, which at the time of the MFF 2007-2013 had only just acceded, has grown considerably (agricultural subsidies, structural funds).
- The already prominent role of the European Council in this respect has been further strengthened by the appointment of a permanent president of the European Council, thus further weakening the role of the rotating presidency.
- The Treaty of Lisbon has considerably reinforced the role of the EP, although it should be noted that the EP is internally divided. The EP is, moreover, inclined to agree as long as the new level of expenditure is higher than the previous level.[28]

A not insignificant difference is the Dutch pursuit of *nominal* instead of *real* growth, de facto resulting in regression of the budget. To this end, the government has in the run-up to the negotiations on the new MFF teamed up with the leaders of four other Member States – Germany, Finland, France and the United Kingdom – which argued that as of 2014 the growth of the European budget should remain below inflation.[29] An increase in the European budget was, in their view, hard to justify at times when drastic spending cuts have to be made at national level.[30] The government's view has been further reinforced as result of a motion tabled by the PvdA (Labour) and the ChristenUnie (small more orthodox Christian party) during the parliamentary debate on the State of the EU on 26 May 2011, exhorting the government, besides going for retention of the Dutch contribution rebate of at least 1 billion, not to agree with a European multiannual budget that goes beyond the nominal zero line.[31] In principle, there is not much to be said against the arguments to modernize the European budget. This could, to begin with, take the form of greater transparency, like that seen in the changes made in the budget template due to the introduction of performance budgeting.[32] A transparent budget forms the basis for a better allocation of available resources and for controlling the legality and efficiency of expenditure, and, as such, contributes to the EU's legitimacy. However, the chance that the above points will be realized now or later seems remote. An indication of the current balance of power within the EU is provided by the consultations that took place

28 The MFF is adopted by the Council and the EP in consultation with the Economic and Social Committee pursuant to the ordinary legislative procedure. Specific programmes are adopted by the Council in consultation with the EP and the Economic and Social Committee pursuant to the extraordinary procedure.

29 Cameron, D. et al. (2010, December 18). *Letter from Prime Minister David Cameron and other European leaders to the President of the European Commission.* London.

30 In this context, the Prime Minister signed a letter together with the heads of state and government of Germany, Finland, France and the United Kingdom to the President of the European Commission, dated 18 December 2010, Dutch House of Representatives, *Kamerstuk* 21 501-20, No. 496.

31 Dutch House of Representatives, *Kamerstuk* 32 502, No. 6.

32 The number of articles was reduced considerably to improve allocation, efficiency and accountability.

in the framework of the above-mentioned Budget Review. They are a good reflection of Member States' views, which are generally stable, irrespective of the composition of the incumbent government coalition.[33]

Figure 14.3 Member States' Positions on Contributions and the Expenditure Ceiling

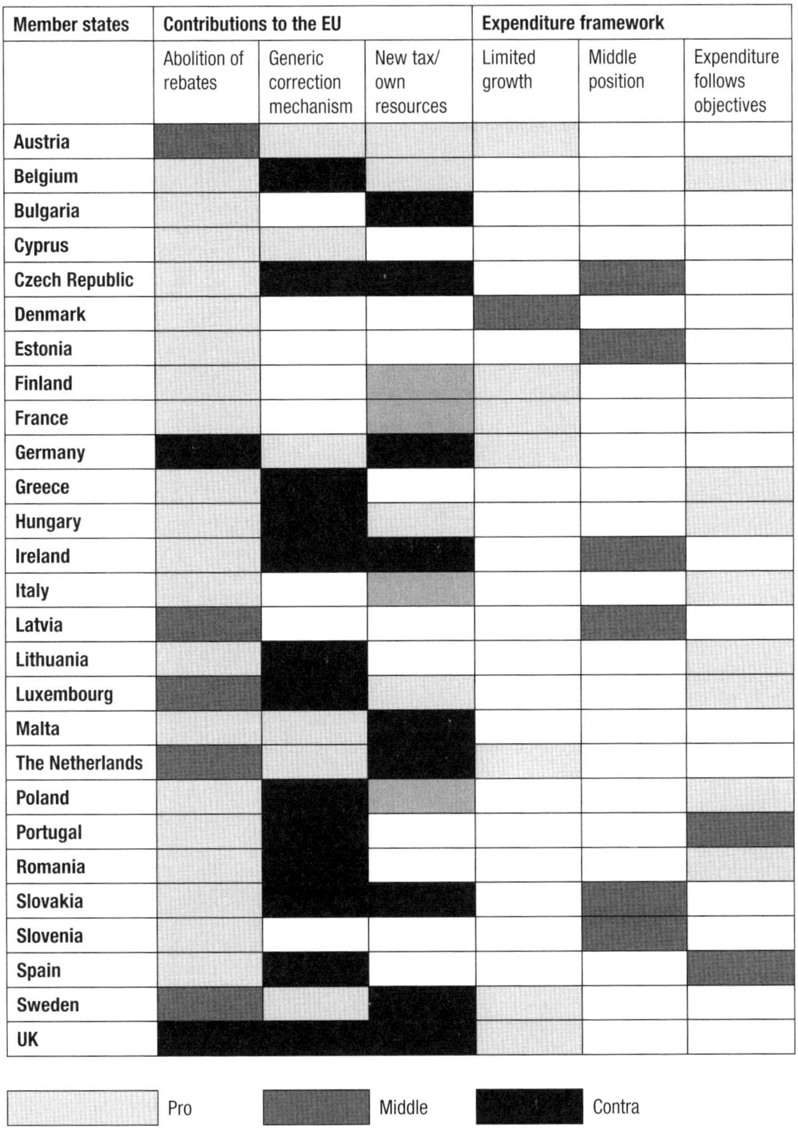

European Commission (2010); Blankenstein, R. (2011). *Onderhandelen over het meerjarig financieel kader van de EU – Een nieuw spel met andere spelers?* [Negotiating the Multiannual Financial Framework of the EU – A new game with different players?]. Thesis, Rotterdam.

33 Lindner, J. (2006). *Conflict and change in EU budgetary politics.* London: Routledge.

Figure 14.4 Member States' Positions on the Agricultural Policy and Structural Funds

Member states	Agricultural budget			Cohesion Fund		
	Budget size	Abolition of income support	National cofinancing of pillar 1	Limiting funds to poor regions in poor Member States	Middle position	Funds for all Member States
Austria			Contra		Middle	
Belgium	Pro	Contra	Contra			Pro
Bulgaria	Pro				Pro	
Cyprus						Pro
Czech Republic	Contra	Pro	Contra		Pro	
Denmark	Pro	Pro	Contra		Pro	
Estonia				Pro		
Finland					Pro	
France		Pro			Pro	
Germany	Pro				Pro	
Greece	Pro		Contra			Pro
Hungary	Pro		Contra			Pro
Ireland	Pro				Pro	
Italy			Pro			Pro
Latvia					Pro	
Lithuania					Pro	
Luxembourg						Pro
Malta	Contra	Pro	Contra			Pro
The Netherlands		Pro		Pro		
Poland	Pro		Contra			Pro
Portugal						Pro
Romania	Pro	Contra	Contra		Pro	
Slovakia		Pro				Pro
Slovenia						Middle
Spain	Pro					Pro
Sweden	Contra	Pro	Pro	Pro		
UK	Contra	Pro		Pro		

Pro Middle Contra

European Commission (2010), Blankenstein (2011).

A majority of the European Member States seem to be in favour of abolishing the rebate on the contribution, which, though, will most probably be vetoed by the UK government. In the last phase of the negotiations on the present multiannual 2007-2013 budget, then Prime Minister Tony Blair did offer an opening as regards the British rebate – he was prepared to give it up in exchange for abolition of the agricultural subsidies[34] – but the door was closed by the then French president Chirac. At that time, the latter was not prepared to talk about restructuring the agricultural policy.[35]

Although the moratorium on phasing out income support in agriculture will expire by the end of 2013, these parties are still polar opposites – judging by the consultations held in the framework of the Budget Review. The same seems to apply to limiting the structural funds to the poorest regions. The Member States cannot agree on this either.
Further analysis shows that the disagreement is considerable. On the one hand, the allocation of the scarce resources should be (more) aligned to the new priorities set in the context of the Europe 2020 strategy. On the other hand, the growth of expenditure should be curtailed, taking the consequences of the sovereign debt crisis into consideration for the budgets of the Member States. It remains to be seen, though, whether the pursuit of modernizing the European budget will lead to merely cosmetic rather than fundamental changes. What will be the Dutch government's fallback position if there indeed proves to be insufficient support for the Dutch position?

14.6 Fallback Position: 'Juste Retour' or 'Self-interest Rightly Understood'?

For some time now, the significance of the EU in the Netherlands seems to narrow down to a discussion on the Dutch net contribution and the place where the EP should meet.[36] In the media, then outgoing Prime Minister Rutte has, on several occasions, spoken in favour of a permanent rebate on the Dutch contribution.[37] However, the rebate is dropping to about 750 million because the Netherlands is

34 *BBC News*. (2005, June 21). Blair says EU rebate 'has to go'. Retrieved 9 April 2012 from <http://news.bbc.co.uk/go/pr/fr/-/2/hi/uk_news/politics/4114180.stm>; Núñez Ferrer, J. (2007). *The EU budget: The UK rebate and the CAP – Phasing them both out*. Brussels: CEPS.

35 *BBC News* (2005).

36 Adviesraad Internationale Vraagstukken [Advisory Council on International Affairs]. (2006). *Europe: A priority!*. The Hague, p. 8; Adviesraad Internationale Vraagstukken. (2007). *The finances of the European Union*. The Hague, p. 10.

37 For the record, a 1-billion rebate on a contribution of around 4 billion does not even amount to 1% of our GNI.

supposed to contribute to the rebates of the other Member States.[38] The Commission proposal, moreover, suggests reducing the part of the traditional own resources that the Member States are allowed to keep from 25% to 10%, thus decreasing the amount to around 500 million.[39] The result is nothing to write home about.[40] The aim of getting a rebate on the Dutch contribution to the EU therefore nets far less than anticipated. The outgoing Rutte Cabinet seems to have been fooling itself, since the amount of 1 billion has already been factored into the coalition agreement. Prime Minister's Rutte words, therefore, seem to be mainly intended for domestic consumption. In this context, it should be borne in mind that the current MFF will indeed continue to apply if no agreement is reached on the MFF for the coming period, but that the temporary rebate will be dropped.[41] In that case, the cabinet will be left completely empty-handed. However, it seems likely that as of 2014 a new retrospective rebate will apply if agreement is reached later than expected.

Considering all this, what is there left to be 'gained'? Restructuring the *revenue* side of the budget, relieving the Netherlands in one go from the accounting discussion on the contribution of port dues and the resulting reputation damage which is hard to express in monetary terms, does not seem politically feasible. Quite the contrary, the Commission even proposes to introduce two *new* own resources – a FTT and a new VAT resource – to make the budget less dependent on Member State contributions. Alternatives should therefore be found on the *expenditure* side of the budget, although it seems impossible to find a majority for either scaling down the agricultural policy or focusing the structural funds on the poorer regions. In the field of administrative costs, there just is not much to be gained. What should – given this starting point – have been the government's position during the negotiations on the new MFF?

First of all, the interest of the Dutch government should lie in a qualitative discussion on the *content* of the budget rather than in a quantitative discussion on its *size*. Instead of thinking in terms of '*juste retour*', the government should focus more strongly on our 'self-interest rightly understood', whereby limitation of the increase in expenditure to inflation correction could be used as a bargaining chip. In line with the Commission proposal, the Dutch government should pursue a

38 Reaction of the cabinet to the Commission proposals for the MFF of the EU for 2014-2020, 2 September 2011, p. 3.

39 *See* Annex 3.

40 This amount, moreover, pales into insignificance compared to the guarantees we issued in the framework of the European emergency fund.

41 The *temporary* rebate on our EU contribution will be dropped, but the *permanent* VAT payment correction – 0.1% instead of 0.3% – will, in principle, be maintained.

reallocation of existing resources in favour of activities that increase productivity and thus competitiveness in economically underdeveloped regions.[42]
A European budget aimed at economic growth is also to the Dutch advantage because, as calculated by the *Centraal Planbureau* (CPB – Netherlands Bureau for Economic Policy Analysis), the Netherlands benefits relatively muchfrom the export of goods.[43] The results of the ECORYS study could serve as a guideline in this context, although control of spending should be tightened in order to ensure that the intended target group is reached and effectiveness increased. Still, effectiveness is not the only criterion by which expenditure should be assessed. The European integration process is based on solidarity. A positive side effect of a strategy aimed at economic growth is that migration flows subside as economic growth in economically underdeveloped regions picks up, thus taking the wind out of populist sails.

14.7 Concluding Remarks: Towards a More Enlightened European Budget

In this chapter, we addressed the Dutch position during the negotiations on the multiannual budget for 2014-2020. The government supported the proposal of the European Commission to modernize the budget. However, given the balance of power, the chance that the revenue side of the budget will be restructured seems slim. In this respect, it should also be borne in mind that the Netherlands had been a net recipient until the Treaty of Maastricht. Improvement should therefore take place on the expenditure side of the budget. The most that can be achieved seems a reallocation of resources in favour of the priorities set in the framework of Europe 2020. Zooming in on those particular issues that are in line with Dutch priorities, such as asylum policy, security policy and preventing climate change, seems the obvious choice. However, in this context it should be noted that the flexibility of the budget is limited.
In addition and in line with the advice already issued at the time by the Sapir study group, the EU budget should focus more on economic growth,[44] or, in the words of Pisani-Ferry, Director of Bruegel in Brussels,

42 Adviesraad Internationale Vraagstukken. (2010). *The EU and the crisis. Lessons learnt.* The Hague. In this context, it is worth considering not relating the growth of expenditure, *a priori*, to inflation, but rather to the Europe 2020 strategy, which is aimed at economic growth and employment.

43 Straathof, B., Linders, G.-J., Lejour, A. & Möhlmann, J. (2008). *The internal market and the Dutch economy: Implications for trade and economic growth.* The Hague: CPB.

44 Sapir, A. (2003). *An agenda for a growing Europe. Making the EU economic system deliver.* Report of an Independent High-Level Study Group established on the initiative of the President of the European Commission. Available from <http://serviziweb.unimol.it/unimol/allegati/docenti/2545/materiale/sapir%20report.pdf>, retrieved 2 April 2012.

> [...] as ECB President Mario Draghi recently said, Europe has a fiscal compact, but lacks a growth compact. To be sure, there are no quick fixes: headline-grabbing initiatives often fail to measure up to the challenge of reviving growth. Nevertheless, serious discussion is needed concerning how to use the EU budget to enhance economic performance, rather than for redistribution only; how to foster pro-growth reforms at the national level; and how to boost investment in the periphery countries' tradable sectors. A credible growth compact would help to overcome immediate hurdles. After all, the post-war Marshall Plan was so successful not because of its size, but because it helped to counteract zero-sum games and self-fulfilling pessimism. That is a lesson to keep in mind today.[45]

To what extent is a European budget that focuses more on economic growth politically feasible? The balance of power indicates that most Member States are in favour of modernizing the budget, but opinions are strongly divided over how that should be achieved. It seems virtually impossible to get all parties to agree, unless the discussion on the European budget is placed in a different context, i. e., that of the sovereign debt crisis. A 'frame shift' is a tried and tested means of breaking a deadlock in negotiations. A revised definition of the problem may reveal new ways of solving the problem, which are moreover easier 'to sell' to grass roots supporters by referring to the sovereign debt crisis.

In answer to the question posed in the title of this chapter, it may be concluded that reallocation of the European budget will not be sufficient to do justice to the priorities set in the context of the Europe 2020 strategy. Increasing the level of expenditure seems inevitable – even if support is found for reallocation – to meet the many, deviating wishes of all Member States.[46] A European budget that focuses more on economic growth may also help to reduce existing macroeconomic imbalances in the eurozone. The budget of the EU will thus implicitly flesh out the G-pillar of the Stability and Growth Pact and the E-pillar of the Economic and Monetary Union, thus eliminating the asymmetry in the institutional architecture.

45 Pisani-Ferry, J. (2012, April 30). France and the Netherlands strike back. *Project Syndicate*. Retrieved 5 May 2012 from <www.project-syndicate.org/commentary/france-and-the-netherlands-strike-back>. According to Angela Merkel, one of the options would be a larger role for the European Investment Bank, which would borrow cheap and then lend the money to banks and businesses on favourable conditions (Pop, V. (2012, April 30). More money for EU Investment Bank as leaders re-focus on growth. *EU Observer*).

46 Since it has been joined by Denmark, Italy, Austria and Sweden, the anti-coalition has more than half of the votes (163 of 345). Those against increasing expenditure may be in the minority, but they can use their veto seeing that the multiannual framework requires unanimity.

Annex 1: Proposal of the European Commission for the Multiannual Financial Framework of the EU as of 2014

Multiannual Financial Framework (EU-27)							(EUR million - 2011 prices)	
Commitment appropriations	*2014*	*2015*	*2016*	*2017*	*2018*	*2019*	*2020*	*total 2014/2020*
1. Smart and inclusive growth	**64,696**	**66,580**	**68,133**	**69,956**	**71,596**	**73,768**	**76,179**	**490,908**
of which: Economic, social and territorial cohesion	50,468	51,543	52,542	53,609	54,798	55,955	57,105	376,020
2. Sustainable growth:								
Natural resources	57,386	56,527	55,702	54,861	53,837	52,829	51,784	382,927
of which: Market related expenditure and direct payments	42,244	41,623	41,027	40,420	39,618	38,831	38,060	281,825
3. Security and citizenship	**2,532**	**2,571**	**2,609**	**2,648**	**2,687**	**2,726**	**2,763**	**18,535**
4. Global Europe	**9,400**	**9,645**	**9,845**	**9,960**	**10,150**	**10,380**	**10,620**	**70,000**
5. Administration	**8,542**	**8,679**	**8,796**	**8,943**	**9,073**	**9,225**	**90,371**	**62,629**
of which: Administrative expenditure of the institutions	6,967	7,039	7,108	7,191	7,288	7,385	7,485	50,464
Total commitment appropriations	**142,566**	**144,002**	**145,085**	**146,368**	**147,344**	**148,928**	**150,718**	**1,025,000**
as a percentage of GNI	1,08%	1,07%	1,06%	1,06%	1,05%	1,04%	1,03%	1,05%
Total payment appropriations	**133,851**	**141,002**	**135,516**	**138,396**	**142,247**	**142,916**	**137,994**	**972,198**
as a percentage of GNI	1,01%	1,05%	0,99%	1,00%	1,01%	1,00%	0,94%	1,00%

Outside the MFF								
Emergency Aid Reserve	350	350	350	350	350	350	350	2 450
European Globalisation Fund	429	429	429	429	429	429	429	3 000
Solidarity fund	1,000	1,000	1,000	1,000	1,000	1,000	1,000	7,000
Flexibility instrument	500	500	500	500	500	500	500	3,500
Reserve for crisis in the agricultural sector	500	500	500	500	500	500	500	3,500
ITER	886	624	299	291	261	232	114	2,707
GMES	834	834	834	834	834	834	834	5,841
EDF ACP	3,271	4,300	4,348	4,407	4,475	4,554	4,644	29,998
EDF OCT	46	46	46	46	46	46	46	321
Global Climate and Biodiversity Fund	p.m.	p.m.	p.m.	p.m.	p.m.	p.m.	p.m.	p.m.
Total outside the MFF	**7,815**	**8,583**	**8,306**	**8,357**	**8,395**	**8,445**	**8,416**	**58,316**

Total MFF + outside MFF	**150,371**	**152,585**	**153,391**	**154,725**	**155,739**	**157,372**	**159,134**	**1,083,316**
as a percentage of GNI	1,13%	1,13%	1,12%	1,12%	1,11%	1,10%	1,09%	1,11%

Annex 2: Net Position by EU Member State in 2009

	Revenue	Payments	Reimbursement 2007-2008	Net
Austria	1,822	2,316	–31	–463
Belgium	2,464	4,661	205	–1,993
Bulgaria	903	390	17	530
Cyprus	197	199	9	6
Czech Republic	2,988	1,374	72	1,686
Denmark	1,400	2,491	144	–947
Estonia	710	159	9	561
Finland	1,230	1,814	110	–473
France	14,228	20,093	1,096	–4,769
Germany	11,865	20,510	–1,736	–10,382
Greece	5,450	2,425	126	3,152
Hungary	3,775	909	51	2,918
Ireland	1,940	1,534	92	498
Italy	9,625	15,418	949	–4,844
Latvia	733	216	12	529
Lithuania	1,803	322	17	1,497
Luxembourg	166	287	17	–104
Malta	65	64	3	4
The Netherlands	2,007	3,337	–2,109	–3,439
Poland	9,543	3,134	146	6,556
Portugal	3,724	1,637	89	2,177
Romania	2,791	1,342	61	1,510
Slovakia	1,236	712	37	561
Slovenia	636	428	19	227
Spain	11,875	11,170	593	1,297
Sweden	1,463	1,855	–609	–1,002
United Kingdom	6,221	10,112	524	–3,377

Source: Algemene Rekenkamer [Court of Audit]. (2011). *EU-trendrapport 2011; Ontwikkelingen in het financieel management van de Europese Unie* [EU trend report 2011; Developments in the financial management of the European Union]. Dutch House of Representatives, *Kamerstuk* 32 624, No. 1, pp. 44-45.

Annex 3: Calculation of Rebate on Dutch Contribution

Gross rebate	1.050	
Contribution to rebate pool	–375	
Contribution UK rebate	75	Dropped
Net rebate	750	
Reduction cost of collection	–250	
Balance	500	

Source: Data provided by the Ministry of Finance.

15 European Agricultural Policy: Innovations Relating to the Agri-Food Chain and Rural Areas

Arie Oskam[*]

15.1 Introduction

Over the years, the Common Agricultural Policy (CAP) has always attracted a lot of attention, usually negative, the main targets being its burden on the European Union (EU) budget and its protectionist nature. Whatever analysis is considered, reference was and is seldom made to the great achievement of Mansholt and his co-workers who succeeded in integrating the highly heterogeneous agricultural policies of the first six EU Member States into a coherent framework, thus laying the foundations for a productivity boost in the European agricultural sector, and ensuring food security.[1]

Analysis of the CAP requires a framework broader than that of the primary farming sector alone, because farming is connected closely to the chain of supplying and processing companies and organizations.[2] There is also an intrinsic relationship between agriculture and rural areas, and thus between both policy areas. Rural policy 'in Brussels' developed from within the CAP. The relationship of agricultural and rural policies led Buckwell et al.,[3] taking a long-term perspective, to argue in favour of broadening the CAP with a Common Rural Policy (CRP). However, the prominent visibility of agriculture in peripheral regions does not imply that the economic importance of agriculture and forestry is accordingly large. As a result of many, and sometimes increasing, other activities (housing, work, recreation) in rural areas, in combination with the reducing economic significance of agriculture, society's demand for a high-quality environment (including biodiversity) has come to play an increasingly important role. This is basically a demand for public goods that can partly be provided by agriculture and forestry. The fact that agriculture is reducing relatively in terms of economic significance is chiefly the result of a long-term fall in real farmgate

---

* The author thanks Herman Stolwijk, Gerrit Meester and Ken Thomson for comments and many editorial improvements. Responsibility for any errors and interpretations lies with the author.

1 Merriënboer, J. (2006). *Mansholt*. Amsterdam: Boom.

2 Berkhout, P. & Roza, P. (Ed.). (2012). *Landbouw-Economisch Bericht 2012* [Agricultural Economic Report 2012]. The Hague: LEI, Wageningen UR, Ch. 3.

3 Buckwell, A., et al. (1997). Towards a common agricultural and rural policy for Europe. *European Economy, 5*.

prices, which is the downside to the strong increase in productivity in the sector, and not of decreasing agricultural production volumes.

This chapter is not so much about the functioning of the current policy. For this, the reader is referred to a book published recently in which the broad area of the EU policy on agriculture, food and rural areas is discussed in great detail.[4] Changes in policy usually come about slowly. Indeed, there is a lot to be said for this. Fast-changing and uncertain policies entail high costs for society.[5] In this chapter, we focus on a long-term vision for policies: a vision aligned as much as possible to changing conditions in society.[6] From this vision, which leaves scope for adjustment, various alternative policies are conceivable within and around the CAP.

When formulating this vision and these alternatives, two aspects are considered essential:

1. A focus on the future, but anchored in the experience gained over the past 50 years
2. Contributions to strengthening the EU and, as a part of this, to the Netherlands

We first look at what the CAP has achieved so far and where bottlenecks remain (Section 2). We then briefly consider the specific position of the Netherlands (Section 3), following which the main policy suggestions are explored in Section 4. The final section provides discussion and conclusions.

15.2 What Has the CAP Achieved, and What Is the Situation with the Present Policy?

The integration of agricultural products into the Common Market and the objectives of the CAP are laid down in Articles 38 and 39 of the EEC Treaty of Rome (now Articles 38 and 39 of the Treaty of Lisbon on the functioning of the EU). Although Article 38 – on market integration – was the most important for the long term and has been fully implemented, Article 39 has often attracted the most attention. According to paragraph 1 of Article 39, the CAP objectives shall be

4 Oskam, A., Meester, G. & Silvis, H. (Eds.). (2011). *EU policy for agriculture, food and rural areas* (2nd ed.). Wageningen: Wageningen Academic Publishers.

5 Oskam, A. (2009, October 22). *Policies for agriculture, food and rural areas: Does science matter?* (Farewell Address). Wageningen: Wageningen University. <www.aepdata.wur.nl/oskam/farewell.pdf>.

6 *See, e.g.*, Veerman, C. (2011). Feeding the planet and the role of the CAP. WASS Lecture, Wageningen. <www.wass.wur.nl/uk/newsagenda/archive/news/2011/lecture_cees_veerman.htm>.

- to increase agricultural productivity by promoting technical progress and by ensuring the rational development of agricultural production and the optimum utilization of the factors of production, in particular labour;
- *thus* to ensure a fair standard of living for the agricultural community, in particular by increasing the individual earnings of persons engaged in agriculture;
- to stabilize markets;
- to assure the availability of supplies;
- to ensure that supplies reach consumers at reasonable prices.

All Treaty reforms have provided for these same objectives in an identical manner. On the face of it, this may seem slightly odd, considering that the context in which agriculture operates has undergone major changes. This is reflected in, for instance, new goals embedded in other articles such as those concerning the environment, sustainability and animal welfare. However, all this need not detract from the above CAP objectives, which, seen from the perspective of the 1960s, have been largely realized, according to Meester.[7]
When the CAP was first framed, and especially when it was established around 1968, it was criticized from various directions. Critics claimed that through market and price support – the core element of the policy at that time – agriculture was 'preserved' at far too high a price level for agricultural products, instead of being 'reformed' and adapted to international developments in supply and demand. Perhaps the most articulate exponent of this criticism was Van Riemsdijk,[8] who, already at that time, argued in favour of introducing (temporary!) direct payments and prices in line with world markets. In 1970-1990, due to increasing production and ever-lower world market prices that were partially a result, criticism mounted from both within and outside the EU. Pressure to reform the CAP continued to rise. In line with dominant thinking in neoclassical economics, a particular case was made for converting the existing market and price policy, with its relatively high internal prices, export subsidies, market interventions, supply quotas etc., into a market-oriented policy with compensatory direct payments to farmers. These compensatory payments should be unrelated to production volumes. Since the 1990s, partly as a result of international discussions within the World Trade Organization (GATT/WTO), the original policy instruments are now subject to restrictions, mainly concerning the level of support

7 Meester, G. (2011). Future developments and policies. In A. Oskam, G. Meester & H. Silvis (Eds.), *EU policy for agriculture, food and rural areas* (2nd ed.). Wageningen: Wageningen Academic Publishers, p. 415.

8 Van Riemsdijk, J. (1968). De landbouw conserveren of vernieuwen? [Preserving or modernising agriculture?]. *Economisch Statistische Berichten, 53*, 590-594.

directly coupled to production. However, the EU still has a wide range of instruments at its disposal to regulate the internal market for a number of products.[9]
The launch of this process (the Mac Sharry reform of 1992) can rightfully be labelled the first major reform of the CAP, and a step on the road from assistance through more or less guaranteed prices to support barely – if at all – coupled to production. The subsequent Agenda 2000 and particularly the Fischler reform of 2003 were a follow-up to the Mac Sharry reform. However, in practice, establishing these three reforms proved difficult,[10] which may have been partly why the ensuing CAP Health Check of 2008 was slightly less ambitious.
In October 2011, the European Commission presented detailed proposals for a further revision of the CAP as of 2014.[11] It is not easy to detect a clear line in the extensive range of these proposals, which concern shifts in direct income support between Member States and groups. 'Basic payments' per hectare and 'greening' of the CAP are the new mantras, and there is a stronger focus on new themes such as climate policy.
Figure 15.1 shows the nominal EU budgetary spending on the CAP.[12] As we can see, over the past few decades there has been a major shift from market and price policy towards direct payments, which in 2009 – together with the rural policy – accounted for more than 90% of the CAP budget. Recent CAP budget expenditures are also the starting point for the budgetary period 2014-2020. No increase is foreseen in the nominal budget.

9 *See* integrated Regulation 1234/2007, laying down the Common Organization of the Market for a total of 21 products. The transition to one Common Organization of the Market was an important step towards rationalization and simplification of the policy. In addition, however, the – again very detailed – policy of direct payments was added by means of Regulation 1782/2003, later replaced by Regulation 73/2009. As a result, the CAP is still a hugely complex policy area only accessible to specialists.

10 Swinnen, J. (Ed.). (2008). *The perfect storm: The political economy of the fischler reforms of the common agricultural policy*. Brussels: CEPS.

11 *See* the special website <http://ec.europa.eu/agriculture/cap-post-2013/index_en.htm>.

12 When interpreting Figure 15.1, one should bear in mind that spending increased at a time when the budget for the market and price policy decreased considerably (*see, e.g.*, Silvis, H. & Lapperre, R. (2011). Market, price and quota policy: From price support to safety net. In A. Oskam, G. Meester & H. Silvis (Eds.), *EU policy for agriculture, food and rural areas* (2nd ed.). Wageningen: Wageningen Academic Publishers, p. 177).

Figure 15.1 EU Budget for Direct Payments and Rural Policy

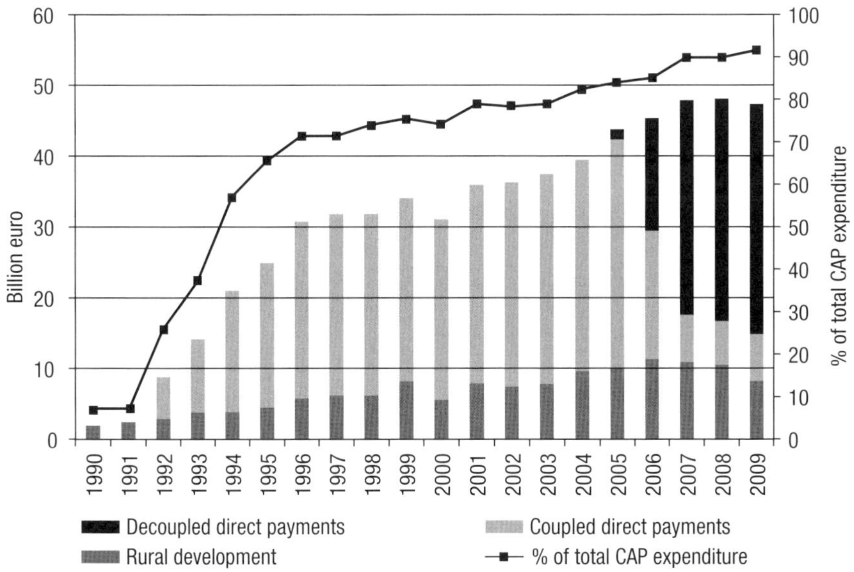

When thinking about the Policy's future, account should be taken of at least one important change in the international markets for agricultural products. It seems that in the first decade of this century the continuous fall in real prices of agricultural products and food has come to a (temporary?) halt. After the food crisis of 2008-2009, plenty of articles predicted that we might be on the eve of an era of rising prices for agricultural raw materials and food. In this context, the main underlying causes are said to be scarcity of resources, including energy, fertilizers and land, an increasing demand for food, especially in Asia, and an agricultural sector that in many developing countries has been neglected for decades.[13] With higher prices for agricultural products, it seems odd to keep compensating farmers in the EU for falls in 'guaranteed prices' that occurred many years ago.[14] When circumstances change, the goalposts should be moved. The policy of the EU and the Member States is not really designed for a period of relatively high prices.[15] In preparing policy, it is useful to take into account such a scenario.

13 *See* FAO, OECD, World Bank etc., or – in the Netherlands – Meester (2011); Meijerink, G., van Berkum, S., Shutes, K. & Solano, G. (2011). *Price and prejudice: Why are food prices so high?* (LEI, Report 2011-035). The Hague: LEI; Veerman (2011).

14 This applies even more to the Member States acceding to the EU in 2004 and 2007. In the framework of 'equal treatment', these countries received higher prices as well as stepwise increasing direct payments.

15 European Commission. (2007). *Scenar 2020. Scenario study on agriculture and the rural world*. Brussels: DG Agriculture and Rural Development; European Commission. (2010, November 18). *The CAP towards 2020: Meeting the food, natural resources and territorial challenges of the future*. COM (2010) 672 final, Brussels.

15.3 The Specific Position of the Netherlands

For years, the Dutch agri-food chain has held a strong international position, as illustrated by the country's substantial net exports. Convincing evidence of this is also provided by the example set by the Dutch agri-food sector to many other countries (such as Chile, China, and South Korea) as well as high scores in broadly based research on international competitiveness. It is with good reason that, in the Dutch innovation policy, two of the nine 'top' sectors are found in the agri-food industry. Still, this does not mean that the agri-food chain is completely without problems. In particular, the substantial environmental burden, especially from the livestock sectors, has been a problem for years.[16]

The net exports of the Dutch agri-food chain account for around 5% of net national income.[17] Since about 80% of these net exports take place in relation to the EU, the Netherlands benefits, practically by definition, from a well-functioning market within the EU. The euro and/or relatively stable exchange rates help to achieve this. European regulation is also crucial. For instance, for a large exporter of agri-food products like the Netherlands, a high level of food safety and food quality is very important. The recent experience with the EHEC bacteria shows that food safety problems not only affect those causing them. They also impact on other producers: in this respect, every exporter of agricultural and food products is in a vulnerable position.[18] Food quality is a broader concept than food safety,[19] and chiefly concerns quality characteristics valued by consumers. If a region, country or the entire EU is regarded as an area where high-quality food is produced, this will not only have positive effects for the producers; it will benefit society as a whole.

According to European standards, the Netherlands has hardly any 'real' rural areas.[20] Areas in the Netherlands that come closest to meeting the EU's rural area criteria are classified, at EU level, as 'less urbanized'. Unlike in most genuinely rural areas in the EU, the per capita income in less urbanized Dutch areas is not much lower than in the rest of the Netherlands. Also, the growth dynamic

16 Stolwijk, H.J.J. & Veenendaal, P.J.J. (1995). *De betekenis van de landbouw voor de Nederlandse economie* [The significance of agriculture for the Dutch economy] (Publication 1.29). The Hague: Landbouw-Economisch Instituut; LEB. (Various years). *Landbouw-Economisch Bericht*. The Hague: LEI.

17 Like any simple standard, the net exports of the agri-food chain, forming part of the net national income, are not without problems either, as the contribution by supplying industries to the economy is – in this context – not explicitly distinguished.

18 Berkhout & Roza (2012).

19 Velthuis, A., Verbeke, W. & Marette, S. (2011). Food quality, food safety and certification. In A. Oskam, G. Meester & H. Silvis (Eds.), *EU policy for agriculture, food and rural areas* (2nd ed.). Wageningen: Wageningen Academic Publishers, pp. 291-301.

20 Terluin, I.J., Slangen, L.H.G., Leeuwen, E.S. van, Oskam, A.J. & Gaaff, A. (2005). *De plattelandseconomie in Nederland: Een verkenning van definities, indicatoren, instituties en beleid* [The rural economy in the Netherlands: An exploration of definitions, indicators, institutions and policy] (Report 4.05.04). The Hague: LEI-WUR.

is sometimes remarkably high, and the share of agriculture in total employment, contrary to 'real' rural areas, is usually below 5%. The objectives of the EU rural policy, focusing mainly on bridging the gap between disadvantaged rural areas and the rest of a country, do not really fit the Dutch situation. There is thus every reason to wonder why the Netherlands (and this also applies to other more highly urbanized Member States and/or regions) has to make use of EU rural policy funds.

15.4 A Few Possible Paths to the Future *for* the EU

Before outlining a few potential paths for EU policy on agriculture, food and the rural areas in the coming decades, we will first briefly consider a few basic principles that should play a role in any discussion on future policy.

15.4.1 *Basic Principles*

Free Internal Market

One of these basic principles is the existence of a free internal market, whereby particular care is taken, through competition rules, to prevent competitive advantages resulting from differences in national policy.[21] This is in the Dutch interest: its sizeable international trade heavily relies on realizing competitive advantages based on economies of scale on the demand side. In view of the small domestic market, this is very important for small countries. However, it should be pointed out that in primary agriculture the economies of scale on the supply side as a result of a larger market quickly reach their limits, and are therefore usually quite limited.

A few years ago, the importance of the internal European market was again studied intensively by the *Centraal Planbureau* (Netherlands Bureau for Economic Policy Analysis).[22] This study showed that for the Netherlands the advantage of the 'single' internal EU market is larger than for the average Member State. This gives rise to two (tentative) conclusions. First, the internal market is very important for the agri-food sector, also due to the significance of intra-EU trade in agri-food.[23] Second, in assessing new EU policy, the most relevant question for the Netherlands is whether it contributes to a better functioning of the Union in gen-

---

21 The agricultural sector is somewhat special in this regard: where elsewhere the aim is to prevent cartels and price-fixing agreements, producer groups or other types of cooperation are sometimes promoted in agriculture. In view of the weak market position of farms as opposed to other links in the chain, there is something to be said for this.

22 Straathof, B., Linders, G.-J., Lejour, A. & Möhlmann, J. (2008). *The internal market and the Dutch economy, implications for trade and economic growth* (CPB Document No. 168). The Hague: CPB Netherlands Bureau for Economic Policy Analysis; *see also* the chapter by Pelkmans in this volume.

23 Berkhout & Roza (2012).

eral and to the internal market in particular. Centring on this question prevents that with each policy change the focus will shift to the narrower question: what are the benefits, in the short term and in budgetary terms?

Subsidiarity

According to the subsidiarity principle, a higher level of governance should not concern itself with policies that can be dealt with just as well, or better, by a lower level. Subsidiarity thus involves bringing decision-making and implementation to a level that, with a view to a socially desirable result, is the most appropriate. In EU practice, this would mean that decisions on basic principles of policy and implementation should be made in Brussels, but that the more detailed policy choices and the policy implementation are a matter for the Member State or region.[24]

This subsidiarity principle was attached as a special protocol to the 1992 Treaty of Maastricht, and can also be found in the Lisbon Treaty[25]; it is one of the fundamental principles on which (in theory) the EU bases its policymaking. National parliaments now also have more possibilities to monitor compliance with the subsidiarity principle, using 'yellow' and 'orange' cards. If by virtue of the subsidiarity principle, the EU decides to transfer certain activities to the Member States, this may also have financial consequences for the Member States.

So subsidiarity means that the EU may act only if objectives are involved that Member States cannot achieve at national level. And if the EU must act, such action will, according to the proportionality principle, remain limited to the absolute minimum. If a proposal does not meet these requirements, it should not be adopted.

The EU's rural policy has always been based on the principle of *partial* subsidiarity. The question is whether national and/or regional authorities could completely take over responsibility in this policy area. In that case, Community involvement could be limited to setting European frameworks. The Community would be required to contribute financially only if the policy had a truly European or, in any case, cross-border character. The Sapir report[26] and the advice of the Socio-Economic Council (SER),[27] for instance, explicitly addressed this question.

24 Gelauff, G., Grilo, I. & Lejour, A. (Eds.). (2008). *Subsidiarity and economic reform in Europe*. Berlin: Springer.

25 TEU, Art. 5.

26 Sapir, A. (2003). *An agenda for a growing Europe. Making the EU economic system deliver: report of an independent high-level study group established on the initiative of the President of the European Commission*. <www.umic.pt/images/stories/sapirreport.pdf>.

27 SER. (2006). *Co-financing of the common agricultural policy* (Advisory Report 06/05). <www.ser.nl/en/publications/publications/~/media/Files/Internet/Talen/Engels/2006/2006_05%20pdf.ashx>.

Stolwijk and Oskam[28] and Grethe[29] elaborate the issue in relation to agriculture. All of them pointed in the direction of shifting responsibility to Member States.

Co-financing

Prevailing practice regarding rural and structural policy is that the EU finances the policy 'in principle', but asks for co-financing by national or regional authorities and/or those directly benefiting from the policy.[30] The percentage of co-financing requested from the Member State, the region or those directly concerned often depends on the per capita income in the areas concerned.

Another approach might be considered: a Member State develops a policy on the basis of a European Framework Directive,[31] and if budgetary resources are required, the Member State will finance the policy and the EU can co-finance a certain percentage. In that case, the Member State need only provide accountability for the policy in question afterwards.

In this way, co-financing closely dovetails with subsidiarity. It confers greater policy responsibility on the Member States, e.g., for direct payments under the CAP. The key question for the SER[32] was to what extent and in what way co-financing of direct payments can contribute to a better (common and national) agricultural policy. In this context, 'better' means more effective and more efficient in realizing future societal objectives that often lie outside the realm of the market (environment, landscape, biodiversity, etc.).

If policy is kept more strictly in line with the subsidiarity principle, and if, following on from this, co-financing is to play a larger role, it is not long before the question arises how to prevent conflicts with internal market rules. The fact is that a national subsidy, whether or not partly co-financed by the EU, will, to a certain extent, always distort competition. Whether it concerns education, research, infrastructure, institutional organization, industrial relations, social services, pensions, taxes, etc., competitiveness will always be affected.[33] But as illustrated by, for instance, Member States' industrial policy, this need not really be

28 Stolwijk, H.J.J. & Oskam, A.J. (2006). Nederland in de Europese Unie [The Netherlands in the European Union]. In C.A. de Kam & A.P. Ros (Ed.), *Jaarboek Overheidsfinanciën 2006* [Annual Government Finances 2006]. The Hague: Sdu Uitgevers, pp. 109-130.

29 Grethe, H. (2008). Agricultural policy: What roles for the EU and the Member States?. In G. Gelauff, I. Grilo & A. Lejour (Eds.), *Subsidiarity and economic reform in Europe*. Berlin: Springer, pp. 191-218.

30 Bos, M. (2011). The EU budget. In A. Oskam, G. Meester & H. Silvis (Eds.), *EU policy for agriculture, food and rural areas* (2nd ed.). Wageningen: Wageningen Academic Publishers, pp. 79-96.

31 Borchardt, K.-D. (2010). *The ABC of European Union law*. Luxembourg: Publications Office of the European Union. <http://europa.eu/documentation/legislation/pdf/oa8107147_en.pdf>.

32 SER (2006).

33 A country that is relatively future-oriented and dynamically and efficiently organized automatically improves its competitive position. But this comes with investments and/or payments (subsidies) that are usually financed by own resources. In addition, such a country contributes to the better functioning of the EU.

a problem. Only in case of obvious and clearly identifiable market advantages will the European Commission intervene. A similar approach could be adopted for agricultural and rural policy.

Do the WTO Green Box Rules Suit the EU?
Discussions within the WTO on market distortion in agriculture, resulting in measures classified according to the extent to which they directly distort the market, may also be useful in this context. Within the WTO, measures causing little or hardly any market distortion are placed in a so-called Green Box.[34] These measures concern, for instance, general government services, government services aimed at agriculture, food and landscape, infrastructure provisions, domestic food aid and decoupled direct payments. Of course, not all Green Box measures are undisputed. Decoupled direct payments in particular are still the subject of discussion, because of the large amount of public funds involved in the EU, United States and Japan.
The question is whether decoupled income support indeed has 'no or only minimal production effects'. In other words, does decoupled income support really belong in the Green Box? On the basis of US data, Weber and Key[35] concluded that it has only a minimal effect at area level. Does this also apply to the EU, where a sudden, sharp decrease in direct payments may substantially affect farm incomes? Answering this question using empirical data is not an easy task: scientific research is still continuing. On the other hand, it may also be argued that there is still no evidence that decoupled direct payments have more than 'minimal' production effects at an aggregate level. This is consistent with the EU's line of argument in the WTO.

15.4.2 Alternative Future Policy Avenues

The Policy Trend
In turbulent times, it is not easy to define the policy trend (i.e., the CAP that may be expected). From a practical perspective, however, the Multiannual Financial Framework proposed by the European Commission[36] may serve as a starting point. This Framework assumes a more or less constant nominal budget for the coming years, and comprises the Commission's proposal for further reform of the CAP. The proposed budgets[37] are in line with those of recent years and are shown in Figure 15.1. The total demand on the budget (in nominal values) in

34 Blandford, D. & Josling, T. (2007). Should the green box be modified? (IPC Discussion Paper). <www.agritrade.org/Publications/DiscussionPapers/Green_Box.pdf>.

35 Weber, J.G. & Key, N. (2012). How much do decoupled payments affect production? An instrumental variable approach with panel data. *American Journal of Agricultural Economics, 94*(1), 52-66.

36 COM (2011) 500 final; *see also* the chapter by Van Nispen and Blankenstein.

37 Off budget, an aggregate entry of nearly €4 billion has been included for crises in the agricultural sector.

2014-2020 will be €19 billion for market and price policy, €302 billion for direct payments and €102 billion for rural policy: €423 billion in total.
The policy trend is to maintain the direct decoupled payments, albeit in a slightly modified form,[38] as well as the financing of rural policy, requiring co-financing by the Member States. Within these budgetary constraints, the direct payments to Bulgaria and Romania until 2016 are phased in, and room is created for new accession states such as Croatia.
What are the alternatives? Below, five possible avenues are discussed.

- *Future Avenue I: Partly Shifting Decoupled Direct Payments to Member State Budgets*[39]

Considering the heavy budgetary pressure in the EU as a whole, Member States can be expected to look for ways to cut spending within the 2014-2020 budget. One possibility is a stricter application of the subsidiarity principle to direct payments. This may be justified by pointing out that direct payments involve only limited supranational interests, but mainly consist of cumbersome income transfers. In addition, these payments are assumed to have no or only minimal production effects. The payments may initially preserve more jobs in the agricultural sector than would otherwise be the case, but in the longer term they will mostly lead to a higher price of land.
Member States might jointly decide to keep, for instance, only 20% of the direct payments under direct responsibility of the EU,[40] while 80% would then be used for reducing the annual contributions to the EU budget, thus releasing funds which Member States can use for, e.g., (1) temporary compensation for producers who used to be entitled to full direct payments, (2) other national policy priorities that may concern both the agri-food chain and rural policy, (3) purposes other than those relating to the agri-food chain and rural policy.
This switch to an 80% budgetary renationalization of direct payments, together with a full renationalization of rural policies, could release an annual sum of around €49 billion for national policy priorities, including a reduction of the contribution to the EU budget. It would, moreover, make negotiations at EU level much easier, because common arrangements with lots of details are avoided.

38 However, so-called cross-compliance is maintained. These are conditions that apply when securing direct payments.

39 A similar alternative (but also a little more complicated because subsidiarity and co-financing already exist) can be developed for the rural policy: *see* future avenue III.

40 Here, it is assumed that around 20% of the direct payments serve a European interest. This interest has been laid down in the cross-compliance and in the rules for 'best agricultural practice'.

- *Future Avenue II: More Focus on Policies to Encourage Innovation in the Agri-Food Sector*

The emphasis on innovation of the agri-food sector resembles some aspects of 'Plan B' of the Dutch Council for the Environment and Infrastructure (*Raad voor de Leefomgeving en Infrastructuur – RLI*).[41] Plan B focuses on reducing direct payments and getting subsidies 'off the ground' for innovations in the agri-food complex. According to the RLI, the current policy already offers Member States room to experiment: 10% of the direct payments. So far, the Netherlands has made limited use of this possibility to skim an annual amount of €80 million (10% of €800 million) off the direct payments and use it for other purposes.[42] If serious thought is given to this alternative, it may be wise to decide and embark on this path so as to gain experience with it.

Although the RLI puts forward a number of suggestions for innovation subsidies, it does not specify in detail how this type of policy should take shape in practice. This means that there is room to further develop this Plan B.

For innovation subsidies, three principles should be observed:

1. The subsidies are granted for innovations in the entire agri-food chain and are balanced with other (national) innovation subsidies.
2. The subsidies are limited because they must fall within the budget released under future Avenue I, and, moreover, are not to be used for the other alternatives mentioned below or still to be developed.
3. The innovation subsidies may not conflict with the Green Box criteria.

- *Future Avenue III: Strengthen the Quality of Landscape, Nature and the Environment in Rural Areas*

While the agri-food chain mainly focuses on producing internationally marketable products, there is also demand for the public goods and services that agriculture and forestry (can) typically produce or support. These public goods and services are succinctly referred to as 'green services'. They play an important role in rural regions, especially those near urban areas. The demand for green

41 RLI. (2011). *European agriculture policy as a transition instrument for agriculture and horticulture.* <http://en.rli.nl/publications/2011/advice/european-agriculture-policy-as-a-transition-instrument-for-agriculture-and-horticulture>.

42 Following the Health Check of 2008, possibilities in this regard seem to have been extended by Arts. 68-72 of Council Regulation 73/2009. Every (*ad hoc*) Member State proposal seems to have been incorporated, with many restrictions derived from the WTO international trade rules. The huge tangle of rules and provisions makes it quite difficult even for a specialist to find out how the policy can be implemented. Thus, the result is another CAP element that is accessible only to super-specialists, and thus completely runs counter to the often expressed wish for policy simplification. The RLI (2011) sees room for innovation subsidies in the agri-food complex, but I cannot find the word 'innovation' in the heap of provisions and terms (in 73/2009), nor in relation to the implementation: overview of the implementation of direct payments under the CAP in Member States in 2012 (Reg. 73/2009) (*) January 2012. <http://ec.europa.eu/agriculture/direct-support/pdf/implementation-direct-payments_en.pdf>.

services strongly depends on the income level of the population and on preferences for living, working and recreating in a rural environment. Over recent decades, the (automatic) availability of green services has decreased as a result of urbanization, growing infrastructure and the modernization of farming.

In large parts of Europe, the development of rural areas is still strongly determined by the agricultural sector. This is far less true of a densely populated country like the Netherlands. Agriculture and forestry do, however, define the visual appearance of rural areas. This also applies to nature reserves, but these areas cover less space. Nature reserves are particularly important in conserving national biodiversity, while they often have a significant recreational function as well.

The emphasis of this third future avenue is on maintaining and promoting green services. An obvious combination of policy instruments can be deployed to protect the public goods and services that are inextricably linked to the (cultural) landscape and natural sites. Compliance with rules at European and national level (such as the Birds and Habitats Directives, the Natura 2000 areas and – in the Netherlands – the National Ecological Network) can be combined with special rewards for nature and landscape management. This immediately begs the question of whether it is really necessary for the government to safeguard the provision of these green services by means of subsidies. Can producers (especially farmers) not be forced to organize their operations such as to preserve the landscape and environmental qualities of peripheral regions, or would reward by the Member State or region still be a more reasonable option? The SER[43] discusses this issue in great detail, ultimately arriving at a qualified answer: sometimes yes, sometimes no, and acknowledging the existence of a grey area. Figure 15.2 serves as a guideline in this respect.

43 SER. (2008). *CAP reform and public services of agriculture* (Advisory Report 08/05). <www.ser.nl/~/media/Files/Internet/Talen/Engels/2008/2008_05/2008_05.ashx>.

Figure 15.2 Diagram of Different Concepts Indicating Whether it is Necessary for the Government To Arrange for the Provision of Public (Green) Services

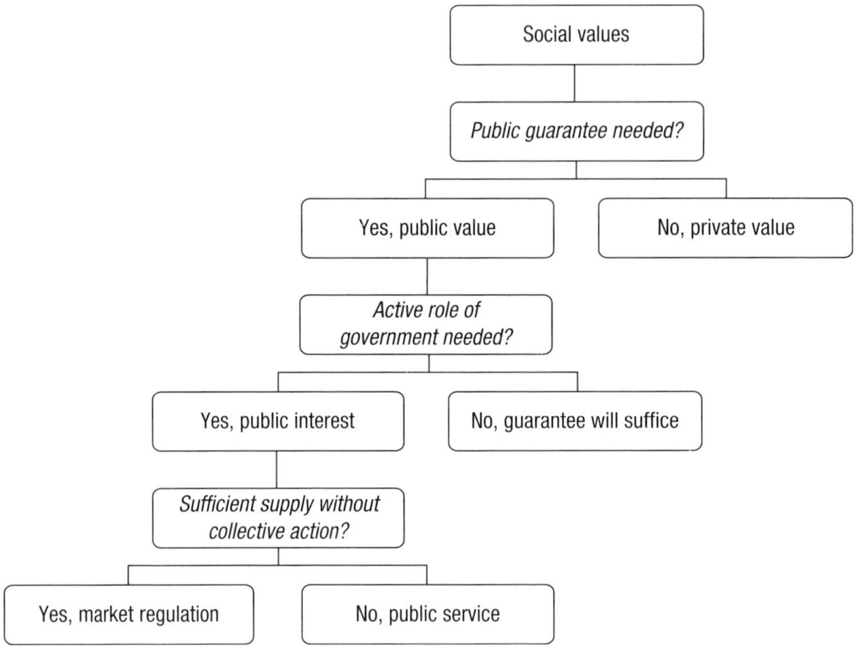

Source: SER. (2008). *CAP reform and public services of agriculture* (Advisory Report 08/05). <www.ser.nl/~/media/Files/Internet/Talen/Engels/2008/2008_05/2008_05.ashx>.

If, according to Figure 15.2, public services are involved, these services can be provided by the national or regional government. Payments are weighed against funds for other public services, are not contrary to the Green Box criteria and are limited by the budget released under Avenue I.

- *Future Avenue IV: A 'Safety Net' in Case of Calamities, and Private Arrangements Aimed at More Stable Market Prices*

For many years, market and price policy – including a wide range of instruments – was at the heart of the CAP.[44] Although the budget is now dominated by direct payments, market and price policy is still an important element for which the EU is responsible. Many agricultural products are still subject to import tariffs, and for a number of products market intervention is still possible and sometimes export refunds/subsidies are granted.

Compared to about 20 years ago, import protection has diminished and direct interventions and export subsidies have decreased markedly: a gradual transition to a safety net approach. This essentially means that the European Commission

44 Silvis & Lapperre (2011).

will intervene in the market only if calamities occur: animal and plant diseases, unexpected problems with or doubts about food safety, exceptional weather conditions, etc. As long as the EU can still apply sufficiently high import tariffs and is, moreover, importing, protection against sudden price drops outside the EU will still be provided by this more traditional mechanism of price policy: increasing import tariffs. However, the intention is to further restrict these possibilities in the future, although there is good reason to doubt that the Doha Round, where such matters are discussed and decided,[45] will (soon) be concluded.

Limiting the risk of excessive fluctuations of internal prices, and thus also reducing the danger of extremely low incomes and large-scale bankruptcies of agricultural enterprises, two types of instruments can be used:

1. A safety net regulated mainly by the EU, aimed at avoiding excessive price fluctuations, both for producers and consumers. This requires maintaining certain market and price policy instruments. This type of policy mainly works in situations of internal price drops. Unexpected low internal prices can (sometimes) be offset by increasing import tariffs or by temporarily storing storable products, assuming that after 2013 the EU can no longer use export subsidies. Unexpected high internal prices can be partly compensated by reducing import tariffs, but this effect stops at a zero tariff. By changing import tariffs, part of the price fluctuation is shifted to the world market (allowed under WTO rules in extreme circumstances).
2. An alternative is to make the market responsible for price stabilization. This can be done in various ways, for instance, by working with contracts between producers and users,[46] but futures markets can also play an important part. In all cases, risks to be avoided are transferred 'at a compensation' to those who are willing to bear those risks. In the EU – particularly in North-West Europe – a number of futures markets for agricultural products are already operational. However, far fewer private possibilities for price stabilization are being developed than in the United States.[47] Whether contracts and/or future mar-

45 Gooren, P., Huige, R. & Stanton, G. (2011). The WTO context. In A. Oskam, G. Meester & H. Silvis (Eds.), *EU policy for agriculture, food and rural areas* (2nd ed.). Wageningen: Wageningen Academic Publishers, pp. 97-111.

46 Recently, a regulation relating to milk entered into force to regulate market relations between suppliers of raw milk and dairy processors through price agreements. *See* Regulation (EU) No. 261/2012 of the European Parliament and of the Council of 14 March 2012 amending Council Regulation (EC) No. 1234/2007 as regards contractual relations in the milk and milk products sector. (2012, March 30). *Official Journal of the European Union.* <http://eur-lex.europa.eu/LexUriServ/LexUriServ.do?uri=OJ:L:2012:094:0038:0048:EN:PDF>. This should be regarded as a 'pilot' to regulate market relations.

47 Pennings, J., Garcia, P. & Oskam, A. (2011). Private market and income stabilization methods. In A. Oskam, G. Meester & H. Silvis (Eds.), *EU policy for agriculture, food and rural areas* (2nd ed.). Wageningen: Wageningen Academic Publishers, pp. 189-195.

kets will work on a larger scale will also depend on how the safety net will be organized. As long as the government irons out price risks without payment, there will be less room for private arrangements (and *vice versa*).

In short, there are both complementarity and trade-off between the safety net based on public funding and private arrangements on the basis of risk premiums which those concerned pay themselves. Complementarity involves hedging major risks through the safety net of the EU. Trade-off means that contracts and futures markets can, to a large extent, absorb price risks for producers and users, who pay for these themselves. The government's task in this context is (1) to exercise restraint in bearing price risks and (2) to facilitate and monitor contracts and futures markets.
The IV(a) approach is a simplified continuation of the EU market and price policy, and must necessarily be implemented at EU level. Under IV(b), the initiative lies with producers and users, requiring only minimal public funding.

- *Future Avenue V: Developing or Strengthening Transnational Chains and Networks*

Since its creation, the policy of the EU has mainly revolved around agriculture itself and only to a limited extent the agri-food chain. This could change. 'Brussels' could focus much more on the chain as a whole. Especially in terms of innovation, logistics, the environment, food safety and animal welfare, such a broader approach seems to have advantages 'on paper'. Interest in the agri-food sector as a *chain* is particularly inspired by aspects of market forces and food safety; more specifically,

1. it is one of the sectors receiving attention in the framework of the competition policy.
2. for a number of products, the market and price policy concentrated on processed farm products (meat, dairy produce, sugar, starch potatoes, etc.). As a result, certain industries processing agricultural products were (and still are) directly affected by the implementation of the market and price policy.
3. where balance in the agri-food chain is concerned, Brussels pays particular attention to whether price movements are sufficiently passed on between agriculture and processing industries.[48] This comes in addition to the competition policy mentioned under the first point.
4. the feed industry, and even more the food industry, plays an important role in achieving food safety in the EU.[49]

The EU can promote the development of transnational chains and networks in the agri-food sector. It is therefore an element for which (temporary) co-financing

48 *See* Regulation (EU) No. 261/2012 (2012).

49 Van der Meulen, B.M.J. & van der Velde, M. (2008). *European food law handbook*. Wageningen: Wageningen Academic Publishers.

by the EU could be considered. This type of policy is in line (in terms of methodology) with the Trans-European Networks or with the interregional policy, and the EU budget required could thus be financed by the cohesion funds.

15.4.3 Evaluative Comments

Each of the above future avenues might, to a greater or lesser extent, replace the existing CAP. But combinations are possible as well. The way EU policy is financed deserves special attention. As stated earlier, the remaining decoupled direct payments lend themselves to renationalization. The current situation, where the EU first asks the Member States to provide (all) the necessary funds and then refunds these to the national authorities, which, in their turn, must arrange for the payments to be made to farmers, seems to conflict with the subsidiarity principle. The change proposed in Avenue I would mostly let the Member States decide to what extent they wish to maintain decoupled direct payments, what alternatives they may be deploying and how they will further develop alternative options. Still, co-financing may be a first step towards full financial renationalization of direct payments. In this context, Member States can be expected to gradually develop new priorities. In all cases, the EU would continue to be involved through (a) co-financing (in case of cross-border effects), (b) monitoring compliance with the conditions set and their implementation, and (c) providing overviews per Member State and for the entire EU so as to increase the transparency of the policy.

15.5 Discussion and Conclusions

For the Dutch economy, especially also for its agri-food chain, it is essential that the EU functions properly. This chapter has discussed the role of the EU agricultural policy in this respect, emphasizing that this role goes further than just agriculture: it impacts on the whole agri-food chain and the rural areas. A striking characteristic of the CAP is its continuous reform. The policy is again under discussion as this is written. Against this background, alternatives have been explored.

Food safety and food quality are of key importance to a country like the Netherlands that is so dependent on the export of agricultural products and food. Relatively high food standards – which are increasingly driven by business and consumers – reflect on the European producers of this food. Considering that attention for food safety and quality is also growing outside the EU, high EU standards offer an advantage when it comes to supplying markets and consumers outside the EU. For this advantage to be realized, innovative entrepreneurs and alert government, as well as good contacts between producers and consumers, are needed.

The current CAP budget is in large part used for direct payments and to a lesser extent for rural policy, including the so-called less favoured areas.[50] This type of policy partly serves as a buffer for agriculture, in order to prevent a far greater reduction in the number of businesses and much bigger drain on employment. Through so-called cross-compliance, i.e., setting requirements which business operations have to meet in order to qualify for direct payments, the CAP also tries to contribute to the quality of the rural environment. In the longer term, both types of policy will probably contribute only little to the dynamics of EU society, seeing that they are too much the product of decisions and discussions at (too high a) Community level and too little adapted to local conditions. In line with the widely endorsed subsidiarity principle, this chapter, therefore, lists a few alternatives that focus much more strongly on national and regional priorities, and are more in line with the Europe 2020 strategy which chiefly aims at less bureaucracy and more 'tailor-made' solutions.[51]

Section 4 briefly sets out five alternatives. A key element of these avenues is to gradually transfer CAP funds, particularly direct payments, to national authorities, which can exploit them much more effectively. The options discussed above go further than those advised by the RLI, but are in line with the latter's arguments for bringing more dynamism to the EU. The options are not exhaustive, but they do share the aim of shifting more responsibility to Member States and regions so as to make the policy more effective as well as more efficient. Generally speaking, subsidies carry the inherent danger of less sensible choices and being captured as 'rents'. However, their justification increases as more positive external effects come into play. Innovation subsidies may apply to this principle by triggering developments that are also profitable for others. Without innovation subsidies, such development might not take place. This is all the more so if in Europe such subsidies are exploited by the different countries, using their special strengths. Bringing decisions closer to entrepreneurs, citizens and local authorities and, moreover, letting them carry a large part of the burden are expected to lead to greater societal involvement and ultimately more dynamism and growth. Subsidiarity and co-financing are important fundamental principles in this context.

The proposal to shift a large portion of the funds spent on decoupled direct payments to the Member States aims to make the policy more efficient, and thus improve the functioning of the EU. On the basis of their own preferences (and within certain limits), Member States could then use these funds to support other forms of policy (innovation, public services, etc.) or to reduce their budgetary contribution to the EU. In EU negotiations, much time and effort are spent on arguing over national or regional priorities, which are often of little interest to

50 *See* Figure 15.1.

51 Dutch House of Representatives. (2011). State of the European Union 2010-2011, *Kamerstuk* 32 502.

Brussels. By setting mere frameworks and leaving the actual elaboration to the Member States, the policy's effectiveness and efficiency can be enhanced.
It is mostly the Member States and the citizens that would benefit from this. Within general frameworks, Member States would have considerable freedom to act. However, freedom brings with it the responsibility to develop proposals and suggest policy choices. The Commission's task would change from one of preparing policy to monitoring and controlling it. Such a development ties in closely with the Dutch views on economic and monetary policy.

16 Party Politics in Europe: Looking for New Directions

Dorette Corbey

16.1 Introduction: the Impotence of Political Parties

Political parties are the pillars of democracy. They are necessary in all corners of society to represent citizens and connect them with their members of parliament and their government. For most political parties times are hard: their membership is waning, and their traditional, stable support is dwindling. Many parties need to update or re-source their message – the search for an appealing vision is a near-permanent one. However, success is dependent not only on effort and vision but increasingly also on party leaders' performance in the media. This may lead to major fluctuations, which, in turn, generate calls for a change of course and reform. In addition, parties face a displacement of political action. Much important decision-making is moving from The Hague to the local level or to Europe, which makes conveying a consistent vision extra complicated. The standing of and trust in politics as a whole are falling.[1]

The struggle of political parties is clearly visible when it comes to taking positions on Europe. Despite evident successes, the European Union (EU) is not popular; peace and prosperity are too much taken for granted. The idea of European cooperation continues to enjoy strong support among the Dutch population, but scorn and derision, rightly or wrongly, about the EU with all its (small) rules, bureaucracy and waste of money are never far away. Admittedly, the loss of popularity is a reaction to years of meekly following, of almost unquestioning loyalty to, the European ideal, which derived its legitimacy from the horrors of World War II: 'Never again'. This naive meekness will never return, which begs the question of how Dutch politics should handle Europe. Europe is a dilemma for nearly all parties: Europe is not popular, but it is a fact. Parties that too eagerly proclaim the blessings of Europe are doomed to the margins. Parties that free-ride on anti-Europe sentiments will only too soon be accused of breaking their promises once they form part of the government. Parties that take the middle ground and advocate a different, a better, a greener, a more social, a more

---

1 *See* Bovens, M. & Wille, A. (2008). Politiek vertrouwen langs de meetlat [Measuring political trust]. *S&D, 10*. Bovens & Wille describe a downward, albeit fluctuating, trend. In 2009, *Binnenlands Bestuur* reported that only one in eight Dutch citizens take members of parliament on their word.

transparent or a more innovative Europe are primarily in the business of lip service politics because the Netherlands cannot do much to change things in the EU.[2] Europe seems a size too big for what parties can handle. This applies to the Netherlands, but similar trends can be seen in other countries as well.

16.1.1 Three Challenges

This chapter explores the possibilities political parties have to help them survive in the context of the EU. It is neither about the democratic deficit nor about the views of political parties, but rather[3] about one of the pillars of democracy: political parties themselves. Political parties in Europe are facing major challenges. The *first* challenge is that party politics within the EU has difficulty developing. Since its establishment, the EU has been largely an apolitical form of governance, and this has not changed much. The *second* challenge is that political responsibility within the Member States is disappearing because important decisions are taken in Brussels – often beyond the reach of political parties. The *third* challenge is that the EU is creating a new social contradiction. Supporters of an international, European orientation are diametrically opposed to those who put the preservation of national identity and national sovereignty first. This contradiction is not adequately expressed in the political debate, thus resulting in pressure being put on the representative function of parties: voters find it increasingly hard to identify with parties.

In this way, Europe undermines the functioning of political parties and thus democracy. A rethink is called for. Can political parties tell an honest story about Europe and involve voters and party members more in European deci-

2 An example is 'Strasbourg'. Nearly all Dutch political parties agree that Strasbourg should no longer be a meeting place of the European Parliament (EP), and they make this an important theme in elections. What they do not mention is that most countries do not agree, that this would require amending the Treaty and that, so far, there has never been a majority in the EP in favour of abolishing its Strasbourg seat. *See also* the chapter by Groenendijk on the impossibility of implementing the plans of Rutte I regarding European migration and asylum policy (the 'Leers agenda').

3 Such analysis has been carried out before. *See* van Rooyen, E. (2010). Wat willen de Nederlandse politieke partijen met Europa? [What do the Dutch political parties want with Europe?]. <www.montesquieu-instituut.nl>; de Jong, G. (2009). Nederlandse politieke partijen en Europa [Dutch political parties and Europe]. *Debat, 22*(2), 9-10; van Keulen, M. (2009, May). Europa? Kiest u maar! Nederlandse politieke partijen over de Europese parlementsverkiezingen [Europe? Take your pick! Dutch political parties on the European parliamentary elections]. *Internationale Spectator, 63*(5), 243-247. Less analysis is available on positions on Europe of political parties in the Dutch House of Representatives. Pijpers, A. (2007). Nationale roerselen in de Nederlandse Europapolitiek [National emotions in the Dutch policy on Europe]. In C.C. van Baalen (Ed.), *Jaarboek Parlementaire Geschiedenis 2007* (pp. 85-96). Amsterdam: Boom, analysed positions of parties in The Hague arena and found that European thinking has become more nationally oriented. The silent pro-European consensus has been broken.

sions? Are political parties capable of shouldering Europe, or should we found democracy on new and different pillars? To answer these questions, Section 2 of this chapter first discusses the political arena in Europe. National politics is addressed in Section 3. The conclusion is that new ways of working are needed. The final section (4), therefore, explores a number of possibilities to indeed incorporate the EU into the political debate and to engage voters (more) in Europe. However, there are no instant, ready-made solutions.

16.2 The European Political Arena

Party politics was taboo at the time the precursors of the EU were established. In the 1950s, the EU started out as an apolitical partnership between states crippled by World War II, the main driving force being peace between them. Peace should not be tarnished by party politics, self-interest or internal fighting. In the European philosophy of progress, party politics and politicians were harmful: politics had to be kept at bay as much as possible. Europe was best governed by independent experts. This has worked well for over 40 years. But in the meantime, the Union has become so much part of the lives of the over 500 million citizens and of the politics of the 27 Member States that the limits of apolitical governance are clearly being reached. Trust in Europe and in European institutions is falling. The Europe for Citizens[4] refuses to become a reality. Great ambitions in the field of economics, competitiveness, innovation, energy, the environment and foreign relations require a good relationship with the 500 million Europeans – starting with the political parties representing them. Here lies an important task for the European Parliament (EP).

Within the EP, parties are organized in the way voters are used to at national level: all major political movements are represented. There is a conservative group including Christian democrats, and there are groups of social democrats, liberals, greens and socialists, and extreme right-wing parties. The EP offers ample opportunity for party politics and principled positions. In practice, however, party-political forces do not have much influence. European policy does not swing to the left whenever left-wing parties win a landslide victory at European elections, or to the right when right-wingers win. Why is that? What buffers offset such fluctuations?

The first buffer is the apolitical organization of Europe. There is no government, there are no government parties and there is no majority in the EP that, in principle, supports the executive. The European Commission, and to an increasing extent the heads of states and government united in the European Council, take (a large part of) the decisions but are not bound to parliament by a political man-

4 European Commission programme to involve the citizens of the European Union more in the Union and in decision-making.

date. Of course, discussions take place between the European Commission and the EP and between the Council and the EP on important legislative proposals or on the political agenda for the next six months. But the half-yearly talks between the EP, the President of the European Commission and the new Council President seldom lead to agreements and hardly ever to fixed political agreements. The debate does not go beyond an exchange of views and does not produce results.[5]

The complex decision-making procedures form a second buffer. Decisions require approval by the Council of Ministers, the EP as well as the European Commission. Legislation requires a second reading in Parliament and must be adopted by a large majority. This means that decision-making takes a long time, but particularly that decisions must be based on broadly supported compromises. First within the EP, but then a compromise will also be required with the Council – i. e., with the ministers of the 27 Member States, who also have to reach agreement amongst themselves. Decision-making is democratic, but political movements are – as stated earlier – hard to identify in European policy. Instead of a democratic deficit, there is a *political* deficit. Brussels decision-making can be compared to an enormous cauldron in which all ingredients simmer into a thick soup. In the final result, the separate ingredients can no longer be distinguished.[6]

16.2.1 All Politics Is National

The third buffer is the mainly *national* orientation of most players in the European political game. This may come as a surprise, the general picture being that everyone in Brussels is constantly working to help move Europe forward, except for a few sharp-eyed parties standing up for national sovereignty. This picture is not entirely accurate. According to Thomas O'Neill, former Speaker of the US House of Representatives, 'all politics is local' in US politics. Representatives' voting behaviour is determined by concerns, views and opinions in their respective constituencies. A politician whose beliefs and actions reflect the views of his/her state or constituency stands a big chance of being re-elected. Vice versa, ideologists, those presenting future vistas and principled politicians do not last long in politics. A similar general rule applies in Brussels: all politics is national. Every political decision in Brussels is the sum of nationally oriented input from government leaders, ministers and members of the European Parliament (MEPs). As the EP gained more power, party politics moved to the background and input

5 Exceptions are the EP's refusal in 2004 to vote in favour of the appointment of an Italian candidate commissioner, and the resignation of the European Commission in 1999 after the majority of the EP had passed a vote of no confidence in a European commissioner.

6 Corbey, D. & Peereboom, D. (2003). De kookpot van Brussel: het Europese onbehagen en het politiek tekort [The Brussels cauldron: The European unease and the political deficit]. *Internationale Spectator, 57*(12), 606-611.

became more nationally focused. In fields where Parliament hardly had (and has) a say, such as foreign policy, party-political coordination within the European political group may be successful. National political parties do not much care how fellow party members vote in the EP when it comes to matters where the Parliament does not have much competence any way. In fields where the EP co-legislates, national preferences are a decisive factor in essential aspects. In such cases, European party discipline will be less relevant. In the EP, it is normal and accepted to deviate from the party line whenever an important 'national' interest so demands. These national interests may involve all sorts of things: car industries that do not want to produce more economical cars, tobacco producers who want subsidy, the right to use traps to kill muskrats undermining dykes, money (payments and subsidies), the right not to apply food safety principles to game products, the right to catch more fish than ecologically sound, free drinking water supply, use of pesticides, etc.

Of course, the political groups in the EP do aim for a certain unity. The dominant culture is even one of not mentioning the national input. Yet every national delegation will first try to make its own view the European group position. If it fails, the European group's vote in the competent committee of the Parliament will not be unanimous. The group's position will then be debated in order to find a compromise. Only after compromises have been reached with other groups and with the Council, will the entire group vote in favour at second reading in the plenary – sometimes reluctantly, though often also quite pleased with the final compromise.[7]

MEPs' loyalty is thus both party-politically and nationally driven, which may lead to clashes. There is a hierarchy, but appearance may differ from reality. However, political parties may also make different choices and focus more or less strongly on national loyalty. The fate of the *Oranjeberaad* is a good example. This concerned a proposal by Wim van der Camp in 2009 – the CDA leader who had just been appointed to the EP. He wanted regular consultations between all Dutch MEPs on issues important to the Netherlands. His proposal failed to appreciate the culture of keeping up party-political appearances. It, therefore, received negative reactions from PvdA and D66, who argued that national input would not be possible (the national interest does not exist!) or not be important. However, this rejection ignores the power of national motives in European politics, particularly also in the EP.

7 Some studies on roll-call votes in the EP conclude that parties in the EP increasingly vote unanimously (Hix, S., Noury, A. & Roland, G. (2006). Dimensions of politics in the European Parliament. *American Journal of Political Science, 50*(2), 494-520). However, this need not be in contradiction with the significance of national motives in the EP. At the time the roll-call vote is taken, part of the compromise has already been reached, and roll-call votes are often about the end result. Besides, it is often about amendments over which there is disagreement that MEPs do not call for a roll-call vote. This prevents the group from losing face, and finding a majority is sometimes easier without taking a roll-call vote.

16.2.2 *Left and Right*

So, is there no distinct left-right division in the European political arena? Yes, there is a contradiction between left and right, but this used to be secondary to the pro-European consensus. Since the 1980s and 1990s, Europe was, according to the Left, mainly (neo)liberal: borders disappeared, and protective rules were abolished for the sake of free market forces. Left parties found it difficult to become enthusiastic about this liberal programme. But they did manage to abandon their reservations, thanks to the strong tradition of international solidarity within social-democratic and socialist parties. Especially the new southern European Member States that had just shaken off their dictatorial chains needed solidarity and European structural funds. In addition, the 'Social Europe' programme was meant to counterbalance the one-sided liberal-economic orientation of European cooperation. Earlier, 'Social Europe' had led to equal rights for men and women, and promised to deliver much more in the fields of social security, protection of employment and work, health and safety at work, and the prevention of the dismantling of social achievements. As a result, the unions and left-wing parties slightly warmed towards Europe. Still, 'Social Europe' has only produced marginal improvements; most left-wing voters have never been able to really identify with Europe.

In the 1970s, those on the right of the political spectrum initially showed little enthusiasm for supranational reveries (rather no integration than a supranational state, as stated by the Dutch employers association). However, the large export-oriented companies were served well by the open markets. But after the millennium, criticism from the business sector increased. It turned out that with the liberalization that started in the 1990s and the abolition of national regulations and market-disrupting rules went a cartload of new European rules to regulate the market. The EU proved less liberal for business than hoped for, but enough to support Europe.

16.2.3 *Political Void*

Now and again, though, the whisper of party politics could be heard in the cacophony of national voices, but politicization has got stuck in the mire of complex decision-making, which, moreover, takes place at a great distance and is quite closed. For instance, there is no European news coverage. In each country, Europe is viewed through a national lens; there are no European media or European political debates or commentaries. In short, the national state is still the framework in which democracy takes shape.[8]

In fact, Europe is still being governed by independent experts. European commissioners as well as the European Commission as a whole are as politically colour-

8 Pijpers (2007).

less as ever. In the Brussels conference rooms, government leaders also guard against too much party politics. As soon as they walk into a European conference room, they shed their party-political colour, and views on Europe or positions in Brussels are affected surprisingly little by changes of government. An example is the Austrian government coalition of Christian democrats and the extreme right FPÖ after the millennium. Brussels viewed the advent of this new Austrian government with trepidation, only to find out after a couple of months that this extreme right-wing/conservative government coalition was presenting normal Austrian positions as usual. The sanctions that had initially been devised against this government with 'anti-European' views were quietly dropped.

Party politics usually has to take second place to national views. But the days that national interests had to give way to the European ideal are definitely over. The anonymity of Europe and of European governance created a void that was filled by national input. Europe did not prove a threat to the national identity. This also means that the nationalism, which the founding fathers had gone out of their way to banish from Europe, is returning in a mild form to the horror of Euro-idealists and federalists who consider every attempt to defend the national interest as a step back towards belligerent nationalism.

The conclusion is that party politics plays a subordinate role in European decision-making. In fact, the political colour of government leaders or the majority of the EP is hardly relevant. European politics can be discussed at length without referring to parties. Manuals on the EU do not, or only marginally, discuss political parties. On paper, there is nothing wrong with democracy in Europe: in practically all policy areas, the directly elected EP co-decides with democratically elected and controlled governments on policy and legislation. Parties and members of parliament do their best to spread their vision of Europe and to propagate European democracy, but often with disappointing results. Political leadership does not come into its own. Far from the national domain – the familiar habitat of political parties – European democracy functions without strong parties. This should give political parties food for thought. How do they fare in their familiar national environment?

16.3 Dutch Politics on Europe

In most Western European countries, political parties have always been organized along religious lines and the contradiction between capital and labour. They were joined by the Green movement in the 1980s. From the 1990s, Dutch political parties at local level got competition from the '*leefbaren*'. The rise of the so-called anti-EU populist parties such as Geert Wilder's Freedom Party (PVV) has drastically changed the political landscape. Similar movements are emerging in other countries as well. In Sweden, Denmark, Belgium, Poland, Hungary, Slovakia and France, for instance, right-wing, often anti-European people's parties enjoy great and/or growing support.

16.3.1 Important Politics Is European

In Europe, the general rule is 'all politics is national', but in the Netherlands, and in other European countries, the opposite applies: 'important politics is European'. Nearly everything of importance has already been decided at European level. There is little or no room for national policy or for an individual approach. Take, for instance, the economic crisis: the Netherlands is at the mercy of European compromises to save the euro and Greece, and has to more or less comply with the 3% rule. Common solutions are more or less supranational, but always still European. The same dependency can be seen in other fields. Energy policy has no more national force or meaning. A transition to sustainable energy will be possible only if similar obligations are imposed on other countries; if not, the Netherlands will price its energy-intensive industry out of the market. Environmental policy requires European coordination because otherwise the effect will be limited and/or Dutch businesses will suffer competitive disadvantages. The Netherlands is increasingly incapable of pursuing its own political course. European preconditions lead national politics into a trap from which there is no escape. Housing associations, hospitals, public transport: Europe is everywhere; the internal market, procurement rules or, for instance, the Services Directive limits autonomy everywhere. The EU is looking over the shoulders of the social partners to check that collective agreements do not contain provisions that adversely affect foreign suppliers. The EU has penetrated into the capillaries of decision-making.

The Dutch House of Representatives has to implement the political decisions that have been made elsewhere – in Brussels. But it is not clear who is in charge. As a result, Brussels is increasingly turning into a black hole that swallows political responsibility. Democratically speaking, this is not really satisfactory. It, moreover, makes political parties' behaviour ambivalent. The European election programme makes a great song and dance about ideals for Europe, for a different, greener, stronger, and more liberal Europe. But the Europe paragraph in the manifesto for the election of the Dutch House of Representatives is small and does not do justice to the EU's real influence.

16.3.2 Wings Versus Roots

The black hole has been described by other authors as well.[9] The EU undermines the functioning of democracy, and there is every reason to defend democracy. But Europe's influence on society and politics goes even further. In all European

9 *See* Cuperus, R. (2009). *De wereldburger bestaat niet, waarom de opstand der elites de samenleving ondermijnt* [The world citizen does not exist, why the revolt of elites undermines society]. Amsterdam: Uitgeverij Bert Bakker; Enzensberger, H.M. (2011). *Het zachte monster Brussel of Europa in de klem* [The soft monster Brussels or Europe in a fix]. Amsterdam: Cossee.

countries, common political trends can be seen. In the vast majority of countries, the political left proved unable to take advantage of the financial crisis; since the start of the credit crisis (2008), liberal and/or conservative parties have come into power almost everywhere. In addition, in many European countries, the contradiction between capital and labour seems to have been eclipsed by that between national and European orientation, i.e., between groups that can be referred to as 'winged' and 'rooted'.[10] This new contradiction is also being politically translated, albeit as yet inadequately. Rooted parties represent voters who feel connected with their national roots and are attached to their country or region with its own culture and history. Winged parties represent voters who are able and motivated to spread their wings, far beyond national borders, and who connect with like-minded people all over the world – also within Europe. Most political parties can be classified in one of these two categories, but a complicating factor is that this contradiction can be found across parties. This is certainly the case with the parties of the political centre, i.e., in the Netherlands, the labour party (PvdA), the christian democrats (CDA) as well as the conservatie liberal party (VVD). Such parties have trouble positioning themselves on the rooted-winged axis. They move to and fro, the result being that voters find it hard to identify with them. They no longer represent a distinct group of voters.

Is the situation that dramatic? Surely not. There are several explanations for the difficult position of the centre parties. And it is not entirely ruled out that their popularity may take a (temporary) turn for the better. Moreover, in each society there are those who feel attached, to a greater or lesser extent, to their country.[11] The difference between winged and rooted, between cosmopolites and provincials, and between world citizens and nationalists is one of all times – latent, and at times intense, when we look further back in history. But something is different now. The distinction between winged and rooted has increasingly become a *contradiction* and has acquired full political significance. To the winged, the EU is an ideal, but it became the subject of ridicule for the rooted – and later also a source of anger. Unintentionally and unwittingly, Europe has driven a wedge in society: by labelling borders as obstructions, by setting openness as the standard, by making international solidarity mandatory, by demanding discipline in regard to national budgets. Whether openness, solidarity and budgetary discipline are good or bad is not the issue here. Very good reasons can be given as to why budgetary discipline within the eurozone is essential and why solidarity is useful. The point is that, within the Member States, there is hardly any room for choices. Europe is on the side of the winged, making them the driving force of history,

10 Most probably, this contradiction also applies at socio-economic level: under that assumption, the rooted work in nationally based professions, such as health care, retail and police, while the winged are found in international business, corporate services etc.

11 *See, e.g.*, Finkelkraut, A. (1988). *De ondergang van het denken* [The demise of thinking]. Amsterdam: Uitgeverij Contact.

and this undeniably provokes a counter-reaction from the rooted. Pulling the handbrake would even be a mild reaction.

16.3.3 Mutual Recriminations

In the second half of the 20th century, the contradiction between capital and labour produced a clear compromise. 'Yes' to open markets and 'yes' to freedom for trade and capital, but in that case also 'yes' to good social conditions for those doing the work. The welfare state became a widely shared ideal in itself. So far, the contradiction between winged and rooted has not generated a clear compromise. There is no appealing idea that provides the centre position with an ideal. The contradiction is not even inciting any meaningful debate,[12] only bitterness. Winged parties deny national identity as well as the force of national motives and interests in Europe, or regard these as a remnant of a history rife with war. They imagine a post-national Europe where the boundary between home and abroad becomes blurred and less important. This is met with bitter reproaches from the rooted. Vice versa, the rooted deny the force of Europe, the prosperity, the results and the need to find itself a new ideal with which people can identify, thus drawing sarcastic reproaches from the winged camp.
It is no coincidence that the parties of the political centre suffer the most from this situation. Both the CDA and VVD, as well as the PvdA, are struggling with Europe, more than D66 and GroenLinks on the winged side, and the SP and PVV on the rooted side. The political centre has no basis in the form of a new social compromise. This makes the power position of the centre parties insecure, as a result of which they are barely capable of offering solutions to tomorrow's social problems.

16.4 Towards a New European Democracy?

The functioning of the political system and of party politics is relevant for the self-confidence of European societies. The triumphant atmosphere of the 1990s, when democracy and capitalism were declared the winners of history, has evaporated. Meanwhile, doubts are growing, politics is losing prestige and there are constant examples of politics not being equipped to solve long-term problems. Some are even looking both enviously and admiringly to autocratic systems or dictatorships which would have an easier time carrying out reforms than the tired European democracy. China, for instance, is very successful, judging by the huge increase in prosperity and the spectacular decrease in the number of people living below the poverty line. The Chinese government is capable of setting clear

12 After the Dutch 'no' to the European 'constitution', a broad social debate was announced, which, however, was called off later.

and ambitious targets and realizing them as well. Our democracy cuts a poor figure next to the Chinese decisiveness. This may not be a problem in day-to-day political concerns, but it is where democracy has to find answers to the major social challenges.

16.4.1 Balance

Europe's multiparty democracy as a model for a peaceful society is worthy of strong support. But on taking stock, we find that democracy in Europe is facing multiple challenges. First of all, political responsibility is disappearing. National politics can still pick up the crumbs that fall off the European negotiating table, but is losing influence and bears no responsibility for Europe. Parties in the national parliament have hardly anything to say about their government's input in Brussels. Parties that then enter the European arena to fight for their ideals for a better, more social, greener, or safer Europe will be disappointed. They soon discover that their input is drowned out by the apolitical organization of Europe. European democracy, moreover, takes a heavy toll, or, in exaggerated terms: the price of peace between states is conflict and mutual distrust within states. The new contradiction increasingly transcends the old party-political contradictions. As a result, representation no longer reflects reality; voters can only partly identify with a party and are only too ready to switch parties. This, in turn, makes it difficult for political parties to develop a consistent vision.
The fundamental problems of politics and democracy in Europe cannot be addressed by technical, instrumental solutions or constitutional amendments. It is up to political parties themselves to make clear choices. It helps if they explicitly position themselves on the rooted-winged axis so as to enhance their identity. But this does not solve everything, seeing that, no matter what, the Union will continue to be a decisive factor in many policy areas. Several attempts have already been made to weave European integration into the political discourse, but these have had little practical effect.[13] Where do we go from here? There are at least three options. The first is to leap forward and accept Europe as a political entity. The second, contrary, option is to accept the apolitical organization of Europe and give priority to seeking national consensus and compromise. The third option accepts the impotence of political parties and looks for new pillars on which to base democracy: the citizens and the Internet.

The First Option: Europe as a Political Unit
The first option starts with accepting Europe as a political entity and provides for the *politicization* of decision-making. This requires a full-fledged party system at European level. MEPs and national parliamentarians of the same party will then

13 *See, e.g.,* Wetenschappelijke Raad voor het Regeringsbeleid (Scientific Council for Government Policy). (2007). *Europa in Nederland* [Europe in the Netherlands]. The Hague: WRR.

convey the same message, but this message will not be developed at national level. Opinions will be in line with those of the European party. This means that at European level the course and content of party programmes will be more fiercely debated. In addition, leadership should be given a chance in Europe, for instance, by holding elections for leaders of political groups and for the president of the European Council.

At European level, strong anti-European parties will have to make themselves heard as well, which will improve representation as well as result in new compromises and new directions in the European debate. The EP will thus be given more weight and more recognizable faces. With strong political parties and strong leadership, Europe will no longer be the anonymous power which enters and dominates Dutch politics and society uninvited.

Realization of this option, therefore, requires radical politicization: the political deficit in Europe should be eliminated quickly. Less complex decision-making, less compromise and clearer political choices are called for. As a result, citizens will be able to identify with European politics.

However, the path of politicization is a difficult one. It will particularly be hard to stomach that opinions will have to be in line with that of the European party. It is therefore difficult to imagine that this will happen and that all political forces will seriously work together towards forming European parties. Politicization thus seems a dead end and will only be feasible if the Netherlands is prepared to become a province of Europe. However, it is difficult to imagine that Dutch politics would wish to be relegated to the provincial level and be put into the straitjacket of ideals thought up in Europe.

The Second Option: National Consensus

The second option is easier as it is more in line with current practice. It starts with the simple recognition that the governance structure is apolitical and that democracy within the EU is hardly based on party politics but rather on nationally biased input from 27 Member States. Such recognition creates a new need to seek *national* consensus, for Europe politics transcends party politics and is a joint responsibility. Agreements and joint positions have to be sought that are *widely* supported in the Dutch House of Representatives and in Dutch society. Elements may include abandoning the pursuit of an ever closer Union, better delimitation of EU competences, a clear exit strategy for the euro, re-nationalization of parts of the current European policy and recognition of the added value of the rest of that policy. Regular public debates between MEPs and members of the Dutch House of Representatives on topical European issues and proposed legislation may contribute to a broad consensus. They link European politics to national politics, and this will help people to identify with political positions. The Dutch House of Representatives will give the government clear mandates for European negotiations. Dutch politics will thus get a better grip on positions adopted by the government and party members in Brussels conference rooms. Responsibility will be spread, and Europe will thus lose its anonymity. Re-introduction of the dual mandate, whereby MEPs are also members of the national parliament, may be an important step in this context.

As a result, European groups in Brussels will be (even) less united, acting as groups of representatives who have something in common but do not chart a common course. This will result in European laws and directives becoming more 'national', i.e., leaving more room for Member States. In the Netherlands, political parties will position themselves more clearly on the winged-rooted axis, thus improving representation. This will also contribute to a more transparent political debate, which, in turn, may facilitate the search for a new, broadly supported consensus and stimulate better representation. For this option to be successful, both the winged and the rooted must form part of the national consensus. If not, support will remain weak.

The Third Option: More Direct Democracy

The third option starts with accepting the impotence of political parties and focuses on the *citizen*. It is quite logical to involve citizens more and more directly in decision-making. Consultation of citizens via the Internet and social media on important legislative proposals is easy to organize. Before legislative proposals are voted on in the EP, the outcome of the referendum should be known. Political parties (national and European) must then take account of the wishes of the citizens, take on board their voters' opinions and be held accountable.

This is not an easy option either. European politicians are still wary of involving citizens in decision-making. The French/Dutch 'no' to the constitution has taken a heavy toll. Of course, opponents of a legislative proposal or measure will put up a fiercer fight, but this will force supporters to at least properly and clearly mark their position and to campaign for their views. The need to reduce legislative proposals to one or a few clear choices will help decrease unnecessary complexity. The third option may reconcile citizens with the Union and inspire political parties to take different views that are based on the referenda. If the EU goes for the third option, 'Europe' will, by definition, no longer be an exclusive elite project. Citizens, proponents and opponents, will find each other via social media and thus create a new political reality which will be transnational as well. Joint – genuinely democratic – transnational decision-making may generate wise decisions, enabling reconciliation and enjoying broad support.

16.4.2 Conclusion

All three options are open, and a combination is conceivable as well. A comparison of options requires reference points. Which option offers democracy the best chances in terms of representation (do citizens identify with politics?), effectiveness (can European democracy solve problems?) and the capacity to bring about reconciliation (a compromise between winged and rooted)? Which is the most feasible option?

Compared with the politicization and national consensus options, the citizens option is the easiest. Online consultation on important decisions can, as it were, be launched by the EP tomorrow. This will, of course, require cooperation with national parliaments. Political parties can position themselves in the campaigns. The second option scores lower on the point of effectiveness since extensive negotiations and broadly supported compromises that are by no means always optimal will always be necessary. However, support may be broader. Under the second option, reconciliation between the winged and the rooted will also be easier. The first option enables European leadership – which, in turn, opens up opportunities in the field of democratic legitimacy.

The conclusion is that there is no ready-made solution: politics in Europe is not an easy matter. However, democracy cannot function without politics that people can identify with. Without a credible democracy, European institutions and the European states lose the trust to solve tomorrow's problems. One or several solutions, therefore, need to be given urgent consideration.

17 Getting a Grip on Europe: National Parliamentary Scrutiny of European Policy

Mendeltje van Keulen

17.1 Introduction

National parliaments were the winners of the most recent round of institutional reforms in Europe. This, let us face it, was not such a feat; after all, they had to come a long way in terms of getting a grip on ongoing European integration. Yes, since the 1980s, following successive Treaty amendments, the European Parliament (EP) – successor to the 'consultative Assembly' of the Treaty of Rome – gradually became a co-legislator to be reckoned with. The European momentum for national parliaments came more than a decade later – but it came fast. The first time parliaments were to play an independent role was in the framework of the European Convention, the joint meeting on the Treaty review to which they were invited in 2002-2003 (unprecedented). Initially, the ever-louder call for national parliamentary empowerment that could be heard there was greeted with considerable scepticism by the Brussels establishment, particularly within the EP, as described by, amongst others, De Bruijn.[1] Paradoxically, the subsequent ratification crisis (May/June 2005), when the end result of the European Convention, the Constitutional Treaty, foundered on the rocks of the French and Dutch referendums, proved most helpful to the supporters of national parliaments. It is precisely in this area that the Treaty of Lisbon (2010) took over a number of characteristic elements from the original Constitution. This mainly concerns Article 12 of the Treaty on European Union, which explicitly recognizes national parliaments as institutions essential to the good functioning of the Union. This provision is developed further in the two Protocols to the Treaty regarding direct provision of information on new European proposals (Protocol 1) and the testing of subsidiarity and proportionality principles (Protocol 2).
Two years later, it is time to take a closer look at the practice resulting from these institutional innovations. This chapter discusses this process in a nutshell, guided by recent practice in the Dutch House of Representatives. It is structured as follows: background and developments, provisional results and the way forward. Moreover, it is an open-ended story. The euro crisis poses considerable risks to

1 De Bruijn, T.J.A.M. (2011, December). De veranderende rol van nationale parlementen in de EU [The changing role of national parliaments in the EU]. *RegelMaat* 2011, 26 (6), p. 327-338

parliaments (the most prominent one being the dilution of the budget right) – but also offers opportunities. However, exploiting these requires not only changes in the institutional domain (procedures, rules, standards) but also at the same time a gradual 're-think' among national parliaments and Members of Parliament towards a new working culture and approach to European issues.

Let us first put things in perspective. The notion of 'national parliaments' suggests a uniformity that in reality barely exists. Judging by practically all conceivable criteria (constitutional powers, size, full-time or part-time membership and thus time and capacity of members and support), the French Assemblée Nationale is quite different from the UK House of Commons. The Finnish Eduskunta resembles the Polish Sejm as little as the Maltese 'Kam'ra dei Deputati' does the Dutch House of Representatives. This is partly why, internally, the national parliaments are neither coherent nor consistent. Relations between coalitions, opposition, big and small parties, spokespersons and back benchers differ – as do, consequently, parliamentary positioning processes. In majority cabinets 'the' European policy of the parliament will largely support that of the government. In political minority cabinets, as are common in Scandinavian countries and which the Netherlands experienced since September 2010 with the Rutte-1 Cabinet, relations between 'coalition' and 'opposition' are less stable, with all the resulting effects on the Europe policy.

Nevertheless, 'the' parliaments are presented as one group of actors in the European discourse. Being legislatures of the Member States, these institutions have one thing in common: both individually (subsidiarity test) and collectively (by forming coalitions for the 'yellow' and 'orange' card) they can make use of the European 'acquis' of parliamentary competences. This begs the question of how, in practice, more than two years after 'Lisbon', national parliaments make use of these opportunities to politicize European Union (EU) affairs at national level. However, to be able to answer this question, we should first look at how parliaments (can) give shape to their European possibilities internally and collectively.

17.2 What Happened?

Since the 1990s, the analytical framework for assessing parliamentary EU involvement at national level has developed along three lines: the information position of parliaments, the timeliness of the debate on European policy and the design of the parliamentary scrutiny of this policy.[2] This involves two levels: first, the European procedure *within* parliaments, such as the development of instruments like the scrutiny reserve, and the *joint* actions of parliaments, to exercise their new powers in mutual cooperation. The relatively small number of comparative studies[3] presents a mixed picture of 'careful first steps' on the way to positioning and cooperation, and, at the same time, great diversity in the design of these processes. Below are some of the findings, focusing in particular on the House of Representatives.

17.2.1 Dependent on Information …

For a long time, national parliaments had been lagging behind in designing European policy, especially due to the ongoing transfer of Member States' sovereignty in an increasing number of policy areas. An important reason for parliaments falling behind was the lack of 'own' European information, that is, independent (in terms of source and content) of that provided by the government. Information on proceedings within the EU Council of Ministers was generally either kept from parliaments, or (at best) forwarded through the ministerial Europe mailbox, annotated or not.

Since the creation of the Working Group for the Assessment of New Commission Proposals (*Beoordeling Nieuwe Commissievoorstellen* – BNC) in 1991, the Dutch parliament, compared with other parliaments, was kept amply informed of new European proposals, by means of information memoranda on new Commission proposals. However, usually these so-called BNC fiches, including a first assessment of the issue at stake, were merely taken note of by both the House of Representatives and the Senate; nor was there much parliamentary interest in European negotiations on ongoing issues in the Council.

17.2.2 Too Late …

The conclusion that, generally, the moment parliaments did actively engage in European issues, little to nothing was left to be changed in the content and form of the proposal in question, had led to increasing frustration with the lack of scrutiny of and grip on Brussels decision-making in the 1990s. On the few occasions that the Dutch parliament did debate European affairs, discussion focused

2 The broadest comparative study, though dated, is still Maurer, A. & Wessels, W. (Eds.). (2001). *National parliaments on their ways to Europe: Losers or latecomers?* Nomos: Baden Baden; more recent insights have been compiled by Raunio, T. (2009). *National parliaments and European integration: What we know and what we should know.* Oslo: ARENA Centre for European Studies; and Kaczynski, P. (2011, February). *Paper tigers or sleeping beauties? National parliaments in the post-Lisbon European political system.* CEPS Special Report. The half-yearly COSAC reports based on survey research among the parliaments also form a source of shared practices.

3 *See, e.g.,* Kaczynski (2011), Raunio (2009).

on the after-phase, that is, the *implementation* of the agreed European rules through national legislation. This sometimes involved quite some political fuss over the allegedly harmful effects of EU legislation that apparently had been adopted earlier and where room for national adaptations proved to have been considerably restricted by 'Brussels' decision-making. Thus, for many years, the House of Representatives' involvement in European affairs could be described as 'too little, too late' and, what is more, as extremely harmful to the public and political image of 'uncontrollable Europe'. Add to this the untransparent nature of European negotiations, where opportunities to exert influence are not automatically obvious, and the problem is clear.

17.2.3 … and Not That Effective

The unique structure of European decision-making works, almost by definition, in favour of the executive (governments and ministers in the [European] Council). Parliaments can test their ministers in advance (*ex ante*) on their intended European commitment, for which all parliaments have different methods. In addition, although feedback during negotiations is provided in different ways everywhere, in all Member States this involves navigating between 'tying the hands' of government (i.e., the need for flexibility during negotiations) and the need for Members of Parliaments to be adequately informed in order to be able to perform their scrutinizing duties. A rough distinction can be made between, on the one hand, 'document' systems, whereby the government informs the House of its position in writing or verbally, which is or is not debated beforehand but following which the minister concerned can freely participate in European decision-making, and, on the other hand, 'mandating' systems, whereby the government is given a mandate by national parliament to be adhered to during EU negotiations.

An example of a mandating system was the Dutch parliamentary debate on proposals in the field of cooperation in Justice and Home Affairs (JHA), in which the Senate in particular was especially interested because some of its members were specialists in this field. For years, these sensitive policy areas had been subject to a special right of assent which the Dutch parliament had negotiated at the time the Schengen Treaty entered into force.[4] An important consideration for instituting this right was the EP's lack of co-decision power. When the Treaty of Lisbon took effect in 2010, the right of assent was limited to those areas where the EP had no co-decision rights.[5] This is, incidentally, one of the characteristics of the traditional European approach within the Dutch parliament: the national parlia-

4 Traa-de Hoop Scheffer motion, Dutch House of Representatives, *Vergaderjaar* 1991-1992, *Kamerstuk* 22 140, No. 20.

5 Title V, Treaty on European Union.

ment would be able to withdraw from those fields where the EP acquired legislative competence.[6]

Regarding *ex ante* political scrutiny, in 1996, it was decided to start, by way of experiment, weekly Europe consultations in the House of Representatives, a regular meeting on Thursday afternoon to discuss the positions of the ministers in all sectoral Councils at EU level in the coming week. In the first few years, these consultations were frequently cancelled, and when they did take place turned out not to be the hoped-for venue for European debate. What did not help was the routinely late dispatch by the government of (annotated) agendas for the European consultations, on which the Members of Parliament almost completely depended, both for their preparation and because they did not have Brussels channels of their own.

The way these problems impacted on the Europe debate in the House of Representatives is described in great detail in the report '*Op tijd is te laat*' (On time is too late), a cry from the heart of VVD Member of Parliament Hans van Baalen (2002).[7] Following the analysis of this pressing problem, the referendum on the European Constitution lost by the government was the proverbial last straw. During 2005, the House of Representatives developed a whole new Europe procedure whereby, partly thanks to a new way of dealing with European proposals in combination with an investment in the internal capacity of EU support, the focus was fully on timely and visible European involvement.

17.3 The House of Representatives on its Way to Getting a Grip on Europe

More than five years later and following a positive evaluation (adopted by the House) of the new procedure, the Europe method can be labelled a success, which is praised in The Hague and Brussels.[8] This is due to a number of ele-

6 *See, e.g.*, the comment of the Procedure Committee in 1986 that deepening national scrutiny undermines the status of the European Parliament. "[...] The real reinforcement of parliamentary scrutiny will have to take place at Community level and thus through the European Parliament." Dutch House of Representatives, *Vergaderjaar* 1985-1986, *Kamerstuk* 19 336, No. 3. Report of the Procedure Committee, p. 2. Besselink, L. (Ed.). (2010). *The role of the States General in the EU*, annual report written for the FIDE congress in Madrid, October, describing practice in both House and Senate until 2006.

7 Dutch House of Representatives, *Vergaderjaar* 2002-2003, *Kamerstuk* 28 632, No. 1.

8 For instance, at the OPAL congress in the framework of the European research project 'National Parliaments after Lisbon', Maastricht, 23-24 February 2012, where the procedure of the House of Representatives was mentioned by several speakers.

ments of the scrutiny system, which below are translated into the three criteria for parliamentary EU involvement.[9]

17.3.1 *Independent Provision of Information …*

Now that parliaments, through the above mentioned right to information (with which they were already familiar because of Commission President Barroso's initiative of the same name), can find all new legislative EU proposals in their mailbox immediately after publication, they are no longer dependent on information from the government for launching a national political discussion. At the same time, developing a way to manage this steady flow of documents (access, selection, transmission with or without official advice) requires considerable investment in parliamentary knowledge, capacity and activity. Forces were joined to take up the challenge posed to parliaments by the second Protocol: shaping the possibility of subsidiarity coalitions ('yellow' and 'orange' card), which is discussed in more detail below.

Over the years, the organization of the House of Representatives has heavily invested in the independent provision of information. To ensure that EU proposals coming straight from Brussels are given the political treatment they deserve on grounds of form and content, a document management system has been designed whereby eight EU advisers who work for the specialized committees in the House (experts with extensive knowledge and experience regarding the EU dimension of the policy areas of these committees) have a crucial signalling and advisory function. With such support of its own, the House is no longer dependent on the government for information on what goes on before and during negotiations in Brussels.

The pivotal role of the specialized committees in this system follows from a deliberate consideration to 'decentralize' European issues. Contrary to the Finnish system of a 'Grand Committee' that deals with all EU affairs for the entire parliament, all Dutch MPs are responsible for EU policy in their own field of expertise and, consequently, for monitoring what happens at respective Council meetings in Brussels. The advantage of this approach is that European affairs end up where they belong, i.e., as an aspect or dimension of the national policy or policymaking on specific issues. A disadvantage is the risk of low, or specialist visibility of the debates, which take place between specialized spokespersons, outside the plenary, and thus often out of sight of press and public.

9 *Kamerstuk* 32 726, No. 1: *Bovenop Europa, evaluatie van de versterkte EU-ondersteuning in de Tweede Kamer 2007-2011* [On top of Europe, evaluation of enhanced EU support in the House of Representatives 2007-2011]. *See also,* Kester, J. & van Keulen, M. (2011, 26(6), 303-314). De Tweede Kamermethode, versterkte parlementaire betrokkenheid bij Europese besluitvorming [The procedure of the House of Representatives, strengthened parliamentary involvement in European decision-making]. *RegelMaat, 6.*

If the House committees incorporate Europe, what is there left for the European affairs spokespersons of the parties? The EU Affairs Committee (EAC) focuses on preparing the European Council, the coordinating General Affairs Council and horizontal or institutional European affairs, such as the accession of new Member States, Treaty amendments and the multiannual budget. In addition, these MPs have been explicitly charged with coordinating the decentralized European procedure, so that they can act as European 'engine' within the party and alert their colleagues whenever influence is to be exerted. Examples of issues which are dealt with by the EAC but which for their development or implementation involve several House committees and thus require intra-parliamentary coordination are the discussions on the European Semester in the framework of the Annual Growth Survey and the EU's Multiannual Financial Framework.

17.3.2 *… Early On in the Process …*

Within the House of Representatives, the Europe spokespersons also coordinate the annual process of selecting European priorities. This selection procedure guarantees timely action by the House regarding European issues. On the basis of the Commission work programme, published by this institution at the end of each calendar year, the specialized committees, advised by EU staff, make a selection of the proposals which, according to the majority, hold special political significance. The list resulting from these consultations will be adopted in plenary as 'the' EU priority list of the House, and also brought to Brussels' attention in the form of an English brochure. Departments and European partners are thus informed at an early stage of the proposals that have special political relevance to the House.[10] During the year, this list may be supplemented with recently published proposals that the Commission did not anticipate but which in view of, for instance, their content or topicality are considered of special importance, as happened with the Schengen border management proposals in 2011. In the case of special procedures (subsidiarity test and/or scrutiny reserve, described below) the House receives a first government assessment in the form of a BNC-fiche within half (i.e., three weeks) of the normal time limit for transmission, so that it can be dealt with soon and swiftly. From being the starting point, the fiche has thus become a follow-up step in the scrutiny procedure for EU dossiers, which starts as soon as the EU proposal in question is published.

In a number of cases the House will already act before the European Commission publishes new legislative proposals. The most eye-catching example is the use made of the opportunity offered by the European Commission to directly

10 The list for 2012 consisted of 60 priorities selected from the work programme, of which 12 proposals were considered eligible for a scrutiny reserve, and 7 of the proposed plans were selected for a subsidiarity test. In 2012, four scrutiny reserves and five subsidiarity tests were executed upon new EU proposals.

respond to Green and White Papers, which present the outlines of new proposed policies. For 30 days before it is sent to Brussels, the government's reaction to these documents is open to inspection at the House. Spokespersons may also decide to inform Brussels of their own views in case of a politically relevant subject. For instance, the Green Paper on public procurement (2011), where the Commission sketches a new approachto this regulation-burdened area which so often meets with domestic resistance, was discussed in special consultations between the spokespersons and the Minister of Economic Affairs, Agriculture and Innovation, and in February 2012, the immigration and asylum spokespersons convened a round table conference on the Green Paper on family reunification. In March 2012, the Committee on Social Affairs and Employment appointed from among its members a 'rapporteur' for the White Paper on Pensions, with a view to presenting a position carried by the House.

17.3.3 … and Binding?

In 2009, the extent to which the parliamentary mandate to the government in European negotiations is binding was central to designing the 'scrutiny reserve' procedure. This instrument, available to the House since the entry into force of the Lisbon Treaty, is actually an enhanced procedure for scrutinizing European plans of special importance to the House: through consultations with the government immediately after a Commission proposal has been published (before the negotiations), the House makes firm agreements on positions of, and provision of information by, the government during the EU negotiations. This means that the scrutiny reserve does not (contrary to what is sometimes assumed and unlike scrutiny practice in other Member States) act as a 'brake' on the European negotiations (which, after all, will hardly have started at this point). It is primarily an incentive for early debate and a guarantee that information is exchanged during the negotiation process. In 2011, for instance, new European proposals to review the common fisheries policy and for legislation on energy saving, subject to a scrutiny reserve, were discussed early in the policymaking process with the government.

However, in other areas there have been setbacks. Since the Lisbon Treaty, the special right of assent which the House had acquired for the entire JHA area when the Schengen cooperation took effect, only applies to new proposals under the special pillar of family and criminal law. As a result, the quality of the annotated agendas which the government sends to the House before JHA Council meetings has seriously deteriorated.[11] One could almost use the term 'dialectics of progress' in reference to the parliamentary commitment to the JHA policy

11 For an overview of the discussion, *see, e.g.*, van Keulen, M. & Mittendorff, F. (2011). Justice and Home Affairs 'At Home': Shaping the AFSJ at the national level. In S. Wolff, F.A.N.J. Goudappel & J.W. De Zwaan (Eds.), *Freedom, security and justice after Lisbon and Stockholm*. The Hague: Asser.

area – which used to be quite a priority – now that the House has made major progress in other areas. In general, there is definitely a shift from the 'ex post' review of European legislation and regulations (according to the adage 'the government governs, the House scrutinizes', as explicitly confirmed more than 15 years ago in the House debate on the parliament and Europe which was primarily about the fear of 'Danish situations'),[12] towards more timely and especially *'ex ante'* involvement in the European decision-making process, or, in the words of Voermans, from an 'intergovernmental' to a 'parliamentary' method, whereby in the latter model, the House's information position is one of independence and equal to that of the government when it comes to adopting national positions.[13]
The above mentioned principle so typical of the Dutch parliamentary scrutiny of EU affairs that in terms of scrutinizing EU policy the national parliament fills the gap left by the EP, and/or can withdraw when competences are conferred on the EP, now seems obsolete as well. Actions by the national parliament to enhance European legitimacy are independent of the EP's actions – or to put it even more strongly: the paths of both legislatures may diverge widely. There are, therefore, still many opportunities to strengthen relations with 'that other' – European – Parliament in Strasbourg. This also seems possible without immediately reaching for the sledgehammer of the 'dual mandate' – which, on paper, is the ultimate solution for optimal mutual recognition and commitment, but, in practice,is a path strewn with obstacles between dreams and reality and was thus abolished for good reason. Also in the current constellation, both sides (national MEPs and MPs) are often insufficiently aware of the opportunities for exchanging information and arguments and of the possibilities that arise when the same European issues are dealt with in the same way. Joint meetings and video conferences offer obvious – still insufficiently exploited – possibilities.

17.4 The Way Forward

The use of the new powers and the capacity to take a European stand when it can still make a difference in the Brussels game begs the question of where and how (action, timeliness) parliaments will adopt individual or joint positions in the European playing field. This concerns a number of issues. Where do opportunities lie for more political involvement at national level, and where for joint

12 Dutch House of Representatives, *Vergaderjaar* 1996-1997, *Kamerstuk* 25 181, No. 2, Parliament and European Union, p. 4, and Dutch House of Representatives, *Vergaderjaar* 1986-1987, *Kamerstuk* 19 336 No. 23. Letter from members Tazelaar and Van Iersel.

13 Voermans, W.J.M. (2007). Invloed van nationale parlementen op Europese wetgeving: hoe doen de buren dat? [Influence of national parliaments on European legislation: How do the neighbours go about this?]. *RegelMaat, 4*, 150-162.

actions of parliaments? How can this be shaped in practice (e.g., who will volunteer as a pioneer or front-runner, and where is the resistance?), and which of the new instruments will be effective in practice? Is there a special role for the Dutch parliament in all this? These questions should be considered more closely and are currently the subject of large-scale comparative researches, e.g., conducted in the framework of the Observatory of Parliaments.[14] Here, there is only room for a few observations.

17.4.1 Towards Parliamentary 'Subsidiarity Coalitions'?

A particular new challenge for parliaments since 'Lisbon' is that they can operate together in forming European negotiating positions regarding new EU proposals. To start with, there is the risk often raised by sceptics in relation to the institutional reforms of Lisbon, namely, that the new 'yellow' and 'orange' card procedures would only lead to unwanted delay or even paralyse European decision-making. The gist of the yellow card is that if, in response to a new European proposal, one third of the national parliaments lodge a subsidiarity objection with the European Commission within eight weeks, the proposal might be reconsidered. If half of the parliaments lodge an objection, the matter will be forwarded to the legislative institutions, i.e., the Council of Ministers and the EP. If, there too, a majority is against the proposal, the Commission may withdraw it.

The scepticism about the obstacles parliaments encounter on the road to swift joint action in Brussels seems realistic. Within eight weeks, parliaments are expected to write a letter containing an analysis even before the first negotiations in the Council working groups about the proposal in question have well and truly started. The supposition that this seemed impossible in parliamentary practice was proved wrong in April 2012 by the first 'yellow' card for a new Commission proposal ('Monti II') for a regulation aimed at clarifying the relation between employees' right to take collective action ('strike') and the freedom of establishment and free provision of services by codifying the case law of the European Court of Justice in this social area.[15] On the day of the deadline, the House of Representatives gave its support to the subsidiarity objection by means of a motion adopted in plenary, and thus a total of 12 '*avis motivés*' could be submitted to the Commission within the eight-week time limit. Since, in this context, a number of unicameral parliaments account for 2 votes, the result was a total of 19 votes, enough for the first yellow card.

Legally, when a 'yellow card' is issued by a sufficient majority of national parliaments, the European Commission has three possible options: maintain, amend or

14 Observatory of Parliaments after the Lisbon Treaty, coordinated by Sciences Po, Paris. Maastricht University takes part on behalf of the Netherlands. The research focuses on, amongst other things, practices in the House of Representatives. *See* <www.opal-europe.org>.

15 COM (2012) 130, the so-called Monti II proposal.

withdraw the contested proposal. On 12 September 2012, the College of Commissioners decided to withdraw the Monti II proposal, highlighting in its side letter, however, political considerations as an explanation for this move, rather than the subsidiarity concerns which had been voiced by national parliaments. Although this motivation could easily be regarded as an attempt to save face, it is indeed in the political signal that national parliaments can give to the EU's legislative branch where the added value of the new procedure lies.

Moreover, when we leave aside this concrete proposal and focus on the actual process of the cards, the parliamentary pro-activity can also be interpreted differently. Indeed, the road to Europe's politicization, at domestic level and when translated as a signal to Brussels, does not primarily lie in waving yellow or orange cards. Rather, it can be found in the possibilities offered by the new procedures within the national parliaments and, at European level, in the Commission, Council and EP, to launch an early discussion on the merits of European proposals. This is exactly where the new 'cards' procedure offers opportunities. Where a national government shares parliamentary objections, it will probably put them forward in the negotiations with great verve, knowing it is backed by its own parliament. If the government's view is different from parliament's as regards the question of whether a proposal can pass the subsidiarity test, this may increase attention for the domestic debate on the proposal concerned, which, in turn, may affect the relevant negotiations at EU level.

17.4.2 *Types of Joint Action*

The fact that all parliaments have been presented with the new possibilities based on the Treaty offers fresh opportunities for interparliamentary cooperation. The challenge for, in particular, representatives of relatively active parliaments is to stimulate others to discuss, internally and *in time* (i.e., within the eight-week time limit), proposals over which political debate is to be expected and to share the outcome both with their own government and at European level.

For the daily exchange of information, parliaments rely on two important channels. First is the contacts between national parties and European political groups, where heterogeneity is the rule. At the moment, most political groups in the House of Representatives have liaison officers working for them, staff responsible for (facilitating and stimulating) exchange of information about issues between Strasbourg, Brussels and The Hague. At institutional level, practically all parliaments have posted parliamentary representatives in Brussels. Currently, 37 Houses from 25 national parliaments are represented in the building adjacent to the EP. One of the 'junctions' of this new network is the weekly meeting of the group in Brussels. A fixed item on the agenda of this so-called Monday Morning Meeting – which, with some imagination, could be typified as a 'parliamentary COREPER' *in statu nascendi* – is the exchange and comparison of individual subsidiarity procedures. In addition, there is a digital forum, the interparliamentary information site IPEX,[16] which is fed by parliaments with documents on discussions of European issues. Parliaments moreover meet on a regular basis. For Europe spokespersons, there is the biannual conference in the country holding the Presidency (COSAC). Although this meeting provides opportunities for discussion and exchange of information, e.g., about the way parliaments obtain independent European information,[17] a complicating factor is the great diversity of this group, precisely because all parliaments have organized their European affairs according to national customs and procedures. And although in the past the permanent secretariat of the club in Brussels made valiant attempts to bring some consistency to the implementation of subsidiarity tests on a number of EU proposals pre-selected by the parliaments, this procedure died a silent death in 2010.

So, in practice, COSAC mainly serves as an information market and marketplace for benchmarks, such as regarding the internal EU organization or the application of subsidiarity tests. For instance, the design of the Dutch scrutiny reserve (an information procedure, but one that does not 'tie our hands' in the Council) was based on a study of how other Member States had gone about this in practice.

All parliamentary EU instruments discussed in this chapter are probably most effective when used appropriately and in moderation, the challenge obviously being to realize this 'moderation' at political level. Instead of splitting European hairs, parliaments should be able (or, be enabled) to, to a certain extent, selectively commit themselves to issues where an urgent national interest is at stake or where at European level political rifts are to be expected. For the exchange of information on such issues, interparliamentary conferences such as COSAC, but also the half-yearly meetings the EP organizes for and on behalf of the parliamentary subcommittees, are a potential information market. The House of Representatives uses these occasions to generate attention and discussion around the abovementioned priority selection from the annual Commission work programme.

17.4.3 *Euro Crisis*

A current challenge in properly exploiting the acquired parliamentary competences is the financial and economic crisis that has held the Union in its grip since 2010. Several commentators have pointed out that the parliament threatens to fall victim to European leaders' frantic search for make shift solutions to the

16 *See* <www.ipex.eu>.

17 In April 2012, the Danish presidency of COSAC initiated a report containing an overview provided by the parliaments regarding what sort of and how EU information is provided by the government and independently. COSAC. (2012). *17th biannual report on EU practices and procedures*. Brussels: COSAC. *See* <www.cosac.eu/eu-information>.

euro crisis and declining market confidence, because these solutions cannot be adequately be discussed in parliament before actions are taken. Some believe this puts the budget right at stake. In this context it should be mentioned, however, that from the very start the House of Representatives was careful to publicly exchange views on the euro crisis and on the measures taken in the form of emergency packages and support structures. For instance, together with the Bundestag, the House of Representatives is the only parliament where, so far, the national positions for all European summits held during the euro crisis have been discussed with the responsible Minister and/or the Prime Minister in public beforehand. The need for rapid market interventions has led to new procedures for ensuring quick and guaranteed provision of information in the event of market interventions whereby confidentiality is guaranteed – traditionally a dilemma for parliamentary involvement.[18]

This has moreover raised the fundamental question to what extent individual parliaments are still or should still be scrutinizing these European budget decisions now that the solution to the euro crisis has acquired such a strong European dimension.[19] Parliaments are explicitly mentioned in the Council conclusions of the European summit of 21 July, the Treaty on budgetary discipline (fiscal compact) includes a special article (13) on parliamentary involvement, and the fourth chapter of the plans of Council President Van Rompuy is dedicated to the democratic legitimacy of the proposed banking union and economic and budgetary cooperation between the Member States. With all the remaining questions as to how this should take shape, it is at least clear that in the coming years parliaments will play an important role in the discussion on the future of the reinforced Economic and Monetary Union.

17.4.4 *Towards Visible Scrutiny*

Visibility then: a *sine qua non* for democratic decision-making. Some say it is not so much parliaments alone that are to be blamed for the weak scrutiny of European policy; rather, it is due to a system error in the relation between parliaments, governments, civil society and the media – for most voters the channel that keeps them informed of discussions on European policy.[20] In the House of Representatives, the great majority of European issues are discussed mainly in committee rooms. This is a result of the decentralized procedure, of the fact that the EU dimension is the responsibility of specialized spokespersons whose field it concerns, and of the fact that only a small part of the deliberations are followed

18 Proposal for the elaboration of scrutiny procedures regarding EFSF/ESM decisions, government letter, Dutch House of Representatives, 21501 No. 877, *Vergaderjaar* 2011-2012.

19 *See, e.g.*, Diamant, M. & Van Emmerik, M. (2011). Parlementair budgetrecht onder vuur? [Parliamentary budget right under fire?]. *Nederlands Juristenblad, 86*(29), 1943-1950.

20 Raunio (2009).

up in plenary. As a result, the discussion of 'day-to-day' European issues often drops off the radar ('the House does nothing with Europe') or is hidden in the abovementioned European debates in times of crisis and in political squabbling in the plenary room ('The House debates on Europe are too heated'),whereas when 'technical' – though no less important – proposals such as on EU border management, the European globalization fund or the cohesion policy are being discussed, the press gallery (and thus the newspapers) stays empty.

In addition, Members of Parliament often receive few external incentives (for instance, through the media or from civil society as a bridge to the electorate) which, as is the case with national issues, can trigger MPs into paying attention to the European aspects of the issues they deal with. In short, they are generally not judged by, or re-elected because of, their European commitment. Based on this conclusion, the *Wetenschappelijke Raad voor het Regeringsbeleid* (Scientific Council for Government Policy), which analyzed the Dutch situation after the referendum on the rejected European Constitutional Treaty, believed that the solution to the legitimacy crisis should not be expected only or primarily from changes that are confined to political or administrative circles.[21] This means that if parliamentary involvement in European policy is to lead to what it was supposed to lead to (more legitimacy of the European process), this process should at least be known to – and subsequently also exploited by – the media, civil society organizations and the business sector when it comes to promoting their own European interests (news gathering, transmitting information, lobbying). Initiatives to focus the attention of these organizations on the annual European prioritization cycle should therefore be seen in this light. However, this and other aspects of the European parliamentary procedure require professional, official support.[22]

Besides new initiatives, existing instruments also require constant monitoring. This still concerns the agreed timing of provision of information to the parliament via the 'fiche'. Informing the House in this way of government assessments and negotiating positions may (now that all EU proposals are sent straight to parliaments) no longer be the first but is still a crucial step in the discussion of new Commission proposals between the government and the House. But also under the new agreements this matter will demand ongoing, constant attention. For

21 Scientific Council for Government Policy. (2007). *Europe in the Netherlands.* Amsterdam: Amsterdam University Press.

22 The EU staff of the Dutch House of Representatives consists of eight members advising on content, and a clerk, also coordinator, as well as the Permanent Representative in Brussels for both House and Senate. The staff of the Scrutiny Committee, House of Commons, has 20 staff members, which makes it the committee with the highest number of staff in the House of Commons. (2009). *The European scrutiny system in the House of Commons.* London: House of Commons, p. 5-6.

instance, in 2011 the parliament still received nearly half of the fiches several weeks too late.[23]

17.4.5 *Implementation and Evaluation*

And then there is the end game in the European policy process: transposition and evaluation. After all, the sting is often in the tail of the process, where spokespersons may consider that agreed European decisions still contain undesirable content. Paradoxically, with all this attention for the 'pre-decision-making phases', it is now almost a task in itself to keep Members of Parliament committed to the transposition of European regulations (which used to be the only phase that would stir their interest). The quarterly quantitative overviews on EU implementation in Dutch legislation provided by the government offer in themselves little insight and urgently need further clarification or context. The big question in this regard is whether the current investments in the preliminary phase will, in due course, indeed translate into less complaining and delay in the transposition of European legislation. The fact that the European policy process takes a relatively long time, from 'shaping' to 'taking' (within which not seldom changes in government/parliament occur), continues to be a special challenge in this context.

17.5 Conclusion

The above description shows the Dutch House of Representatives, basing itself on the new Treaty, has taken the much-needed steps towards more, and more timely, involvement in European policy and decision-making – from Europe as a 'whim' of a single spokesperson and from the few debates in the after-phase (transposing or transferring EU regulations ['taking']) to developing the grip that parliaments as a whole should have on European policymaking (influencing or'*shaping*' policy); from merely mentioning or generally discussing the ministerial Council meetings beforehand (including in the House of Representatives), or even only after the meeting in question (e.g., the Polish Sejm), to debates immediately after new legislative proposals are published so as to be able to monitor the negotiations. How far are we in reaching the original aim of the changes discussed in this chapter, that is, increased parliamentary scrutiny of and involve-

23 *See* the study of the *Rekenkamer* (Netherlands Court of Audit) of 2004. *Kamerstuk* 29751, No. 2, and the discussion in the House of Representatives, *Vergaderjaar* 2008-2009, *Kamerstuk* 22 112, No. 884. In the recent discussion of the review of the common fisheries policy – which the spokespersons considered a priority proposal – the fiche was delayed by the government for weeks, pleading the recess of the House of Representatives.

ment in European decision-making for the sake of the legitimacy of European policy?

On the whole, the experience of national parliaments as 'new kids on the European block' seems to be one of selectively exploiting early innovations. The institutional achievements mentioned above came about at a critical time, affecting national parliaments in practically all Member States. The rise of Eurosceptic parties is but one small crack in the legitimaticy of European actions. Adequately strengthening 'input legitimacy' (democratic bodies exercising *ex ante* scrutiny of European decision-making) may be a solution in this respect, in the form of elected Members of Parliament acting as 'liaison officers' between the government operating at EU level and the citizen 'at home', who feels powerless and put at a distance. In various parliaments (Germany, the Netherlands), this problem analysis, as most acutely formulated by the Bundesverfassungsgericht in 2010, has resulted in reinforced and more timely examination of European proposals, whether or not accompanied by new instruments such as the European 'scrutiny reserve' of the House of Representatives. Growing insight into the effect of new initiatives regarding information exchange and into the possibilities of more regular information sharing between parliaments in the form of national practices and best practices will show whether parliaments can realize that which their new European commitment was supposed to achieve: to act as intermediary between the European and national levels of governance.

Annex: Main Dutch Political Parties

VVD. The People's Party for Freedom and Democracy is a conservative-liberal party. It is a member of the European Parliament's Alliance of Liberals and Democrats for Europe (ALDE). Founded in 1948, the VVD has frequently been in government as a member of a coalition. Since 2010, for the first time in its history, the party has provided the Prime Minister, Mark Rutte, who, from 2010 to 2012, led a minority government (together with the Christian Democrats (CDA) and supported by the Party for Freedom (PVV)) and, since November 2012, a majority government of the VVD and the Social Democrats (PvdA). Though traditionally a strong supporter of European integration, in particular in the area of market integration and free trade, and opposed to political integration, the VVD has recently become more Euro-critical, especially where it concerns the deepening of economic integration and further enlargement of the EU. This can partly be explained as a response to the rise of the Eurosceptic Party for Freedom (PVV).

PvdA. The Labour Party is a social democratic party. It is a member of the European Parliament's Party of European Socialists (PES). The PvdA has a strong foothold in the welfare system. Founded in 1946, it has often been in government, including providing the Prime Minister. Since November 2012, the PvdA has been in a coalition with the VVD, in the second Rutte cabinet. Though sceptical about European integration in the fifties, the PvdA has, over the last decades, always been in favour of further European integration. Also during the years before 2012, when the party was in opposition, it supported the then governments (e.g. the first Rutte cabinet) in the efforts to strengthen the euro zone and deepen, in particular, economic integration. On the other hand, the PvdA is in favour of the subsidiarity principle, especially where it concerns European intervention in the welfare state, the national health system, public housing and public services in general.

CDA. The Christian Democratic Appeal is inspired by Christian values. It is a member of the European Parliament's European People's Party (EPP). It was founded in 1977 as a result of the merger of the Catholic People's Party (KVP), the Anti-Revolutionary Party (ARP) and the Christian Historical Union (CHU). The CDA (and its predecessors) have been part of most post-Second World War

Dutch governments, often providing the Prime Minister. Most recently, its then political leader, Jan-Peter Balkenende, was Prime Minister from 2002 to 2010. Presently, the party – which lost the last two elections – is in opposition. The CDA and its predecessors have always been strong supporters of the European integration process. Though in favour of the subsidiarity principle, the CDA supports the deepening of integration, in both the economic and political domain.

PVV. The Party for Freedom is a Eurosceptic populist party. In the European Parliament, the PVV operates as an independent group. The party is led by Geert Wilders, who left the VVD in 2004, in response to the positive stance of that party on Turkey's membership of the EU. In 2005, Wilders founded his own party, the PVV, which was very successful at the elections of 2010 (going from 9 to 24 seats in Parliament). As a result of these elections, a minority government of VVD and CDA was formed, led by Mark Rutte. That government was officially supported by the PVV. Highly critical of the budgetary policies of the Rutte cabinet and in particular of its support of measures to save the euro, Wilders decided to withdraw his support for the minority government in April 2012. During the subsequent election campaign, the PVV's main political issue was withdrawal of the Netherlands from the EU. However, the party lost quite substantially at these elections and has been in opposition since. The PVV is an anti-European party, very much opposed to further enlargement of the EU and opening up the EU borders for free movement of people, and in favour of the Dutch withdrawing from the EU.

SP. The Socialist Party is a left-wing socialist party. It is a member of the European Parliament's European United Left/Nordic Green Left (GUE/NGL) group, and has an originally Maoist background. However, since it entered Parliament in 1994, the party has become more moderate and has moved from a Maoist-inspired political programme to a socialist approach to society, focusing specifically on the position of the weak and the poor. The party is highly critical of European integration and was one of the main opponents of the European Constitution. The SP is particularly against the foundation of what is called a European super-state and the EU's interference in the Dutch welfare system. Yet, with the prospect of an election victory in 2012 and hoping to be seen as a party willing to take responsibilities, the SP had toned-down its anti-EU campaign.

Smaller parties: **D66/GroenLinks/ChristenUnie.** D66 was founded in 1966 as a protest party. It is now a left-wing liberal party and has been in government several times. The party is a member of the European Parliament's Alliance of Liberals and Democrats for Europe (ALDE) and is strongly in favour of European integration, especially of a federal Europe and a strong European Parliament. GreenLeft was founded in 1989 as the result of the merger of a number of left-wing parties. Originally a protest party mainly focusing on environmental issues, it has become more of a left-wing liberal, libertarian party. GreenLeft is strongly pro-European and a member of the European Greens in the European Parliament. The ChristianUnion was founded in 2000 following the merger of two more orthodox Christian parties. Though critical of further European integration, it has recently supported the Rutte cabinets in the matter of deepening economic integration in the EU. The ChristianUnion is a member of the European Conservatives and Reformists in the European Parliament.

Authors

Richard Blankenstein is a graduate student in public administration at the Erasmus University, under the supervision of Frans van Nispen. He wrote his master's thesis on the Dutch position and strategy in the multiannual financial framework of the European Union. As part of his MA thesis he did an internship at the Ministry of Finance. Furthermore, he is a member of the city council of Breda for the Dutch social democratic party (PvdA).

Monica den Boer holds a position at the Police Academy of The Netherlands and is a Member of the Committee on European Integration of the Advisory Council on International Affairs. After obtaining a PhD in 1990 from the European University Institute she worked at Edinburgh University, the Netherlands Study Centre for Crime and Law Enforcement, the European Institute of Public Administration, Tilburg University, and the European Institute of Law Enforcement Co-operation. She was professor of Comparative Public Administration at the VU University Amsterdam, served as a Member of the Iraq Investigation Committee, and participated in the Defense Future Survey Group. She has published widely on European internal security co-operation and engages in teaching, coaching as well as supervision.

Dorette Corbey was Member of European Parliament for the labour party (PvdA) from 1999 to 2009. She is now president of the Dutch Emissions Authority, chair of the Committee for Biomass Sustainability Issues, and director of the Advisory Council for Science and Technology Policy. Dorette Corbey studied social geography and worked at Clingendael Institute and at the Dutch Trade Union Confederation (FNV). She published in *International Organization*, *Internationale Spectator*, and in other scientific journals and periodicals.

Paul Dekker studied political science in Nijmegen and Berlin. He is Professor of Civil Society at Tilburg University, and head of the Participation and Government research unit of the Netherlands Institute for Social Research (SCP). His research focuses on civil society broadly understood: social and political involvement and participation, the non-profit sector, public opinion, political attitudes and values.

Margriet Drent is a Senior Research Fellow at the Research Department of the Netherlands Institute of International Relations 'Clingendael' and Assistant Professor at the International Relations Department of the University of Groningen. She specialises in international security issues with particular attention for the EU as a security actor. She is also a member of the Peace and Security Committee of the Advisory Council on International Affairs (AIV). Until 2004, Margriet Drent was the Executive Director of the Groningen-based Centre for European Security Studies.

Willem van Eekelen studied law at Utrecht University and political science at Princeton University. He was a member of the Netherlands foreign service with postings in New Delhi, London, Accra, and the delegation to NATO. In 1977 he was elected to parliament and served in three cabinets, as state secretary for defence, state secretary for European affairs and minister of defence. He was secretary-general of the Western European Union (1989-94) and upon his return was elected senator. He participated in the European Convention of 2003 and wrote 'Debating European Security' (1998), 'From words to deeds, the continuing debate on European security' (2006) and several occasional papers on civil-military relations for DCAF Geneva.

André Gerrits is professor of Russian History and Politics and chairs the MA programmes in International Studies and European Union Studies at Leiden University. Gerrits studied History and Slavic Studies at the Free University and the University of Amsterdam. He also was a Jean Monnet Professor of European Studies at the University of Amsterdam and a senior research fellow at the Netherlands Institute of International Relations 'Clingendael'.

Kees Groenendijk is emeritus Professor of Sociology of Law at the Radboud University Nijmegen, research fellow of its Centre for Migration Law, and chairman of the Standing Committee of Experts on international immigration, refugee and criminal law (Meijers Committee). He is a member of the Odysseus Network of Experts on European Migration and Asylum Law and the EU Network Free Movement of Workers. He has widely published on the social and legal status of immigrants in Netherlands and the EU, immigration and race relations legislation, integration of immigrants and nationality law.

Corina Hendriks is staff member of the Mr. Hans van Mierlo Stichting, the scientific office of D66. She holds a Ph.D in political science (University of Amsterdam). She is editor of the political-scientific journal of the Van Mierlo Stichting (*Idee*), and works on topic such as labour markets policies, political and economic governance, consensual politics, civil society and sustainability.

Mendeltje van Keulen is clerk of the European Affairs Committee of the House of Representatives of the Dutch parliament. She advises the Members of Parliament on European dossiers and interparliamentary co-operation. She held previous positions at the Netherlands Institute for International Relations 'Clingendael', the Scientific Council for Government Policy (WRR) and various advisory boards. Her PhD concerned a case-study of EU interest representation by the Dutch government.

Frans van Nispen has served for several years as policy analyst for the Dutch ministry of Finance before returning to academia. At the moment he is Associate Professor of Public Administration at the Erasmus University of Rotterdam and responsible for the Masters Program on International Public Policy and Management. He has published in various journals, primarily on issues at the interface of policy analysis and public budgeting in the international and European context. He has done consultancy for international organizations, such as EU, OECD and World Bank.

Arie Oskam is a dairy farmer's son, who studied different subjects in Delft, Wageningen, Rotterdam and Utrecht and, from 1971 to 2009, worked at Wageningen University. He did his PhD at the University of Amsterdam. Research, teaching and PhD supervision were central to his activities. Besides in the Netherlands, he taught courses in USA and China and provided courses on 'EU policy' to professionals in Europe. He was editor of the European Review of Agricultural Economics and – later – scientific director of Mansholt Graduate School, finalising his career as Professor Emeritus Agricultural Economics and Rural Policy.

Jacques Pelkmans is Senior Fellow at CEPS (Brussels) and visiting professor at the College of Europe (Bruges). In addition, he has been associated professor of economics at the European University Institute in Florence, professor of Economics at the European Institute of Public Administration (Maastricht) and professor for European Economic Integration at Maastricht University. He also held part-time positions at the WRR (think-tank of the Dutch Prime minister), acted as founding Director at the European Institute of Asian Studies in Brussels and professor in 'Business & Europe' at the Vlerick Business School (Gent, Leuven, Beijing, St. Petersburg). Dr. Pelkmans has been advisor to the European Commission, the OECD, the World Bank, UNIDO, ASEAN and governments in Europe and Asia.

Jan Rood is senior research fellow at the Clingendael Institute en professor in European integration from a global perspective at Leyden University. He is also chief editor of the Dutch monthly *Internationale Spectator* and chairman of the Netherlands Society for International Affairs. His main areas of expertise concern European integration, the role of the EU in the world and Dutch foreign policy.

Adriaan Schout is deputy director for research and heads the EU studies group at the Netherlands Institute of International Relations 'Clingendael'. His book with Andrew Jordan won the UACES (Journal of Common Market Studies) prize for the Best Book in Contemporary European Studies. He worked for seventeen years as trainer of the rotating EU presidency and has done consultancy work for national governments and EU institutions e.g. on EU aviation policy. He has numerous publication in international academic journals and is currently visiting professor at the University of Victoria (Canada).

Alfred van Staden is professor of international relations at Leiden University and member of the Netherlands' Government Advisory Council on International Affairs. From 1995 till 2005 he served as director of the Clingendael Institute in The Hague. He published extensively on topics of international security, European integration, and foreign policy.

Amy Verdun is Jean Monnet Chair Ad Personam, professor of political science at the University of Victoria (UVic, British Columbia, Canada). She is an expert on the politics of monetary integration in the EU and has authored numerous books on European integration, including *Ruling Europe: The Politics of the Stability and Growth Pact* with Martin Heipertz (Cambridge University Press 2010). Amy Verdun is also editor, together with Michelle Cini (University of Bristol), of the *Journal of Common Market Studies*. In 2009, she was awarded the annual prestigious Craigdarroch Silver Medal for Excellence in Research op de University of Victoria.

Jan Marinus Wiersma holds a degree in history and is Senior Visiting Fellow at Clingendael. He is an expert on EU enlargement. As member of the European Parliament (1994-2009), he was closely involved in the accession of new member states in 2004 and 2007. He was rapporteur for Slovakia. He publishes regularly on the topic. Together with Joost Lagendijk he wrote, *Brussel, Warschau, Kiev. Op zoek naar de grenzen van de Europese Unie (Brussels, Warsaw, Kiev. Pushing the boundaries of the European Union)*, Amsterdam, Balans, 2001. He was one of the editors of *EU enlargement anno 2012. A progressive engagement.* Brussel: PES, 2012.

Arjen van Witteloostuijn is Professor of Organization and Strategy at Tilburg University in the Netherlands, and Research Professor of Economics and Management at the University of Antwerp in Belgium. In the 1980s, 1990s and 2000s, he was affiliated with the University of Groningen, University Maastricht, Utrecht University and Durham University, and he visited New York University and Warwick Business School. He holds degrees in business, economics and psychology. Apart from many (chapters in) books, and articles in Dutch dailies and journals, he has published widely in such international journals as the Academy of Management Journal, Academy of Management Review, Accounting, Organizations & Society, American Journal of Political Science, American Sociological Review, Economica, Industrial Relations, Journal of Economic Psychology, Journal of International Business Studies, Journal of Management Studies, Journal of Public Administration Research and Theory, Management Science, International Journal of Industrial Organization, Organization Science, Personality and Individual Differences and Strategic Management Journal.

Sarah Wolff is Lecturer at Queen Mary, University of London, and Senior Research Associate Fellow at the Netherlands Institute for International Relations. Her research focuses on justice and home affairs and EU external relations, in particular with Mediterranean countries. She is also Visiting Lecturer on the external dimension of EU migration policies at the University of Pompeu Fabra in Barcelona, Spain. Prior to academia, Dr Wolff worked for the European Commission and as a parliamentary assistant in the European Parliament.